CANCER AND
THE FAMILY LIFE CYCLE

CANCER AND THE FAMILY LIFE CYCLE

A Practitioner's Guide

Theresa A. Veach, Ph.D.
Donald R. Nicholas, Ph.D.
Marci A. Barton, Ph.D.

BRUNNER-ROUTLEDGE
ALERE · FLAMMAM
Taylor & Francis Group

USA	Publishing Office:	BRUNNER-ROUTLEDGE *A Member of the Taylor & Francis Group* 29 West 35th Street New York, NY 10001 Tel: (212) 216-7800 Fax: (212) 564-7854
	Distribution Center:	BRUNNER-ROUTLEDGE *A Member of the Taylor & Francis Group* 7625 Empire Drive Florence, KY 41042 Tel: 1-800-634-7064 Fax: 1-800-248-4724
UK		BRUNNER-ROUTLEDGE *A Member of the Taylor & Francis Group* 11 New Fetter Lane London EC4P 4EE Tel: +44 (0) 20 7583 9855 Fax: +44 (0) 20 7842 2391

CANCER AND THE FAMILY LIFE CYCLE: A Practitioner's Guide

1 2 3 4 5 6 7 8 9 0

Printed by Edwards Brothers, Lillington, NC, 2002.
Cover design by Nancy Abbott.

A CIP catalog record for this book is available from the British Library.
The paper in this publication meets the requirements of the ANSI Standard
Z39.48-1984 (Permanence of Paper).

Library of Congress Cataloging-in-Publication Data is available from the publisher.

ISBN 1-58391-016-6

*This book is dedicated
to Elaine Nicholas Underhill,
August 18, 1943, to January 3, 1996*

CONTENTS

PREFACE

It is 4:00 p.m. on a busy Friday afternoon. Tired after a full week, I receive a psychooncology consult for yet another family recently diagnosed with cancer. I start to think defeating thoughts about my work in the mental health field: *What can I possibly say to help this family? What can I do to make things better for them? How are they going to respond to me, a total stranger, when I approach them about this life threatening illness? I feel like an intruder on most sensitive and private ground.*

We understand that this book, *Cancer and the Family Life Cycle: A Practitioner's Guide*, cannot replace genuine human compassion, empathy, and superior listening skills, but it does provide a conceptual "road map" for helping patients and their families adapt to one of the most ubiquitous of life threatening illnesses, cancer.

Cancer affects more than 30% of the individuals in Western societies alone. From a broader perspective, not only does cancer have an impact on the individual patient, but also on the entire family system. It has been estimated that three out of four families will suffer from some form of cancer during the course of a lifetime (American Cancer Society [ACS], 1998). Cancer can thus be regarded as a "disease of the family system." This book integrates the current literature on families of adult cancer patients and places it within the rich context of family systems theory to provide a guide for working with cancer patients and their families.

Increasing numbers of professionals from many specialties are being called upon to help families adapt to the immediate and long-term effects of cancer. Due to advances in cancer treatment, the focus of practice and research has shifted from one of coping with loss and bereavement to one of adapting to prolonged life with cancer. Rather than concentrating solely on quantity of life concerns, quality of life now has become important. Thus, more and more families are in need of therapeutic assistance in coping with long-term treatment regimens, treatment side effects, cancer rehabilitation, and survival concerns. The growing subspecialty of psychooncology is addressing these needs via empirical research and clinical accounts of family adaptation to cancer.

This book is an integration of much of the current psychosocial literature on families of adult cancer patients. It has been written to assist psychologists, marriage and family therapists, counselors, social workers, clergy, oncology nurses, and all other professionals who are helping to facilitate family adaptation to cancer. This book is a synthesis of two broad frameworks: the clinical course of cancer (i.e., diagnosis, treatment, rehabilitation, survivorship, recurrence, and the terminal phase) and the family life cycle (i.e., single young adults, newly forming couples, families with young children, families with adolescents, families launching children, and families in later life). The six phases of the clinical course of cancer and their specific effects on each of the six family life cycles are highlighted in the individual chapters.

The first section of each chapter focuses on specific medical variables. For example, during the diagnostic phase, pertinent medical information includes (1) symptoms and "lagtime," (2) the diagnostic workup, (3) cancer severity continua, and (4) treatment decision making. The second section of each chapter is an integration of the psychosocial literature on families of adult cancer patients. Again, this information is specific to each phase of the clinical course of cancer. For example, during the diagnostic phase, specific psychosocial information includes (1) the existential crisis, (2) the patient's search for meaning, (3) predictors of individual distress during the existential crisis, (4) predictors of distress in the family system, and (5) family assessment during the diagnostic phase. The final section of each chapter constitutes the application of both the medical variables and the psychosocial information via the use of case studies. Suggestions for therapeutic interventions are included.

Six families are followed as they progress from the existential crisis of the diagnostic phase, through the daily long haul of the treatment phase, and into the rehabilitation and survivorship phases of the illness. Other families from each of the six life cycles are introduced in the last chapter. These case studies illustrate family systems as they face cancer recurrence, advancing disease, cancer metastasis, and the terminal phase of the illness.

This book can be used as both a general guide for professionals working with multiple families throughout all phases of the clinical course of cancer, or it can be used as a quick reference for professionals working with a particular family during a specific phase of the clinical course of cancer. For example, when working with a cancer patient who has adolescent children and is currently undergoing cancer treatment, chapter three, "Treatment and the Family Life Cycle: The Long Haul," is the most pertinent chapter. Thus, much of the current literature regarding families of adult cancer patients has been organized to provide a framework for facilitating healthier family adaptation to cancer. It is hoped that by organizing the literature and by providing a solid theoretical foundation, increased therapeutic assistance, comfort, and care can be given to families in any life cycle, during any phase of the clinical course of cancer.

☐ Reference

American Cancer Society (ACS). (1998). *Cancer Facts and Figures—1998*. New York: Author.

ACKNOWLEDGMENTS

We owe a debt of gratitude to the many people who have educated us and who have inspired and challenged us to write a book about how to help the families of cancer patients. At the top of our list are the many courageous and remarkable families whose lives have been touched by the human experience of cancer. We are thankful to them for the honor of joining them in the process of living lives affected by cancer.

In addition, there are many people who directly helped in the production of this book. Our oncology experts, Dr. Steve Tilmans and Patricia Avila, OCN, helped us correctly explain the basics of cancer. We are thankful for their helpful comments in reviewing early editions of the book. Melody Crabtree, Barb Cox, Rhonda Harmon, Lesley Langona, Marcy Moore, and Drs. Gregg Dickerson, Bill Fisher, Fred Francis, Joe Songer, Doyle Stephens, and Paul Walker, all staff at Ball Memorial Hospital, have supported the provision of psychological services to cancer patients, as well as the training of graduate students in counseling psychology. Without their continued support over the past 10 years, we would not have had the clinical experience to complete this project.

In writing a book about families, each of us has come to recognize the importance of our own families and are grateful for their support. I (TAV) would like to express my deepest gratitude and devotion to my family, especially to my husband, Todd, and my daughter, Kaitlin, who taught me what forever is for. Also, I would like to thank Tammy Montgomery for her undying encouragement.

My (DRN) personal experience of being part of a family forever touched by the experience of cancer has served as a source of continual inspiration, purpose, and renewal. I want to acknowledge the courage and inspiration of my family members: Mom, Sam, Craig, Doug, Carol, Joanie, Ken, and Bob, during Elaine's illness and death, and the unconditional love and support of my immediate family: Pam, Leah, AJ, and Jacob.

I (MAB) would like to thank my coauthors for the opportunity and joy of working together on such a meaningful project. I would also like to express my deep appreciation for God's presence and purpose in my life. I am truly grateful for my husband, Jim, and his unending love and support and for the love and devotion of my family and friends: Mom, Grandma, Matt, Trish, Kyla, and the Morris and Barton crew. I also appreciate the encouragement and inspiration from the WVU faculty, the 5-S team at CAMC Memorial Hospital, and the staff at the David Lee Cancer Center.

Finally, we want to thank the editorial staff of Brunner-Routledge for their help in the production of this book. In particular, we would like to recognize Bernadette Cappelle for sharing our vision of this book and helping to give us the opportunity to write it, Katherine Mortimer for keeping the book's "developmental momentum" moving along, Liz Ebersole for her ability to be as warm as she is professional, Jean Anderson for her uncanny eye for detail, and George Zimmar, Emily Epstein, and David Hull, all of whom we have been blessed to have as editors on this project.

Theresa Veach
Don Nicholas
Marci Barton

Introduction and Purpose

More than 8 million new cases of cancer will be diagnosed worldwide during the course of one year (Parkin, Pisani, & Ferlay, 1999). The number of new cancer cases has increased by 37% over the last 15 years, a growth rate higher than that of the world's population (Parkin et al., 1999). The most recent global estimates suggest that in one year cancer causes more than 5 million deaths, with 55% of those deaths occurring in developing countries (Parkin et al., 1999). In the United States alone, more than 1,500 people die every day from cancer. Each of these deaths has had a tremendous impact on the American family with estimates that three out of four families will be faced with the crisis of cancer (American Cancer Society [ACS], 1990; Zimpfer, 1992).

With such large numbers of cancer patients, many professionals working in a variety of settings are being called upon to help patients and their families as they adapt to cancer. Oncologists, nurses, social workers, psychologists, family therapists, nutritionists, clergy, and many other professionals are essential members of the family's health care team. For the practitioner working with families of cancer patients, it is important to understand (1) basic medical information about cancer, (2) the clinical course of cancer and its phases, and (3) how cancer affects the family life cycle. This book is an integration of each of these components. It has been written to provide a basic framework for the many professionals who strive to comfort and assist families in their adaptation to cancer. Although this is a book about adult cancer and its impact on the family system, much of the information can be applied to families who have children with cancer. In addition, it is hoped that this book has been written with sensitivity and understanding regarding the cultural, ethnic, racial, religious, and socioeconomic diversity of the American family as well as the diversity of families throughout the world.

☐ Cancer Basics

What Is Cancer?

The human body is made of millions of cells, each one containing 23 pairs of chromosomes. Chromosomes carry genetic information that directs cellular growth and functioning. In normal cell development, cells have the ability to reproduce themselves through a process called mitosis (Bullock, 1992). This process allows new cells to replace old cells, with a turnover rate of more than a billion cells a day. Cancer is a disease that originates from normal, healthy cells that lose their ability to control their growth and proceed to divide without control or order (National Cancer Institute [NCI], 1997). When mutations in cellular division and chromosomal reproduction occur, the abnormal cell loses its ability to grow in an orderly fashion, and a mass or lump can result from the excessive cell division.

Cancer is not one disease, but a group of more than 200 different diseases resulting from uncontrolled abnormal cellular growth. During the earliest stages of abnormal cellular growth, cancer cells are confined to the particular layer of cells in which they first developed. This is known as carcinoma in situ, or noninvasive cancer. In situ cancers are generally curable if they are treated before the confined cancerous cells have had a chance to grow enough to become invasive (Dollinger, Rosenbaum, & Cable, 1997). If the cancer cells continue to grow, the tumor invades and destroys surrounding healthy tissue. When a cancer begins this spreading process, the growth proceeds to compress, invade, and damage normal tissue, often producing debilitating local and distant effects.

Three Types of Cancer and Primary Sites

Malignant tumors can be classified into one of three broad categories: *carcinomas*, which are tumors that develop in *epithelial* tissues that cover or line the surface of organs and passageways (epithelium); *sarcomas*, which are tumors that develop in supporting or connective tissues such as muscle, bone, or tendons; and *lymphomas/leukemias*, which are tumors that develop in either the lymphatic system (lymphomas) or from the cells in bone marrow that produce and manufacture blood cells (leukemias). These three types of malignant tumors can be found in many different body locations, or sites such as lung, breast, prostate, pancreas, stomach, rectum, esophagus, colon, and the head and neck. Cancer type, site, and stage are directly related to the severity of the disease.

Staging of Cancer

The seriousness or the severity of disease can range from minimal to life threatening, depending on the type of cancer, its location, the size of the initial tumor, its stage at the time of diagnosis, and whether the disease has spread (metastasized) to other parts of the body. It is the staging of the disease that most directly indicates severity. There is a variety of staging systems that have been developed, but recent efforts to standardize the process have utilized the TNM system. In this system, T stands for the size of the tumor and the degree of local invasiveness, N for the degree of spread to the lymph nodes, and M for the presence of metastasis. From these categories, a composite of the TNM system is then converted to a stage, with the severity of disease increasing from stage I to stage IV. Treatment options and long-term prognoses are determined by the stage of the disease. Dollinger, Rosenbaum, and Cable (1997) provide an excellent reference to help understand cancer from a medical context.

Incidence

More than 8 million people in North American report a history of cancer and one million new cases are expected to be diagnosed each year in the United States alone (American Cancer Society [ACS], 1999). Although no one is immune to cancer, cancer risk increases with age and with certain genetic, behavioral, and environmental risk factors. According to ACS (1999), during the course of a lifetime men have a one in two chance of developing cancer and women have a one in three chance of developing cancer. A family history of cancer also increases one's risk of developing cancer. For example, women who have a first-degree relative with breast cancer are twice as likely to develop breast cancer than women with no family history of breast cancer (ACS, 1999).

Some cancers are the result of behavioral factors such as tobacco use or excessive alcohol consumption. Smokers are 10 times more likely to develop cancers of the lung, pharynx, larynx, and esophagus. Excessive exposure to the sun's harmful rays as well as to asbestos and benzidine-based dyes also contributes to many types of cancers. Some cancers are related to nutritional factors and sedentary life styles (ACS, 1999). Behavioral interventions such as recommended smoking cessation, a nutritional diet, and increased exercise can substantially decrease the risk of cancer development (ACS, 1999). However, the majority of cancers occur because of a combination of multiple genetic factors in conjunction with behavioral and environmental factors (Lerman, Rimer, & Engstrom, 1991).

Social Economic Status, Minorities, and Cancer

Social economic status and education level have been correlated with cancer risk and survival (Balfour & Kaplan, 1998). Many types of cancers, including lung, oral and esophageal, stomach, uterine, cervix, and pancreas, are associated with lower socioeconomic status and education levels. Other types of cancers, such as colon, rectum, testis, prostate, breast, uterine, and skin, have been shown to be associated with a higher socioeconomic status (SES; Balfour & Kaplan, 1998). However, these patterns have not remained stable across time (i.e., lung cancer was associated with affluence prior to the midtwentieth century), nor are they consistent across every population (i.e., lung cancer increases with affluent Italian women and with higher socioeconomic status residents of Columbia; Balfour & Kaplan, 1998).

Cancer risk also differs for minorities. African Americans are more likely to develop cancer than are Caucasians (ACS, 1999). While the overall incidence of cancer has decreased .8% per year for Caucasians, it has increased 1.2% per year for African Americans. Although cancer mortality rates for both Caucasians and for African Americans have been declining, African Americans are still 30% more likely to die from cancer (ACS, 1999). These differences have been attributed to later diagnoses and difficulties in receiving medical treatment for many minorities. Screening behaviors and beliefs regarding medical interventions also differ between various racial and ethnic groups (ACS, 1999).

Cancer Prevention and Screening

Early detection and treatment of cancer can substantially reduce cancer mortality. The ACS (1998) outlines specific guidelines for the early detection of cancer. Persons between the ages of 20 and 40 should have cancer-related checkups every three years, particularly for cancer of the thyroid, oral cavity, skin, lymph nodes, testes, and ovaries. Both men and women over 50 years old should follow regular cancer examination schedules. All women over the age of 18 should conduct monthly breast self-exams in addition to having an annual Pap test and pelvic examination. Women over the age of 40 are encouraged to have an annual mammogram as well as an annual clinical breast exam. Men 50 and older should have both the prostate-specific antigen (PSA) blood test and the digital rectal examination conducted annually. Younger men considered at high risk for prostate cancer should also follow these guidelines.

The family can exert a large influence on cancer screening behavior. For example, physicians' recommendations along with family members' influence have been shown to play a significant part in promoting sigmoidoscopic screening for the detection of colorectal cancer (Holt, 1991). Further, specialized counseling programs have been shown to increase proactive behaviors of sisters and daughters of breast cancer patients. Certain programs have been shown to be effective in increasing mammograms and self-examination for the early detection of breast cancer (Houts, Wojtkowiak, Simmonds, Weinberg, & Heitjan, 1991). By providing screening evaluations and information to high-risk individuals, doctors can detect cancer as soon as possible. Early detection and treatment are essential to increased rates of survival.

Death and Survival Rates

One in four deaths in the United States are due to cancer (ACS, 1999). Within the last decade there have been more than 5 million cancer deaths in the United States. During the course of a year, it has been estimated that more than 500,000 Americans will die from cancer. The good news is that the national cancer death rate fell 2.6% from 1991 to 1995 and continues to fall as screenings are allowing for early detection, new treatments for cancer are being discovered through clinical trials, and behavioral changes such as smoking cessation are being made (ACS, 1999).

Earlier in this century few patients had any hope of long-term survival, but by the 1930s one in four patients could be expected to reach the five-year survival mark (ACS, 1999). Now, four out of ten cancer patients will be alive at least five years after diagnosis. When these rates are adjusted for normal life expectancy factors, there is now a 60% relative five-year survival rate (ACS, 1999). Regular cancer checkups, preventative medicine, early detection, and compliance with medical treatment all play a part in cancer survival. Because of increasing cases of survival, cancer is now being viewed not only as a terminal illness leading to issues of bereavement and loss, but also as a chronic illness with all the implications of long-term survival.

☐ The Clinical Course of Cancer and Its Phases

Families will be faced with many different challenges during the fluctuating course of the disease. The severity and trajectory of the clinical course is determined by the type of cancer and the stage of the disease. With cancers such as early-stage breast cancer, early-stage prostate cancer, or melanoma, the cancer experience can be minimized, leaving some families with relatively little impairment following diagnosis and treatment (Sherman & Simonton, 1999). Other cancers such as head and neck cancer, later stage lung cancer, and cancer that has recurred or metastasized will place heavy demands on the family, which in turn may lead to greater family disruption. Thus, the clinical course of cancer affects the severity of the demands that will be faced by the family.

The Four Trajectories of the Clinical Course of Cancer

There are four major trajectories or clinical courses that cancer may follow (Holland, 1989a):

(1) symptoms/cancer diagnosis, primary treatment, and rehabilitation/remission, resulting in *long-term survival and cure;*

(2) symptoms/cancer diagnosis with *no primary treatment possible,* resulting in terminal illness and death;

(3) symptoms/cancer diagnosis, *primary treatment with no response,* resulting in terminal illness and death; and

(4) symptoms/cancer diagnosis, primary treatment, and rehabilitation/remission with cancer *recurrence or metastasis,* resulting in terminal illness and death (pp. 78–79).

These clinical courses have been described as the various "roller-coaster rides" of cancer (Holland, 1989a, p. 79). Some families will be blessed with a brief roller-coaster ride consisting of primary treatment leading to rehabilitation and long-term survival. For families with more advanced stages of cancer, the clinical course may be short, moving directly from diagnosis to palliative care and death. The clinical course of cancer can also be an exhausting, long, and drawn-out experience, with families undergoing the many hardships of treatment and recurrence, only to suffer the pain of loss and bereavement.

Within each of the different clinical courses there are disparate phases of the cancer experience. Families of adult cancer patients face unique medical, emotional, and psychosocial difficulties during each phase of the clinical course of cancer. Knowing the phases of the family's unique clinical course can help to clarify treatment planning and goal setting. This, in turn, can help to empower and educate the family regarding what might be expected, medically and psychosocially, during each of the various phases (Rolland, 1995). On the other hand, knowing the clinical course can assist the family in being alerted to emotional and behavioral warning signs that may warrant professional assistance. Figure 1.1 highlights the clinical course and its phases and Table 1.1 provides information on common family tasks typically associated with each of the phases.

Although the clinical courses of cancer consist of many phases—some running concurrently with one another (e.g., treatment and terminal phases)—they do have specific points at which families appear to have increased levels of stress and potential for dysfunction, depression, and anxiety. A disease continuum of these critical points has been previously presented in the literature (Holland, 1989a; Loscalzo & Brintzenhofescoz, 1998; Nicholas & Veach, 2001). All of the clinical courses share the common phases of symptom/diagnosis and treatment planning. After these initial phases, the course can begin to differ dramatically. For our purposes the clinical course can be organized into the following six phases: (a) symptoms/diagnosis/decision making, (b) primary treatment/no possible primary treatment, (c) treatment completion/rehabilitation/remission, (d) long-term survivorship, (e) recurrence/metastasis/advancing disease, and (f) treatment failure/palliative care/terminal illness/bereavement.

Symptoms/Diagnosis and Decision Making

Rarely does the diagnosis of cancer come as a complete surprise to the patient. The first phase of the clinical course of cancer has been described as the period in which the patient identifies suspicious symptoms (Holland, 1989a). During this first phase unusual bleeding or discharge, a lump in the breast, blood in the urine, difficulty swallowing, or other signs and symptoms are experienced. The patient typically feels a general sense of unease and suspicion. Patients may choose to keep these symptoms a secret, or tell select family members. At this time the family has important influence over the patient. Sometimes patients may believe that "what they don't know won't hurt them" and delay or fail to seek treatment. Family members can provide a safe and encouraging environment so that the patient seeks medical care, typically with his or her primary care physician. Upon

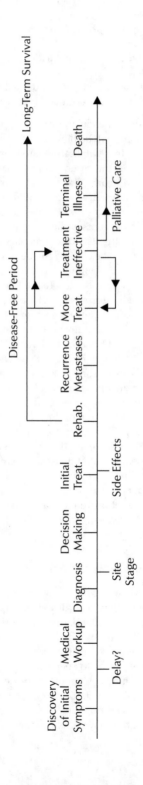

FIGURE 1.1. The clinical courses of cancer.

TABLE 1.1. Common Family Tasks Associated with the Phases of the Clinical Course of Cancer

Diagnostic Phase
    temporary reassignment of roles
    temporary shifts in power and responsibilities
    facilitation of clear communication regarding diagnosis and treatment options
    regulation of the family's emotional distress
Treatment Phase
    facilitation of clear communication about treatment
    time-specific role and responsibility shifts
    balancing treatment demands with the family's daily routine
    adapting to the patient's physical changes
    continued regulation of emotional distress and hopefulness
Rehabilitation/Remission Phase
    restoration of previous roles and responsibilities
    resumption of previous power structure
    adaptation to ongoing functional limitations
    return to a "normal" daily routine
    balancing mixed emotions
    living with uncertainty
Long-Term Survivorship
    living with long-term disabilities
    changes in planned family structure
    financial restrictions
    fear of recurrence
Recurrence/Metastasis/Advancing Disease
    maintaining hope and meaning
    another readjustment of roles and responsibilities
    persistence despite emotional exhaustion
    more permanent shifts in power structure
    anticipatory grief
Terminal Illness/Bereavement
    permanent reassignment of roles and responsibilities
    determining caregiving roles
    advocate for palliative care
    anticipatory grief and bereavement
    planning for life after the death of a loved one

Note: Information from Loscalzo & Brintzenhofescoz, 1998; Sherman & Simonton, 1999.

seeking medical care, patients will undergo a medical workup consisting of a variety of diagnostic procedures such as X rays, computerized tomography (CT) scans, blood tests, and biopsies (Dollinger et al., 1997). Following this workup a diagnosis is determined and a referral made to the physician specialists (e.g., surgeon, oncologist).

When a definitive diagnosis of cancer is made, the family moves into the acute phase of hearing the diagnosis, understanding and comprehending, and making decisions about treatment. Rowland (1989) has described patients' reactions to a diagnosis of cancer as involving worries and concerns about the five D's: distance, dependence, disability, disfigurement, and death. Often anxiety levels are so high that it is virtually impossible to digest all the medical information that needs to be communicated. Thus, it is important that a family member or friend be present during these initial physician visits. Some patients have even suggested that tape recording the doctor's presentation of information can be helpful. The family may feel bombarded by information at this time, and questions and concerns may often need to be addressed over and over again. Important questions regarding the patient's prognosis, treatment planning, and decision making will continue to surface throughout this phase. In fact, the physician informing the patient of the diagnosis of cancer will frequently offer information about treatment options at the very same time. Thus, patients and families are faced with the dual tasks of (a) comprehending the significance and meaning of the diagnosis, and (b) beginning to decide about treatment. This often occurs at a time when patients and families are experiencing significant confusion and fear.

Primary Treatment/No Possible Primary Treatment

Following a diagnosis and a period of decision making, patients and families enter the treatment phase of the clinical course. The initial treatment might involve surgery, chemotherapy, radiation therapy, biological (hormonal) therapy, or some combinations of each. In some unfortunate situations, no primary treatment is available. Treatment options depend largely on the type and severity of cancer, and the initial treatment course can vary from a brief surgical intervention to a lengthy course involving combination treatments, extending for months.

The variety of psychosocial issues that arise during the treatment phase will vary and be determined largely by the interaction between individual patient reactions, family reactions, and medical variables (e.g., stage, primary site, treatment). Common psychosocial issues during the treatment phase include (a) specific fears and worries about treatment procedures and side effects, (b) developing and maintaining satisfactory relationships with health care professionals, (c) incorporating the rigors and demands of treatment into previously established daily routines, and (d) regulating ongoing emotional distress.

As the family begins to adjust during the treatment phase, family members often want to understand more about how to cope with different treatment regimens and their side effects. Many families want to learn how to strengthen and draw upon needed resources, how to reassign roles within the family, and how to help the sick family member feel better (i.e., special diet, antinausea, and antidiarrheal medications). In addition, they often want to know how to maintain a balance between living individual lives, attending to the needs of the family, and caring for the ill family member.

Treatment Completion/Rehabilitation/Remission

Following the initial treatment course, patients and families enter the rehabilitation and remission phase. For some, the time since initial diagnosis might still be a matter of weeks (e.g., surgery with no further treatment), while for others it could have been months since diagnosis. The planned treatment is now completed, and following a period of rehabilitation and recovery, patients and families enter a phase during which they hope for long-term remission, while remaining vigilant for any recurrence. They must adapt to life with uncertainty.

Once again, the psychosocial issues that arise will vary and be determined largely by the interaction between individual patient reactions, family reactions, and a variety of treatment-related variables (e.g., late effects of treatment, continued side effects, disabilities, chronic symptoms). Individual patient reactions may include remnants of continued "psychic numbing," shock, and denial, while for others sufficient time will have passed to recognize that their assumptions about how their life will proceed have changed forever.

Most patients will encounter mixed emotions that will center on an uncertain future. Potential mixed feelings may include gratitude and anger, relief and fear, meaning/purpose and meaninglessness, denial and hypervigilance, enhanced interpersonal relationships, and loneliness.

Following an extended course of treatment, some patients experience a sense of abandonment and heightened anxiety from the reduction in frequent contact with health care professionals. During this time problems such as financial concerns or other long-term ramifications of the disease are addressed. The family will often begin to evaluate the impact of the disease and how their system has changed—for the better or for the worse.

This is a phase that is generally marked by a discrepancy between the patient's emotional recovery and the family's emotional recovery (Sherman & Simonton, 1999). During treatment, the entire family may have been mobilized into action with each member focusing on the illness. After treatment ends, family members may want to "get on with their lives" and "leave the disease behind them." It is difficult for some family members to understand that the patient may be slower to heal emotionally. Although the overt physical aspects of the disease may be waning, patients may still be dealing with the temporary ramifications of treatment, such as fatigue and hair loss. Or, in more severe cases, patients may be struggling with permanent losses such as the removal of a breast or the loss of speech. When losses are great, the patient is left to develop a new identity, one that may have a heightened sense of vulnerability. Because of these patient-specific challenges, the family may not be able to understand why the patient can't "move on" and join the family in the continuation of their shared developmental processes.

Long-Term Survivorship

Long-term survivorship follows a period of rehabilitation and remission. As vigilance for recurrence slowly fades and the likelihood of longevity increases, patients become long-term survivors. Although the definition of cure varies by type of cancer, a five-year disease-free period is often used an operational definition of cure. Five-year relative survival rates, for all cancers, have risen from 49% in 1974–1976 to 60% in 1989–1994 (ACS, 1999). In 1998, the ACS estimated that approximately 8 million Americans, still living, had a history of cancer. During the 1980s attention shifted from a focus on quantity of survival to an appreciation for the importance of quality of survival. As this shift occurred, research on the specific issues of long-term survival (Dow, 1991; Henderson, 1997) exposed a variety of patient concerns that include physical, social, sexual, employment, and insurance problems (Kornblith, 1998). Recent reviews of this literature (e.g., Kornblith, 1998) suggest that psychosocial adaptation will vary considerably, once again, by patients' individual differences, family reactions, and a variety of medical variables. Individual patient concerns may include (a) fears of recurrence, (b) body image disturbances, (c) job discrimination, (d) insurance problems (e.g., difficulty acquiring health or life insurance), (e) vocational reentry problems, (f) relationship difficulties, and (g) sexual dysfunctions (e.g., infertility, impotence).

Family members may react with understandable fears about recurrence or with needs for reassurance from the medical staff. Even though the treatment phase may be long past, episodes of anxiety and depression may still occur. This is a time for mourning lost opportunities, both past and future. Opportunities during treatment may have been missed due to the physical and emotional stress of treatment protocols. Future opportunities such as having children may be mourned for patients with gynecological or testicular cancers, or for patients with treatment-induced infertility. Conversely, cancer may leave the family system with new priorities, direction, and meaning.

Recurrence/Metastasis/Advancing Disease

Unfortunately, not all cancers are curable. Many recur (come back at or near the original site) or metastasize (spread throughout the body to distant sites/other organs) or both as the disease advances. A hope for cure and long-term survival often gives way to a focus on remission and "containing" the spread of disease. A second round of treatment is often offered. Patients and families are once again faced with understanding, comprehending, and deciding on a course of treatment. At the same time, they typically often are experiencing shock, disbelief, and significant despair. During this phase the individual patient concerns are significantly heightened, and many report that this is the single most distressing phase of the clinical course (Holland, 1989a). Individual patient reactions may include (a) fear; (b) heightened awareness of death; (c) loss of control; (d) intensified search for meaning; (e) helplessness.

Treatment Failure/Palliative Care/Terminal Illness/Bereavement

If treatments fail and the disease advances, patients and families enter the terminal illness, palliative care, and bereavement phase of the clinical course. Sherman and Simonton (1999) have written about healthy and unhealthy family responses during the progressive illness phase. Families who appear to adapt better will find this a time of life review, a time for the resolution of long-standing family conflicts, and a time for communicating important messages and meaningful good-byes. Families who tend to have greater difficulty in adapting to this phase regard death as a taboo subject. They often demonstrate trepidation toward the discussion and acceptance of death. Some family members with particular difficulty will continue to search for increasingly aggressive treatment options, long after the patient and other family members have accepted the patient's impending death. If the discrepancies between seeking further treatment and treatment discontinuation are not resolved, they could result in enduring family rifts based on guilt and resentment (Sherman & Simonton, 1999).

In addition to relational concerns, almost one third of families lose their primary source of income when cancer strikes, and just as many lose all of the family savings (Covinsky et al., 1994). Families that are poorer and younger are often the hardest hit financially. It is sometimes difficult to discuss financial concerns during the poignant time of grief and loss. However, in addition to their grief, family members must also carry the weight of day-to-day functioning.

Transitions from Phase to Phase

Not only are the specific phases important to consider, but the transitions from one phase to the next are also critical to assess. Individual and family functioning must become flexible enough so that important shifts in behavioral patterns can take place. For example, modifying patients' daily routines so that they may adapt to the physical stress of treatment is a common occurrence. Even though a transition from the treatment phase into a more long-term remission or chronic phase is necessary, these modifications may no longer be of use and they may only hinder the family in its successful transition from one phase to the next (Jacobs, Ostroff, & Steinglass, 1998).

The diagnosis, treatment, remission, and bereavement phases each place specific demands on the family. Even the long-term survival phase presents with different requirements that need to be met by the family. Rait and Lederberg (1989) describe the requirements of acute, chronic, and resolution phases, which correspond with Rolland's (1995) crisis, chronic, and terminal phases.

Acute Phase Transitions.   Acute (or crisis) phase requirements take place during diagnosis, the beginning of treatment, at the time of relapse, and during unexpected complications. During times of acute stress, family members respond with asynchronous individual responses, each with their own level of need for accurate and understandable information. Families also have a tendency to pull inward during times of crisis in order to increase cohesion, to mobilize resources, and to support one another. The family is grieving the loss of the life they knew before the illness while attempting to adapt to new treatment protocols and daily schedules. During acute crises phases "the family needs to create a meaning for the illness that maximizes a sense of mastery and competency" (Rolland, 1995, p. 496). Relationships with health care team members may be able to help the family gain a sense of mastery and control and to discover meaning during a time of crisis.

Chronic Phase Transitions.   After the initial acute and crisis phase, the family enters into a chronic phase marked by disease constancy, progression, or episodic change (Rolland, 1994). During chronic phases, the family has attempted to integrate the illness into the daily routine. The family's need for increased cohesion can relax as they attempt to resume normal developmental tasks and to resolve conflicts between the needs of the patient and other family members. Although chronic phases are generally regarded as a "neutral time," there is often a paradoxical increase in psychological symptomatology within certain family members (Lederberg, 1998). Emotions that had been pent up or put aside during acute phases may now surface. Emotional, interpersonal, and financial difficulties incurred during the crisis phases may need to be addressed and resolved.

Resolution Phase Transitions.   Last, during the resolution or terminal phase, the inevitability of death becomes apparent for most family members. The family must move from aggressive attempts at controlling the illness and warding off death toward a process of letting go and accepting death (Rolland, 1995). The family must begin to visualize life after a great loss and to adapt to the long-lasting emotional ramifications of the cancer experience.

☐ Cancer and the Family System

It has been noted that "psychological factors play a more important role in family well-being than do illness factors, even with procedures as rigorous as bone marrow transplants" (Lederberg, 1998, p. 981). It is therefore extremely important to understand the psychological and functional dynamics of the patient's family system.

There are many varied and complex definitions of "family." In addition to the traditional nuclear family, there are single-parent families, blended families, gay and lesbian families, multigenerational families, couples without children, and countless other familial configurations. Broadly defined, "families comprise people who have a shared history and a shared future. They encompass the entire emotional system of at least three, and frequently now four or even five, generations held together by blood, legal, and/or historical ties" (Carter & McGoldrick, 1995, p. 1). The family system is the patient's most immediate and intimate social system. Most often the family provides the environment in which the patient attempts to heal from cancer. The family exerts influence over many aspects of the cancer experience, including treatment decisions and the general recovery process. However, during the crisis of cancer the family is often called upon to function at its best during a time when stress levels are at their highest. Families are expected to participate in treatment decision making, handle finances, help with at-home treatment procedures and diet, all the while providing emotional support and hope for the future.

A Brief History of Cancer and the Family

We are only just beginning to understand cancer's impact on the family. Although the details of cancer and the family have not yet been extensively examined, cancer's general impact on the family has a long history (see Holland, 1989b). Table 1.2 provides an overview of the history of cancer, its perception in our culture, and the impact on families.

In the early part of the 1800s a definitive diagnosis of cancer was hard to determine. Surgical treatment had not come into use. High mortality rates were expected, and a shroud of shame surrounded the diagnosis of cancer. There was great fear in transmitting infectious diseases, one of which was believed to be cancer. All involved felt helpless. The patient often died at home, leaving the family confused, hopeless, and without much medical, emotional, or social assistance. In the 1940s and 1950s new advances in chemotherapies were on the rise, with the first remission of acute leukemia taking place. This was followed by the first cure of choriocarcinoma by chemotherapy alone. However promising the new treatments for cancer had become, the diagnosis of cancer was typically

---

TABLE 1.2. The History of the Perception of Cancer and the Family

---

1800–1920: Cancer is equated with death. Confusion, hopelessness, and shame surround the cancer patient and the family. Patient dies at home under the care of the family.

1920–1940: Successful surgical removal of some cancers. Radiation therapy is developed and used for palliative care. The beginning of the psychosomatic movement. Physicians assume a paternal role in the decision-making process, thus removing the power from the families as well as the patient.

1940–1950: Chemotherapies and cures for some types of cancers are developed. Research on life events and personality factors as causes of cancer take place. A diagnosis of cancer is only revealed to the family of the patient, not to the patient. This places the burden solely upon the patient's family and squelches communication among family members.

1950–1970: The first survivors of childhood leukemia and Hodgkin's disease. New ways of holistically treating the cancer patient come to the foreground. Research on cancer prevention and behaviors contributing to cancer are conducted. Increasing interest in death with dignity and the bereavement process.

1970–1990: New medical treatments for cancer continue to come into play. "Quality of life" becomes an issue for cancer patients. First National Conference on psychosocial research in oncology (1975) and Project Omega take place (1977–1984). Families of cancer patients are beginning to be recognized in the psychooncology literature.

1990–present: First overall reduction in cancer mortality. Psychopharmacologic, psychosocial, and behavioral intervention trials come to the foreground in psychiatry and psychology. Families are regarded as the "unit of treatment" for cancer. A family systems approach is used to address the biopsychosocial needs of the patient and the family.

Note: Information from Holland (1989b).

only revealed to the family members and seldom to the patient. The patient was thought of as being too weak to handle the diagnosis. The burden of knowledge was placed on a family system that was already weakened by the secrecy of the disease and by the lack of necessary communication.

The 1960s brought about new ways of treating cancer patients. Combined-modality treatments led to successful treatment of Hodgkin's disease. Psychiatrists and psychologists paved the way for more open discussion concerning cancer and its impact on the individual as well as on the family system. Subsequently during the late 1970s, the family, rather than the individual, was defined as the unit of treatment for cancer (Quinn & Herndon, 1986; Rait & Lederberg, 1989). The advent of taking a family systems approach to healing cancer was due to our culture's broadening view of the nature of illness in general. Cartesian mind–body dualism began being replaced with a biopsychosocial approach toward treatment (Engel, 1977; Zimpfer, 1992). In conjunction with the physical needs of the patient, the emotional and psychological needs of the patient and of the patient's family were now being taken into consideration.

Current advancements in treatments for some cancers are now prolonging the lives of many patients so that cancer is becoming regarded as a chronic disease rather than a terminal one. Thus, the patient's "quality of life" has become of paramount importance, and the family plays a significant role in the patient's quality of life. Although the importance of the family is currently being recognized, most professionals still place emphasis on the patient and perceive the family system as peripheral. Opportunities to centrally engage the family in the process of recovery from cancer, and thus to draw upon its influence and resources, are oftentimes overlooked in an oncology setting.

Psychosocial Oncology Literature: Cancer and the Family

The growing body of literature about the quality of life of cancer patients addresses the behavioral, psychological, and pharmacological management aspects of cancer. This psychosocial perspective encompasses not only the behavioral variables that may play a part in cancer risk and survival—a question of quantity of life—but also focuses on the emotional impact that cancer may have on the patient and the family—a question of quality of life. Currently, research in psychosocial oncology is also addressing the needs of family members of cancer patients within a family systems paradigm. The patient is now not alone in the diagnosis, but rather the family is being recognized, not only as a source of support for the patient, but *in need* of support as well. Many needs and concerns of the family have been recognized in the literature (Koch & Beutel, 1988; Rait & Lederberg, 1989; Schulz, Schulz, Schulz, & Von Kerekjarto, 1996). These concerns include fear of loss; fear of physical contact, including sexual difficulties; increased emotional distance; strain from additional tasks; uncertainty about the future; and confrontation with suffering and dying (Schulz et al., 1996, p. 234). Additional family-centered aspects of cancer include marital quality of cancer patients, psychosocial status of patients' next of kin, and the development of new measures that assess family adaptation to cancer (Veach & Nicholas, 2000).

Although recent research regarding the family's needs is currently being conducted, there are still many methodological problems that exist (Schulz et al., 1996). The perspective of the patient and not that of the family system still predominates. Sample sizes are often quite small and thus many results are not generalizable. Concepts such as quality of life, coping, and family cohesion are not easily operationalized and vary across studies. Further, most research is focused on the acute phases of the illness (i.e., diagnosis or recurrence) and consequently adaptational processes that take place during the chronic and intermediate phases are less understood. Despite these methodological problems, the current state of the literature is now being organized so that needs of the family system can be better realized (Sherman & Simonton, 1999; Veach & Nicholas, 1998).

Family Systems Theory and Cancer

Family systems theory, as opposed to individual theories, emphasizes patterns of relationships (von Bertalanffy, 1968; Green, Harris, Forte, & Robinson, 1991). Each member who makes up the system is also involved in countless other systems, all of which may affect participation and behavior in the current subsystem. Family systems theory is the direct application of general systems principles theory to family functioning (von Bertalanffy, 1968; Green et al., 1991). Using family systems theory, we can assess adaptation to cancer in the context of the family's unique dynamic. This process of adaptation can be best understood with reference to a number of key system principles. Table 1.3 presents definitions and explanations of a number of principles that will be used throughout this book.

A family system can be regarded as an open system that is constantly engaging with the environment. This engagement is not a passive reaction to stimuli. Family members par-

---

TABLE 1.3. Key Family Systems Principles

Family Systems Theory
Definition: The application of general systems theory to family functioning. Emphasizes patterns of behavior and the relationships between family members.

Cohesion
Definition: Emotional connection that family members feel toward one another. Includes areas of emotional bonding, coalitions boundaries, and how family decisions are made within the family system. "Enmeshed" families have decreased member independence and increased levels of family consensus that limit individuation. "Disengaged" families demonstrate an increase in separateness and limited attachment to the family as a unit.
Healthy families: Members are able to be independent from, yet still connected to, their families (i.e., midrange levels of cohesion).
Unhealthy families: Families that demonstrate excessive degrees of either enmeshment or disengagement.

Adaptability/Flexibility
Definition: The degree of appropriate and necessary change in the family's leadership, control, discipline, negotiation styles.
Healthy families: Flexible enough to meet the changing requirements of the phases of the clinical course of cancer. Midrange levels of flexibility are important family adaptations to cancer.
Unhealthy families: Families who resist necessary change (i.e., "rigid" family structures), as well as families that lack leadership and clear rules (i.e., "chaotic" family structures).

Communication
Definition: The governing dimension of movement for both family adaptability and cohesion. It is measured by the family's ability to keep family issues in perspective while working to understand other family members' points of view.
Feedback loops: Patterns of interaction that either reduce the likelihood of change (i.e., negative feedback loops) or increase the likelihood of change (i.e., positive feedback loops).
Healthy families: Clear communication and organized problem-solving skills. Family members work to understand other members' points of view.
Unhealthy families: Family secrets, assumptions, or misinterpretations hinder clear communication and problem solving.

TABLE 1.3. Continued

Family Structure

Definition: Organized patterns of family interaction. The examination of these patterns can be used to describe sequences of behavior that are predictable. Includes the family systems concepts of subsystems, boundaries, roles, and rules.

Subsystems: Smaller units made from the larger family system determined by generation, gender, or function.

Boundaries: Emotional barriers used to protect the integrity and autonomy of the subsystems by regulating the amount of contact with others. Rigid boundaries result in family member isolation. Diffuse boundaries result in family member overdependency. Clear boundaries help to clearly define family subsystems and their functions (i.e., parental subsystem with financial and disciplinarian-nurturing functions).

Roles: Expected behavior of an individual within the family system. In healthy families, role expectations differ across the generations and are clearly defined. In unhealthy families there can be role conflict and confusion that can lead to symptom manifestation in one or more family members.

Rules: Behaviors that govern family transaction and structure. Healthy rules are comprehensive, yet flexible. Unhealthy rules are narrow, unclear, limited, and are used regardless of appropriateness.

Healthy families: During the crisis of cancer, the family system strives for stability by filling in for the altered role of the sick family member, coping with excessive demands and potential losses, meeting the emotional needs of all family members, and continuing to perform regular family functions.

Unhealthy families: Difficulties occur when family remains "stuck" in overregulated patterns of behavior that are no longer needed.

Types of Change

Definition of first-order change: Changes in behavior that are still governed by the same family rules and therefore do not have the depth to alter family structure or meaning.

Healthy uses of first-order change: Using first-order change to pave the way for more stable second-order changes.

Unhealthy uses of first-order change: Using first-order change as a barrier to necessary second-order changes.

Definition of second-order change: Changes that require alterations in the family's rules, structure, and meaning.

Healthy uses of second-order change: Using second-order change to promote family adaptability and flexibility so that family tasks can be resumed successfully.

Unhealthy uses of second-order change: Using second-order change to pull family "inward" thus leading to unclear boundaries and confused patterns of communication.

Movement

Definition of centripetal movement: The drawing of the family inward necessitating cohesion and unity.

Definition of centrifugal movement: The pushing away from the center of the family. Individual goals are emphasized and the boundaries around the family are loosened.

Patterns of Adjustment

Triangulation: Involvement of a third person into a two person conflict in order to detour the conflict and to stabilize the two-person relationship.

Fusion: Blurring of emotional and psychological boundaries between an individual and others.

Reactive distancing: Flight from an unresolved difficulty within the family system. An extreme form of reactive distancing is total emotional cutoff.

Differentiation: Emotional and psychological balance between self and others that fosters autonomous functioning and healthy attachments.

ticipate actively in the enhancement of the self as well as in the creation of the family's identity (Nichols & Schwartz, 1991). Impetus for change can be found outside as well as inside the system. For example, in response to cancer, the family must change in order to adapt to the external force of the cancer as determined by the medical variables of the disease (i.e., type and stage of cancer). During the crisis of cancer, the family system must also attempt to remain stable and organized by filling in for the lost role of the sick family member, coping with excessive demands and potential losses, meeting the emotional needs of other family members, and continuing to perform regular family functions (Lederberg, 1998). Conversely, the family must remain flexible enough to meet the changing requirements of the various phases of the clinical course. When the family system is placed in a medical crisis, most families tend to increase the need for stability and regularity in order to adapt to the demands of the illness (Jacobs et al., 1998). Thus, hypervigilance toward maintaining the status quo may temporarily impede family development and change. However, this necessary increase in overregulation is usually temporary, and many adjusted families will return to a more balanced position between meeting the needs of stability and those of change. Difficulties in family adaptation to cancer occur when this balance is not regained and thus the family remains "stuck" in attempting to hold onto overregulated patterns of behavior that are no longer needed (Jacobs et al., 1998).

Concepts such as family cohesion, adaptability, feedback loops, and family structure are often used when working with family systems. Cohesion, or marital/family togetherness, is defined as "the emotional bonding that family members have toward one another" (Olson, 1993, p. 103). This dimension of family functioning includes areas of emotional bonding, coalitions, boundaries, and the process of how family decisions are made within the family system. Healthy families are able to be both independent from yet still connected to their families. These types of families typically tend to be more functional when faced with an anxiety, such as cancer.

On the other hand, families can react to cancer by becoming enmeshed or disengaged. In enmeshed families, there is little member independence and too much consensus within the family, which can limit autonomy and individuation of each family member. This type of family discourages member autonomy.

Disengaged families are characterized by family emotional separateness and limited attachment or commitment to the family unit. This type of family is seen as one where members "do their own thing" in relation to time, space, and interests. The enmeshed and disengaged family types are hypothesized by Oslon's circumplex model to be problematic for both individual members and familial relationship development (Olson, 1993).

Another dynamic is family adaptability, or family flexibility. Flexibility "is the amount of change in its leadership, role relationship, and relationship rules" (Olson, 1993, p. 107). Here, the areas of interest are leadership, control, discipline, negotiation styles, role relationships, and family rules. The dynamics that are hypothesized to be most beneficial for healthy families include the ability to instigate change when appropriate and in a semidemocratic, equalitarian leadership style within the family system. Families who resist change and are highly controlling are seen as rigid family structures, whereas families in which there is a lack of appropriate leadership and unclear rules are characteristic of chaotic family structures. Both of these extreme family types present problems for the family and its individual members.

Communication is regarded as the governing dimension of both family adaptability and cohesion (Olson, 1993). Communication is the one "dimension that can facilitate a family's movement among the family types and levels of adaptability and cohesion" (Green, Harris, Forte, & Robinson, 1991, p. 57). The family communication patterns are measured by the ability to listen, speak, clarify, track, self-disclose, and respect. This area is important to the entire model of family functioning because negotiation and problem-solving skills can be enhanced or hampered depending on the levels of communication. Families in balanced systems tend to have good communication and problem-solving skills, whereas those outside of those balanced regions struggle with problem solving and have poor communication skills (Olson, 1993).

Rather than focusing on individuals and linear cause–effect relationships, family systems therapists focus on "circular causality" or sequences of interactional feedback loops that occur within and across systems. Feedback loops are patterns of interaction that either reduce the likelihood of change (negative feedback loops) or increase the likelihood of change (positive feedback loops). Inherent in the concept of feedback loops are several key phenomena: (1) family rules or the range of behaviors that are acceptable by the system; (2) negative feedback that is used to enforce those rules; (3) sequences of family interaction that characterize family reactions to a problem; and (4) ineffective negative feedback loops that necessarily become positive feedback loops, which amplify the need for change (Nichols & Schwartz, 1991). For example, consider a family where the father has been diagnosed with metastatic lung cancer. This family has incorporated the rule of no in-depth discussion about death and loss. The adolescent daughter makes several attempts to discuss the impending incredible loss of her father, but her parents maintain their old patterns of avoidance, which preclude any meaningful discussions about death. Rather than reducing the daughter's need to address death and loss (thus maintaining the rule and homeostasis), the parents' negative feedback results in the opposite effect. The daughter continues to demand meaningful communication with her parents and begins to demonstrate increasing levels of depression and anxiety. In this way, the family's original negative feedback loop of avoidance of death has become a positive feedback loop; their reaction amplifies rather than diminishes deviant and problematic behavior. The family is caught in a vicious cycle that threatens to destroy the unity of the family system.

In addition to feedback loops, the crisis of cancer often necessarily leads to a reexamination of the existing structure, so that family adaptation can occur. Family structure is "the organized pattern in which family members interact. . . . It describes sequences that are predictable" (Nichols & Schwartz, 1991, p. 449). Families are divided into subsystems that are determined by their functions (i.e., the parental subsystem with financial and disciplinarian-nurturing functions). Boundaries define the subsystems within the family and lay the foundation for family rules. Boundaries can be rigid, clear, or diffuse. Rigid boundaries result in decreased communication and support between familial subsystems, which leaves family members relatively disengaged, isolated, and autonomous. Diffuse boundaries result in individuals or subsystems that are overreliant and dependent.

Family systems theory incorporates many other concepts to identify patterns of adjustment and interaction within the family system. Some of these include "triangulation," where a third family member is used to stabilize dyadic interactions under stress. Other family patterns include "fusion," "reactive distancing," and "total cutoffs," which are reactions demonstrated by family members attempting to create and maintain comfortable emotional bonds. Last, "differentiation" is a pattern that refers to a balanced interaction of autonomy and emotional connectedness with others (Carter & McGoldrick, 1995).

☐ Cancer and the Family Life Cycle

The concept of the family life cycle has been added to family systems theory in recognition of the various developmental requirements performed by families as they move through time. The family is regarded as a system, containing a number of existing subgroups, coalitions, and alliances, which may span several generations. With the family life cycle perspective, the individual cancer patient who comes to therapy is a part of a family system that is traversing the family life cycle elements with different tasks to accomplish at each of its phases. Each member of a family's "individual life cycle takes place within the family life cycle, which is the primary context of human development" (Carter & McGoldrick, 1989, p. 4). Even though the time frame that is emphasized in this model is linear, the focus on the family process is by no means linear. This nonlinear, but circular, focus provides the underlying basic assumptions about patients and their families. Recent life cycle frameworks have shifted from the idea of an "invariant epigenetic process" toward a more encompassing recognition of cultural, socioeconomic, ethnic, racial, and gender influences on family development (Rolland, 1995, p. 500). Multigenerational frameworks also have been applied to the family life cycle, highlighting the complexities of family development (Combrinck-Graham, 1988; Nichols & Schwartz, 1991).

Many family therapists do not view stages of development as discrete segments of time, but rather, the stages are continuous, requiring smooth transitions from one stage to another (Combrinck-Graham, 1988). Events such as the union of a partnership, the birth of a first child, and the last child leaving home are some of the "markers" that highlight transitions from one cycle to the next. Through predictable transitions and unpredictable life events, a family can be derailed from the appropriate developmental momentum of the system. The goal of the practitioner working with families of cancer patients is to help reestablish the family's developmental momentum in light of a serious illness. Since each life cycle stage requires different developmental tasks, the practitioner must first determine the family's current developmental stage. Following this identification, the determination of how well the family is managing that life cycle sequence must be made.

Families of cancer patients can have difficulty meeting the demands of their respective life cycles. Adapting to cancer takes up much of the family's available energy, and consequently family development will often follow a path of least resistance rather than the path of greatest usefulness (Lederberg, 1998). For example, cancer may break apart an already shaky marriage, or it may increase already occurring feelings of isolation or dependency. Professional assistance may be required to help families of cancer patients to successfully complete cycle-appropriate developmental requirements.

Although many different life cycle frameworks have been suggested, each with varying numbers of stages (Carter & McGoldrick, 1989; Duvall, 1977), for our purposes six general stages of family development will be addressed: the single young adult, the new couple, families with young children, families with adolescents, families launching children, and families in later life (Carter & McGoldrick, 1995). The family life cycles and cancer's impact on their corresponding developmental tasks are depicted in Table 1.4.

The Single Young Adult

The single young adult is beginning to experience the self as separate from the family of origin and to take on greater emotional and financial responsibilities. Although many theorists of individual development have focused on independence and autonomy (Erikson, 1963, 1968), family systems theorists tend to focus on a continuity of interpersonal development in which individuals learn to balance connectedness and separateness. This process of learning to become functionally interdependent can be regarded as the cornerstone of conceptualizing individual development within the context of the family. Single young adults are thus learning to identify with their families of origin while simultaneously developing a strong sense of self in connection with others outside of the family system.

Young adults from many different ethnic, racial, and socioeconomic backgrounds de-

TABLE 1.4. Cancer's Impact on the Family Life Cycles

	Emotional Process	Cancer's Potential Impact
Single Adult	Accepting emotional and financial responsibility for self	Impede differentiation and the development of peer relationships and career goals
New couple	Commitment to new system	New family system may not be stable and solidified. Patient may return to family of origin.
Families with young children	Accepting new members into the system	New roles and tasks must be assigned. Potential generational boundary confusion.
Families with adolescents	Increasing flexibility of family boundaries	Family members may become enmeshed in family issues, or may disengage from the system prematurely.
Launching children	Accepting multiple exits from and entries into the family system	Older children may remain home to care for the sick parent, indefinitely delaying development of the system.
Families in later life	Accepting the shift of generational roles	Adult children may begin to care for the parent (role reversals), or there may not be an adult to care for the patient (resource vacuum).

From Elizabeth Carter, Monica McGoldrick, *Changing Family Life Cycle,* 2nd Edition. Copyright © 1989 by Allyn & Bacon. Reprinted/adapted by permission.

pend upon their families of origin for emotional support and encouragement (Fulmer, 1995). Families set examples and pave the way for the quality of work and relationships that the young adult will foster. Young adults are learning to transform their life interests into salable commodities. This process may take quite some time, as the young adult balances the need for financial independence with the need for creative self-expression. When difficulties arise in obtaining satisfactory jobs, young adults will either remain on their own or return home to further prepare for adulthood. Living at home may be difficult for some young adults who are struggling to create their own standards and values apart from the family system, while still needing financial assistance. It becomes nearly impossible to become emotionally independent when remaining financially dependent (Fulmer, 1995).

The experience of young adulthood can differ according to gender, sexual orientation, racial identification, and socioeconomic class. Males may attempt to exaggerate their "maleness" by demonstrating aggressive behaviors. Women may feel pressured to relinquish their own needs so that they may tend to the needs of others. Gay men and lesbian women are likely to feel rejected and marginalized. Minority young adults may find it difficult to work successfully in a society that often regards them as second-class citizens. Much of the current socioeconomic structure does not account for the cultural and financial needs of minority young adults. For these young adults, as well as for young adults from lower socioeconomic classes, there is a great need for competent and willing mentors who model new ways of forming work relationships and career goals.

The New Couple

The new couple begins to form during a time of courtship. In the past few decades, this joining process is decreasing in frequency (Bumpass, Sweet, & Cherlin, 1991). The current trend in American society is for individuals to delay committing to a permanent relationship to allow for an increased focus on accomplishing personal goals, such as education and career building. Typically, a relationship is established in order to meet the intimacy needs of the couple. These needs are met through the sharing of each other's lives, including the joys and the pains.

During this time of joining, the relationship and the new partner are both idealized, and the enormous task of integrating two family systems is often overlooked. Research has shown that this early period of relationship development is the highest in marital satisfaction, but, in reality, the joining process can be difficult as each couple must attempt to form a cohesive unit, combining and altering family rituals, behaviors, and beliefs. A successful relationship often is based on the values that each individual member holds and the joint concept of marriage. This can present a challenge to couples who may vary in their values or belief systems, namely, around issues of religion, intimacy, time, and money. These couples also may find themselves having difficulties realigning with their families of origin and may struggle with a new system definition.

All new couples have several common dimensions that must be incorporated into the new union. These include finances and emotions, intimacy and power, distribution of work and leisure activities, and the formation of the couple's boundaries in relation to other family members and friends. Thus, forming a balanced relationship within all of these complex dimensions is often a difficult task. This can be challenging for any couple, but particularly if the couple is coming from very diverse families of origin, or if the couple is not validated by their families or by society.

Families with Young Children

The birth of a child, particularly the first, changes the family system substantially and permanently. The challenges of raising a child are often much more than the young couple had expected, with sleepless nights, demands for time, and countless added responsibilities. The arrival of a first-born child often can alter the couple's established balance of power and intimacy. After the birth of the first child, the balance of power may swing to the primary wage earner, leaving the other partner feeling dependent and dissatisfied. These power struggles may affect the couple's level of intimacy and result in sexual problems and feelings of isolation. When these difficulties are not resolved, they can lead to overall marital dissatisfaction and, ultimately, divorce.

Relationships with extended family members are usually drastically altered with the birth of a first child. In these families, the couple is required to accept new members into the system and to realign the system to include parenting and grandparenting roles. These new emotional and functional systems may present problems when new roles and boundaries are not discussed and agreed upon. The new parents may feel bombarded by information and advice about how to raise their child. New boundaries and alignments, oftentimes with well-meaning parents and grandparents, may need to be created.

The couple, and at times the extended family, must agree upon many aspects of child care. Important issues such as how to discipline, who will discipline, who will provide day-to-day care, and who will provide for the family financially are often major sources of dispute. These crucial concerns are difficult to negotiate when both parents work, when the child is from a single-parent home, or when there are few familial and societal sources of support.

Families with Adolescents

In families with adolescents, the family system is working toward the integration of spousal, parent, and sibling subsystems. During this time, profound changes in relationships across the generations occur. Adolescents begin to push the family's limits in order to gain a sense of their own autonomy and independence. Thus, this is generally a time of confusion and reorganization, as families alter boundaries and rules to make room for their growing adolescents.

All adolescents are undergoing physical, emotional, and sexual changes. These intense changes can lead to unpredictable behaviors and mood swings, which can lead to creating difficulties for a family system that is not flexible enough to alter the balance of former relationships. Structural changes must often take place, involving at least three generations of relatives (Garcia Preto, 1989). Parents of adolescent children often redefine their relationships with their own parents, as they take on the responsibilities of raising teenaged children. Grandparents begin to have more mature relationships with their adolescent grandchildren.

Parents and other guardians must agree on specific rules and guidelines for their adolescent children. A parental subsystem that does not have agreed-upon limits and consequences can add to the confusion of this life cycle. This process may be difficult, especially if the parents are divorced or living apart. For parents still together, it is a time of reevaluating their own relationship. Although it may be easy for parents to focus solely on the activities and disciplinarian needs of their growing children, they must also take time for themselves in order to ensure the longevity of their marital relationship after the children have grown.

Families Launching Children

The family system changes dramatically when the children begin to leave home, especially when the last child has gone. Many parents face this time of their lives with mixed emotions—sorrow at the loss of day-to-day interaction with their children, and happiness at the new freedom this brings. Many mothers go back into the workforce or return to school. Fathers may have a difficult time during this life cycle, especially if they are feeling the irrevocable loss of missing out on their children's formative years. Parents can now begin to focus more on their own marital relationship. They may find that it is a time of marital happiness and sharing, or that it is a time of marital dissatisfaction and emptiness. The absence of children can thus either enhance a good marriage or break apart one that cannot survive without the focus of child-rearing activities.

This is one of the longest phases of the family life cycles, lasting 20 years or more. It is a time of changing roles and redefining relationships. Middle and upper socioeconomic families usually experience this life cycle as a time of ease and enjoyment. There is a relaxation of routine and a freeing up of time that used to center around the children and their activities. However, it is often a difficult time for lower- and working-class families. Poor families often lack access to health care, health insurance, and steady income. For them, this may be a time of increased physical decline and uncertainty.

During this time of midlife, parents of adult children redefine their relationships with their own parents, often becoming their caregivers. Families that view this caregiving process as natural, as do Latino, Asian American, African American, and Native American families, will have a less stressful time than families that view this time as a burden (Blacker, 1995). For caregivers and their aging parents, shifts in power and responsibility take place. The caregivers face role reversals with their parents and are now responsible for their safety and well-being. Caregivers may also undergo boundary changes with their parents, as they take care of their parents' intimate physical care. These family members are at a great risk for burnout, and setting appropriate limits to caregiving tasks may be necessary to successfully navigate this life cycle.

Families in Later Life

Families in later life are beginning to accept the shifting of generational roles. During this life cycle, parents are becoming grandparents and even great-grandparents. Relationships with their grandchildren may be particularly enjoyable, because they have the opportunity to form special bonds with another generation without the complications of day-to-day discipline and obligations. During this life cycle, older adults begin to accept their own mortality and special place in the family life cycle. Many take pleasure in watching their families grow and in seeing the continuation of the family system develop through the lives of their progeny (Walsh, 1995).

Many older adults must face the death of a partner or spouse and the loss of their siblings and friends. Women often become widows relatively early in life and have many years of life still ahead of them after the death of their partners (Walsh, 1995). Thus, women in later life must redefine themselves and take on new roles. For both aging women and men, this is a life cycle of transcendence, when life choices and paths are reflected upon, and meaning for these choices is created. Spiritual and religious beliefs can assist greatly in the comfort and well-being of the aging adult.

The risk of cancer and chronic disease increases with age, and the number of elderly adults within our society is increasing dramatically. Thus, families are taking care of their elderly family members in greater numbers than ever before. Caregiving is a major stressor for many families. Some caregivers provide assistance numerous hours each day, taking responsibility for the feeding, shopping, meal preparation, toiletries, and dressing of their elderly parents and grandparents. Home health care is a growing problem, leading to caregiver burnout, high levels of stress, and in severe cases, abuse of the elderly. Medical, personal, social, and rehabilitative services are now being combined to provide a spectrum of integrated services for families with health care needs (Institute for Health and Aging, 1996).

Transitions and Life-Structure-Maintaining Periods

Like the transitions between the phases of the clinical course of cancer, the transitions between the various life cycles are also important. Times of transition are often periods of upheaval and confusion, requiring a type of "centrifugal" momentum, or a push away from the center (Rolland, 1994). New responsibilities are being undertaken and new roles and boundaries are usually created. The family system opens itself to change, and marker events such as a new union or marriage, or the birth of a child, herald the beginning of a new life cycle. These events are often demarcated by rituals, celebrations, or ceremonies such as weddings, christenings, and funerals.

Because transitions are a time of change and thus of centrifugal momentum, they are at direct odds with the centripetal nature of the crisis phases of the clinical course of cancer (i.e., diagnostic or recurrence phases of cancer; Rolland, 1994). The centripetal force of the crisis draws the family system inward, necessitating cohesion and unity in reaction to the crisis event. For example, a family in the launching stage (i.e., a centrifugal life cycle) may need to pull its family members inward in response to the diagnosis of cancer. This response delays the launching process of the family system. When cancer strikes a family during a transition period, there is an increased risk for the illness to become unnecessarily embedded in the family structure (Rolland, 1994). The family system that is in transition may pull inward in response to the needs of the crisis, but never regain its appropriate, centrifugal momentum after the demands of the illness have shifted into a more chronic phase. During the chronic phases of cancer (i.e., the treatment phase and remission), the illness does not require as much family cohesion, and the family can resume its previous centrifugal momentum. Conversely, the transition tasks of the family may be so important to some family members that the weight of the illness is ignored in pursuit of the current developmental tasks. Under this circumstance, the family does not develop the cohesion needed to address the crisis, but continues in a centrifugal state, altering the family structure without including the demands of the disease.

Life-structure-maintaining periods are times of plateau and relative stability. These times depict the living out of decisions and choices that were made during the previous transition (Carter & McGoldrick, 1989). The family system requires greater cohesion so that it can maintain its structure and equilibrium. When cancer strikes a family during periods of cohesion, it will have a much different effect than when diagnosed during a transition period. If the cancer type and stage are less severe, the family may only undergo minor behavioral and structural changes. However, if the cancer diagnosis is severe, the family may be pushed into a life transition for which it is not prepared (Rolland, 1994). For example, a couple busy maintaining their new partnership may need to have an elderly parent who has been diagnosed with cancer move in with them. This event may push the new couple into the semblance of a "family with young children," wherein a dependent family member is added to the system. Cancer itself can be regarded as an additional family member with needs and cyclical patterns all of its own (Rolland, 1994). The family system must then alter its structure to include the needs of this "new family member."

The timing of the disease also has important consequences for the family system. Timing can be regarded as "normative," or in keeping with the expected developmental tasks of later life, or "nonnormative," which is experienced when cancer strikes a young system. When cancer occurs during untimely or nonnormative periods of development, the expected unfolding of life events and the natural momentum of development is greatly disrupted (Rolland, 1994). This can be especially true for young adults, or families with young and adolescent children. During these stages, cancer can be particularly devastating, because of its untimely occurrence combined with the already existing stress and responsibility of those particular family life cycles.

☐ Summary

In this introductory chapter, we have introduced the reader to the basic concepts necessary to understand subsequent chapters. First, the basics of cancer were presented with explanations of the three general types of cancer, the process of staging, current incidence data, socioeconomic differences, the importance of early detection and screening, and current survival rates. Second, the common trajectories along which families travel as they experience the course of the disease were explained and divided into the six phases of the clinical course of cancer: (a) diagnosis, (b) treatment, (c) rehabilitation, (d) survival, (e) recurrence, and (f) terminal illness. Third, key family system principles were presented

TABLE 1.5. The Clinical Course-Life Cycle Framework

Family Life Cycle	Diagnosis "Existential crisis"	Treatment "The long haul"	Rehabilitation "Living in limbo"	Survivorship "Sword of Damocles"	Recurrence "Life in the balance"	Terminal "Strange land"
Single, young adult	Disruption to the process of separating from the family of origin	Disruption in establishing self in world of work and in creating intimate relationships	Disruption to body image, sexuality, fertility; can begin to regain developmental momentum	Young adult may need to reevaluate career goals, intimate relationships, and plans for childbearing	Crisis may draw young adult back into family of origin; major disruption to "assumptive world"	Family & friends are drawn inward; community becomes involved
Newly forming couple	Disruption to the creation of a new system	Balance of power may be disrupted due to "patient" "caregiver" roles	Renegotiate balance of power; address sexuality conerns, fertility, body image	Address fears of recurrence and cancer's impact on the new couple	Can be more difficult than initial diagnosis; assess for depression and anxiety	Prepare for loss; create meaningful rituals and memories
Families with young children	Centripetal crisis can overwhelm young families resulting in role strain	Possible role strain, may need to mobilize external resources; decide what/how to tell children	Developmental momentum may be resumed; address fears for cancer recurrence	Address body image, fertility, sexual dysfunction, altered plans for the future; assess cancer's impact on family	Assess for pain, anxiety, depression, suicidal ideation, need for external resources	Prepare advanced directives; plan for care of children; create meaningful rituals

Families with adolescents	Crisis may delay the relaxing of boundaries needed for adolescent development	During treatment adolescents may experience role strain resulting in enmeshement or disengagement	Developmental momentum may be resumed; family members and patient may have differing recovery times	Address fears for recovery, body image, sexuality, and impact cancer has had on family system	Assess caregiver burnout, role strain, anxiety, depression, self-efficacy regarding parenting	Prepare advanced directives; create meaningful rituals
Families launching children	Centripetal crisis is in direct conflict with centrifugal launching of children	Developmental delay may occur for children about to leave the home; identify tasks that are put on hold	Risk of illness becoming embedded in family system; facilitate family's momentum	Address fears of recurrence, body image; address resuming work and life cycle tasks	Assess for depression, anxiety, suicidal ideation; assess for role strain and caregiver burnout	Discuss death and loss; create meaningful rituals
Families in later life	Centripetal crisis causes shifts in generational roles	For older adults, there may be a "resource vacuum" or role strain for sandwich generation	Address all rehabilitation needs; review impact on multigenerational life cycle	Integrate experience of cancer into multigenerational history	Assess cognitive functioning, pain, anxiety, suicidal ideation; assess for caregiver burnout	Prepare advanced directives; create meaningful rituals

and briefly explained, and then the six family life cycles were introduced: (a) single young adult and (b) newly forming couple and families (c) with young children, (d) with adolescents, (e) launching children, and (f) in later life.

The remainder of the book follows this six-by-six clinical course by family life cycle framework as presented in Table 1.5. Chapter two begins with the diagnostic phase and is followed in order by chapters on the treatment, rehabilitation, survival, recurrence, and terminal phases of the clinical course. Each chapter begins with information about medical variables and psychosocial considerations of importance to that phase and is then followed by detailed case examples of each family life cycle. Each case example consists of recommendations regarding family assessment, goals, intervention strategies, and outcomes.

☐ References

American Cancer Society (ACS). (1999). *Cancer facts and figures–1999.* New York: Author.

American Cancer Society (ACS). (1998). *Cancer facts and figures–1998.* New York: Author.

American Cancer Society (ACS). (1990). *Cancer facts and figures–1990.* New York: Author.

Balfour, J., & Kaplan, G. (1998). Social class/socioeconomic factors. In J. C. Holland (Ed.), *Psychooncology* (pp. 78–90). New York: Oxford University Press.

Blacker, L. (1995). The launching phase of the life cycle. In E. Carter & M. McGoldrick (Eds.), *The changing family life cycle: A framework for family therapy* (3rd ed., pp. 287–306). New York: Gardner Press.

Bullock, B. (1992). Cells: Structure, function, organization. In B. Bullock & P. Rosendahl (Eds.), *Pathophysiology: Adaptations and alterations in function* (3rd ed., pp. 4–31). Philadelphia: J. B. Lippincott Company.

Bumpass, L., Sweet, J., & Cherlin, A. (1991). The role of cohabitation in the declining rates of marriage. *Journal of Marriage and the Family, 53,* 913–927.

Carter, E., & McGoldrick, M. (Eds.). (1989). *The changing family life cycle: A framework for family therapy* (2nd ed.). Needham Heights, MA: Allyn and Bacon.

Carter, E., & McGoldrick, M. (Eds.). (1995). *The changing family life cycle: A framework for family therapy* (3rd ed.). New York: Gardner Press.

Combrinck-Graham, L. (1988). Adolescent sexuality in the family life cycle. In C. Falicov (Ed.), *Family transitions.* New York: Guilford.

Covinsky, K. E., Goldman, L., Cook, F., Oye, R., Desbiens, N., Reding, D., Fulkerson, W., Connors, A., Lynn, J., & Phillips, R. (1994). The impact of serious illness on patients' families. *Journal of the American Medical Association, 272,* 1839–1844.

Dollinger, M., Rosenbaum, E., & Cable, G. (1997). *Everyone's guide to cancer: How cancer is diagnosed, treated, and managed day to day* (3rd ed.). Toronto, Ontario, Canada: Somerville House Books Limited.

Dow, K. H. (1991). The growing phenomenon of cancer survivorship. *Journal of Professional Nursing, 7,* 54–61.

Duvall, E. (1977). *Family development.* Philadelphia: Lippincott.

Engel, G. (1977). The need for a new medical model: A challenge for biomedicine. *Science, 196,* 129–135.

Erikson, E. H. (1963). *Childhood and society.* New York: Norton Press.

Erikson, E. H. (1968). *Identity and crisis.* New York: Norton Press.

Fulmer, R. (1995). Becoming an adult. In E. Carter & M. McGoldrick (Eds.). *The changing family life cycle: A framework for family therapy* (3rd ed., pp. 215–286). New York: Gardner Press.

Garcia Preto, N. (1989). Transformation of the family system in adolescents. In E. A. Carter & M. McGoldrick (Eds.), *The changing family life cycle: A framework for family therapy* (pp. 256–284). New York: Gardner Press.

Green, R., Harris, R., Forte, J., & Robinson, M. (1991). Evaluating FACES III and circumplex model: 2,440 families, *Family Process, 30*(1), 55–74.

Henderson, P. A. (1997). Psychosocial adjustment of adult cancer survivors: Their needs and counselor intervention. *Journal of Counseling and Development, 75,* 188–194.

Holland, J. C. (1989a). Clinical course of cancer. In J. C. Holland & J. H. Rowland (Eds.), *Handbook of psychooncology: Psychological care of the patient with cancer* (pp. 75–100). New York: Oxford University Press.

Holland, J. C. (1989b). Historical overview. In J. C. Holland & J. H. Rowland (Eds.), *Handbook of psychooncology: Psychological care of the patient with cancer* (pp. 3–12). New York: Oxford University Press.

Holt, W. S. (1991). Factors affecting compliance with screening sigmoidoscopy. *Journal of Family Practice, 32*(6), 585–589.

Houts, P. S., Wojtkowiak, S. L., Simmonds, M. A., Weinberg, G. B., & Heitjan, D. F. (1991). Using a state cancer registry to increase screening behaviors of sisters and daughters of breast cancer patients. *The American Journal of Public Health, 81,* 386–388.

Institute for Health and Aging, University of California, San Francisco. (1996). *Chronic care in America: A 21st century challenge.* Princeton, NJ: Robert Wood Johnson Foundation.

Jacobs, J., Ostroff, J., & Steinglass, P. (1998). Family therapy: A systems approach to cancer care. In J. C. Holland (Ed.), *Psycho-oncology* (pp. 994–1003). New York: Oxford University Press.

Koch, U., & Beutel, M. (1988). Psychische Belastungen und Bewaltigungsprozesse bei Krebspatienten. In U. Koch & R. Stegie (Eds.), *Handbuch der Rehabilitationspsychologie* (pp. 397–434). Berlin: Springer-Verlag.

Kornblith, A. B. (1998). Psychosocial adaptation of cancer survivors. In J. Holland (Ed.), *Psycho-oncology* (pp. 223–254). New York: Oxford University Press.

Lederberg, M. S. (1998). The family of the cancer patient. In J. C. Holland (Ed.), *Psycho-oncology* (pp. 981–993). New York: Oxford University Press.

Lerman, C., Rimer, B., & Engstrom, P. (1991). Cancer risk notification: Psychosocial and ethical implications. *Journal of Clinical Oncology, 9*(7), 1275–1282.

Loscalzo, M., & Brintzenhofescoz, K. (1998). Brief crisis counseling. In J. C. Holland (Ed.), *Psycho-oncology* (pp. 662–675). New York: Oxford University Press.

National Cancer Institute (NCI). (1997). *Questions and answers about metastatic cancer* [Booklet]. Bethesda, MD.

Nicholas, D. R., & Veach, T. A. (2001). The psychosocial assessment of the adult cancer patient. *Professional Psychology: Research and Practice, 31,* 206–215.

Nichols, M. P., & Schwartz, R. C. (1991). *Family therapy: Concepts and methods.* Needham Heights, MA: Allyn and Bacon.

Olson, D. H. (1993). Circumplex model of marital and family systems: Assessing family functioning. In F. Walsh (Ed.), *Normal family processes* (pp. 104–137). New York: Guilford Press.

Parkin, D. M., Pisani, P., & Ferlay, J. (1999). Global cancer statistics. *Cancer Statistics, 49*(1), 33–64.

Quinn, W. H., & Herndon, A. (1986). The family ecology of cancer. *Journal of Psychosocial Oncology, 4*(2), 45–59.

Rait, D., & Lederberg, M. (1989). The family of the cancer patient. In J. C. Holland & J. H. Rowland (Eds.), *Handbook of psychooncology: Psychological care of the patient with cancer* (pp. 585–597). New York: Oxford University Press.

Rolland, J. S. (1995). Chronic illness and the family life cycle. In B. Carter & M. McGoldrick (Eds.), In J. C Holland & J. H. Rowland (Eds.), *The changing family life cycle: A framework for family therapy* (3rd ed., pp. 492–511). New York: Gardner Press.

Rolland, J. S. (1994). *Families, illness, and disability: An integrative treatment model.* New York: Basic Books.

Rowland, J. H. (1989). Developmental stage and adaptation: Adult model. In J. C. Holland & J. H. Rowland (Eds.), *Handbook of psychooncology: Psychological care of the patient with cancer* (pp. 25–43). New York: Oxford University Press.

Schulz, K., Schulz, H., Schulz, O., & Von Kerekjarto, M. (1996). Family structure and psychosocial stress in families of cancer patients. In L. Baider, C. L. Cooper, & A. Kaplan De-Nour (Eds.), *Cancer and the family* (pp. 226–255). New York: John Wiley and Sons Ltd.

Sherman, A. C., & Simonton, S. (1999). Family therapy for cancer patients: Clinical issues and interventions. *The Family Journal: Counseling and Therapy for Couples and Families, 7*(1), 39–50.

Veach, T. A., & Nicholas, D. (2000). *The family adaptation to medical illness inventory (FAMILLI): The making of a measure for second order patients.* Unpublished doctoral dissertation, Ball State University, Muncie, IN.

Veach, T. A., & Nicholas, D. R. (1998). Understanding families of adults with cancer: Combining the clinical course of cancer and stages of family development. *Journal of Counseling and Development 76,* 144–156.

von Bertalanffy, L. (1968). *General systems theory.* New York: George Braziller.

Walsh, F. (1995). The family in later life. In E. A. Carter & M. McGoldrick (Eds.), *The changing family life cycle: A framework for family therapy* (pp. 312–334). New York: Gardner Press.

Zimpfer, D. G. (1992). Psychosocial treatment of life-threatening disease: A wellness model. *Journal of Counseling and Development, 71,* 203–209.

2

CHAPTER

Diagnosis and the Family Life Cycle: The Existential Crisis

The diagnostic phase has many medical and psychosocial variables that affect each stage of the family life cycle. The diagnostic examination is often physically and emotionally stressful. The patient may have to go through many uncomfortable diagnostic procedures and then often wait for test results. It is a time of emotional disequilibrium that reverberates throughout the family system. This is a time of increased anxiety, uncertainty, and anxious apprehension during which family members begin to prepare themselves for very frightening and threatening news.

Biomedical Variables during the Diagnostic Phase

Cancer stage and illness severity have been consistently linked to levels of distress in the family (Sales, Schulz, & Biegel, 1992). Thus, the early identification of the signs of cancer, the early detection of cancer, and the early treatment of cancer are crucial in maintaining both physical and mental health.

Symptom Recognition and Help Seeking

The ACS lists seven warning signs of cancer that form the acronym "CAUTION":

1. Change in bowel or bladder habits
2. A sore that won't heal
3. Unusual bleeding or discharge
4. Thickening or lump in the breast or elsewhere
5. Indigestion or difficulty swallowing
6. Obvious change in a mole or wart
7. Nagging cough or hoarseness

The cancer experience begins with these, and related, physical signs and symptoms. Given the variety of individual differences in response to identifying possible signs of cancer, there could be an immediate response or a significant delay in seeking help (Mor, Masterson-Allen, Goldberg, Guadagnoli, & Wool, 1990). Thus, there can be a lag time between the recognition of suspicious symptoms and seeking medical attention, during which persons gather the necessary intrapersonal coping skills to prepare for a possible cancer diagnosis. Understandably, this is a time of increased anxiety and dread. Beliefs about cancer also play a part in early diagnosis and detection. Many families still regard all cancers as a "death sentence," and do not understand that early detection can lead to possible cure. The family can play a large role in the expediency of the formal diagnostic examination. Families that have little or no medical insurance will often delay seeking treatment. Other families may have difficulty with access to health care and thus put off seeking medical attention. Since early detection and treatment are usually crucial for an increased chance of survival, families that lack insurance and access to health care are more likely to die from cancer, even cancers with substantially increased survival rates (Balfour & Kaplan, 1998; Cella et al., 1991). Different family configurations, financial circumstances, and shared belief systems all impact the initial diagnostic phase.

The Diagnostic Workup

There are four major goals of the diagnostic examination or workup: (1) to determine whether the tumor (or mass) is benign or malignant, (2) to determine the tissue type of the malignancy, (3) to determine the primary or original site of the malignancy, and (4) to determine the extent to which cancer has spread throughout the body (i.e., metastasized). The diagnostic procedure begins with a thorough physical examination and a comprehensive history of the patient's known risk factors (i.e., type of job, smoking habits, alcohol consumption, diet, amount of exercise, family history, etc.). The rest of the diagnostic approach is based upon the patient's specific symptomatology, the patient's ability to tolerate invasive diagnostic procedures, the diagnostic equipment readily available in the hospital or surrounding communities, and the biological characteristics of the suspected malignancy. Procedures may involve laboratory studies, tumor imaging techniques, or more invasive examinations such as endoscopies or biopsies.

The patient may undergo a series of imaging techniques. Radiographic studies, or X rays, can identify problems in dense structures such as bones and are used to distinguish between normal and abnormal body structures. Mammography and occasionally ultrasound (for breast cancer) are radiographic techniques that are used in the detection of breast cancer. CT scans can be ordered to investigate areas of the inner body such as organs and tissue. The CT scan provides multiple images as an X-ray beam circles the body followed by a computerized combination of these scans, which provides a cross-sectional image and detailed evaluation of the brain, chest, abdomen, and pelvis. For example, a chest CT would often be obtained for a patient with lung cancer. CT scans are often used to determine the stage of cancers, as well as provide information about the local and regional extent of disease. Magnetic resonance imaging (MRI) techniques look at thin cross sections of the body. An MRI uses radio waves and strong magnets, which provide a more detailed image than a CT scan, especially in the brainstem and the cerebellum. This procedure enables doctors to identify any additional lesions or tumors that a CT scan may not detect. An MRI evaluation would typically be ordered for a patient with a brain tumor to provide better detail than a CT scan. It is also used to evaluate tumors of the extremities or pelvis, such as soft tissue sarcomas. Ultrasound procedures use sound waves to identify tumors of the prostate, breast, or ovaries. For example, a prostate ultrasound is performed at the time of biopsy, and an ultrasound evaluation can also accompany a mammography to provide additional information regarding a breast abnormality. Two other types of diagnostic procedures include positron emission tomography (PET) scans and angiography.

Sometimes more invasive tests must be used. Endoscopies, or the use of thin (rigid or flexible) telescopes, can be performed to directly visualize inner parts of the body. A bronchoscope can be used to directly examine the lungs, a cystoscope can be used to examine the bladder, and a gastroscope or colonoscope can be used to see the stomach or colon and to collect samples for tissue confirmation. Cytological studies (i.e., the study of cells) and bone marrow analyses are other invasive means used in the confirmation of cancer. Cytological studies (the study of cells) are used to examine cells removed by natural means (coughing up phlegm), or by scraping the surface of an organ. The Pap smear is a cytological study used to detect cervical cancer. Pathologists will examine these cells under a microscope to detect atypical or cancerous changes. Bone marrow also can be analyzed to determine the presence of blood or bone marrow cancers. Small amounts of bone marrow are drawn into a needle (usually via the pelvic bone) and then examined under a microscope to check for leukemia, lymphoma, or other cancer cells.

The most definitive way to confirm the presence of cancer is to perform a biopsy. During a biopsy, tissue is taken directly from the tumor site for a microscopic examination. This can be done using an incisional biopsy (a partial removal of the tumor), an excisional biopsy (complete removal of the tumor), or a needle aspiration. Since biopsies are often performed during surgery, tissue samples from the lymph nodes and nearby organs may also be taken. This helps to determine the presence and the extent of cancer metastasis.

Cancer Severity Continuum

Cancers differ significantly in long-term prognoses, ranging from those that are immediately life threatening to those that only temporarily interrupt the flow of family life. These variations in prognoses form a severity continuum from very good to very poor chances of survival. Thus, although any individual prognosis is influenced by many factors (e.g., type, stage, metastases), a general overview of severity is best understood by examining five-year relative survival rates. Figures 2.1 and 2.2 present survival rates for various types of cancers, ranging from those with good to poor prognoses.

Relative five-year survival rates include individuals who are disease-free, in remission, or still being treated for cancer. These rates are adjusted to take into account persons who had cancer and have died from other means such as heart disease or old age (American

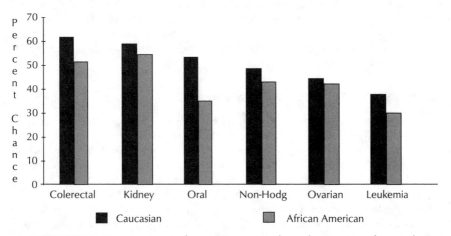

FIGURE 2.1. Five-year survival rates: Cancers with moderate rates of survival.

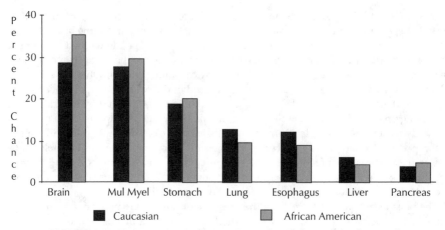

FIGURE 2.2. Five-year survival rates: Cancers with low rates of survival.

Cancer Society [ACS], 1998). For Caucasians, there are several types of cancer with relatively high five-year survival rates (above 70%). These include cancers of the thyroid, testis, prostate, melanoma, breast, endometrium, urinary–bladder, cervix, and larynx and
Hodgkin's disease. When these cancers have been detected early and are still contained,
there is an increased chance of survival. Other types of cancers have more moderate survival rates (40%–65%). These cancers include colorectal, kidney, oral, and ovarian, and
non-Hodgkin's lymphoma and leukemia. Again, early detection, early treatment, and individual factors all contribute to the patient's unique chances of survival. Cancers such as
brain, multiple myeloma, stomach, lung, esophagus, liver, and pancreas are more severe
types of cancers and have relatively low (less than 30%) five-year survival rates. The cancer
severity continuum for Caucasians complete with five-year survival rates associated with
specific cancers are shown in Figures 2.1 and 2.2.

Survival rates differ between Caucasians and African Americans. African Americans
have fewer types of cancer with five-year survival rates over 65%. These cancers include
thyroid, testis, prostate, and breast, and melanoma and Hodgkin's disease. There are more
types of cancer with moderate five-year survival rates (between 33%–66%) for African
Americans. These include urinary–bladder, cervix, kidney, endometrium, larynx, colorectal,
ovarian, brain, oral, non-Hodgkin's lymphoma, and leukemia. More severe cancers (less
than 30% five-year survival rate) for African Americans are multiple myeloma, stomach,
lung, esophagus, pancreas, and liver. The cancer severity continuum for African Americans is also summarized in Figures 2.1 and 2.2.

Diagnosis and Developmental Stage

Different types of cancers are more likely to occur at specific ages and thus during different stages of development. For example, acute leukemia, Hodgkin's disease, lymphoma,
testicular cancer in men, and breast cancer in women are more likely to be diagnosed for
younger adults (Rowland, 1989). Patients from about 35 to 45 have a greater chance of
being diagnosed with lung, breast, colon, rectum, uterine, ovary, and brain cancers, as
well as leukemia and lymphoma (Rowland, 1989). As age increases, so does the risk of
developing cancer. Thus, most families of cancer patients will have an older family member with cancer. The common cancers in later life include lung, breast, colon, rectum,
prostate, pancreas, ovary, uterus, stomach, and brain cancers.

Treatment Planning and Decision Making

Diagnosis is a time of crisis, an acute phase in which the patient and the family system must be mobilized. This is also a time of shock, confusion, anxiety, depression, anger, and denial. Many patients and families report a type of "psychic numbing" during this time. While these emotions are both understandable and normal, they can interfere with the many important, life-altering decisions to be made about treatment. Treatment planning involves medical, personal (age, health, individual desires), and quality of life considerations and typically occurs immediately after diagnosis. It is a time that calls for effective family communication regarding potentially life and death decisions.

The confusion and the emotional intensity of the decision-making process necessitate the presence of a family member or friend when discussing treatment options with the physician. Vast amounts of important information are discussed during the initial physician visit, including the severity of the illness, treatment options, and prognosis. The physician will take many factors into account when presenting the diagnosis and formulating the best treatment plan. The stage of the disease, the cancer type, the biology of the tumor, recommendations from interdisciplinary case conferences, and the unique characteristics of the patient are all taken into consideration. Because patients may not be able to absorb all the information, family members can help to understand, record, and assimilate all that the doctor has to say.

The type and stage of the tumor are usually the most critical factors in determining treatment options. If the tumor has had a long time to grow and to spread, cancer may be present in other parts of the body. It is important to note that the type of cancer is determined by the original site of the cancer. For example, if cancer originates in the breast and has spread to the lungs it is still breast cancer. The type of cancer and its expected behavior (growth rate, chance of spreading) will play a large role in determining recommended cancer treatments. Physicians also have the input of many other specialists to help guide treatment planning. Medical oncologists, radiation oncologists, pathologists, surgeons, oncology nurses, medical physicists, and dosimetrists all contribute to treatment planning. Thus, it is important to stress to the family that they are not alone in this process.

Main treatment options include surgery, radiation therapy, chemotherapy, and biological therapy. Surgery may be limited to only a biopsy, or it may involve a radical procedure. For example, in small cell lung cancer, lymphoma, or Hodgkin's disease, the role of surgery is primarily limited to a biopsy. On the other hand, surgery for breast cancer ranges from lumpectomy to mastectomy, and usually is accompanied by a lymph node dissection or sectional lymph node evaluation. Radiation therapy uses ionizing radiation to alter a cancerous cell's genetic structure (DNA). This results in cell death, or inhibited replication. Radiation therapy can be delivered externally or internally. High energy radiation therapy, from linear accelerators, can be given externally and aimed at the tumor through a series of beams. The internal delivery of radiation therapy is known as brachytherapy and involves implanting radioactive "seeds" near the cancer site. Radiation therapy may be used following surgical treatment, or as a prophylactic or palliative treatment. Prophylactic treatments are those in which radiation may assist, for example, in preventing brain metastases in patients with lung cancer, while palliative radiation treatment is therapy designed to relieve symptoms of the tumor.

Chemotherapy is the use of chemicals (i.e., drugs, medicine) to destroy cancer cells. These drugs may be given orally, through an injection into the blood stream, or by direct placement into a cavity or organ, such as the cerebralspinal fluid, or the lining of the abdomen (American Brain Tumor Association, 1996). The chemotherapy affects tumor cells because the chemotherapy drugs are absorbed by actively dividing mitotic cells. This, unfortunately, means that some healthy mitotic cells may also be affected. It is often these healthy cells that when under the influence of chemotherapy produce the side effects of nausea and fatigue. There are many different types of drugs used in chemotherapy, and thus specific side effects will vary according to the established treatment plan. Biological therapies involve boosting the patient's immune system to treat cancer by using proteins such as interferon and interleukin-2.

Cancer treatment can also be used in various combinations. Combination or multimodality treatments are often used to treat aggressive cancers. Large tumors may necessitate radiation or chemotherapy in order to shrink the tumor before surgery. Conversely, radiation or chemotherapy may be administered after surgery to help decrease recurrence risk. Adjuvant chemotherapy, or chemotherapy after surgery, is given to destroy cancer cells that may be too small to be detected or to kill any remaining cancer cells. Adjuvant therapy is common in the treatment of breast cancer (Dollinger et al., 1997).

☐ Diagnosis and Psychosocial Considerations: The Existential Crisis

Regardless of the type of cancer, its stage, or treatment, the diagnosis of cancer often leaves the patient and the family in a state of "existential crisis" (Weisman & Worden, 1976). The existential crisis marks a period of time, estimated to be the first 100 days after receiving the diagnosis, during which the cancer patient and family show increased concern for issues of life and death (Germino, Fife, & Funk, 1995; Weisman & Worden, 1976). This is a time when families must learn to renegotiate their family structure, reassign their roles and rules, and reevaluate their basic assumptions about how life will unfold. During this time, it becomes clearly evident that cancer is more than a medical disease. Cancer is an illness that impacts multiple dimensions of life. In particular, Donnelly (1995) made an important distinction between the concepts of cancer as disease (biological) and cancer as illness (psychosocial). *Cancer as a disease* places primary focus on the biological processes of tumor size, cell characteristics, and tumor response to treatment. This focus has been criticized as ignoring the person with the disease, forgetting that diseases happen to people, not organisms. The view of *cancer as an illness* places primary focus on the psychosocial aspects of cancer, recognizing the effect cancer can have on multiple dimensions of life, such as family, finances, work, emotions, and basic life assumptions. Although the initial understanding of cancer begins with the medical variables (cancer as a "disease"), the practitioner can gain a broader perspective by addressing the family's unique interpretation of the illness and its meaning (cancer as an "illness").

The Need for Meaning

During the existential crisis, patients and their families reach a peak of vulnerability (Weisman & Worden, 1976). Their very existence and way of life is endangered, and many individuals will search for some kind of meaning to ascribe to the illness regarding the "whys" (Why did this happen? Why now? Why me?) and "wherefores" (How does cancer change me and my life? What is the significance of cancer in my life?), particularly during the diagnostic phase (Taylor, 1995). However, not all family members may need to restructure their lives or to find meaning for the illness. For some, the impact of cancer may be slight and transient, negating the need to address life and death issues (Weisman & Worden, 1976). When the individual's assumptive world is not challenged by the diagnosis, there may be no need to search for meaning (Fawzy, 1994).

Others may have a need for meaning, but respond to the need in less conspicuous ways. Taylor (1995) identifies three less apparent ways in which patients may respond to the need for meaning: through resignation, reconciliation, and remonstration. Through resignation, patients may assume a passive role in the search for meaning by resigning themselves to beliefs such as, "It is impossible to know a reason," or "The reasons don't matter" (p. 38). Others reconcilers may take a more active approach and believe, "There is a reason for this illness. I don't know what it is, but I am reconciled to whatever that reason may be" (p. 38). Remonstrators will continue to search for meaning throughout the course of the illness. The search may be painful, and satisfying answers may not be forthcoming. These patients or family members may find it difficult to accept the illness and become increasingly plagued by a search for meaning, which ultimately leads to discontent and despair (p. 38). Conversely, patients who are able to search for meaning, find or create meaning, and then use that meaning as a source of support, appear to adapt more easily during the diagnostic phase (Germino et al., 1995; Taylor, 1995; Weisman & Worden, 1976).

The Patient's Search for Meaning

The patient's search for meaning, particularly during the time of diagnosis, has been well noted in the psychooncology literature (Donnelly, 1995; Germino et al., 1995; Lewis, 1993; O'Connor, Wicker, & Germino, 1990; Taylor, 1995; Weisman & Worden, 1976). Persons who attempt to find meaning often report that they are more than just coping with the illness; their lives have changed for the better because of the experience (Taylor, 1995). Patients can use meaning to reorganize their priorities and to revitalize their lives and their relationships. The significance of the illness can be integrated into a new model of life, often empowering the patient and leaving a legacy of positive effects (Taylor, 1995).

The coping process involved in the search for meaning requires a balance between the realities of the illness that can, and should, be accepted and those issues that can be harmlessly ignored (Weisman & Worden, 1976). There is a delicate interplay of denial and acceptance that shifts throughout the course of cancer. Denial can be used as a protective mechanism, shielding the patient from distress that is too difficult to cope with at the time. While most patients are able to cope with the reality of the diagnosis, at least enough to begin treatment planning, 10% of cancer patients have been shown to deny the diagnosis of cancer even after lengthy discussions with their doctors (Weisman & Worden, 1976). This level of denial is harmful and potentially lethal. Although most patients will not deny the diagnosis to this extent, some may confuse coping strategies with defensive responses. Some helpful distinctions can be made if coping is conceptualized as the active resolution of a problem, and defense is conceptualized as relief through avoidance and denial. For example, temporary distractions can be used to help calm and protect the patient and thus serve as coping strategies. However, these same distractions can be used to avoid important treatment planning and thus serve as defensive responses. The consequences of emotional and behavioral responses are important in determining the distinction between active, engaged coping and avoidant denial.

During the coping process, individuals may search for causal explanations underlying the illness. Heredity, age, environment, and chance factors are causal reasons often cited for cancer occurrence (Taylor, 1995). Causal explanations are more easily attributable to cancers with specific, known causes. With illnesses such as breast cancer, where there is no known cause, individuals often make multiple determinations regarding causality (i.e., chances are I would get breast cancer, breast cancer runs in the family, stress probably caused it, I am bound to get cancer at my age, etc.). After determining the causal reasons for cancer, responsibility may be attributed to some single, key factor (toxins caused my cancer, therefore I am not responsible). Responsibility may be viewed as either controllable or noncontrollable, where controllable events often lead to blame (Taylor, 1995). Blame can be placed on others, the environment, the self, and even God. When patients blame themselves or other family members for cancer, the impact of the illness can be extremely destructive to the family system (Vess, Moreland, & Schwebel, 1985). When God is held responsible and blamed for the illness, cancer is often perceived as a punishment and the diagnosis can leave the patient guilt ridden and full of self-doubt (Taylor, 1995).

The process of creating meaning also includes a "life review" (O'Connor et al., 1990). The life review can take place on an individual, specific level—the search for meaning *in* life—or on a broader, spiritual level—the search for the meaning *of* life. Patients may view their lives as "well spent" and that they "have no regrets" (O'Connor et al., 1990). These patients have an easier time finding meaning in their lives. Some patients may take stock of their religious or spiritual beliefs and measure themselves accordingly. Patients who believe that they have "lived in accordance with a larger plan" and are a part of "something greater than themselves" often can come to terms with their existential crisis more easily (Germino et al., 1995; Taylor, 1995).

Supportive Components in the Search for Meaning

Hope acts as a supportive component in the personal search for meaning. Hope has been defined as the expectation of achieving realistic goals that are personally significant and satisfying (O'Connor et al., 1990). For cancer patients and their families, hope often centers around the goal of seeing family events such as birthdays, weddings, and other family occasions. Patients and their families often find hope from their doctors, trusting that the treatment is going to be effective and that the patient is going to be cured. Hope can be found even in the most dire of life and death circumstances as witnessed by the patient who simply looks forward to a "peaceful death without pain," or for the patient who perceives "good coming from the illness" (i.e., others quit smoking due to lung cancer diagnosis; O'Connor et al., 1990, p. 173).

Strong religious or spiritual beliefs are often cited as supportive factors during the existential crisis (O'Connor et al., 1990). Some patients may find renewed faith in their church, while others may have an increased appreciation for nature or the "simple things" in life. The patient's priorities often shift so that relationships, particularly with family members, are viewed as the highest priority in life. Depth, strength, and the enduring qualities of the family have been shown to provide the ultimate social support during this time of existential crisis (Germino et al., 1995).

Predictors of Individual Distress during the Existential Crisis

In their landmark study defining the "existential crisis," Weisman and Worden (1976) reported that patients who had regrets about the past, histories of psychiatric treatment or suicidal ideation, more physical symptoms, and less support from their families demonstrated high levels of emotional distress. Patients from multiproblem families, who were extremely pessimistic, who had marital problems, and patients who were widowed or divorced also had higher rates of vulnerability (Weisman & Worden, 1976). Conversely, patients with fewer marital problems, fewer life changes, and fewer physical symptoms had low levels of emotional distress. Patients with colon cancer and malignant melanoma demonstrated peak vulnerability during the diagnostic phase and lung cancer patients were by far the most distressed (Weisman & Worden, 1976). Recent studies have built upon Weisman and Worden's initial work regarding patient responses during the existential crisis to include members of the family system (O'Connor et al., 1990; Taylor, 1995). For example, children of cancer patients have been shown to have increased levels of stress, anxiety, and depression during the diagnostic phase (Compas et al., 1994). Young children demonstrate higher levels of overall stress, whereas older children respond with negative affect such as anxiety and depression. Stress responses in older children have been shown to be a function of the interaction between the sex of the child and the sex of the sick parent (Compas et al., 1994). Adolescent girls were more likely to have difficulties when their mothers were diagnosed with cancer and adolescent boys were more likely to exhibit stress responses when their fathers were diagnosed with cancer (Compas et al., 1994). In addition, adolescent girls whose mothers had cancer were shown to be at high risk for anxiety and depression (Compas et al., 1994). Adolescent girls may be in a particularly high-risk group when a parent has cancer, because they gain greater caretaking responsibilities within the family system (Compas et al., 1994).

Other studies have focused on predictor variables and spousal reactions to the cancer diagnosis (Blanchard, Albrecht, & Ruckdeschel, 1997). During the existential crisis period, predictors of strain for spouses include cancer stage, the emotional adjustment of the patient, gender, age, marital adjustment, and overall family functioning. Specifically, spouses of cancer patients are at an increased risk for psychosocial distress when the patient has been diagnosed with an advanced stage of cancer (Blanchard et al., 1997). Moreover, females, younger spouses, and couples with lower socioeconomic status have greater difficulties with adaptation to the diagnosis of cancer. Spouses of cancer patients who have adequate social support, good communication with their partners, and more flexible family systems are more likely to be able to meet the demands of the diagnosis (Blanchard et al., 1997).

The Family System's Search for Meaning

Families also search for meaning when their collective, assumptive worlds have been challenged (Germino et al., 1995; Lewis, 1993; O'Connor et al., 1990). The very concept of a "family life cycle" implies that the family system will typically follow a common course during which life cycle tasks are completed and mastered. The single young adult usually desires to meet a life partner, to become established in the world of work, and to create a life that is separate from the family of origin. Families with children want to see their children grow, launch their children into adulthood, and retire from fulfilling jobs. Families in later life want to review a life well lived and to see their progeny carry on in the multigenerational life cycle. The crisis of cancer can shatter these expectations, leaving the family in a world that seems devoid of order and meaning. When meaning is created by the family system, it can make the difference between a family that is vulnerable to dysfunction and a family that is strong and flexible enough to meet the demands of the diagnosis.

During the coping process, the family often goes through a time of "destructuring," during which old patterns of behavioral interaction and communication no longer work (Lewis, 1993). The family must restructure the system by establishing new ways of viewing the world, planning for the future, and functioning from day to day. Although the coping process may eventually result in decreased levels of anxiety and depression, the family must first undergo an increase in interpersonal tension (Germino et al., 1995; Lewis, 1993). At first, families will tend to use coping strategies that worked for them in the past. Few individuals or families will change their life styles if the illness does not necessitate that they do so (Weisman & Worden, 1976). However, when these initial strategies do not work, the family must begin to make second-order changes and find new ways to communicate, behave, and define themselves in the family system.

The adult partners, as the executive unit of the system, provide the foundation for the perceptions of the illness for all family members (Germino et al., 1995). The individuals in the executive dyad may have shared needs for creating meaning and shared coping strategies. When this happens, the process of coping with the diagnosis is easier to navigate. However, there may be times when needs and meanings diverge and the coping process becomes more difficult. Some partners search for meaning to find some positive significance from the illness. Others may need to cope with cancer by avoiding it or by attempting to maintain the family's status quo at all costs. Partners with divergent needs and perceptions may result in a family system that is disorganized and chaotic.

Timing of communication is another important factor to consider (Germino et al., 1995). Some partners may wish to discuss the meaning of cancer early in the experience, whereas others may need to wait until later in the process to discuss how cancer has affected their lives. Although family members may have divergent interpretations of the illness, a convergence of shared meaning does not have to take place in order to facilitate successful adaptation to cancer. When family members remain flexible toward, and accepting of, the divergent interpretations of the illness, the family system can be strengthened (Germino et al., 1995).

Each member of the family may have different beliefs regarding the cause of the illness. These may include biological explanations (i.e., virus), societal explanations (i.e., toxins, pollution), family dysfunction (i.e., anxiety, stress in close relationships), and supernatural explanations (i.e., God, wrong morals; Rolland, 1994). Families who are flexible with their causal explanations, and take into consideration multiple biological and psychosocial healing strategies, adapt to the diagnosis easier than families who attribute blame and shame to cancer's cause (Rolland, 1994). Families who blame specific members for the cause of the illness demonstrate greater amounts of tension and difficulty in each phase of the clinical course of cancer. Transitions into new phases of the clinical course of cancer often escalate negative feelings of guilt and shame, particularly during the terminal phase of the illness (Rolland, 1994). The causes attributed to cancer by each family member can be addressed early in the clinical course so that new and flexible causal explanations can be explored.

Predictor Variables of Distress in the Family

Although many families will have little difficulty in finding meaning for the illness, or continuing with life cycle tasks, some families will struggle with the crisis of cancer. Predictor variables of strain have been shown to be either objective factors of the illness, or the contextual variables of the family system (Sales et al., 1992). Medical variables that are indicative of high levels of distress include the severity of the disease as well as the presence of metastatic disease. The family's contextual variables also can be used to predict levels of family distress. Younger families show greater emotional distress, while families in later life have greater difficulty with caregiving demands (Sales et al., 1992). Female members of the family often exhibit more distress than males, and they also provide more physical and emotional support for male patients (p. 15). Families with a lower socioeconomic status and families with recent additional life stressors (loss of job, death in the family) also are at high risk for distress.

Other predictors of family strain may be noted by the hospital staff. For example, there may be a general absence of patient care and support or there may be disruptive family behaviors in the hospital setting (Lederberg, 1998). There may be apparent conflict between the patient and the rest of the family or signs of anxiety and depression in the patient or other family members. In general, families with unhealthy patterns of interaction coupled with negative medical prognoses are more likely to have difficulty coping with the diagnosis (Weisman & Worden, 1976).

Cancer patients and their family systems have been examined using the circumplex model of family cohesion and adaptability (Schulz, Schulz, Schulz, & Von Kerekjarto, 1996). Spouses and children of cancer patients reported that family adaptability was important. Families with the lowest levels of distress demonstrated moderate levels of adaptability. These families demonstrated a balance between knowing their roles and rules and remaining open and ready for change. The importance of flexibility is seen by the adjustment of the family structure, the allocation of tasks, and the juggling of daily responsibilities. These qualities may be more important to the family members of cancer patients than for the patients themselves. Cancer patients have been shown to be more concerned with emotional bonding and family cohesion and find it important to have midrange levels of family cohesion. Thus, while maintaining optimal levels of adaptability is important for spouses and children of cancer patients, patients tend to focus on the need for family cohesion. Although cancer patients need cohesive family systems, sometimes there can be "too much of a good thing." Overcompassionate behavior and exaggerated care can interfere with the patient's adaptation to the diagnosis (Schulz et al., 1996). Flexible family systems, or families that are neither rigid nor chaotic, demonstrate the highest levels of functioning. Flexible family systems are able to diffuse and reduce anxiety and reestablish emotional equilibrium in response to a crisis such as cancer (Kerr, 1981).

Family Assessment during the Diagnostic Phase

Psychosocial interventions can occur as early as the medical workup. The medical workup is often a time of increased anxiety, and families need information regarding (1) the types and purposes of the diagnostic examinations to be performed, (2) when to expect to hear about test results, (3) who will be coordinating the health care, and (4) the normal emotional reactions that may surface while waiting for the diagnosis (Northouse & Peters-Golden, 1993).

The diagnostic phase is the optimum time for the mental health practitioner to meet the family and to become recognized as an essential member of the treatment team (Campbell, McDaniel, & Seaburn, 1992). Rolland (1994) emphasizes the importance of taking a preventive, normative approach toward assisting family adaptation to illness. By including the family from the onset of the illness at least four therapeutic tasks can be accomplished: (1) a family systems consultant is introduced as a member of the health care team, (2) the family system is defined as the unit of care, (3) the expectation of psychosocial strains for the family are normalized in a nonblaming way, and (4) feelings of helplessness and isolation that can lead to family dysfunction are reduced (p. 199). When the family is referred for psychosocial assistance only during later phases of the clinical course of cancer (i.e., recurrence or terminal phases), the family is more likely to feel a sense of shame and failure. By introducing the mental health practitioner during the initial diagnostic phase, these feelings of shame can be alleviated and the therapeutic bond can take place more readily. The overall goal of the therapeutic relationship during the diagnostic phase thus becomes "the optimization of the immediate situation, the provision of immediate emotional comfort, and the creation of an extended, flexible and long-lasting system of support" (Lederberg, 1998, p. 989).

When a family systems approach is not taken by other members of the health care team, the mental health practitioner is more likely to be consulted regarding an individual patient's adaptation to the illness. However, there are five key scenarios that are indicative of an increased need for family involvement: (1) when the family is first informed about the illness; (2) when the family cannot provide care for the patient; (3) when conflict and communication difficulties take place between the patient, family, and health care team; (4) when a family member has current psychiatric symptomatology and is having difficulty adapting to the illness; and (5) when transitions between active and chronic phases occur (Jacobs, Ostroff, & Steinglass, 1998).

When the family is defined as the unit of treatment, there are specific areas that are helpful to address. Lederberg (1998, p. 989) has outlined the necessary components of a family needs assessment: (1) the medical facts about the disease, (2) the preexisting roles in the family system, (3) the required patient care, and (4) the family's available resources. When families do not understand the medical variables, including the patient's prognosis or treatment options, they often feel isolated and hopeless. Informing family members about the facts of the disease and available treatments can help families to have a sense of control, cooperation, and hope. When families demonstrate limited knowledge about the medical variables, or have a fatalistic attitude toward cancer (e.g., "cancer is an automatic death sentence"), the importance of treatment planning and treatment compliance can be negated. Misinformation regarding the medical components of the illness may need to be addressed so that the family will continue with treatment planning.

An assessment of the preexisting family system is also important. The family's structure, boundaries, rules, roles, and levels of cohesion and adaptability can change dramatically in light of a medical crisis. Developmental tasks may need to be put on hold, boundaries may need to shift to accommodate family functioning, and levels of cohesion and adaptability may need to change throughout the clinical course of the illness (Rolland, 1994).

The family can also use this time to formulate how the system will function from day to day. The family can be informed about the patient's expected symptoms, the patient's emotional and physical needs, and added activities of daily functioning, including transportation to treatment and doctor's appointments (Lederberg, 1998). Some families with limited resources may need to be informed about the availability of community, hospital, and private resource agencies. To assist in the assessment of family adaptation, Jacobs, Ostroff, and Steinglass (1998) have provided specific questions regarding the "who," "when," and "what" to tell during the diagnostic phase:

> Do family members understand the diagnosis?
> Are they informing key members of the patient's social network?
> Are family members taking the steps necessary for making sound treatment decisions?
> After the initial shock is over, are any family members visibly struggling with guilt, denial, anger, depression, or anxiety?
> Are family members making realistic plans for the treatment phase? (p. 996)

Recognizing the characteristics of functional family systems can provide a gauge by which to assess family adaptation to the diagnosis of cancer (Fogarty, 1976; Gillies, 1987; Sedgwick, 1981; Taylor, 1990). Here are specific characteristics of successful family functioning: (1) the family system maintains flexibility during transitional stages and periods of stress; (2) emotional disturbances in particular family members are viewed as a function of the system, rather than of the particular individual; (3) generational boundaries are maintained without blurring of authority; (4) overcloseness is avoided; (5) distancing is not used to problem solve; (6) scapegoating or triangulation is not used to problem solve; (7) differences are tolerated within the family system; (8) children have age-appropriate responsibilities and privileges that are negotiated by parents; and (9) each spouse maintains a balance of affective expression, relationship focus, and caretaking.

Family System Assessment Goals during the Diagnostic Phase

Specific goals for assessment during the diagnostic phase include (1) meeting and creating a therapeutic relationship with the family system; (2) identifying the family's structure and preillness roles, rules, and patterns of communication and behaviors; (3) examining the family's understanding of the medical variables; (4) examining the family's beliefs about cancer and how those beliefs will affect family functioning and treatment planning; (5) identify developmental tasks that may need to be put on hold during the crisis phase of the illness; and (6) begin treatment planning and setting goals for the future.

☐ The Six Family Life Cycles during the Diagnostic Phase: The Importance of Assessment

The diagnostic phase has a unique effect for each of the family life cycles. An encapsulation of the impact of the diagnosis on each of the six family life cycles is illustrated in Table 2.1. The impact and meaning of cancer on the family is often determined, in large part, by the extent of disruption of life cycle tasks. Life cycle tasks are usually defined by the activities associated with a particular stage of development (Eisenberg, Sutkin, & Jansen, 1984). Meaning and purpose in life can also be defined by the activities, tasks, and roles each family member has in the system. For example, the father who has been diagnosed with cancer and who can no longer perform life cycle tasks of work and parenting must go through extensive changes in role functioning and thus will give greater meaning to the cancer experience. Moreover, changes in role functioning have been associated with higher levels of distress (O'Connor et al., 1990).

Thus, careful assessment of the many ways in which cancer can impede functioning and disrupt life activities is important during this phase of the illness. Central to the assessment of the family system during the diagnostic phase are the elements of (1) patient background, including developmental tasks and important life activities; (2) background of the patient's family of origin; (3) preillness family structure; (4) medical information, including type of cancer, severity of the disease, and treatment options; and (5) the family's potential existential crises. Case conceptualization then provides the foundation for specific goal setting and intervention.

Regardless of the family life cycle and the disruptions to their tasks, the family system can be successful at coping with the diagnosis of cancer. Families that are successful are able to integrate their previous assumptive worlds with the present state of disorder so that new and more mature systems can be created (Taylor, 1995). These families are able to balance the demands of the illness with the family's activities and daily functions and to create renewed and strengthened family systems (Lewis, 1993). Although most family systems are successful at adapting to cancer, even healthy family systems may need assistance at various points along the clinical course of cancer. The following cases exemplify "normal" family functioning in response to the diagnosis of cancer.

☐ The Single Young Adult during the Diagnostic Phase

When cancer strikes the single young adult, the diagnosis has ramifications for several generations of family functioning. The young adult's family of origin will be affected by the diagnosis, and the patient's grandparents will also feel the impact of the untimely

(text continues on page 44)

TABLE 2.1. Diagnostic Phase and the Family Life Cycle: The Centripetal Force of the Existential Crisis

	Life cycle tasks	Cancer's potential disruption to the system	Psychosocial interventions	Specific topics of communication
Single young adult	Differentiate from the family system	Disrupt process of establishing self in work/intimate relationships; centripetal force of the phase is at odds with the need to differentiate	Provide young adult with information, resources, and help maintain developmental momentum	Discuss interpretation/meaning of illness, understanding of prognosis and treatment options, identify ways to balance dependence and independence during crisis phase
Newly forming couple	Break from families of origin; negotiate the balance of power in the new system	Disrupt the forming of the new system; disrupt balance of power in the new system because illness creates new roles of "patient" and "caregiver"	Provide couple with information; help couple to establish newly forming system in light of a serious illness; help couple determine boundaries with families of origin	Discuss divergent meanings attributed to the illness; discuss impact of the diagnosis on the new system; negotiate patient and caregiver roles
Families with young children	Define new roles for both parents and grandparents; nurture young children	Centripetal force of diagnosis may compound the system's existing inward pull resulting in role strain/confusion	Help family to address fears and needs during the crisis phase; assist family in reallocating roles	Help parents decide what and how to tell young children; discuss divergent meaning attributed to the illness

Family stage	Developmental task	Impact of illness	Intervention	Existential/meaning
Families with adolescents	Create flexible boundaries to accommodate adolescent development	Centripetal force of diagnosis may delay the creation of flexible boundaries; possible role confusion/strain; ambivalent feelings may arise for adolescents	Assist family in temporary developmental dealy; help them to resume tasks after crisis subsides; help to reallocate temporary role	Discuss all family members' understanding of the diagnosis; discuss existential meaning attributed to the diagnosis; identify divergent meanings
Families launching children	Family is learning to accept multiple exits and entries from the system	Centripetal force of the crisis may disrupt centrifugal momentum of the launching process; may delay launching of older children	Assist family in temporary developmental delays; establish more cohesive boundaries until crisis subsides	Discuss interpretations of the illness; discuss individual family member's developmental delays
Families in later life	Adjust to retirement; accept death of peers; form relationships with grandchildren	Disruption to plans and dreams in later life; may have possible resource vacuum or role shifts with adult children	Assess concurrent illnesses, cognitive functioning; assess external resources; prepare for potential role changes	Discuss existential meaning, life review, support, role of patient in multigenerational life cycle

disease. In addition, the young adult's siblings, peers, colleagues, and newly developing intimate relationships will all be affected by the diagnosis. Important decisions regarding the creation of the family's next generation may need to be altered, as the young adult makes decisions regarding marriage, childbirth, and parenthood in light of a life threatening disease. Patterns of relationships will begin to change as each system begins to adapt to cancer in its own way (Lynam, 1995). Parents and grandparents may want to draw the young adult back into the family system so that they may care for him or her on a daily basis. Thus, during the diagnostic phase, the young adult may need to delay the developmental tasks of disengaging from the family of origin, establishing work, and creating a sense of self outside of the family system. A diagram of cancer's impact on the single young adult's generational family system is depicted in Figure 2.3.

The way in which the young adult left the family of origin will also play a role in how the family responds during the diagnostic phase. The young adult who has previously disengaged from the family of origin will have a decision to make regarding either returning to the difficulties of the family system or remaining autonomous from the family and tackling the difficulties of cancer on his or her own. Conversely, if the young adult is overly dependent on the family system, emotionally, financially, and functionally, the diagnosis may thwart any differentiation the young adult has accomplished thus far.

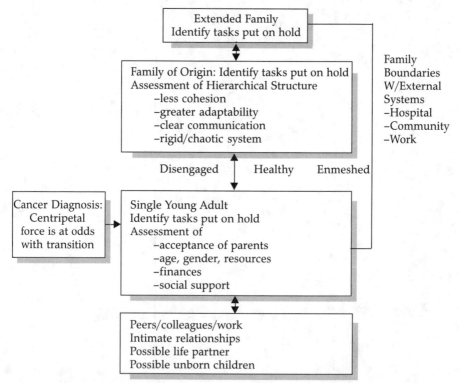

Emotional Process of Transition: Accepting emotional and financial responsibility
 1) **Differentiate from family of origin**
 2) **Develop intimate peer relationship**
 3) **Financial independence**

FIGURE 2.3. Diagnosis and the single young adult.

In the following case, a young single male has been diagnosed with testicular cancer. For males between the ages of 20 and 34 years, testis tumors account for up to 22% of all cancers and are ranked first in cancer incidence (Small, Torti, & Yagoda, 1997). In addition, cancer of the testis is the second most common cancer for men aged 35 to 39, and third most common for men aged 15 to 19. While testicular cancer makes up about 7,200 cases in the United States, only 350 of those cases will result in death each year (Small et al., 1997). Thus, testicular cancer is a highly curable form of cancer.

CASE EXAMPLE 1. The Single Young Adult: A Case of Testicular Cancer

Mark, a single 22-year-old male, with one older brother Mitchel, age 26, and one younger sister, Missy, age 19, was diagnosed with testicular cancer. Mitchel is currently engaged to Margaret, age 25. The family's genogram is pictured in Figure 2.4. Mark has been attending college away from home for the last three years. He describes himself as independent and driven to become a "mechanical engineer, like my brother." He stated that he has had to work very hard at his coursework and has little time for friends, although he has been seeing his girlfriend, Marie, for about eight months. He also works part time in the engineering lab at the university to help finance his education and independent living arrangements. Mark made reference several times to his older brother, Mitchel, who became a mechanical engineer and has made a "successful life for himself." Mark stated that he had always had to do things "the hard way," while things seemed to come easily for Mitchel. He reported that he had always been in good health, he liked to play several sports, and usually ate a healthy diet, so he could not understand why he would get cancer.

Preillness Family Structure

Prior to diagnosis, Mark's family system appeared to be fairly structured. Developmentally, Mark was in the process of creating a sense of self apart from his family of origin. Each family member seemed to have his or her own role in the family, and deviations from those roles were not readily accepted. Communication patterns were also structured, with the parental unit valuing communication with each other, but infrequently with Mark or the other children. The children rarely found time to talk with one another, as they were involved in their own activities such as sports and social events. The family did not have much time to sit down together to have dinner, which left each family member on his or

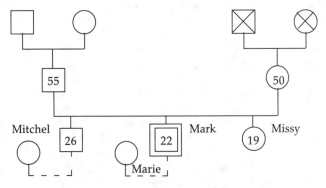

FIGURE 2.4. The single young adult genogram.

her own. The family system was oriented toward goal achievement, and little deviation from those goals was tolerated. The focus of the family system on goal achievement and the developing autonomy of the family members were congruent with this stage of the family life cycle.

Mark's Medical Information

Mark began to discuss his illness by stating, "At first I thought I just had an injury from playing basketball or something." He remarked that one of his testicles had become swollen and painful. He thought he had pulled a groin muscle or had exerted too much energy. When the pain and swelling did not subside after a couple of weeks, Mark decided to tell his brother about his symptoms. His brother began to speak for him, "I didn't think it was anything like cancer! Still, I thought he should go to the student health clinic on campus and get it checked out." After another week, Mark went to the health clinic where he was treated for epididymitis (inflammation of the spermatic cord). His primary physician wanted to see if antibiotics would reduce the swelling and relieve Mark's discomfort. Mark continued to have swelling and discomfort two weeks following antibiotic therapy. His physician then recommended further testing to rule out other diseases.

Mark and his family reported their shock at the diagnosis of cancer, and all the members of the family believed the diagnosis to be life threatening. They understood little about treatment for testicular cancer and were concerned with sterility, nausea, and pain. Mark's father stated that they had discussed radiation therapy treatment with their oncologist, but that they were afraid radiation treatment meant that Mark's cancer was serious and that he would probably not recover. In addition, they expressed concerns about Mark becoming "radioactive" and endangered because of exposure to radiation. Mark was fearful that cancer treatment would debilitate him and prevent him from continuing his education and his job. He also worried that his new relationship with his girlfriend would end because of the disruptions cancer and its treatment would cause. He stated that he did not want to move back in with his family, no matter "how horrible treatment was." He perceived moving back home as an act of "failure," and he did not want to disappoint his family by becoming weak and dependent.

Assessing Psychosocial Considerations: The Family's Existential Crisis

The news about testicular cancer devastated Mark. He was fearful that cancer meant that he "didn't have much time left," and that if he did live long he would never be able to have children, and that "no woman would ever want me." He perceived the diagnosis to be a result of overwhelming stress in his life. He often made self-deprecating comments about the course of his life, how he was a "failure," and how the diagnosis of cancer proved this. He believed his parents would be disappointed in him because of the cancer diagnosis, and thus would view him as a failure. He often asked, "Why me? Why now?" He reported not having a "good relationship with God," and now he "was madder than ever at Him for the pain He has caused." Mark believes that his stress caused his cancer and that the disease proves him to be a failure. Both Mark's mother and father stated that cancer is due to "chemical disruptions in the body, and that no one is responsible for the disease." Mark's parents did not accept Mark's beliefs about cancer, so, therefore, they did not address them. Mitchel remarked that the diagnosis was "really no big deal" and that anything can be "licked if you put your mind to it." When asked what her thoughts were about the diagnosis, Missy stated that the reasons "can't be known and so you just have to trust that everything will be alright."

Diagnosis and the Single, Young Adult: Case Conceptualization

For the family system, the diagnosis of cancer made it necessary for the family system to come together in adaptation to a medical crisis. Patterns of communication, belief systems, long-standing rules, and clear boundaries were challenged by the crisis. All of the members of the family seem to have misconceptions about the severity of the diagnosis and thus its relatively positive prognosis as well as the risks and benefits of cancer treatment. The family must become more informed about Mark's specific cancer diagnosis and options for treatment. Long-term ramifications of different cancer treatments need to be discussed in greater detail with their oncologist.

Mark's family is currently in transition. Prior to the diagnosis, the developmental tasks of differentiating from the family system were taking place with relatively minor difficulties. The centrifugal momentum of the transition (i.e., pushing the family outward from the center of the system) is in direct contrast to the centripetal momentum of the diagnosis (i.e., pulling the family inward toward its center, or family of origin). This "pulling inward" of the family system is also difficult because of the centrifugal momentum of this particular family life cycle. Family members also hold different existential beliefs about the diagnosis, and the existing family structure and communication pattern could impede them from accepting one another's existential viewpoints. Mark equates his diagnosis with being a family or personal failure, while Mitchel does not put much existential weight on the diagnosis. Mark's parents have more biological reasons for the whys and wherefores of the diagnosis. The family may need to become more open to hearing differing beliefs underlying the diagnosis and to become more accepting of alternative perceptions of the illness.

Mark is currently contemplating life-altering decisions regarding career choices, marriage, and even having children in the future. The parental subsystem is also in a time of transition, as they launch their children and renegotiate their marital relationship. They have set new goals for both their marriage (i.e., taking trips and "having fun") and individual development (i.e., goals of becoming a nurse). The family system is also busy with providing a flexible structure for their adolescent daughter, Missy. Missy's developmental tasks involve forming peer relationships and beginning to form an identity apart from her family of origin. Her confusion regarding her responsibilities toward her brother and the diagnosis is developmentally appropriate. Mark's older brother, Mitchel, is in the life-structure maintenance phase of young adulthood. He has an established career, and his developmental position in the family system is thus the most stable (i.e., he has successfully completed the appropriate developmental tasks for his current position in the life cycle), and may therefore be the least disrupted by the diagnosis.

Communication patterns within the family system enforce rules such as "Be highly responsible at all costs," and "Success in your career is of utmost importance." These rules may pose some difficulties for Mark, especially since he believes that he is now a "failure." Mark assumes that any disruptions or setbacks to his goals make him a failure and disappointment to his family. Because of the centrifugal momentum of their stage of family development, there has been a decrease in active family communication. This lack of communication leaves little opportunity for Mark to accurately evaluate his assumptions. Therefore, the rigid communication patterns and boundaries may need to be addressed so that Mark's fears can be heard and his needs be taken care of during the treatment phase of the illness.

Goals of Intervention

Mark's family of origin is functioning within the normal limits of family adaptation to a cancer diagnosis. Goals of intervention during the diagnostic phase for the family are to (1) foster caring relationships within the family system and other support systems; (2) help the family to become more informed about the medical variables, including treatment, treatment dangers, and its long-term ramifications; (3) help the family to alter patterns of communication to promote flexible boundaries and rules within the system; (4) help Mark to establish clearer understanding of the ramifications of the diagnosis, and to identify/rectify feelings of "failure" and "disappointment"; (5) help the family to remain flexible with regard to the challenges of the next phase of the illness; (6) remain apprised of Mark's support system and available resources; and (7) help Mark to become more flexible with exercising his options regarding seeking family support. These goals can be achieved by helping the family to become more knowledgeable about the prognosis and treatment options of testicular cancer, and assisting the family in establishing an active communication pattern. This can be done by helping the family to loosen boundaries and role requirements. An active communication pattern will help the family members to evaluated their perceptions and assumptions regarding their roles and rules within the family. This will also lead to more flexible patterns of interaction so that adaptation to the challenges of the next phase of the illness can be made. Specifically, if Mark's fears of failure and of disappointing his family are heard and validated by his family system, his needs may be more readily met during treatment. Direct communication with his oncologist may relieve some of his fears regarding radiation treatment and its ramifications. The more Mark is informed about treatment procedures and the dangers of treatment, the more he can make realistic plans regarding a future career choice, marital commitment, and decisions about child rearing.

Mark's family has requested that Mark return home for emotional and physical support. Mark's fears of disappointing his family may keep him from returning to his family of origin during treatment, if needed. Since Mark has reported a lack of social support at school, and high levels of stress at the university and in his job, he may need to consider returning to his family of origin during the treatment phase of the illness. While Mark reports that he is currently able to financially support himself, the physical stress of cancer treatment may mean that he has to leave his job or some of his coursework or both. Further, his available support systems and resources need to be examined in detail to assure him the emotional and physical support he may require during treatment. However, returning to his family of origin may require additional family systems work in renegotiating rules, roles, boundary formations, and patterns of communication. Mark's return to his family of origin is counter to his developmental tasks. Failure to modify the family structure in a manner that accommodates Mark's new sense of autonomy could reinforce Mark's perception of being a "failure." The temporary delay of Mark's developmental tasks should thus be emphasized if he returns to his family of origin.

Specific Intervention Strategies: Process and Outcome

Specific therapeutic interventions were chosen and designed to meet the aforementioned goals. The first and second goals were met by creating a therapeutic bond with the family from the onset of the diagnostic phase. By first developing an early relationship with the family system, and allowing each member to tell his or her story, the practitioner can help to normalize the reactions to the crisis of the diagnosis. The second goal was addressed through a family meeting with the oncology nurse to clear up confusion regarding Mark's diagnosis, prognosis, and treatment options.

The next two goals were met by identifying the communication patterns in the family system and by using the family's strengths in order to become a more flexible system. First, the psychosocial considerations specific to the diagnostic phase were explored. Each member of the family system had applied a different existential meaning to the diagnosis. Mark's own beliefs regarding the illness were particularly revealing, because he believed that the illness was a metaphor for his "failures" in life. His parent's causal beliefs differed greatly from his. Both of his parents attributed causal explanations of the illness to biological or physiological occurrences in the human system, and in no way held Mark responsible for the diagnosis. Each family member was encouraged to listen to and validate other members' beliefs without attempting to change them. They used a reflective listening technique, where each member was directed to "mirror" back each family member's beliefs without judgment. They were also encouraged to accept one another's beliefs for the time being. By allowing this exchange of information, Mark felt heard by his family regarding his overwhelming feelings of failure, which were now surfacing in response to the cancer diagnosis. Through active communication, Mark was beginning to challenge his misperceptions regarding his role in the family and his sense of self-worth.

Mark's developmental tasks of differentiating from the family of origin were also discussed during the initial session. Mark's family system left little room for self-disclosure or for self-exploration within the context of family interaction. The parents' push to make swift career choices and to quickly differentiate from the family system was causing concern for Mark. These issues were being exacerbated by the diagnosis of cancer. Since Mark was delayed in making a swift career choice and functionally differentiating from the family system, he often mentioned perceiving himself as a "failure" in the family. Mark's fear of being a "failure" was hypothesized to be a ramification of low self-esteem, caused, in part, by implicit parental messages and a lack of active communication in the family system about family rules and expectations. Self-esteem has been defined as the result of a comparison between the current self-concept and the ideal self (Pope, McHale, & Craighead, 1988). A four-step intervention process adapted from Cobb and Jordan (1993) was used to explore Mark's level of self-esteem in relationship to his perceptions of other family members' expectations of him. First, Mark listed objective descriptors about his roles in the family and in his own life. Second, he listed all of the behaviors he would currently be doing in order to meet his goals in each of his roles. He discussed these expectations and goals openly with his family. Mark described himself as a "son trying to prove myself in a family with high expectations and certain demands." When asked what these "demands" were, he stated, "I must be a strong student in an acceptable job with a good future. So, I followed my brother, who is a 'god' to them, and am studying mechanical engineering." The third step entailed Mark evaluating the degree to which he was meeting current expectations. Mark stated that he felt that he often fell short of his parents' expectations and that "it was killing" him. To Mark, the stress of trying to reach his parents' expectations may have even given him cancer and was "robbing him of his entire life." Last, Mark was asked to describe his own values and goals without attention to his parents' expectations. Mark replied that he would rather describe himself as an artist, a musician, or as a man with a more creative focus in his life's work. He was not sure what this new focus would be, and this uncertainty made him feel like a "failure." The confusion that Mark is feeling at this stage of development was normalized for both him and his family. Often, young adults move in and out of their family system, in search of their own identities in relation to career and intimate relationships (Carter & McGoldrick, 1989).

After much discussion, Mark's parents assured him that "although we want you to have a good career and to be independent, we can tolerate some confusion right now."

The last goals pertinent to the diagnostic evaluation were met by assessing Mark's available resources and by helping Mark to examine all of his available support systems. Mark's available support systems included his few friends at school and his family of origin. Since he spent much time with work and with school, he had made little time for friends and leisure activities. After our initial meeting, Mark became increasingly aware of the support available to him through his family of origin and the hospital staff. By bolstering his support system, and by helping him to become aware of increased options for social and emotional support, preventative measures were taken to ensure greater adaptability during subsequent phases of the illness.

Outcome of the Diagnostic Phase for the Single Young Adult

Mark's family became more knowledgeable regarding Mark's prognosis and treatment options. Mark was diagnosed with early stage seminoma. It was recommended that Mark undergo an orchiectomy (unilateral removal of the testis) with adjuvant radiation therapy. Since testicular cancer is not necessarily life threatening, and radiation therapy is not painful, the family became more at ease in making treatment and developmental decisions. Mark was also given information regarding sperm banking and testing. Since the surgery would also leave Mark disfigured, therapy to discuss sexuality concerns was also recommended by his oncologist.

The family began to become more flexible with communication patterns and role requirements. Each member's existential beliefs were stated and heard by the other family members. Mark's fears of disappointing his family, particularly with regard to his career choice, were validated, and he was assured that he was not perceived as a "failure." His parents told him repeatedly how they were proud of him and that cancer was due to biological reasons, and not for reasons of punishment or blame. These active communication patterns resulted in Mark's increased sense of self-esteem, and a decreased sense of anxiety and stress.

Because Mark began to feel supported and validated by his parents, he decided to take a semester off from his school work and to return home during the course of his treatment. Because of more effective communication leading to a more accurate self-perception, he made these decisions without feeling like a "failure" to his family. His few close friends and his girlfriend were encouraged to visit him on the weekends. Mark thus made the most of his social and emotional support systems during the existential crisis.

During this initial crisis phase, the family's developmental tasks were put on hold in order to meet the challenges of the disease as a cohesive family system. Specifically, Mark's developmental tasks of differentiating from the family of origin were delayed, and thus the family system's task of launching was also delayed. Mark's mother also delayed her own career goals for a short time in order to care for Mark at home during the initial course of his treatment. Because of the mother–son parallel process of delaying developmental tasks, Mark's mother helped to role model healthy adaptability during the diagnostic phase. The family began to make plans for the "long haul" of the treatment phase, and to determine any changes and adjustments that would need to take place in the family system. This longitudinal perspective helped to keep the family focused on recommencing their developmental tasks and on the necessity to remain flexible in order to meet both the demands of the illness and of the family system.

☐ The Newly Forming Couple during the Diagnostic Phase

During the diagnostic phase, newly forming couples may have difficulties in creating new family systems apart from their families of origin. With the stress of the diagnosis, the couple may break apart, with the patient or partner or both returning to the stability of the original family system. If the new partner has not been validated by the patient's family of origin, the patient's family may attempt to disregard the new partner's role in decision making, financial planning, and other requirements of the diagnostic phase. If the new couple is to remain intact, it may be necessary for them to create distinct boundaries that respect the integrity of the new system.

For newly forming couples, the perception of the diagnosis and its long-term ramifications can mean the difference between the solidification of the new union and disintegration of the system. This can be exemplified by the recently married woman diagnosed with breast cancer who told her husband, "If you want a divorce, I can understand why, because it's not as if I'm a whole person now" (O'Connor et al., 1990, p. 171). The task of forming a new union and finding meaning and purpose in the creation of a lasting bond can be severely disrupted when cancer strikes a newly forming couple.

The forming of a new couple, and thus a new family system, is perhaps one of the most complex and difficult transitions of the family life cycle (Feldstein & Rait, 1992). The new couple is beginning to negotiate the tasks of daily living while attempting to bridge two separate families in order to create a more complex network of systems and subsystems (Feldstein & Rait, 1992). When cancer strikes a newly forming couple, the impact can result in increased difficulty not only for the couple themselves, but also for their families of origin and their extended family systems. Cancer's impact on the new couple's multigenerational life cycle is depicted in Figure 2.5.

The couple's families of origin will also have difficulty as they attempt to accept a new member into their family while merging with in-laws and their customs, rituals, and general patterns of communication and life-style habits. Cancer may wreak havoc on newly forming couples who have a history of enmeshment with their families of origin, making it particularly difficult to differentiate and to begin their own lives. New partners who have cut themselves off from their families, attempting premature and pseudoindependence from their origins, may also have difficulty since the diagnosis of cancer often brings to the surface life and death issues, which may need to involve the family of origin. Both the well and the sick partner's relationship with their in-laws may also become intensified during the crisis phase of the illness. If the sick partner's family of origin has had difficulty in letting go of the patient, and in accepting the new relationship, the family may pull the patient back into the system, particularly during the crisis phase when the centripetal momentum of the disease is at a peak.

In the following case example, a newly married young woman has been diagnosed with breast cancer. Breast cancer is the most common malignancy in women; it affects one out of nine women, or 181,600 new cases each year in the United States (Dollinger et al., 1997). Although breast cancer is highly treatable when detected during its early stages, more than 40,000 women die each year from advanced-stage breast cancer. However, the evaluation and treatment for breast cancer has advanced considerably over the last 20 years (Dollinger et al., 1997). Treatment options include various types of limited surgeries and mastectomies, radiation therapy, and chemotherapy. A number of options for breast reconstruction are now available to breast cancer patients (Dollinger et al., 1997). Breast

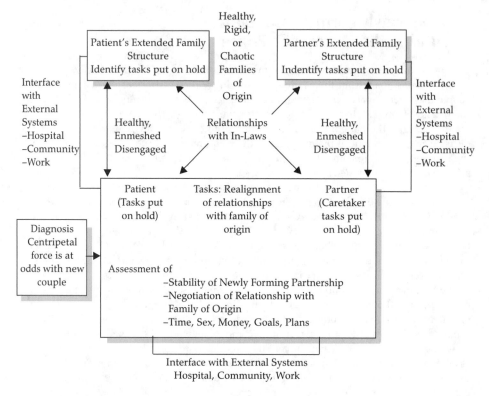

FIGURE 2.5. Diagnosis and the new couple.

cancer will have a different impact depending upon the patient and the family's current life-cycle stage (Oktay & Walter, 1991). Thus breast cancer will be discussed within the following context of a young female, and will later be illustrated by a woman with breast cancer in midlife (see Case Example 5: The Family Launching Children).

CASE EXAMPLE 2. The Newly Forming Couple: A Case of Breast Cancer

Brenda, a 25-year-old female in her first year of marriage to Bob, who is 27, was diagnosed with breast cancer. Their family genogram is pictured in Figure 2.6. Brenda has a college education and practices nursing at the same hospital in which she was diagnosed. She reports that she has always worked very hard at staying healthy and keeping up with all breast exams, even at her young age. She is devastated by the diagnosis and feels betrayed by her profession, modern technology, and her own body. She remarked that Bob has been her strongest support system and that they are very committed to each other, especially since the diagnosis. During the clinical interview, Brenda discussed her family of origin. Brenda's parents are still married and live only a few miles from Brenda and Bob. They all attend the same church regularly. Brenda also has two older brothers who live

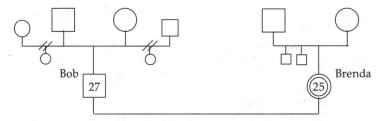

FIGURE 2.6. The newly forming couple genogram.

about an hour away. Brenda stated, "I have always been the baby in the family. My brothers have always protected me and made sure that I was safe. In fact, they are having a hard time approving of my marriage to Bill. I have no idea what this diagnosis is going to do to my parents and to my brothers. I can't tell them about it. It will devastate them."

Bob works as a computer programmer and has been successful in creating and maintaining his own business. Bob reported that his family is very different from Brenda's. "My family doesn't really see each other very much. I mean, my parents are divorced and all of my family lives far away from each other. My older half sister and I have never really been close. My mother remarried when I was almost 17 and she had my younger sister with her new husband. We are from two different, and very separate, families." Brenda had only met Bob's mother, step-father, and half sister once; it was at their wedding almost a year ago. Brenda has never met Bob's biological father, who left the family when Bob was five years old.

Preillness Family Structure

Brenda and Bob discussed their relationship and their struggle to negotiate their own boundaries, rules, and roles for their new system. Brenda stated that although "she was the baby in her family, she knew she had to get a good education and work hard for herself." She has a degree as a nurse practitioner and has worked since her graduation. She describes herself as independent "but deeply in love with my husband." She also reported that it was difficult to make a commitment to Bob because her family could not seem to "let her go." Bob commented that it was hard for him too, because he felt like an "outsider, always wanting to be included and feeling left out." However, he reported that the "situation is changing and they are beginning to accept me." Brenda and Bob appear to have been successful in negotiating their own rules and boundaries within their own subsystem, but reported difficulty with Brenda's enmeshed system and Bill's disengaged one. At this point in the clinical course, both Brenda and Bill did not want to tell the diagnosis to either of their families.

Brenda's Medical Information

Both Brenda and Bob reported having a good understanding of the medical variables involved in Brenda's diagnosis. Brenda was diagnosed with stage II breast cancer. Her type and stage of cancer had a high rate of survival. She was currently in the treatment decision-making process and was considering undergoing a lumpectomy, radiation therapy, and adjuvant chemotherapy. Bob was in agreement with her decisions; however, he reported that he had not dismissed the idea of Brenda having a radical mastectomy "to make sure they get all the cancer out and it doesn't spread." Brenda disagreed with his opinion:

"The lumpectomy with radiation and chemo will be enough," she said. They did not proceed to discuss their disagreement.

Although Brenda and Bob understood their medical diagnosis and prognosis, they reported being very angry with the hospital and with modern technology in general. Brenda remarked that her nursing education had lead her to believe in modern medicine and in the advances of technology for use in early cancer detection. She reported that she had gone in several times to have a lump examined and that the first three times, the exam came back negative. "If I hadn't gone back in a fourth time, who knows where I would be—probably with metastatic cancer by now. How could the doctors have let me down so badly?" Brenda felt betrayed by her profession, the hospital, and the doctors she had trusted. Her faith in her own work as a nurse was also shaken.

Assessing Psychosocial Considerations: The Family's Existential Crisis

Brenda reported that the diagnosis of cancer made her feel vulnerable and out of control. Prior to the diagnosis, both she and Bill had attended the same church for several years together and had enjoyed a life of education and monetary success. Brenda stated that she now felt like "Everything is out of control and I don't know what to do about it." Brenda and Bob stated that they were attending counseling with their minister at their church in order to understand "why God would do this kind of thing." The security that they had found in their faith and in Brenda's medical training had thus been altered, and both of them were going through a change in their relationship with God. Further, Brenda remarked that her plans for the future had also changed. Where once she knew "without a doubt" that she wanted children, she was no longer sure that she would be a good mother now that she was sick. Thus, her meaning goals in life also had been altered by the diagnosis. Bob did not hold this same belief. He said "Of course you can still be a good mother. You are going to come out of this stronger and wiser than ever." At this, Brenda's eyes teared and she shook her head. They did not acknowledge their disagreement with their existential views regarding the diagnosis.

Diagnosis and the Newly Forming Couple: Case Conceptualization

This new couple is in the beginning stages of their family development. They have found it difficult to negotiate the external boundaries of their own developing system with those of Brenda's family. Brenda's family of origin has reportedly demonstrated characteristics of an enmeshed family system. Both Brenda's parents and her brothers have been overly protective of her and have even made it difficult for Brenda to leave the system and begin her new life with Bill. Brenda fears that her family will begin to overcompensate and may insist on cooking the meals, driving her to treatments, and doing the yardwork. Subsequently, Bob has often felt left out of the extended family, of decision making, and has had to struggle to create a separate subsystem with his new wife. The centripetal momentum of the diagnostic phase has made both Brenda and Bob fearful that Brenda's family of origin will begin to assert their influence over their newly forming system and to threaten the marital boundaries Brenda and Bob have created for themselves. They are attempting to maintain their pseudoindependence by not telling their extended families about the diagnosis.

The new couple's relationship with Bill's family of origin is quite different. Bill's family of origin has demonstrated characteristics of a disengaged family system, rarely seeing one another and only being mildly interested in one another's lives (i.e., only meeting Brenda once at the wedding). Brenda and Bob have decided not to tell Bob's family of origin about the diagnosis, believing that "they really wouldn't care much anyway."

Brenda and Bob reported having little difficulty negotiating the rules, roles, and levels of intimacy within their own relationship. They both stated that they wanted to have children, and both appeared to respect each other and thus demonstrated respect and a balance of power within their own system. However, communication appeared blocked or detoured when important subjects such as treatment decision making and children were discussed. It appeared that neither Brenda nor Bob wanted to broach subjects that might upset their equilibrium. The couple has a tendency to withdraw from each other when communicating about sensitive topics. This mutual distancing in communication pattern is commonly called referred to as "silent steamers," where the couple stews about the issues at hand, instead of working toward consensus (Notarius & Markman, 1993). If important topics of communication remain blocked for them, they may encounter difficulty in subsequent phases of the illness. There are at least four areas of discussion that need to be addressed when the couple is ready: (1) Bob's feelings about Brenda's treatment decisions; (2) their differing existential views regarding the illness, and the upset to their religious faith; (3) their desire to keep the illness a secret from their families of origin; and (4) their differing perspectives on having children.

Goals of Intervention

The new couple is functioning within the normal limits of family adaptation to a cancer diagnosis. Thus, primary interventions at this point along the clinical course of cancer are designed to (1) establish a working relationship with the newly forming couple, respecting their boundaries and past communication and behavioral patterns; (2) ensure that the couple has sufficient medical information and that they are comfortable with their treatment decisions; (3) facilitate effective communication within the new system and between the new system and the extended families, while supporting the new system's need to remain independent; (4) discuss existential difficulties and feelings of betrayal to promote successful adaptation to cancer and a trusting relationship with the medical staff; (5) help both Bob and Brenda make sure their thoughts and feelings are being heard with regard to treatment decisions, existential concerns, and future plans; and (6) help the new system to maintain its balance of power and to prepare for the long haul of the treatment phase of the illness.

Brenda and Bob have a sufficient understanding about Brenda's diagnosis and prognosis. However, they are at odds regarding treatment decision making, which could lead to difficulties in the future. It may help both of them to take some time to discuss all the treatment options with their oncologist or oncology nurse. Bob has often felt left out of the decision-making process within their family system, and his thoughts and feelings could easily get pushed aside during this crisis. Because they are in the beginning stages of negotiating power within their system, the diagnosis of cancer may leave the couple feeling out of balance, as Brenda becomes a "patient" and Bob becomes a "caregiver." These roles are very different from the ones they are used to assuming. This imbalance of power could render the newly forming system vulnerable to the strong influence of Brenda's family of origin. The couple already reports not wanting to tell Brenda's family of origin about the diagnosis, but alternative options and ways of communicating important information can be addressed during follow-up sessions with the couple.

Specific Intervention Strategies: Process and Outcome

The specific therapeutic interventions were chosen to help meet the above-mentioned goals for the new system. Goals one and two were accomplished by joining with the new system as a valued member of the health care team and making sure that the couple has adequate information regarding their diagnosis, prognosis, and treatment options. However, meeting goal one was more difficult, given Brenda's feelings of betrayal by professionals in a hospital setting. As a working nurse who has taken active steps toward early detection of cancer, Brenda feels betrayed by her profession for not recognizing sooner that the lump in her breast was cancerous. These feelings of betrayal can impede the forming of a trusting relationship with her health care team. It was important to listen to Brenda's interpretation of her medical crisis. An intervention described by Bardill (1993) was used to address Brenda's feelings of betrayal and anger. Communications. theorists have shown that "relationship considerations about right/wrong differ from the considerations that apply to content level" (p. 186). Specifically, Brenda's feelings of betrayal can be viewed from either content considerations (i.e., factual mistakes occurring at the pathology lab that can be categorized as "right" or "wrong" actions), or from relationship considerations that defy "right" and "wrong" categorization. For the first step, Brenda was asked to discuss her experiences with the health care profession from a relational vantage point.

Brenda was asked to recount, in detail, the past couple of years as she went in for her breast exams. She described an incompetent health care team that did not listen to her fears and concerns regarding the lump in her breast. She was "sure that they didn't care at all" about her, and did not take adequate time in pathology. She "knew that they did things too fast and without care for the people they serve." She reported that she had to "force them to listen and to do further examinations, even after they told her repeatedly nothing was wrong with her . . . that the lump was due to stress." Brenda was visibly distraught as she relayed the details of her "battles with the profession" over the last two years. After discussing and validating her feelings of betrayal and being "let down by a profession she had loved her whole life," Brenda was asked to try and retell the events of the last two years without making the professionals "wrong" or "incompetent." Since her feelings were so strong, she had a difficult time getting started, but with a little assurance, she was able to manage.

> I have always wanted to be a nurse, and, as a little girl, nurses seemed like angels to me. They could do no wrong. They helped soothe and cure, and ease the pain and suffering in this world. I always knew I wanted to be like that. I have always had this type of respect for doctors too, and I guess medical technology falls into that category. You know, it can't fail somehow. Then, when the mammogram failed to detect the malignancy in my breast, I just couldn't believe it! It was like this perfect thing, this wonderful profession, had become so flawed, so wrong. Having this much faith in something could have cost me my life! Now, although it is still difficult, I see that for all of our technological advancements, and for all of our knowledge, we still can't be perfect. I can't be protected from everything in this life, even though my family and my profession has tried to protect me.

The content considerations of Brenda's and Bob's relationship with the health care team, and with each other, centered on their understanding of their treatment options and their ultimate treatment decision-making process. Brenda and Bob were encouraged to meet with their oncology nurse and to discuss all treatment options, taking into consideration both Brenda's and Bob's views on treatment. Bob stated, "I don't really mind giving Brenda the final word on her treatment, but I do want to be heard. I have fears too, and I am a part of this family, so I guess I just want my feelings to matter a little."

Brenda and Bob both exhibited distancing communications patterns, where important decisions and feelings were often disregarded or ignored. The diagnosis of cancer was making it necessary for them to change these patterns and to begin to open up to discussing important life-altering decisions. Some of these decisions include the above-mentioned treatment options. A communication strategy was used to help the couple begin to listen to each other with warmth and validation, called the "speaker–listener" exercise. Here, the couple takes turns being the speaker and the listener, while focusing on reflective listening while in the listener role. The speaker is encouraged to use "I" statements as a way to communicate feelings and thoughts. With the addition of this technique, Brenda and Bob can make sure that they clearly understand each other, while at the same time validating each other's opinions. By using this communication strategy, boundary formation and other communication concerns with their extended families could be addressed. The centripetal momentum of the diagnosis was pulling Brenda and Bob inward to create an separate marital subsystem, while differentiating from their families of origin. At this early stage in their crisis, Brenda and Bob were simply asked to think about how they would ultimately want to interact with their families of origin. The couple was presented with a question that forced them to think about and articulate their ultimate goals for their family interactions. When Brenda was asked, "If a miracle occurred overnight, and your relationship with your family was just how you wanted it to be, what would be different?" She responded that she could be close to her family, yet, at the same time, her family would be more accepting of her husband and of their new marriage. When Bob was asked the same question, he indicated that he would like to have a good relationship with Brenda's family, where he would feel like he had a place in decision making as well as be respected as Brenda's husband.

Importantly, both Brenda and Bob were going through existential crises as a result of the cancer diagnosis. They were beginning to question their relationship with God and with their meanings for life and in life. Their meanings for life focused on perceptions of being betrayed by a higher power, while their meanings in life centered on their decisions regarding children. Since Brenda and Bob were active in their own church, they were encouraged to seek spiritual assistance to help them sort out the existential crisis and their meaning for life. Since they differed in terms of their future meaning in life and their decisions regarding children, they were encouraged to listen to each other during this time of crisis, but to delay attempts to change one another, or to make any final decisions at this early stage.

Outcome of the Diagnostic Phase for the Newly Forming Couple

Brenda began working on reembracing her profession, while at the same time recognizing that modern medicine and health care professionals are imperfect. She also found herself to be more empathetic to patients, because she was a patient herself. Because of the diagnosis, she was beginning to mature and to gain a sense of strength, even during this time of vulnerability. This strength, in turn, helped both her and Bob to begin to establish their own ideas about their new system in relationship to their families of origin. They were able to communicate more effectively, which greatly facilitated their decision-making process. Although they were uncertain about when they would tell their extended families, they began to formulate plans to tell them in the future, "after we have gotten on our feet and made some of our own decisions." Because of Brenda's newly found strength and the use of new communication strategies, Bob reported feeling "heard" by Brenda. His thoughts and feelings regarding the cancer diagnosis, cancer treatment, and any long-term ramifications of cancer, were increasingly being taken into consideration by Brenda. Their newly forming system was being increasingly fortified by their identification of sabotaging coping patterns, the implementation of healthy, effective communication, and the development of more stable second-order changes.

Brenda and Bob discussed their existential concerns with their minister and during follow-up counseling sessions. Brenda's feelings of betrayal began to diminish as she came to terms with her new views of God, and her own sense of vulnerability in an imperfect world. Paradoxically, the vulnerability generated during this time of existential crisis made both Brenda and Bob feel stronger and more solidified in their new marriage. This strength was demonstrated by their courage to discuss and to debate important issues of cancer treatment, by their boundaries with extended family systems, and by their willingness to accept differing existential perceptions of the diagnosis.

☐ The Family with Young Children during the Diagnostic Phase

Families with young children often encounter many difficulties during the diagnostic, decision-making phase. When a parent has been diagnosed with cancer, the experience can devastate the family system, upsetting the family's roles, rules, and boundaries. If the diagnosis is particularly severe, the family system's structure may change dramatically. In essence, the family shifts from a two-parent structure into the semblance of a single-parent home with an added dependent family member—the illness itself (Rolland, 1994). The ill family member must take on the new role of "patient" and the well family member must assume the role of the "caregiver." Both of these new roles can dramatically change the dynamics of the family system. Cancer's impact on the multigenerational life cycle of a family with young children's is illustrated in Figure 2.7.

For families with young children, the patient's functional role of parent can be challenged. The parent's meaning in life may center around the important task of raising children. A sense of purpose may be found in taking a large part in their development and daily activities. Patients with more severe diagnoses may not have the energy to continue with parenting tasks. Newly diagnosed cancer patients may feel "stopped in their tracks" and unable to fulfill their roles as nurturers and providers. For a parent, meaning in life may be greatly altered by a diminished sense of purpose in the family and in the world (O'Connor et al., 1990). For the single parent who has been diagnosed with cancer, the stress of decision making and treatment planning may be too great, and extended family members may need to help in day-to-day functioning.

It is often difficult determining what and how to tell children about the illness. Communication patterns within the family system need to be assessed, and age-appropriate information can be determined before breaking the news of the diagnosis to young children. Children under three years cannot understand the illness but usually have concerns about their own needs (Rittenberg, 1996). Helpful ways to assuage the concerns of a small child include (1) closely following routine schedules, (2) encouraging contact between the ill parent and child, (3) reassuring the child that he or she will not be abandoned, and (4) avoiding any offhand remarks that could be easily misinterpreted by the child (Rittenberg, 1996). Moreover, treatment for cancers of the reproductive system may greatly alter the family's plans for having additional children. Thus, the family's multigenerational structure and development will be changed because of the diagnosis of cancer.

The following case example describes a young mother who has just been diagnosed with cancer of the cervix. Invasive cervical cancer accounts for 6% of cancers in women (Stern, 1997). In addition, 500,000 new cases of preinvasive cancer, or squamous

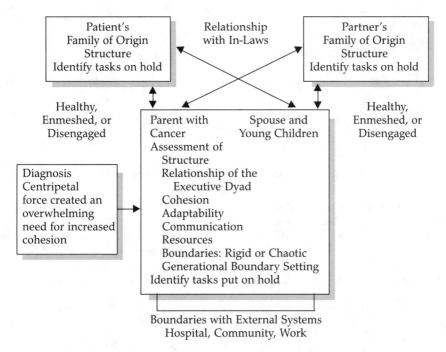

Boundaries with External Systems
Hospital, Community, Work

Emotional Process of Transition: Accepting New Members into the System
  1) **Adjusting marital dyad to include children**
  2) **Joining of childrearing, finances, and household tasks**

FIGURE 2.7. Diagnosis and families with young children.

intraepithelial lesions, will be diagnosed each year in the United States (Stern, 1997). Treatment for cervical cancer typically involves a hysterectomy (Stern, 1997), and thus this type of cancer has a tremendous impact on women and families who have not completed their plans for having children.

CASE EXAMPLE 3. The Family with Young Children: A Case of Cervical Cancer

Sally, a 34-year-old female with two children was recently diagnosed with cervical cancer. Her family's genogram is pictured in Figure 2.8. Sally has been married to Sam for eight years. Sally remarked how all of her friends from high school seemed to get married right after graduation, but she wanted to go to college first. During her last year at a local university, she met Sam and they dated for four years before deciding to get married. "Getting married and having children were the most important decisions I ever made. I knew that Sam and I could build a good family and raise several children together. We always planned on having a pretty big family, at least three or four children." Sally also commented on her family of origin. She stated that she was very close to her mother, but her father always seemed elusive and indifferent toward her. "Sam is different. He pays lots of attention to both me and our two children. They are the most important people in the world to us and we don't want to upset them with this horrible news. How do we tell them

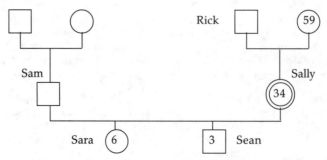

FIGURE 2.8. The families with young children genogram.

their mother has cancer? Would they even understand?" Both Sally and Sam discussed their fears about telling the children about the diagnosis of cancer. They believed that their youngest child, Sean, who is three years old, wouldn't understand much and might get fearful if told the news. "Our six-year-old, Sara, may understand a bit more. But still, we don't want to put any burden on her or cause her to have any fears or concerns. Still, she is pretty smart and she seems to notice everything. We are not sure at all what to tell her and what not to tell her." Sally and Sam felt that they needed more time and more information before telling other family members, especially their children, about the diagnosis.

Preillness Family Structure

When asked, Sally and Sam discussed their preillness family structure. "I guess you could say we are pretty family oriented," Sally remarked. "I worked as a business consultant for a while before Sara was born, but after I had her, I knew I wanted to stay at home with her and our future children. Sam has a pretty good job at a factory here in town, so we can make ends meet. Thank God we have insurance to help us with this." Sally also talked about her mother and how close they are. She expressed fears over telling her mother the news about the diagnosis of cervical cancer. "I know it will devastate her. My mother kind of flips out over stuff anyway, and this will put her over the edge. I don't think that I can tell her, yet, on the other hand, I can't hide it from her either. I guess, too, I am afraid that I can't deal with her reactions and my own at the same time. I have to wait until Sam and I have a hold on the situation."

Sally's Medical Information

Sally and Sam seemed to be in a state of questioning and decision making. Sally reported that she had not been experiencing any symptoms, and that she still felt "very healthy." She had gone in for a routine gynecologic examination and to discuss discontinuing birth control because both her and Sam wanted to have another child. "I thought everything was fine! I had to go in for test after test and they kept coming back "abnormal." Finally, my gynecologist sent me to an oncologist. We are planning on having more children. Now, instead of thinking about life and birth and all of that, we are faced with cancer and possible death! How can we begin to deal with that?" Sam stated that this was the first time Sally had put their fears into words. Since they had little information regarding the specific stage of the cancer, the recommended treatment options, and the long-term ramifications of treatment, Sally and Sam were not able to address the crisis with concrete information and goals. Sam remarked, "I know that our doctor told us more information about Sally's cancer and our treatment options. We just can't seem to register all this information right now."

Assessing Psychosocial Considerations: The Family's Existential Crisis

Sally and Sam were going through the beginning stages of the existential crisis. Both of them were having a difficult time fully accepting the diagnosis, and neither of them was obtaining needed medical information. The diagnosis had completely disrupted their ideas about how their normal, assumptive worlds would unfold, particularly since the diagnosis came at a time when both of them were (1) concentrating on the development of their family system; (2) responding to the centripetal needs of their young system; (3) wanting more children, and thus increasing the inward pull of their system; and (4) feeling healthy and asymptomatic. Neither Sally nor Sam had begun to verbalize the myriad possible ramifications the diagnosis could have on their family system.

Since both Sally and Sam reported drawing much of their strength from their family, the diagnosis of cervical cancer will have a direct impact on their meaning in life and their meaning for life. Both Sally and Sam reported being "family oriented" and they both appeared to derive much meaning and life satisfaction from raising their children and planning for their family's development. Cervical cancer, or any type of cancer of the reproductive system, is going to drastically alter the structure and the meaning of the family system, particularly when it is diagnosed in younger families. Sally and Sam's existential views regarding the diagnosis can be discussed later, after the initial shock has dissipated, and after they have obtained more concrete information regarding treatment, treatment side effects, and long-term prognosis.

Diagnosis and the Family with Young Children: Case Conceptualization

This young family is in a life-maintenance stage of family development. They have had the time and the opportunity to establish their family system as separate from their families of origin while still maintaining contact. Since their family is young, with two small children in the home, the family system is already experiencing a centripetal pull set in motion by the developmental needs of their small children, in particular, and the needs of the young family system, in general. The diagnosis of cancer will more than likely exacerbate the inward pull of the family system, potentially creating role strain because of the added demands and confusion due to the change in the family's stability. Information regarding cancer stage (indicating severity and long-term prognosis) and treatment options will help them to reorganize their family structure and to evaluate how much outside help they will need. Neither Sally nor Sam has demonstrated any patterns of disengagement or "cutoffs" from their families of origin. Because of this, they will be able to utilize necessary outside family support that is needed when a young family is diagnosed with cancer. However, since this young family has little information, they cannot begin treatment planning or seek the support they need.

The diagnosis of cervical cancer will have a direct impact on Sally's reproductive system, and thus on their family's future structure. Sexuality concerns and difficulties also may surface. At this time, Sally and Sam report having a "good marriage" and that they "can talk about anything." However, communication between the couple and their oncologist appears to be blocked at this time. Both Sally and Sam were encouraged to write down specific questions before their next appointment. In addition, it was suggested that they tape record their discussion with the doctor so that they could review it in more detail after their anxiety levels had decreased. Five additional areas of discussion may need to be addressed when the couple is ready: (1) treatment options and the long-term effects of cervical cancer treatment; (2) what and how to tell the children and other outside family members; (3) what types of support their young system needs, now and during subsequent phases of the illness; (4) how cancer has changed the couple's meaning in life; and (5) the long-term implications of the illness on their lives.

Goals of Intervention

Primary interventions for this family are designed to (1) support the young system as they obtain needed information and begin treatment planning; (2) facilitate effective communication between the couple and the medical team; (3) provide counseling on how and what to tell both their children and their families of origin; (4) prevent any possible future breakdowns in communication between the couple and the medical staff, or the couple and the other members of the multigenerational family system; and (5) help the young system to maintain their life structure and to obtain any needed support from either other family members or outside services.

Specific Intervention Strategies: Process and Outcome

The specific intervention strategies were chosen to help meet the above-mentioned goals for the young system. The first two goals were achieved by meeting with the couple and hearing their stories while offering support for their needs. This process encourages Sally and Sam to articulate the specific questions they need to ask their oncologist. Since cervical cancer requires specialized care, there are several important questions Sally and Sam can ask at this point. First, Sally's specific stage of cervical cancer and its recommended treatment should be discussed. Other questions of importance include (Stern, 1997):

1. What qualifications do you have for treating cervical cancer? Will a specialist in gynecologic oncology be involved in my care?
2. What is the advantage of surgery versus radiation therapy?
3. Will a staging surgery be performed? Why or why not?
4. Is adjuvant chemotherapy with radiation therapy beneficial? (p. 405)

Although Sally and Sam understood the importance of obtaining needed medical information, both of them appeared hesitant to ask their oncologist questions. Sally said that she was so "shocked by the news" that she found it difficult to put her questions into words. By writing the questions down and discussing the importance of each question, Sally and Sam felt they were ready for their next appointment with the oncologist. In addition, they met the oncology nurse and several other members of the medical team, including the nutritionist and the social worker. By becoming introduced to the members of the oncology team, they felt they had the support they needed to address the diagnosis with minimal levels of denial.

Next, Sally and Sam wanted to discuss how and what to tell their children. At first, they did not want to discuss Sally's illness with either of the children. However, they were both aware that too little information can result in children filling in missing gaps with mistaken information that can be worse than reality. They decided to tell Sean, since he is only three years old, information that will help him to feel safe and cared for. They decided that, for them, appropriate information for Sean at this time included: (1) mommy is sick and that special doctors are caring for her, (2) there is nothing that he or his sister did to cause this sickness, (3) he is loved and will be cared for by all the family, just as before, and (4) he can talk about the sickness and ask questions if he wants to. Sally and Sam thought that Sean might be able to understand all this information, particularly if they discussed it with him in several different ways and when he appeared ready to receive small bits of information. They also decided to tell Sara much the same things, except they also wanted her to know that Sally's illness was not "catchy." Some young children may be afraid that the well parent may get sick too, or that they did something to cause the illness. Sally and Sam wanted to reassure Sara that she did nothing to make Mommy sick, and that she would be cared for and loved just like before. The couple was also encouraged to have family activities, within Sally's physical well-being, which will help to reinforce the healthy family system and demystify Sally's illness. It may also be beneficial for each child to have "Mommy time," where they are individually able to receive attention from their mother. This will help to buffer against feelings of alienation and abandonment. Sally and Sam were also prepared to recognize any future psychosocial symptoms that Sara may exhibit (e.g., bed wetting, acting out, anger, nightmares) that could be indicative of difficulties in adaptation.

Sally was also concerned with what to tell her mother and when would be the best time. She decided to wait and discuss her illness with her mother until after she had obtained more medical information. Sally realized that her mother could be a tremendous source of support for the entire family system during Sally's treatment and rehabilitation. Still, both Sally and Sam felt that they needed to come to terms with the illness before discussing it with Sally's mother. In preparation for the discussion with her mother, Sally reflected on (1) what details of the illness she wanted her mother to know, (2) what type of emotional support she needed from her mother, (3) what range of emotions she was prepared to share with her mother, and (4) what tangible help the family system needed from her mother during the treatment phase of the illness. If necessary, Sally's mother was also invited to meet the treatment team and to join future counseling sessions.

Outcome of the Diagnostic Phase for the Family with Young Children

At a follow-up consultation, Sally and Sam reported that they were able to discuss Sally's stage of cancer, long-term prognosis, and treatment options with their oncologist. "We felt a little silly asking the same questions over and over again. But this time we wanted to make sure we had all the information we needed to make clear and informed decisions." Sally and Sam found out that Sally's cancer was stage I and that it was confined to the cervix. They also learned that there are at least two treatment options to consider: either undergoing a radical hysterectomy or receiving external-beam radiation followed by an intracavitary cesium insertion. Although Sally and Sam were still demonstrating higher levels of anxiety, they did report being relieved that Sally's overall chance at cure was from 65% to 95%. Sally reported that she felt that she and Sam were now "getting a better picture of it all. I think we can begin to cope with this better now that it is sinking in and we are getting more and more information. I swear, I had to ask the doctor six times about my long-term prognosis. I wanted to make sure I heard her right!" Now that Sally and Sam realize that the illness is not necessarily life threatening at this point, and that there are successful treatment options available to them, they can begin to share the news with other family members. "I think now I can tell my Mom. I can tell her that although it is serious, I do believe I can beat it and come through alright. Sally and Sam also decided to tell their children about the illness. They reported that the children seem to understand and that they "are coping well at this point."

At this time, Sally and Sam are busy coping with the pertinent tasks associated with the crisis phase of the illness. They are beginning to decide on the best treatment possible, and they are beginning to determine the boundaries of communication between their family system and others. Soon, Sally and Sam will need to address the long-term implications of the illness and the lasting effects it will have on their family system. According to Sally, "I don't think I will be able to have more children though. And I just can't think about that right now. We'll discuss that with the health care team later." Right now, Sally and Sam are discussing their treatment options and preparing the family system for the treatment phase of the illness.

☐ The Family with Adolescents during the Diagnostic Phase

The diagnostic phase can be particularly disruptive to families with adolescent children. The family system may already be in upheaval because of the family's changing rules and structure. The crisis of the diagnosis may pull the family back into a preadolescent cycle, wherein the adolescent feels trapped and developmentally delayed. Conversely, the crisis may take the focus off of the adolescent's needs for limits and consequences, leaving the adolescent with no clear-cut boundaries. Adolescents may respond to the diagnosis with varied reactions. Some teens may become preoccupied with illness and their own mortality. For example, daughters of mothers with breast cancer are likely to have increased anxiety regarding their own health and futures (Compas et al., 1994; Compas, Worsham, Ey, & Howell, 1996). Others may withdraw completely, tending to their own developmental needs to be with their peers.

School-aged children most often worry about taking on additional chores and responsibilities (Northouse, 1995) and about being rejected by their peers (Rittenberg, 1996). Details regarding the parent's illness can be given to this age group, since open communication can minimize fantasies, misconceptions, and guilt (Rittenberg, 1996). Parents can (1) allow school-aged children to talk to doctors and nurses, (2) work with teachers to facilitate healthy interaction at school, (3) give the child tasks that can be mastered both at home and at school, and (4) let them help with specific duties in the home (Rittenberg, 1996). The effects of cancer on the multigenerational family with adolescents are illustrated in Figure 2.9.

The following case example depicts a father of three adolescents who has recently been diagnosed with Hodgkin's disease (a type of lymphoma). Hodgkin's and non-Hodgkin's lymphomas account for only about 6% of cancers diagnosed each year, so it is a relatively uncommon type of cancer (Horning & Hardy, 1997). However, Hodgkin's disease is an important type of cancer to note, due to its substantial cure rate (Horning & Hardy, 1997). In fact, the systematic approach that has been taken with diagnosing, staging, treating, and creating clinical trials for the curing of Hodgkin's disease has set a standard for modern cancer therapy (Horning & Hardy, 1997). Hodgkin's disease occurs in a bimodal age distribution. Specifically, incidence rates rise after the age of 10 and peak during the late twenties. After the late twenties, incidence rates decline until the age of 45, when incidence rates begin to steadily increase with age (Rosenthal & Eyre, 1995).

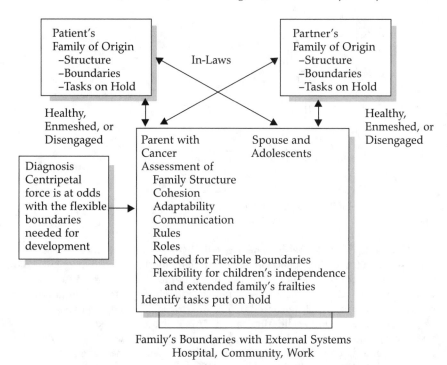

Family's Boundaries with External Systems
Hospital, Community, Work

Emotional Process of Transition: Increasing Flexibility of Family Boundaries
  1) **Shifting of parent–child relationships to permit adolescent independence**
  2) **Refocus on midlife of marital and career issues**
  3) **Beginning shift toward joint caring for older generation**

FIGURE 2.9. Diagnosis and families with adolescents.

CASE EXAMPLE 4. The Family with Adolescents: A Case of Hodgkin's Disease

Frank, a 45-year-old male, married with three adolescent children, was recently diagnosed with Hodgkin's disease. Frank, his wife Anne, and two of their children, Alexis age 13 and Fred age 15, were present for the initial consultation. The family's genogram is pictured in Figure 2.10. Frank has been a carpenter for more than 25 years. He worked with his father when he was an adolescent and inherited the family business after his father died of lung cancer two years ago. He and Anne met in high school and were married shortly after graduation. Anne has her own small catering business and is very busy raising their three adolescents and running her business.

Anne and Frank discussed their families of origin and their own family system. Anne comes from a large family, with four sisters and two brothers. She remarked that they were all close, sometimes "too close." Anne's family lives in a nearby town and the sisters frequently get together to help with the catering business. Conversely, Frank comes from a family of three boys. Frank noted, "None of us see each other very much anymore. I guess we got enough of each other when we were kids." Frank did state that he often

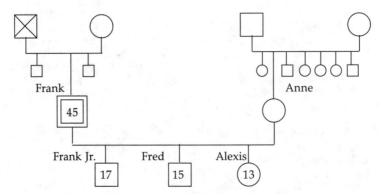

FIGURE 2.10. The families with adolescents genogram.

called his mother, but he rarely saw her since she lived several states away. Both Frank and Anne stated that they "had good kids, but that their oldest son, Frank Jr. (age 17) did not want to hear about the diagnosis or have any part of it." Fred remarked that his brother was being a "jerk" and that he could not understand why he did not want to come to the counseling meeting. Frank remarked that "Frank Jr. was probably pretty scared because he just saw his grandfather die from cancer." Anne also mentioned how close Frank Jr. was to his grandfather. "Frank Jr. was so upset when his Grandpa died. We didn't really even see Frank Jr. for about a month after his death. Whenever he was home, he stayed in his room all the time."

Preillness Family Structure

Due to the centrifugal momentum of this family with adolescents, the boundaries of the system are becoming increasingly open in order to allow for the growth of the children. Communication patterns, too, were open and flexible, with the children and the parents interacting without rigid boundaries. Anne and Frank commented that the children were becoming increasingly involved with their friends and outside activities. However, the boys still work with their father after school and on some weekends. They were paid for their help, but were also expected to "keep their grades up and help at home." Alexis has recently begun helping her mother and her aunts with the catering business. Thus, roles, boundaries, and communication patterns are becoming more relaxed and flexible as the children have become adolescents.

Frank's Medical Information

Since the family had just witnessed the death of a loved one to cancer, they were all understandably shaken when Frank received the news of his diagnosis. Frank had gone to the doctor to have the swelling in the lymph nodes of his underarms examined. Frank had been experiencing the swelling, weight loss, and skin irritation for a few weeks. Frank reported that "at first I thought I was just working too hard and that it was too hot outside. But things kept getting worse." Frank had waited almost two months before seeking medical attention. His signs and symptoms were nebulous, and he believed the swelling would subside on its own. Frank stated, "I never even thought it might be cancer. My Dad had cancer. He coughed and lost so much weight. He was in pain almost all the time. There was no way I had cancer too." Like Frank Jr., the other children were afraid that their father was going to die like their grandfather did. They associated the word "cancer" with death. The family was encouraged to speak to their oncologist and oncology nurse to find out more about Frank's particular stage and treatment options for Hodgkin's disease.

Assessing Psychosocial Considerations: The Family's Existential Crisis

The family discussed the meaning the diagnosis of cancer had for each of them. Frank remarked how he had always followed in his father's footsteps and that he was not surprised that he has cancer now. Frank attributed the cancer diagnosis to genetics and stated that "since my father died of cancer, I figured I would probably get it too. I just didn't know it would be so soon." Cancer, for Anne, had a different meaning. Anne stated that Frank's father had smoked and chewed tobacco for years and that is why he developed lung cancer. She said, "You don't smoke, Frank. So it is nothing that you did wrong. It is probably because I don't go to church anymore with my family." Anne interpreted the diagnosis as being a "punishment from God." Because of this, Anne felt responsible for her husband's disease. Anne also believed that she could help cure her husband of his illness if she returned to her family's church and "made things right with God."

The children appeared to be hurt by Anne's interpretation of the illness. Both of them remarked often about how "She is a great mother," and "None of this was her fault." Alexis commented that she believed "There is no reason for Dad's illness. We just have to deal with things as they come," and Fred remarked, "Dad works too hard. He should learn to take it easy more. Then he wouldn't get sick." Each of the family members has very different meanings attributed to the diagnosis of cancer. Still, all felt that the disease was life threatening and were very fearful of losing Frank.

Diagnosis and the Family with Adolescents: Case Conceptualization

The family system is currently in an early state of transition, with the three children becoming adolescents. Thus, the boundaries, roles, rules, and communication patterns within the system are changing. The centripetal pull of the diagnosis of cancer has brought most of the family system inward to deal with the crisis. However, the oldest son, Frank Jr., has chosen to become disengaged from the family due to the stress of the diagnosis. The rest of the family system has allowed Frank Jr. to establish his own boundaries, even though his absence from the family meeting caused slight disruption to the system. Although Frank Jr. was not present at the session, his absence can most likely be attributed to his developmental stage. Teens can respond with ambivalent feelings toward the diagnosis of cancer. On one hand they may feel drawn in more tightly to the family system. On the other hand, they may feel drawn toward their friends and their own independent lives. Although it is difficult for the family members, they are currently allowing Frank Jr. to respond to the diagnosis in his own way. However, the rest of the family members appear to be having a difficult time accepting Frank Jr.'s choice to disengage from the family system during a time of crisis.

Communication patterns in the family are flexible and seem to enforce rules such as "You can speak freely," and "It's safe to express emotions." Because of the flexibility of both the family system's boundaries and communication patterns, the family is more likely to (1) accept differing meanings attributed to the illness, (2) accept changing roles during Frank's treatment, (3) maintain their developmental momentum as a family with adolescents, and (4) become strengthened as a family system.

Goals of Intervention

Frank and Anne's family appears to be functioning well within the normal limits of family adaptation to cancer. Primary interventions will be aimed at (1) supporting the family system during a time of crisis and helping the system to prepare for the next phase of the illness, (2) helping the family to maintain its centrifugal momentum in light of the centripetal pull of the crisis, (3) encouraging this family's natural tendencies to be flexible and open to diverse meanings attributed to the illness, and (4) encouraging the adolescents to maintain a balance between engaging in the family system during a time of need while still developmentally differentiating from the system.

Since Frank's diagnosis of Hodgkin's disease is probably not a life-threatening one, the permanent disruption to the family system will probably be minimal. However, the family has recently lost a loved one to cancer, so the effects of even a highly curable form of cancer may be exacerbated by the family's previous health-related experiences. Frank and Frank Jr.'s relationship to the deceased is of particular importance. Although Frank Jr.'s absence from the session may be due to his stage of development, an important goal in this family's assessment is to ensure that Frank Jr. is able to adapt well to his father's diagnosis.

Specific Intervention Strategies: Process and Outcome

The first two goals were accomplished by scheduling a follow-up appointment with the family to discuss Frank's long-term prognosis, to decide upon treatment, and to assess the family's potential to adapt during treatment. Frank Jr. was especially invited to attend this follow-up consultation. The entire family was present during this session, which was scheduled to take place directly after their consultation with the oncologist. The family was pleased to report that Frank's type of cancer is highly curable with concurrent radiotherapy and combined chemotherapy treatments. Frank was diagnosed with stage II Hodgkin's disease (involvement of two or more lymph node regions on the same side of his diaphragm; Horning & Hardy, 1997). Frank was scheduled to begin his treatment the following week.

After fully understanding the type of cancer Frank has, its severity, and their treatment options, the family's ascribed meanings behind the diagnosis changed. Frank remarked that he now understood that he didn't get Hodgkin's disease because his father had lung cancer, nor did he get it from working too hard. "But I can tell you that even though I probably am not going to die from this, it did change my life. I want to spend more time with my family doing fun things. I want to get to really know my kids and my wife." The meaning behind the diagnosis also shifted for Anne. "I still believe that this diagnosis was a wake-up call for our family. God wanted to pull us back to church and to help us come together as a family. We have been growing away from Him and our family seems to be coming apart too."

To meet goals three and four, the family was encouraged to discuss how they viewed their system now that the children were getting older. The dynamics of the centrifugal momentum of the family were normalized. In addition, the family was helped to understand how the pull of the diagnosis was bringing them together in order to meet the needs of the crisis phase. However, each family member was encouraged to discuss his or her own needs and how those needs could still be met even while taking care of their family during an illness. The rules and roles were discussed, and new tasks were assigned to each of the children to fulfill during the treatment phase. However, the children also stated that some of their more important differentiating tasks must also be met. Alexis wanted to make sure that she could continue her dancing lessons and to have friends over, when appropriate. It was important to Fred that he continue to play on the basketball team. He wanted to finish out the season, which would be over in three weeks. Frank and Anne both thought that these needs could easily be met.

To continue to assure that each family member was receiving the appropriate amount of autonomy, while also contributing to the family needs, weekly family meetings were encouraged. At these meetings, the family was encouraged to discuss the dissemination of chores and tasks, while also becoming apprised of upcoming social events and obligations. This encouraged flexibility and open communication throughout the course of treatment and beyond.

Frank Jr. was also encouraged to discuss his perceptions of the illness, as well as his grief over the loss of his grandfather. He stated that at first he was really scared his father was going to die. "I just wanted to run away and hide. If Dad dies, then that will mean that I have to become the man of the family and I am not ready for that. I am still pretty much just a kid." Frank Jr. was also afraid that much of the responsibility of the family business would fall on him during his father's treatment. Frank and Anne were able to discuss their expectations of him during treatment, but they were also able to stress that any added responsibilities were only temporary. Frank's developmental needs of differentiating from the family system were also listened to. Frank stated that he needed some time to spend with his friends and with his new girlfriend. Although he would work for his father on the weekends, Frank was permitted time for his own needs each week.

Outcome of the Diagnostic Phase for the Family with Adolescents

The family was able to become more knowledgeable regarding Frank's diagnosis and treatment. During the first few weeks of the existential crisis, the family system's boundaries became slightly more rigid and impermeable to outside family members. However, Anne's mother was able to help out during the week by getting the children to and from their school sports, activities, and dance lessons. Anne took a few weeks off from her catering business and allowed her sisters to do most of the work. The family system was able to remain flexible with their roles, rules, and communication patterns in order to meet the needs of the diagnostic phase. Frank Jr. reported that he was slightly overwhelmed by school and work, but he also knew that his new role in the family system was only temporary. Both Anne and Frank were still making sure that Frank Jr. did get time to meet his own personal needs, and that his developmental momentum was only slightly delayed during this phase. Each family member's developmental tasks will be reevaluated during the next phase of the illness.

☐ The Family Launching Children during the Diagnostic Phase

The diagnosis of cancer during this life cycle has ramifications for many generations of the family. Age-appropriate children may be anticipating or already participating in the creation of their own lives outside of the family system. They may be drawn back to their families of origin to help care for their sick parent, or for younger siblings. For enmeshed families, or for families with difficulty launching their children, the diagnosis of cancer can become a reason for remaining in a more desirable prelaunching stage. For families that are disengaged, or for families that have looked forward to launching their children, the necessity of keeping the children home for additional help may be a disappointment

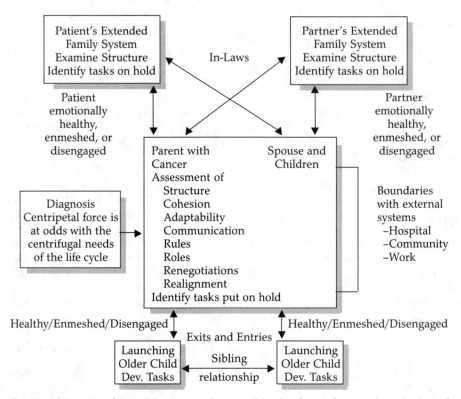

Emotional Process of Transition: Accepting a multitude of exits from and entries into the family system
   1) **Renegotiation of marital system as a dyad**
   2) **Development of adult-to-adult relationships between grown children and parents**
   3) **Realignment of relationships to include in-laws and grandchildren**

FIGURE 2.11. Families in the launching stage.

for everyone. When the cancer diagnosis is severe, grandparents may also need to be called back to help the family. Cancer's impact on families launching their children is illustrated in Figure 2.11.

Families launching children may be affected by cancer depending upon where they are in the launching process (Rolland, 1994). Families with children who are becoming well established in their own lives may need to adjust their daily routines to assist during the crisis phase. However, this type of disruption is different from the disruption cancer has on a family just beginning the launching stage. Families with children anticipating leaving home, or making concrete plans to do so, may be faced with difficult decisions. Adult children may have to alter life plans and to postpone the differentiating process in order to remain home during the crisis. If the developmental tasks of launching children are not resumed after the crisis subsides, the illness can imbed itself into the family structure, leaving the family stuck and without the developmental momentum needed to resume and complete the launching process. When this happens, adult children can remain indefinitely taking care of the family of origin, often sacrificing their own developmental needs.

The following case is about a woman in midlife who has just been diagnosed with breast cancer and how cancer affects her role as an individual, a wife, and mother of grown children. Although breast cancer has already been depicted in a previous case example, it is one of the most common diseases to affect women, with almost as many women dying from breast cancer *each* year as the total number of people who have died from the AIDS epidemic (Oktay & Walter, 1991) and thus warrants further attention. In addition, breast cancer has a different impact on women and families depending upon the developmental stage of the patient and the family's life cycle.

CASE EXAMPLE 5. The Family Launching Children: A Case of Breast Cancer

Claire, a 47-year-old, married mother of two adult children, was recently diagnosed with stage II breast cancer. Claire was unaccompanied to the initial consultation. Claire reported that she had been married for 23 years and had two grown children, Katherine, age 21, and Peter, age 23. Their family genogram is pictured in Figure 2.12. Her son had graduated from college the previous year and was working at a pharmaceutical company in a nearby town. Katherine was completing her bachelor's degree in journalism and was planning to travel to Europe with friends after graduation.

Claire also discussed her husband, Greg, who could not be with her today. "Greg and I have a different kind of marriage I guess. Well, at least I think it is different now that the children have left home." Claire noted that she felt distant from her husband and that they had little in common now that they were not focusing on the children and their development. "Greg is a writer and I think that he spends much of his time in his own world. When he is not writing or interviewing people, he is usually fishing. We never really see each other anymore." When asked about her family of origin, Claire stated that she had three sisters and two brothers; one of the brothers died when he was only four years old. Claire remarked that she was close to her family, "But since they all live so far away, I don't feel that they are a big part of my life right now." Claire also reported that she felt "alone" most of the time and that "Everyone seems to be caught up in their own lives and I am left behind."

Preillness Family Structure

Claire's family is highly disengaged. The children have moved to college and have been successfully "launched" from the family system. While Greg has his work and individual

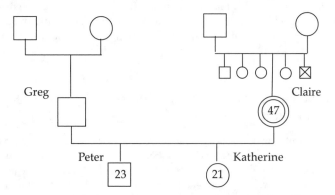

FIGURE 2.12. The family launching children genogram.

interests to help him adjust to this stage of the family life cycle, Claire has had difficulty adapting. Claire had just begun classes at the local college in pursuit of a degree in elementary education. She claimed, "Life was passing me by and I had to do something." Claire reported that communication was good with her two children, especially her daughter. "I talk to her at least once a week to keep caught up with her life. But that still isn't like having her here at home." She talked less often with Peter, now that he is busy working and is in a "serious relationship." When asked about communication with her husband, Claire stated, "I don't know how to talk to him anymore. Without the kids there just isn't much to say."

Medical Information

Claire discussed her medical condition and seemed very knowledgeable regarding her disease, its stage and severity, and her treatment options. "I noted a lump in my breast a few weeks ago while I was taking a shower. I have always had slightly lumpy breasts, so at first I didn't think anything of it. But the lump began to change and to grow. Then, I knew this lump was different. I didn't tell Greg about it. I am not sure why. I guess I am afraid he won't care. I went to have it biopsied a couple of weeks ago. I received a phone call from the physician's office at around 8:00 one evening when Greg was out fishing. I'll never forget that phone call. The woman on the phone told me the lump was malignant and that I should come in to discuss treatment. Can you believe it? I still haven't had the guts to tell Greg. He doesn't even know I am here."

Assessing Psychosocial Considerations: The Family's Existential Crisis

As Claire talked about her family and her medical condition, she appeared to grow increasingly despondent. Verbalizing the diagnosis of cancer often brings home the reality of the illness and its ramifications. During the consultation, Claire remarked about the "emptiness" in her life. "I feel as if life has no meaning for me. My kids are gone. I have no marketable skills, and I feel as if I am alone." For Claire, the diagnosis of cancer drove home the message that "life is over" for her. The diagnosis of cancer was the severing blow between her and the rest of her family, between her and her own desire to seek any joy from life. Claire remarked that Greg would probably either want to leave the marriage or, even worse, not care one way or the other. "I am more scared for my daughter than for me or anyone else. Although she knows I found a lump, she doesn't know about the diagnosis. I am afraid she will alter her own plans and want to be with me during treatment. Then how do you think I will feel? Guilty and depressed. That's how." Thus, the diagnosis of cancer also meant that Claire was the "bad mother," the "destroyer of plans," and a "burden to her husband."

Diagnosis and the Family Launching Children: Case Conceptualization

This family is currently finishing up the launching phase of family development. Although Claire is proud of her children and how they have been able to establish themselves in their own studies, plans, and careers, she also misses them and feels devoid of meaning in her own life. Too, the marital dyad has not been successful at completing this stage of the family life cycle. During the launching stage, the marital dyad must take the time to (1) renegotiate the relationship, (2) recommit to the marital subsystem, and (3) discover new and creative ways to share life that are apart from meeting the needs of the children and the family system. In essence, Greg has become absent from the marital subsystem. Further, rather than attempt to rebuild their subsystem, Claire now confides in her daughter, Katherine, and has thus triangulated Katherine with her marital relationship with Greg. This shift in boundaries and communication has created subtle changes both within the marital subsystem as well as in the boundaries between the marital subsystem and the children's subsystem. Because of the launching stage of the family system, it is appropriate to loosen boundaries and to renegotiate roles and relationships. However, this renegotiation should not take place at the expense of the marital relationship.

Claire was beginning to develop her own interests and to make her own career plans by beginning classes. While this would help her to create meaning and substance in life, and to gain a sense of generativity that would last into later adult life, her newfound plans would not necessarily help the marital subsystem. After the launching of their children, Claire and Greg experienced a breakdown in communication that has lasted for about three years, which had resulted in Claire feeling isolated and lonely, and it is hypothesized that Greg may be experiencing these feelings too.

Goals of Intervention

Largely due to the preillness structure of the family system, Claire is not adapting well to the initial diagnosis of cancer. Although she is well informed regarding her diagnosis, stage, severity, and treatment options, she reports feeling isolated and apathetic regarding the future. Goals will thus be focused on (1) supporting Claire during the diagnostic phase and helping her to articulate how to tell her family the news about the diagnosis, (2) facilitating communication between Claire and her husband, (3) using both effective communication strategies and the natural centripetal pull of the diagnostic phase to bring the disengaged system back to a healthier mode of functioning, (4) helping the family to prepare for the demands of the treatment phase, and (5) detriangulating their daughter while still upholding the stability of the family system.

Specific Intervention Strategies: Process and Outcome

To meet the first goal, it was recommended that Claire first discuss the news of the diagnosis with her husband rather than with her daughter. This intervention focused on supporting and upholding the marital system. Although this did not feel as safe for Claire as it would be if she told her daughter first, Claire realized that by confiding in her husband she was accomplishing two important goals: (1) opening communication patterns between her and her husband, and (2) breaking the pattern of triangulation that was taking place between her, her husband, and their daughter. It was further recommended that Greg be invited to accompany Claire to a follow-up session.

Claire and Greg were both present at the next session the following week. Both of them had just had a consultation with their oncologist to decide upon Claire's best treatment option. Claire began the meeting: "This week everything is so different. I was able to tell Greg everything. I just said, 'Greg, I need to talk to you about something important.' I began by telling him about the lump I found and about the results of the biopsy. He couldn't believe that I had held all this inside for so long." Greg commented, "Yeah, here I am just going along like everything is fine. I had no idea what she was going through!" They had decided to wait to tell their children until after discussing treatment regimens and treatment side effects with their oncologist.

Claire began, "We have already decided on treatment. We agree that I should have a mastectomy followed by chemotherapy. The chemotherapy will take place over the course of several months. Although I am scared, I feel better now that Greg knows about the diagnosis and that he is here with me now." Both Claire and Greg wanted to increase the effectiveness of their communication. Until the diagnosis of cancer, neither of them had fully realized how distant they had become from one another. First, we discussed the three parts to a relationship as defined by Satir (1988): the "you," the "me," and the "us." Greg had established the "me" portion of the relationship by continuing to work and to fish as he had always done. On the other hand he seldom paid much attention to the "you" or the "us" necessary in maintaining a healthy marital relationship. Claire was beginning to redefine the "me" in their relationship by beginning her classes and developing plans of her own now that the children had left home. She, too, was neglecting the "you" and the "us" important to the relationship. Claire and Greg decided to spend more time cultivating the "us" portion of their marriage, and the centripetal pull of the crisis made this mandatory to do so. Throughout the duration of the first few months of the diagnostic and early treatment phase (i.e., the existential crisis), Greg and Claire continued to come to counseling. The technique of "caring behaviors" was suggested to the couple, where they identify activities that would express their care for one another and then act on those identified needs. The need for these caring behaviors was emphasized through the metaphor of a bank account (Notarius & Markman, 1993; Campbell, McDaniel, & Seaburn, 1992), where the current status of the couple's marital bank account was in the "red." The couple's account status prior to the diagnosis was fairly depleted, and the cancer was the event that caused the couple to seriously contemplate the account status of their relationship. Through the use of caring behaviors, the couple was able to make behavioral deposits into their relationship that will sustain them throughout the long haul of cancer treatment. They also began to work on enhancing their communication skills by using the three basic interactional steps in communicating wants: (1) declaration of wants, (2) confirmation of wants, and (3) verification of wants (Forisha, 1993). In the declaration of wants, the first partner expresses the particulars of a current want or desire. In the confirmation of wants, the second partner restates what he or she has heard, confirming that the want has been heard. In the last interactional step, the second partner seeks to verify the confirmation by asking, "Is that correct?" This step is completed by the first partner, who responds either "yes" or "no." Claire, in particular, was learning how to declare her wants during the existential crisis. Moreover, Greg was learning to hear her wants and to respond accordingly. In doing so, an existential shift began to occur in Claire. Although she was facing a life threatening illness, she began to cultivate new meaning in her marriage and to be inspired to continue to work on her relationship with Greg. Claire stated, "Now I feel I have so much to live for. I have my marriage, we have our children, we may be grandparents some day. I also have my school and my own goals, which I am still planning on pursuing. It seems so ironic that the threat of death can bring about so much love for life."

Outcome of the Diagnostic Phase for the Family Launching Children

Claire and Greg continued their counseling sessions during the weeks that Claire received her chemotherapy, and during the times when she felt physically up to the sessions. The first few weeks of the existential crisis were a turning point in their marriage and thus for the entire family system. Since Claire was able to discuss the diagnosis with Greg first, before confiding in her daughter, Claire was able to break the pattern of first discussing matters of importance with her daughter, and subsequently shutting off her husband and their need to communicate. Although Claire and her daughter are still close, the triangulation of the daughter with the marital dyad no longer takes place.

As Claire had expected, Katherine wanted to leave school and cancel her plans to go to Europe the following summer in order to take care of her mother. Both Claire and Greg were able to sit down with their daughter and reassure her that Greg would be able to help her through the surgery and through chemotherapy treatments. By strengthening the marital dyad, Katherine was allowed to continue her developmental tasks of differentiating from the family and establishing herself in her own world of school, work, and intimate relationships. Peter was also concerned about his mother. He, too, felt reassured when his father told him that his mother would be alright under his care. Because of the children's concern for their mother, communication was increased, specifically around the role of the children in their mother's illness. These new communication patterns assisted to reunify the family while also respecting the developmental needs of the children.

☐ The Family in Later Life during the Diagnostic Phase

Cancer risk increases with age, and thus this is the family life cycle that is most often hit by the diagnosis of cancer. The multigenerational impact of cancer in later life is illustrated in Figure 2.13. Older adults may feel "cheated" out of their retirement years, a time that many have worked and saved for much of their adult lives. Families in later life may struggle to integrate the diagnosis with their previous plans of retirement and with the process of the life review: "I spent the last seven years working toward retirement. But having this thing right here has changed this. I might not make it five years" (O'Connor et al., 1990, p. 170). Being useful to others, living a fulfilling life, and creating meaning from life-long relationships are tasks that may be disrupted during the diagnostic phase for older patients. They may also worry about the increased likelihood of other family members getting cancer. In addition, their concerns about becoming a burden to their families may have a direct impact on treatment decision making (Germino et al., 1995). Older patients may refuse treatment for fear of placing financial and emotional burdens on their families. Older adults may be struggling financially, and the diagnosis of cancer may pose economic devastation.

These concerns will often weigh heavily on the older cancer patient who must face giving up independence and autonomy. If the diagnosis is severe, and cancer treatment is to be extensive, the older patient may decide to move in with adult children in order to receive daily care. Available resources should be evaluated as early as possible, so that both the patient and the potential caregivers can become emotionally and functionally prepared for the next phase of the illness.

The following is a case example about a male in later life who has been diagnosed with prostate cancer. Prostate cancer is the most common type of cancer diagnosed in males over the age of 65 and is the second leading cause of cancer death for men (Zinner & Brosman, 1997). Although more than 300,000 new cases of prostate cancer are diagnosed each year, it is highly treatable when it is diagnosed in its early stages—before it has had a chance to metastasize beyond the prostate gland (Zinner & Brosman, 1997). Because of advances in diagnostic testing, particularly the development of a specific blood test that checks for the levels of a "prostate-specific antigen" (PSA), fewer than 5% of all prostate cancer diagnoses will be metastatic. Thus, when detected early, prostate cancer is now a highly treatable form of cancer.

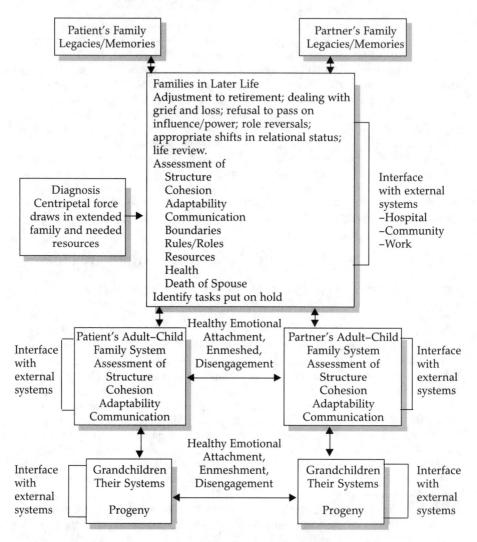

Emotional Process of Transition: Accepting the shifting of generational roles
1) Maintaining own and/or couple functioning and interests
2) Exploration of new familial and social role options
3) Making room in the system for wisdom/experience of the elderly
4) Supporting the middle generation without overfunctioning for them
5) Dealing with the loss of spouse, siblings, and other peers

FIGURE 2.13. Diagnosis and families in later life.

CASE EXAMPLE 6. The Family in Later Life: A Case of Prostate Cancer

Red, a 72-year-old, married male was recently diagnosed with early-stage prostate cancer. His wife, Rachel, accompanied him to the initial consultation. Rachel and Red have been married for almost 50 years and "never do anything without the other." They discussed their three sons and two daughters and their eight grandchildren. Their family genogram is pictured in Figure 2.14. Red commented, "We have a pretty big family and we try and keep in contact with them all. They are all spread out across the country, so we make a special trip every summer to visit each child for a few days." Both Red and Rachel are retired elementary school teachers. They both taught at the same elementary school for almost 40 years. Rachel retired early, due to the advancing of her arthritis.

Both of them reported being in good health because of "taking care of each other." Red stated, "When she needs to go in for a checkup about her arthritis, I make her go. We are just like that with each other. When she gets too tired, hungry, or grouchy, I just make her sit down and rest. She is always pushing herself, especially with her gardening and cleaning. She just loves to make everything look nice." Rachel also noted that she takes good care of Red: "I made him go and get his physical, even though he likes to put it off. This time, I am really glad he went when he did."

Preillness Family Structure

Rachel and Red noted that their extended family system "kept in touch much of the time." They were more frequently in touch with their youngest daughter, Rene, who was struggling with their grandson who has Down's syndrome. Although they talked with Rene often, the extended family system was noted to be slightly disengaged, with Rachel and Red having clear boundaries around their marital subsystem. "We raised our children to be independent and that's what they have become. They each have their own families and their own lives," Rachel commented. Rachel and Red also discussed their friends who live near them in their small community. Although Rachel and Red report being "private people," they do get together with a few of their neighbors once a week to play cards. Thus, their preillness family structure appears healthy with developmentally appropriate and clearly defined boundaries around their marital subsystem.

Medical Information

Red reported that he was feeling "fine" and was experiencing no disturbing symptomotology. At Rachel's request, he had gone in for a routine physical examination. His primary physician had discovered a small, hardened area within the prostate via a digital rectal examination. Red also noted that there was an elevation in his PSA level, which was determined by a blood test. Due to the results of these two tests, Red's primary physician referred him to an oncologist and Red was diagnosed with early-stage prostate

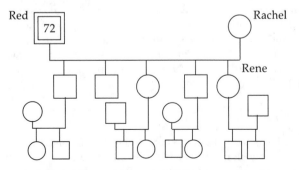

FIGURE 2.14. The family in later life genogram.

cancer. Although the word "cancer" had initially caused great concern for both Red and Rachel, their oncologist assured them that Red's prostate cancer was caught in its early stages. Red reassured Rachel, "Doc said that I have 'Grade 3' prostate cancer and that he can take care of it with radiation treatment." (Here, Red is referring to the "Gleason grading system," a scale denoting the level of aggressive cancer cells in the body. See Zinner & Brosman, 1997, p. 637.) Red was scheduled to receive interstitial radiation (brachytherapy), which consists of radioactive pellets or seeds that are directly placed into the prostate. Several factors went into the decision to have radiation treatment. Red reported, "Doc even said that "watchful waiting" may be best at this point. He said that my cancer was slow growing and that it would probably take about 10 to 15 years to cause any real problems. But we decided we couldn't sit back and do nothing, so we are going ahead with the radiation treatment." They decided on using brachytherapy instead of either surgery (to remove the prostate) or external beam radiation since Red is in excellent health, has a PSA value of less than 10, has a low Gleason score, and has relatively small amounts of cancer. Red also wanted to reduce the risks of sexual dysfunction and fecal incontinence that could result from surgery or external beam radiation therapy (Flannery, 1992).

Assessing Psychosocial Considerations: The Family's Existential Crisis

Since the diagnosis of cancer for this particular family is not severe, Red and Rachel will probably not experience severe psychosocial difficulties related to "an existential crisis." However, both of them noted that the diagnosis had put them into a paradoxical bind. The diagnosis of cancer initially made them more cognizant of the "important things in life"— their marital relationship and the yearly visit with their children and grandchildren. "Now that Red is going to have this implant procedure done this summer, we are not sure if we can visit our children or not," Rachel said. Red commented, "It is funny how cancer has made me appreciate my kids and grandkids even more—but because of the treatment, I may not be able to see them!" They both realized that this setback was temporary, and that different arrangement could be made later. Rachel remarked "I know we can't live forever, but this diagnosis—and just hearing the word 'cancer' does bring the reality of death just a little closer to home for us."

Diagnosis and the Family in Later Life: Case Conceptualization

Red and Rachel's family system is going through a life-structure maintenance stage. Both of them have been retired for several years, and both of them have been enjoying their time together. Although their extended family system appears to be slightly disengaged, particularly due to lack of proximity between the marital subsystem and their children's families, Red and Rachel appear to be able to meet their own needs and to have external resources in the form of friends, neighbors, and church members. Since the diagnosis and its treatment does not warrant extended care or additional resources, Red and Rachel are adapting well to the initial crisis phase.

Goals of Intervention

This family in later life is well within the normal limits of adaptation to the diagnosis of cancer. A few important goals must still be considered: (1) with Rachel's assistance, ensuring that Red comply with necessary treatment; (2) remaining apprised of any treatment side effects Red may experience as a result of his brachytherapy; (3) making sure that Red and Rachel have adequate information regarding the management of treatment side effects and nutrition; and (4) continuing to monitor Red's and Rachel's psychosocial adaptation during the treatment phase.

Specific Intervention Strategies: Process and Outcome

The first two goals were attained when Rachel and Red scheduled an appointment with their oncologist where Red was to receive his interstitial implant. This procedure took about an hour, and Red was able to resume his normal activities within a couple of days. Red was glad to have Rachel to take care of him: "She has been so wonderful to me these past few weeks. I still feel pretty good and I know it is because I have her around me." Both Red and Rachel met other members of the health care team, including the oncology nurse and the nutritionist. Both of these team members would be able to help Red manage any treatment side effects he may experience during the next phase of the illness. In addition, Rachel and Red's psychosocial adaptation to the next phase of the clinical course of cancer was to be assessed during a follow-up consultation.

Outcome of the Diagnostic Phase for the Family in Later Life

The diagnostic phase did not present with many physical or psychosocial difficulties for this family. Red and Rachel decided to telephone each of their children to let them know about Red's diagnosis, his treatment, and his potential for long-term recovery. They reported that their children seem concerned, but they also appeared to be handling it well. Red and Rachel were also happy to report that most of their children were going to come and visit *them* this summer—after Red had fully recovered from his treatment side effects. Rachel said, "Our oldest might not be able to make it, but all the others are coming into town in mid-July. With the money we would have spent on traveling, we are going to help them all with hotel accommodations. We couldn't be more pleased with this idea!" At this point along the disease continuum, Red and Rachel appear to have adequate sources of support, a flexible extended family system, and open communication regarding the diagnosis and cancer treatment.

☐ Summary

In this chapter the focus was on the family during the initial diagnostic phase of the illness. Biomedical variables of importance during the diagnostic phase and the major psychosocial issue of the existential crisis were explained. Next, important considerations for the six family life cycles, during the diagnostic phase, were presented, followed by a detailed case example relevant to each life cycle. In each case example the importance of a thorough assessment of the family system was emphasized. In addition, a family systems case conceptualization was offered, followed by goals, intervention strategies, and outcomes of the diagnostic phase.

The next chapter will explain important biomedical information and psychosocial considerations relevant to the treatment phase of the illness. This will be followed by further elaboration of the six case examples, with an emphasis on the importance of flexibility while facing the long haul of treatment.

☐ References

American Brain Tumor Association. (1996). *A primer of brain tumors: A patient's reference manual* (6th ed.). Chicago, IL: Author.

American Cancer Society (ACS). (1998). *Cancer facts and figures–1998.* New York: Author.

Balfour, J., & Kaplan, G. (1998). Social class/socioeconomic factors. In J. C. Holland (Ed.), *Psychooncology* (pp. 78–90). New York: Oxford University Press.

Bardill, D. (1993). The tell-it-again intervention. In T. Nelson & T. Trepper (Eds.), *101 interventions in family therapy.* New York: The Haworth Press.

Blanchard, Ch., Albrecht, T., & Ruckdeschel, J. (1997). The crisis of cancer: Psychological impact on family caregivers. *Oncology, 11*(2), 189–202.

Campbell, T. L., McDaniel, S. H., & Seaburn, D. B. (1992). Family systems medicine: New opportunities for psychologists. In T. Akamatsu, M. Stephen, S. Hobfoll, & J. Crowther (Eds.), *Family health psychology* (pp. 193–215). Washington, DC: Taylor and Francis.

Carter, E., & McGoldrick, M. (Eds.). (1989). *The changing family life cycle: A framework for family therapy* (2nd ed). Needham Heights, MA: Allyn and Bacon.

Cella, D., Orav, E., Kornblith, A., Holland, J., Silberfarb, P., Won Lee, K., Comis, R., Perry, M., Cooper, R., Maurer, L., Hoth, D., Perloff, M., Bloomfield, C., McIntyre, O., Leone, L., Lesnick, G., Nissen, N., Glicksman, A., Henderson, E., Barcos, M., Crichlow, R., Faulkner II, C., Eaton, W., North, W., Schein, P., Chu, F., King, G., & Chahinian, P. (1991). Socioeconomic status and cancer survival. *Journal of Clinical Oncology, 9*(8), 1500–1509.

Cobb, N., & Jordan, C. (1993). Self-esteem: Everyone's favorite. In T. Nelson & T. Trepper (Eds.), *101 interventions in family therapy.* Binghamton, NY: The Haworth Press.

Compas, B. E., Worsham, N. L., Epping-Jordan, J. E., Grant, K. E., Mireault, G., Howell, D. C., & Malcarne, V. L. (1994). When Mom or Dad has cancer: Markers of psychological distress in cancer patients, spouses, and children. *Health Psychology, 13*(6), 507–515.

Compas, B. E., Worsham, N. L., Ey, S., & Howell, D. C. (1996). When Mom or Dad has cancer: II. Coping, cognitive appraisals, and psychological distress in children of cancer patients. *Health Psychology, 15*(3), 167–175.

Dollinger, M., Rosenbaum, E., Benz, C., Goodson III, W., Friedman, G., Sickles, E., Margolis, L., Meyler, T., Tripathy, D., & Henderson, C. (1997). Breast (pp. 356–384). In M. Dollinger, E. Rosenbaum, & G. Cable (Eds.), *Everyone's guide to cancer therapy: How cancer is diagnosed, treated, and managed day to day.* Toronto, Ontario, Canada: Somerville House Books Limited.

Donnelly, E. (1995). Culture and the meaning of cancer. *Seminars in Oncology Nursing, 11*(1), 3–8.

Eisenberg, M. G., Sutkin, L. C., & Jansen, M. A. (Eds.). (1984). Chronic illness and disability through the life span: Effects on self and family. In T. W. Backer (Ed.), *Springer series on rehabilitation* (vol. 4). New York: Springer.

Fawzy, F. (1994). The benefits of a short-term group intervention for cancer patients. *The Journal of Mind-Body Health, 10*(2), 17–19.

Feldstein, M., & Rait, D. (1992). Family assessment in an oncology setting. *Cancer Nursing, 15*(3), 161–172.

Flannery, M. (1992). Reproductive cancers. In J. Clark & R. McGee (Eds.), *Core curriculum for oncology nursing* (2nd ed., pp. 451–469). Philadelphia: W.B. Saunders Company.

Fogarty, T. (1976). System concepts and dimensions of self. In P. Guerin (Ed.), *Family therapy theory and practice* (pp. 144–153). New York: Gardner.

Forisha, B. (1993). Facilitating marital dialogue: A few fundamental components (pp. 74–81). In T. Nelson & T. Trepper (Eds.), *101 interventions in family therapy.* Binghamton, NY: The Haworth Press.

Germino, B., Fife, B., & Funk, S. (1995). Cancer and the partner relationship: What is its meaning? *Seminars in Oncology Nursing, 11*(1), 43–50.

Gillies, D. A. (1987). Family assessment and counseling by the rehabilitation nurse. *Rehabilitation Nursing, 12*(2), 65–69.

Horning, S., & Hardy, R. (1997). Lymphoma: Hodgkin's disease (pp. 549–557). In M. Dollinger, E. Rosenbaum, & G. Cable (Eds), *Everyone's guide to cancer therapy: How cancer is diagnosed, treated, and managed day to day.* Toronto, Ontario, Canada: Somerville House Books Limited.

Jacobs, J., Ostroff, J., & Steinglass, P. (1998). Family therapy: A systems approach to cancer care. In J. C. Holland (Ed.), *Psycho-oncology* (pp. 994–1003). New York: Oxford University Press.

Kerr, M. (1981). Cancer and the family emotional system. In J. Goldberg (Ed.), *Psychotherapeutic treatment of cancer patients* (pp. 273–315). New York: Collier Macmillan Publishers.

Lederberg, M. S. (1998). The family of the cancer patient. In J. C. Holland (Ed.), *Psycho-oncology* (pp. 981–993). New York: Oxford University Press.

Lewis, F. (1993). Psychosocial transitions and the family's work in adjusting to cancer. *Seminars in Oncology Nursing, 9*(2), 127–129.

Lynam, M. J. (1995). Supporting one another: The nature of family work when a young adult has cancer. *Journal of Advanced Nursing, 22,* 116–125.

Mor, V., Masterson-Allen, S., Goldberg, R., Guadagnoli, E., & Wool, M. S. 1990. Pre-diagnostic symptom recognition and help seeking among cancer patients. *Journal of Community Health, 15,* 253–266.

Northouse, L. (1995). The impact of cancer in women on the family. *Cancer Practice, 3,* 134–142.

Northouse, L., & Peters-Golden, H. (1993). Cancer and the family: Strategies to assist spouses. *Seminars in Oncology Nursing, 9*(2), 74–82.

Notarius, C., & Markman, H. (1993). *We can work it out: How to solve conflicts, save your marriage, and strengthen your love for each other.* New York: Penguin Putnam Inc.

O'Connor, A., Wicker, C., & Germino, B. (1990). Understanding the cancer patient's search for meaning. *Cancer Nursing, 13*(3), 167–175.

Oktay, J., & Walter, C. (1991). *Breast cancer in the life course: Women's experiences.* New York: Springer.

Pope, A., McHale, S., & Craighead, W. (1988). *Self-esteem enhancement with children and adolescents.* New York: Pergamon Press.

Rait, D., & Lederberg, M. (1989). The family of the cancer patient. In J. C. Holland & J. H. Rowland (Eds.), *Handbook of psychooncology: Psychological care of the patient with cancer* (pp. 585–597). New York: Oxford University Press.

Rittenberg, C. N. (1996). Helping children cope when a family member has cancer. *Supportive Care Cancer, 4,* 196–199.

Rolland, J. S. (1995). Chronic illness and the family life cycle. In B. Carter & M. McGoldrick (Eds.), *The changing family life cycle: A framework for family therapy* (3rd ed., pp. 492–511). New York: Gardner Press.

Rolland, J. S. (1994). *Families, illness, and disability: An integrative treatment model.* New York: Basic Books.

Rosenthal, D., & Eyre, H. (1995). Hodgkin's disease and non-Hodgkin's lymphomas. In G. Murphy, W. Lawrence, Jr., & Raymond Lenhard, Jr. (Eds), *American Cancer Society textbook of clinical oncology* (2nd ed.). Atlanta, GA: American Cancer Society.

Rowland, J. (1989). Developmental stage and adaptation: Adult model. In J. C. Holland & J. H. Rowland (Eds.), *Handbook of psychooncology: Psychological care of the patient with cancer* (pp. 25–43). New York: Oxford University Press.

Sales, E., Schulz, R., & Biegel, D. (1992). Predictors of strain in families of cancer patients: A review of the literature. *Journal of Psychosocial Oncology, 10*(2), 1–26.

Satir, V. (1988). *The new peoplemaking.* Palo Alto, CA: Science and Behavior Books.

Schulz, K., Schulz, H., Schulz, O., & Von Kerekjarto, M. (1996). Family structure and psychosocial stress in families of cancer patients. In L. Baider, C. L. Cooper, & A. Kaplan De-Nour (Eds.), *Cancer and the family* (pp. 226–255). New York: John Wiley and Sons Ltd.

Sedgwick, R. (1981). *Family mental health: Theory and practice.* St. Louis: Mosby-Yearbook.

Small, E., Torti, F., & Yagoda, A. (1997). Testis. In M. Dollinger, E. Rosenbaum, and G. Cable (Eds)., *Everyone's guide to cancer therapy: How cancer is diagnosed, treated, and managed day to day* (pp. 684–694). Toronto, Ontario, Canada: Somerville House Books Limited.

Stern, J. (1997). Cervix. In M. Dollinger, E. Rosenbaum, & G. Cable (Eds). *Everyone's guide to cancer therapy: How cancer is diagnosed, treated, and managed day to day* (pp. 397–405). Toronto, Ontario, Canada: Somerville House Books Limited.

Taylor, C. (1990). *Mereness' essentials of psychiatric nursing* (13th ed.). St. Louis: Mosby-Yearbook.

Taylor, E. (1995). Whys and wherefores: Adult patient perspectives of the meaning of cancer. *Seminars in Oncology Nursing, 11*(1), 32–40.

Vess, J. D., Moreland, J. R., & Schwebel, A. I. (1985). An empirical assessment of the effects of cancer on family functioning. *Journal of Psychosocial Oncology, 3*(1), 1–17.

Weisman, M. D., & Worden, J. W. (1976). The existential plight in cancer: Significance of the first 100 days. *International Journal of Psychiatry in Medicine, 7*(1), 1–15.

Zinner, N., & Brosman, S. (1997). Prostate. In M. Dollinger, E. Rosenbaum, & G. Cable (Eds.), *Everyone's guide to cancer therapy: How cancer is diagnosed, treated, and managed day to day,* (pp. 634–649). Toronto, Ontario, Canada: Somerville House Books Limited.

Treatment and the Family Life Cycle: The Long Haul

The treatment phase has many medical and psychosocial variables that affect each stage of the family life cycle. The treatment phase begins with developing an understanding of the various types of cancer treatments and their side effects. Psychosocially, the family system is adapting to the "long haul" of day-to-day life with cancer. The centripetal momentum of the diagnostic phase begins to relax and the family system can begin to incorporate cancer treatment regimens into daily functioning.

☐ Medical Variables during the Treatment Phase

There are several different treatment procedures that are used in an attempt to cure cancer, improve quality of life, or to relieve pain and suffering (palliative care). The most common cancer treatments include surgery, radiation therapy, and chemotherapy. Other treatment modalities include bone marrow transplants (BMTs), biological therapy, and laser therapy.

Surgery

One of the oldest and most widely used types of cancer treatment is surgery. Surgery as a primary treatment is often used when a tumor has been confined to a specific area of the body, and when the tumor can be safely removed (Pellegrini & Byrd, 1997, p. 41). During this type of surgery, the primary mass or tumor is removed along with adjacent areas of normal tissue and the associated lymph nodes. These tissues are analyzed by a pathologist to determine the specific type of tumor and the extent of disease. Because important information usually takes a few days to determine, the "success" of the surgery and the patient's prognosis cannot be discussed in detail until a few days following surgery (Pellegrini & Byrd, 1997). Surgery is sometimes followed by chemotherapy or radiation therapy to treat cancer cells that may have spread to other parts of the body. However, surgery can also be performed after chemotherapy or radiation therapy has been used to shrink the tumor's size. When cancerous tumors are causing particularly severe symptoms, surgery may be conducted for palliative care rather than for curative purposes. For example, tumors can block the gastrointestinal tract, as well as compress nerves. If these tumors cannot be entirely removed safely, surgery can still be used to unobstruct passageways or to relieve the discomfort and pain of compressed nerves (Pellegrini & Byrd, 1997).

Surgery is also used to implant ports, catheters, or pumps that can be used during chemotherapy. Ports are small chambers underneath the surface of the skin that have attached tubes that run along the inside of veins. These ports can be accessed easily so that the administration of drugs can take place relatively painlessly. Catheters are also used to run tubes along the inside of veins. However, unlike ports, the end of the catheter is left outside of the skin. Catheters can have multiple lines of infusion so that different drugs or types of nourishment can be given at the same time. Pumps are mechanisms that are implanted inside the body that consist of drug-filled chambers. Driven by the body's heat, pumps can administer a constant flow of drugs into a specific vein or artery leading directly to a targeted organ.

Radiation Therapy

Over half of all cancer patients receive radiation as part of their treatment protocol (Holland, 1989; Kramer, Hanks, Diamond, & Maclean, 1984). Radiation is used to kill cancer cells by destroying their ability to divide. Radiation treatment involves extensive assessment and treatment planning. If external beam radiation therapy is to be used, the patient will undergo a simulation procedure. A simulation is conducted to determine the optimal treatment approach. The treatment fields or portals are marked on the patient's skin with colored ink so that the radiation beam can enter an exact, targeted point of entry (or port) each time radiation is administered. During assessment and treatment planning, the radiation oncologist will consult with a medical physicist and a dosimetrist to devise a specific treatment plan. The amount of radiation to be received requires a balance between maximum effectiveness in destroying the tumor cells and minimal damage to the surrounding healthy tissue. The total dosage of radiation to be administered is divided into a number of segments (fractionation), so that smaller amounts of radiation can be administered daily, typically for about two to eight weeks. Giving smaller, daily doses of radiation, rather than one dose all at once, helps to give the healthy cells time to recover and to repopulate.

Radiation can be administered from a source outside of the body (teletherapy) or from inside the body (brachytherapy). Megavoltage equipment, such as linear accelerators, have deep ranges of penetration and can be used to treat multiple types of cancer. Brachytherapy uses sealed sources of radioactive material that are placed near or directly into the tumor (e.g., prostate cancer). Permanent implants are made of small radioactive seeds that deliver a specific dose of radiation to the tumor over a period of several weeks. However, many implants are temporary and involve ribbons, tubes, needles, grains, or seeds that contain radioactive substances that are removed within minutes to days.

Side effects from radiation treatment are usually specific to the type of cancer being treated and thus the port of entry. For example, patients typically will not experience hair loss except in cases where radiation treatment is being used for brain cancer. Likewise, nausea may be experienced by patients receiving radiation treatment to the abdominal area, and patients receiving radiation to the head and neck will often experience irritation of the membranes lining the mouth (mucositis) (Rosenbaum, Dollinger, Piper, & Rosenbaum, 1997). The most common side effects for patients receiving radiation treatment are fatigue and localized skin irritations such as slight redness and inflammation.

Chemotherapy

Chemotherapy is the use of chemical agents (drugs) to treat cancer. While surgery and radiation therapy are localized forms of cancer treatment, chemotherapy is a general or systemic type of treatment that affects many organ systems. Thus, chemotherapy is often used to treat systemic types of cancers (i.e., leukemias and lymphomas) that cannot be treated by surgery or radiation therapy. The goals of chemotherapy treatment are to either eradicate all malignant cells or to control the disease and its symptoms. These goals include eliminating the tumor, reducing the tumor's size, extending the patient's life, and improving the quality of the patient's life.

The scheduling of chemotherapy is important to consider. Adjuvant chemotherapy is used after surgery or radiation therapy to destroy cancer cells that are too small to be detected and that have spread to other parts of the body. Neoadjuvant chemotherapy (also known as induction, primary, or synchronous chemotherapy) is administered before surgery or radiation therapy to provide early treatment for cancer as well as to promote the reduction of overall tumor size. Chemotherapy can involve a single drug, but more than likely multiple types of cancer-fighting drugs will be used in various combinations. There are many different types of chemotherapeutic drugs used to treat cancer. Some of these different types include alkylating agents, which prevent cell replication; nitrosureas, which interfere with DNA formation; antibiotics, which block DNA directed RNA and DNA transcription; plant alkaloids, which arrest mitosis (cellular division); and hormones, which alter the hormone environment of the cell and thus disrupt cellular proliferation (Dollinger & Rosenbaum, 1997).

Chemotherapy can be administered in a variety of ways and over varying lengths of time. Usually drugs can be administered intravenously, using catheters, which extend into large veins; implanted infusion ports; and ambulatory pumps. Chemotherapy used to treat specific cancers, such as acute leukemia, can be delivered directly into the central nervous system via lumbar punctures or by using spinal reservoirs (Dollinger & Rosenbaum, 1997). Intra-arterial drugs can be given by delivering the drugs through specific arteries in the liver, head, and neck areas. The administration of chemotherapy can be done during hospital stays, during day visits to the hospital, at the doctor's office, or by oncology nurses at home.

Before the administration of each chemotherapy treatment, blood counts must be taken. Chemotherapy affects the growth of all rapidly growing cells, including healthy ones. White blood cells (which assist in immune system functioning) and platelets (which assist in the clotting of blood and thus to stop bleeding) are rapidly growing cells that are important to healthy functioning. Although blood counts are expected to drop during chemotherapy, if the patient's blood counts are too low, the treatment may need to be delayed until blood counts recover (Dollinger & Rosenbaum, 1997).

Bone Marrow Transplants

The bone marrow manufactures the blood cells that are necessary for life. BMTs are recommended for those cancers (e.g., leukemias) that affect the production of blood cells in the bone marrow, or for cancers where high doses of chemotherapy or radiation therapy damage the bone marrow (Armitage, 1997). BMTs have been found to be more successful for younger patients and when conducted early in the course of the disease process (Armitage, 1997).

There are two types of BMTs: allogeneic and autologous transplants. In allogeneic transplants the transplanted marrow is from a matched donor, while in autologous transplants uses the patient's own marrow, previously "harvested" and stored for later transplant. In both types, the transplanting of the marrow is preceded by very high dose chemotherapy. This chemotherapy is designed to destroy all cancer cells before transplanting the healthy marrow. After the transplant, the healthy marrow is then used to stimulate the growth and production of healthy, noncancer blood cells. Risks in BMTs are high, sometimes involving threats due to transplant rejection (graft versus host disease), pneumonia, excessive bleeding, and infections.

Other Types of Cancer Treatment

Examples of other types of cancer treatments include biological therapy, laser therapy, hyperthermia, and hyperthermic perfusion therapy. Biological therapy treats the immune system with highly purified proteins such as interferon and interleukin-2 to help bolster immune functioning, so that cancer cells can be more readily recognized and destroyed by the body's own immune system (Mitchell & Catane, 1997). Laser therapy uses high-intensity light beams to destroy cancer cells. To date, laser therapy is used to relieve symptoms such as bleeding and obstructions caused by cancer, rather than to cure cancer (i.e., palliative therapy; Pellegrini, Rosenbaum, Dollinger, 1997). Hyperthermia cancer treatment, or using heat to destroy cancer cells, can be used in combination with radiation therapy to destroy cancer cells that are poorly oxygenated. Moreover, heat seems to improve the effects of some types of drugs used in chemotherapy (Sneed, 1997). Hyperthermic perfusion, or regional perfusion, can be used to administer drugs to parts of the body that can be isolated readily from the circulatory system (i.e., arms and legs). Heat helps to destroy the isolated tumor without affecting the entire circulatory system (Sneed, 1997).

Complementary and Alternative Treatments

In addition to traditional forms of cancer treatment, increasing numbers of cancer patients are receiving alternative or complementary treatments (Holland, Geary, & Furman, 1989). It is important to distinguish between these two terms. Alternative treatments are typically treatments provided "in place of" traditional cancer treatments, and are often provided with claims of treatment cure. They include a wide variety of therapies, some of which have some basis for their claims, while others are clearly fraudulent. Distinguishing the differences is difficult and thus patients and families should be advised to "proceed with caution" and consult available resources that summarize many of these treatments and give advice on how to evaluate their efficacy (e.g., Cassileth, 1997; see also the ACS website [www.cancer.org] and the Oncolink website at the University of Pennsylvania [www.oncolink.upenn.edu]).

Complementary treatments, in contrast, are typically provided "in addition to" traditional treatments and are more typically focused on improving a patient's quality of life. They do not offer a cure, but rather offer educational information and support that can result in improved psychological well-being and emotional health. Many are provided by licensed professionals (e.g., psychologists, social workers, registered dietitians, oncology nurses) who are well qualified to provide such services. Most recently, some comprehensive cancer centers are providing complementary treatments in an "integrated" fashion, in which they involve cancer patients in educational and supportive treatment programs in the same setting in which they receive their traditional treatments. This allows for a safe, comprehensive, holistic approach to patient care, in a setting where all relevant health professionals can provide a team approach to patient care.

Preparation for Treatment

The individual cancer patient and the family will be best able to manage the long haul of treatment when armed with information. Preparation for treatment can include (1) touring the oncology clinic, (2) reviewing videotaped presentations of patient models coping with treatment procedures, (3) discussing concerns about treatment with a practitioner, and (4) receiving written information about treatments and how to manage side effects (Burish, Snyder, & Jenkins, 1991). Enhanced preparation for treatment facilitates coping with treatment, and being prepared is best accomplished with information. Available sources of information include the ACS (www.cancer.org), the NCI (www.cancernet.nci.nih.gov), and an excellent cancer website at the University of Pennsylvania (www.oncolink.upenn.edu).

Managing the Side Effects of Treatments

The most common side effects of cancer treatments are nausea/vomiting, hair loss (alopecia), and fatigue. Side effects of chemotherapy vary by the type of drugs used and by individual patient differences (ACS website). In general, chemotherapy side effects are caused by the effect that the drugs have on faster growing healthy cells of the body. These cells make up hair follicles, bone marrow, and the linings of the mouth, stomach, and bowels. Thus, the common side effects are hair loss, nausea, vomiting, diarrhea, constipation, and overall fatigue. Nausea and vomiting are common side effects of chemotherapy and some forms of radiation therapy in which the gastrointestinal system receives radiation. Nausea and vomiting are not the same thing, and should be considered separate, but related, entities. Nausea is the subjective, unpleasant, wavelike sensation that often precedes (but not always) vomiting; while vomiting or emesis is the forceful emptying of gastric contents (Morrow, Roscoe, & Hickok, 1998). Not all patients experience nausea and vomiting, but estimates suggest that about 60% of patients experience some nausea and 50% report vomiting (Morrow et al., 1998) after chemotherapy. Postchemotherapy nausea and vomiting (PNV) typically begin anywhere from a few minutes to a few hours after the administration of chemotherapy, and can be controlled by a variety of antiemetic medications that can be administered intravenously or orally during, or soon after, cancer treatment.

In contrast, anticipatory nausea and vomiting (ANV) are nausea or vomiting or both symptoms that occur *prior to the beginning of a new cycle* of chemotherapy, in response to conditioned stimuli. After a few prior chemotherapy treatments, anticipatory nausea occurs in approximately 29% of patients, while anticipatory vomiting appears to occur in about 11% of patients (Pickard-Holley, 1991; Stone, Richards, & Hardy, 1998). Both are conceptualized as classically conditioned responses to the unique environmental cues of the chemotherapy treatment setting (e.g., smells, chemotherapy room, nurse) and can be managed by learning a variety of nonpharmacologic interventions such as systematic desensitization, progressive muscle relaxation, hypnosis with imagery, and biofeedback (Rigatos, 1992).

Hair loss, or alopecia, is another common side effect of cancer chemotherapy and is also determined by the type of chemotherapy drugs administered. Some drugs may not affect hair at all, while others may cause partial hair loss (thinning), and others will result in complete hair loss. Once chemotherapy begins, damage to the hair follicles occurs, but actual hair loss usually does not occur until a few weeks later. Since hair follicles are rapidly dividing cells, they regrow and hair growth typically returns about a month or two after completing all chemotherapy treatments.

Fatigue is a commonly reported side effect of cancer treatments, but since it is a subjective experience, it has been difficult to define and is generally not well understood. It may be best defined as a condition characterized by physical, mental, and emotional distress and decreased functional status related to a decrease in energy (Pickard-Holley, 1991; Stone et al., 1998). As many as 78% to 96% of all cancer patients report fatigue, with the incidence being highest during treatment (Vogelzang et al., 1997). No current standard of care is available for the treatment of fatigue, and yet a variety of management strategies have been developed (Ortho Biotech, Inc., 1994).

☐ Treatment and Psychosocial Considerations: The Long Haul

Transition from the Existential Crisis to the Long Haul

The transition from the existential crisis of the diagnostic phase to the long-haul challenges of the treatment phase requires the family system to remain flexible to the demands of treatment while sustaining household functioning (Sherman & Simonton, 1999). The developmental tasks of the family system and of its individual members will often remain "on hold" during the treatment phase. However, it helps the family to understand that this developmental delay is temporary and that momentum should be regained once adaptation to the illness, and its day-to-day demands, is made (Rolland, 1994). After the crisis of the diagnostic phase, the family's strengths and resources can be used to (1) accommodate treatment interventions, (2) cope with adverse treatment side effects, (3) rearrange family schedules, (4) modify financial plans, and (5) shift the family's roles and responsibilities (Sherman & Simonton, 1999). By drawing upon the family's unique strengths, the developmental needs of the system can be met with success even during the treatment phase of a life threatening illness. The specific tasks and needs of the family system during the treatment phase are illustrated in Table 3.1.

The transition from the crisis phase to the chronic phase marks an important time of reevaluation for the family system. Unfinished business from the previous phase can cause difficulties for families entering the next phase of the illness (Rolland, 1994). Belief systems, communication strategies, and differing ways of responding to the illness, if not acknowledged during the crisis phase, can continue to impede family adaptability during the chronic phase. Moreover, a shift in momentum must take place, from the "pulling together" of the family system during a time of crisis, to a more long-term, viable life style for the long haul of the treatment phase. Rolland (1994) recounts a family in which a single young woman began caring for her ill mother during the crisis phase of the disease. Since she had been so effective during the crisis phase, all other possibilities for caregiving and assistance from other family members and outside support resources during the long haul of treatment were overlooked. For this family, "The successful crisis structure assumed a life of its own and became permanent" (Rolland, 1994, p. 51). By overlooking options and by becoming inflexible to change, both the caregiver's and the patient's development became frozen in a system that no longer worked successfully for its members. It is necessary that the family completes smooth transitions that take into account many possible courses of action and adaptation. When considering caregiving options, the primary goal becomes meeting the needs of the patient while adequately maintaining each individual family member's autonomy and developmental momentum, despite the pull toward dependency and focused caregiving (Rolland, 1994).

Women with Cancer and the Family System

The specific impact of cancer in women on the family system has been studied extensively (Baider & Kaplan De-Nour, 1988; Northouse, 1995; Schag, Ganz, Polinsky, Fred, Hirji, & Petersen, 1993). When mothers have cancer both the emotional and functional aspects of the family system can be disrupted. Family functioning is particularly important during the treatment phase (Northouse, 1995). Mothers who have increased difficulty adapting during the treatment phase are those with less social support, less optimism, more uncertainty, concurrent stressors, and are those receiving chemotherapy (Northouse, 1995).

Short-term effects of cancer treatment such as nausea and vomiting and decreased libido are often temporary for the patient, and the patient's body image can be recovered shortly after treatment has ended. However, when cancer treatment leaves the patient permanently disfigured, such as after a mastectomy, the patient's attractiveness and body image may need to be the focus of much detailed conversation. Opportunities to speak with other patients who have undergone radical changes in body image, sexual counseling for patients and their partners, and family counseling focusing on changes in plans regarding having additional children, can begin to take place during the treatment phase to help patients and their partners who are encountering psychosexual difficulties.

Children of Cancer Patients and the Long Haul

Many children of cancer patients are no different than normative samples with regard to emotional or behavioral problems (Howes, Hoke, Winterbottom, & Delafield, 1994). Many children adapt quite well to their parents' illnesses. However, successful adaptation has been linked with the adaptability of the mother, with higher functioning in the mother being related to greater adaptability in the family (Howes et al., 1994). Mothers who report having greater psychological distress due to their illness have been shown to have children with increased psychological and emotional problems (Downey & Coyne, 1990; Howes et al., 1994). However, the influence on family adaptation may be reciprocal within the family system. For example, women with breast cancer who report greater emotional support from family members also report increased personal adaptation (Zemore & Shepel, 1989). Therefore, family members may be in more distress when the mother is having difficulty adapting to the illness, but this elevated stress level may be due to the mother's perceived lack of support by family members (Northouse, 1995; Zemore et al., 1989), or to a poor prognosis (Northouse, 1995).

Fears of abandonment and confusion may be experienced by young children in the family. Safety concerns, questions regarding the diagnosis and the future, and erroneous information should be addressed (Northouse, 1995). It is often difficult to know how and what to tell young children about cancer. Although young children may not be able to understand the complexities of the disease, if left with too little information they may fill in missing gaps with mistaken ideas about cancer that can be worse than reality (Rolland, 1994). Young children may feel responsible for the illness, may be experiencing grief over the potential loss of a parent, and may be suffering from fear, anger, and resentment about being pushed aside by their preoccupied parents (Lederberg, 1998). The family system is the young child's entire world, and these fears can be extremely overwhelming. In addition, a lack of clear boundaries may leave the child fearful and overly dependent.

(*text continues on page 92*)

TABLE 3.1. The Treatment Phase and the Family Life Cycle: The Importance of Flexibility during "The Long Haul"

	Life Cycle Tasks	Cancer's Potential Disruption to the System	Psychosocial Interventions	Specific Topics of Communication
Single young adult	Differentiate from the family system; establish self in the world of work and in creating new system	Cancer treatment can delay development and become embedded in the family system as a permanent way of life	Help young adult to maintain a balance between dependency needs and establishing independency; help establish caring relationships	Discuss boundaries with family of origin; discuss life/death concerns; discuss putting limits on cancer; address side effects of treatment
Newly forming family	Establish new system with roles, rules, boundaries; plan for future family development	The treatment phase can become embedded in the new system, resulting in permanent "patient" or "caregiver" roles; must set limits on these roles; help new system to create their own boundaries during treatment	Help couple to establish new system and to determine their balance of power; help couple to meet the demands of treatment by becoming flexible in role allocation	Discuss meaning emerging from the illness and its treatment; discuss modified plans for the future; remain flexible regarding future planning and childrearing
Families with young children	Establish adult roles as parents; make room in young system for new members; nurture young children and create sibling subsystems	The treatment phase can add a new member, "the illness," causing role strain; ill parent can lose self-efficacy regarding parenting abilities; well parent can become overwhelmed by responsibilities; remain flexible with regard to role reallocation and communication boundaries	Help young family mobilize external resources; identify family members who may serve as sources of support without crossing boundaries	Continue to discuss the illness with the children in an age-appropriate manner; modify future family planning

Families with adolescents	Loosen boundaries to accept external influence on children and family system; remain flexible with boundaries and roles	Parents may become overwhelmed by the demands of treatment; adolescents may become sullen, withdrawn, angry, or may experience role strain	Identify tasks that are put on hold; maintain balance between meeting the demands of the illness and the demands of the life cycle	Discuss the effects of caregiving on the family; discuss the needs of all the family members
Families in later life	Formulate life review; create a sense of generativity in life and meaning for life	Older adults may experience guilt over "being a burden" during the treatment phase; may need to rely heavily on spouse or adult children	Help older adult to maintain a sense of worth and value during the course of treatment	Discuss feelings of guilt and being a burden; identify ways older patient can maintain a sense of generativity

Changes in sleeping patterns or bed wetting may occur. The child may begin to act out and get into trouble at school and at home, testing the family's structure, rules, and boundaries. Giving young children age-appropriate information and responsibilities may help them, and the family system, to adapt more effectively.

Adolescent children have been reported to have more difficulties during the treatment phase than young children (Nelson, Sloper, Charlton, & While, 1994). It has been suggested that difficulties raising adolescents can be exacerbated when added responsibilities and role changes due to the illness are required (Wellisch, 1979). In addition, adolescent children who are ignored or not given sufficient information demonstrate increased levels of anxiety, depression, and anger, which can last years after the treatment phase has ended (Rosenfeld & Caplan, 1983). Adolescents who are at risk for psychosocial distress are those who are not given information about the illness at the time of diagnosis, are unable to discuss the parent's illness with anyone, and must give up extracurricular activities and time with friends (Nelson et al., 1994). It helps both the young child and the adolescent when (1) they are informed about the illness and its treatment, (2) they are afforded time to spend with peers in their own activities, (3) they are given appropriate and clear-cut roles and responsibilities, and (4) they are able to spend time with the well parent (Lewis, Hammond, & Woods, 1993).

Spouses of Cancer Patients and the Long Haul

The spousal subsystem has the most influence on overall family functioning (Broderick & Smith, 1979). Moreover, it has been noted that "instead of coping with the illness, it appears that the family is coping with the couple's ability to negotiate the illness successfully" (Lewis et al., 1993). Thus, although the medical variables and the demands of treatment play a large role in patient and subsequent family functioning (Northouse, 1995), it has been theorized that it is the couple's ability to negotiate that has the most bearing on successful adaptation to cancer (Lewis et al., 1993). Couples who are able to integrate the demands of treatment into their daily lives are more likely to experience higher levels of marital adjustment and family adaptability (Burke & Weir, 1982; Lewis et al., 1993).

The marital dyad has been reported to be both strengthened (LeFebvre, 1978) and torn apart by the illness (Baider & Sarell, 1984). The couple's level of communication is pivotal in their adaptation to cancer. Since cancer necessarily conjures feelings of fear, sadness, helplessness, and even anger, the couple's ability to successfully discuss these intense feelings is important to facilitate increased levels of intimacy and adaptability (Keitel, Cramer, & Zevon, 1990). When emotions about the illness and its treatment are not discussed openly, both the patient and the partner may experience unnecessary feelings of isolation and abandonment.

Spouses of cancer patients may feel overwhelmed with responsibilities in many areas of daily functioning including childrearing, general household management, and financial concerns. When anger or resentment are expressed, or even felt, by spouses of cancer patients, they may experience guilt and question their own self-image (Oberst & James, 1985). To reduce feelings of guilt, spouses may then become overly attentive to the patient, paradoxically leaving the patient feeling more distressed, helpless, and fatalistic (Newsome & Schulz, 1999). Successful marital adaptation to cancer is thus associated with adequate and appropriate amounts of caregiving and helping behavior (Newsome & Schulz, 1999), as well as frequent feedback, reflection, and discussion (Lewis, Woods, Hough, & Bensley, 1989). It also benefits the spouses of cancer patients to know (1) the type and length of treatment the patient is to undergo, (2) any anticipated side effects and when they may occur, (3) the ways to manage treatment side effects, (4) the likelihood of temporary role changes in the marital dyad, and (5) the availability of cancer education and support groups in the area (Northouse & Peters-Golden, 1993).

Special Considerations: Caregiving during the Treatment Phase

Due to decreased acute care in the hospital setting, the focus of patient care has recently shifted from the hospital staff to the family system (Laizner, Yost, Barg, & McCorkle, 1993). Monitoring the side effects of treatment, making sure the patient gets to scheduled appointments, and listening to the patient's fears and distress are all components of the caregiving experience (Bowers, 1987). Caregivers must tend to (1) the personal needs of patient care such as bathing, hygiene, and mobility; (2) the instrumental needs of patient care like meal preparation, housework, shopping, transportation, home health, and child care; and (3) the administrative needs of patient care such as financial advice, legal advice, and information about the disease (Laizner et al., 1993).

Families who are able to allocate roles and responsibilities within the nuclear family, rather than outside of the system, have been shown to experience less conflict and greater amounts of family cohesion (Northouse, 1995; Vess, Moreland, & Schwebel, 1985). However, when the family system becomes overloaded with responsibilities, there is a decrease in family cohesion, and anger and resentment can mount, particularly for the primary caregiver (Northouse, 1995). This often occurs when the patient loses much of his or her ability to function in the family, thus leaving other family members to assume additional responsibilities.

Spouse as Caregiver

Difficulties can arise for both spouses of cancer patients, and for adult children caring for their parents with cancer. There are several factors that can affect spousal distress. Illness-related variables such as the stage of the disease and the patient's emotional adjustment can affect the distress levels experienced by the primary caregiver. Advanced disease and poor emotional adjustment in the patient has been correlated with higher distress in spousal caregivers (Blanchard, Albrecht, & Ruckdeschel, 1997). Contextual variables, such as gender, age, SES, additional life stressors, personality constructs, and social support also have been related to caregiver adaptation. Specifically, both age and SES are inversely related to emotional distress, while caregiver optimism and perceived coping efficacy may mediate the effects between caregiver strain, depression, and functional status (Blanchard et al., 1997; Kurtz, Kurtz, Given, & Given, 1995). Variables that are specific to the marital relationship and overall family functioning also have been shown to be related to caregiver distress (Blanchard et al., 1997), with effective communication and moderate levels of adaptability (i.e., family systems that are neither rigid nor chaotic) correlating with decreased levels of caregiver distress.

Spousal distress often occurs due to a lack of effective communication about the illness demands and fears regarding the future. Often spouses of cancer patient do not want to discuss their burdens or fears with the cancer patient for fear of disturbing the patient even further and being perceived as pessimistic and fearful. Interventions targeted to increase spousal communication and overall marital satisfaction have been shown to be effective in the reduction of spousal caregiver burden.

Adult Children as Caregivers

In addition to spouses as caregivers of cancer patients, adult children of elderly cancer patients often take on the caregiving role, leaving themselves little time or energy for their immediate families, or for themselves. In families where caretaking of the elderly is believed to be a natural process of the family life cycle, the caregiving role is less stressful (Carter & McGoldrick, 1989). Adult children who live far from the sick parent may feel guilty for not being readily available to the patient (Welch-McCaffrey, 1989). Special efforts to communicate information to these family members help to decrease feelings of isolation for both the patient and the other family members. With some patients in later life, there may be no caregiver to help meet the demands of the treatment phase. Thus, a "caretaking-vacuum" (Rait & Lederberg, 1989, p. 590) is created, leaving the patient with no available resources.

Caregivers have both objective and subjective needs (Montgomery, Gonyea, & Hooyman, 1985). Objective needs are the concrete activities associated with caregiving (i.e., amount of privacy, time, and personal freedom), whereas subjective needs are the attitudes and emotional reactions of the caregiver to the experience of caring for an ill family member. One important objective need of caregivers is lack of freedom due to the many responsibilities of caregiving, including, for example, feeding, toileting, bathing, dressing, managing money, doing laundry, preparing meals, doing house/yardwork, providing transportation, and running errands. This lack of freedom appears to be the central concern for many caregivers (Montgomery et al., 1985). Interventions aimed at reducing the functional aspects of caregiver burden, and thus giving the caregiver more freedom, have been shown to be helpful (Montgomery et al., 1985). However, there are several barriers to the utilization of the available resources that could reduce caregiver burden. The practitioner should be aware of any barriers that could impede seeking and obtaining assistance. These barriers include (1) lack of awareness about available services, (2) lack of knowledge about how to access those services, (3) possible financial constraints, (4) stigma of asking for and accepting help, (5) family resistance, (6) transportation difficulties, and (7) already overworked existing services (Laizner et al., 1993).

Many caregivers of elderly cancer patients must face role reversals with their parents for which they are not prepared. Adult children who care for their sick parent can range from the single young adult, to adults with children and adolescents in the home, to those in the pre- and postlaunching phases of the family life cycle. It is therefore necessary to assess the family life cycle in which the role reversal is taking place. Role reversals during any of the family life cycles often involve complex role and relationship issues (Germino & Funk, 1993).

Role concerns for the adult caregiver include (1) developing the role of a support person for the ill parent, (2) adapting to role changes in the family system, (3) adjusting to the parent's problems with the changing roles, (4) balancing the demands of the illness, (5) attending to their parent's desires to maintain their role as a parent, and (6) having difficulty meeting their own needs (Germino & Funk, 1993).

Relationship issues often include the need to (1) be closer to the ill parent, (2) resolve past relationship issues, (3) develop or heal the relationship with the other, well parent, (4) maintain a strong marital relationship, and (5) have extended family members provide assistance and care (Germino & Funk, 1993).

☐ The Six Family Life Cycles during the Treatment Phase: The Importance of Flexibility

The challenges of the treatment phase will vary according to the patient's individual stage of development. The treatment phase and its impact on the family life cycle are outlined in Table 3.1. Rather than examine the patient's needs in isolation, the developmental tasks of the cancer patient can be viewed as a complex interchange between the needs of the patient and the patient's family system. Thus, flexibility in areas of interpersonal functioning such as communication, collaboration, respect, negotiation, and interdependence is important in successful adaptation during the treatment phase. Rowland (1989) has outlined several specific areas of interpersonal functioning that can be affected by severe or chronic illness. These include (1) altered relationships, (2) balance between dependence and independence, (3) achievement disruptions, and (4) body image and integrity. When cancer strikes, the force of its impact in any of these areas will vary, depending upon the patient's developmental stage and life context.

☐ The Single Young Adult during Treatment

The general impact of the treatment phase will differ according to whether the young adult has established a stable life apart from the family of origin (i.e., in a life-structure maintenance stage), or if the young adult is just beginning to differentiate and create a life of his or her own (i.e., still in a life cycle transition). Periods of transition mark a time of important decision making. Subsequently, these decisions are lived out during the life-structure maintenance phase of the life cycle (Carter & McGoldrick, 1989). When cancer treatment takes place during a time of transition, it is more likely to become either embedded in the decision-making process or ignored when making important life decisions (Rolland, 1994). For example, the single young adult who is in transition and going through treatment may encounter disruptions to the development of intimate relationships and a satisfying career. Cancer treatment can affect the young adult's ability to care for himself/ herself and to meet financial and functional needs. Peer relationships may be altered during treatment, as the patient begins to question the development of close bonds. Friends of the single young adult may become overwhelmed by the demands of treatment and its side effects (i.e., seeing their friend lose hair and weight, and become fatigued and nauseated), and withdraw from the relationship (Lynam, 1995). The young adult may question forming an intimate relationship with another person, and the healthy partner may question continuing a relationship with an individual who has cancer (Rowland, 1989). This could result in social and emotional isolation for the cancer patient. Having friends who help the patient to maintain social relationships and intimate friendships is important to successful adaptation to cancer, particularly during the treatment phase when the ramifications of cancer are so physically apparent (Lynam, 1995).

The achievement needs of the single young adult may also be put on hold during the course of treatment. The young adult's developmental tasks of defining himself or herself in the world of work and career may need to be temporarily delayed so that time and energy can be devoted to treatment protocols and eventual rehabilitation. However, during the later phases of rehabilitation and survivorship, achievement tasks can be resumed (particularly when the patient has a good prognosis), and developmental momentum can be regained (Rolland, 1994). Young cancer patients struggling with issues of body image and more permanent changes in physical appearance (loss of a breast or testicle), can have significantly greater difficulty in resuming developmental momentum due to the need to alter life plans and goals in terms of forming intimate relationships and families.

The young patient must also attempt to find a healthy balance between learning to be dependent on others during treatment and establishing an independent self outside of the context of the disease. The young adult can be helped to assume a dependent role when treatment procedures and side effects make it necessary (i.e., being driven to treatments, having others help with the preparation of meals, and responsibilities when in the throes of the side effects of treatment). On the other hand, the patient should also be encouraged to maintain an active level of participation in treatment regimens and in the management of treatment side effects. Although the developmental tasks of the young adult may be disrupted, and the young adult patient may be pulled toward remaining dependent upon others during treatment, a balance between dependence and independence should be encouraged (Rowland, 1989). At the extreme, rebellious young adults may not comply with needed treatment, or they may become overly dependent upon the family system and treatment team long after the completion of the treatment phase. Interventions to help the young cancer patient to maintain interpersonal relationships and a balanced sense of interdependency include encouraging (1) visits by friends, (2) usual role functions when possible, (3) open discussions about attitudes and beliefs regarding the patient's present and future relationships, and (4) the discussion of the impact of cancer treatment on the patient's career and relationship plans and goals (i.e., Will cancer treatment have long-term ramifications on my ability to work or to have a family?).

CASE EXAMPLE 1 (Continued). Mark's Treatment Protocol and Side Effects

Mark and his family were encouraged to discuss their questions regarding his prognosis in more detail with the oncologist and the oncology nurse. They were able to broach sensitive subjects such as Mark's chances of survival, his ability to have children, and sexuality concerns. Mark and his family reported that they were relieved to hear, once again, that Mark's chances of survival were around 98% based on his diagnosis of early-stage seminoma. In addition, since Mark was not diagnosed with advanced stage testicular cancer, he would not undergo chemotherapy treatment. However, Mark was recommended to have surgery to remove one of his testicles which would leave him disfigured and possibly impotent. Due to the nature of the surgery, Mark was also given information regarding sperm banking and planning for his future family. Radiation therapy was also recommended as adjuvant treatment for his early-stage seminoma. Treatment side effects would be minimal, and recovery was expected to be nonremarkable.

Although the recommended treatment protocol and its ramifications were distressing for Mark and his family, they were able to obtain uplifting information regarding his chances for survival. Moreover, psychosocial and sexual concerns could be addressed, now that Mark and his family have a better understanding of the recommended treatment plan, short-term treatment side effects, and the long-term ramifications of the disease and its current treatment options.

Psychosocial Considerations: The Nature of Family Work during the Long Haul

Since Mark had decided to take some time off from school and to return home during his cancer treatment it became necessary to help him to balance his treatment dependency needs with his developmental independency needs. In order to successfully negotiate the balance between dependence and independence during the treatment phase, Mark and his family had to adapt to cancer in several areas, including (1) establishing caring relationships, (2) acknowledging the possibility of death, (3) putting the illness in its place, (4) looking toward the future, and (5) recognizing the roles of others in supporting the young adult" (Lynam, 1995, p. 120).

During the treatment phase, Mark began to establish a network of caring relationships with both family and friends. For Mark, caring relationships were defined by the amount of actual physical presence, actions, and understanding his family members and friends were able to provide (Lynam, 1995). He said, "It's funny, I thought I knew who my real friends were, but now I see that friends can come from places and people you never thought possible. One friend of mine, who I thought was one of my best friends, has pretty much disappeared. Then, there is this guy I know from one of my classes who has become a really close friend to me now. His Mom died of cancer a couple of years ago, so he can talk to me about stuff that other people don't want to talk about. He comes over to our house all the time now." Mark's definition of caring relationships in terms of friends and colleagues has taken on a deeper meaning during the treatment phase. Mark also commented, "I can even talk about how it felt to hear that I have 'cancer.' My family, a few friends like Marie, and I have learned to talk about life and death now. We don't try to hide our feelings and fears like we used to. It seems like we respect each other as adults, which allows us to talk about our feelings more. We get it out without dwelling on it too much—but at least it's out. We don't pretend that nothing is happening." Thus, Mark's family was learning to communicate their feelings and fears more freely regarding both life and death. In doing so, they were becoming more flexible and less rigid in their rules governing communication within the system. Subsequently, they were allowing growth and second-order change to take place for the family system.

Mark's mother and father were beginning to perceive Mark as a competent, capable, and independent member of the family (Lynam, 1995). This perception of their son was making it easier for Mark to continue his personal development even though the illness delayed his education, financial independence, and emotional differentiation from his family of origin. According to Mark's father, "Although Mark is living at home right now, we all accept this as a temporary situation. We still encourage Mark to help around the house, and to be of assistance to his sister." By encouraging Mark to maintain an appropriate level of independence and responsibility, his developmental momentum was being sustained in light of a serious illness. In addition, the illness was also being "put in its place" (Lynam, 1995, p. 121). Mark's family let him know that his illness-related changes (slight disfigurement, fatigue) were not nearly as important as who he is and who he wants to become as a person. Mark's mother commented, "For the first time we are seeing Mark as separate from our own plans and expectations. His diagnosis and treatment of cancer has really changed how all of us look at life. We are now more interested in being together, rather than seeing every one of our kids be successful. We are trying to use this illness to help Mark 'determine his own path,' so to speak. I think that the surgery really bothers him still, makes him feel like he is deformed and unattractive, maybe. But he is getting stronger because of it and we have to support that as a family. He is even questioning his previous career plans now." In essence, Mark's family system was becoming more flexible in their expectations of Mark regarding his development in the world of work.

This flexibility was also apparent in the ways in which Mark and his family discussed the future. Mark stated, "I always thought I would end up like my brother. I thought I should become a mechanical engineer, get married soon after I graduated from college, and have a small family. Since going through treatment for cancer, my plans have changed. It feels like I have looked death in the face and said, 'Is this what I want from my life? Now, I am not so sure.'" Mark's career interests appeared to be easier for him to contemplate and to discuss than the complexities of marriage and family. This can be considered normal for young adults, since decisions about marriage and family are very personal and can thus be tightly interwoven into the experience of cancer (Lynam, 1995). Mark reflected, "I am not sure at all how I feel about marriage and children. I mean, I am not sure if I can even help produce children, and that doesn't seem at all fair to a future wife. Then I think, if I have kids, I could die on them, and then what kind of a father would I be—no father at all! If I did get cancer again, and I didn't have a wife and children, it would all be so much easier on everyone. But then I think, I don't want to live the rest of my life alone and in fear! So what am I to do? Just wait, I guess."

Outcome of the Treatment Phase for the Single Young Adult

For the time being, it was recommended that Mark and his family continue to remain flexible in their communication, roles, rules, and in their expectations regarding the future. Both Mark and his family were also beginning to recognize the importance of social support. Mark was encouraged by his family to maintain his relationships with his friends by inviting them to the home, supporting him when he wanted to go out with his friends, and by helping his friends to discuss uncomfortable topics such as the surgery, radiation therapy and its side effects, and the ramifications treatment will have on Mark's future. This increase in support helped to normalize Mark's fears while providing him with the resources necessary to meet the challenges of his illness. Since Mark was encouraged to foster his relationships with his friends and girlfriend, he was able to maintain his developmental momentum and to find balance between his dependency and independency needs.

☐ The Newly Forming Couple during Treatment

For newly forming couples, patients may encounter disruptions to their relationships, their interdependency, their needs for achievement, and their body images (Rowland, 1989). The new partner with cancer may have great difficulty in becoming dependent during the treatment phase. Similarly, the healthy partner may question his or her role as a caregiver in a new partnership. This demanding role may be more than what the new spouse had anticipated. Newly forming couples are just beginning to negotiate boundaries, emotional comfort levels, the allocation of roles and responsibilities, and issues regarding sex, time, and money. For the newly forming couple, this struggle to find a balance between dependence and independence is exacerbated during cancer treatment. The diagnosis of cancer may disrupt the newly formed equilibrium, taking away one partner's sense of power by becoming a "patient," while adding increased responsibility for the other partner who becomes a "caregiver" (Rolland, 1994). High levels of dependence can force the system to become off balance, and can result in anger and resentment for both the patient and the well partner (Rowland, 1989). The boundaries of caregiving and care receiving should be clearly outlined so that optimal balance between dependence and independence can be maintained by both partners in the new system (Rolland, 1994).

Concerns about body image and diminished attractiveness are common for the cancer patient (Rowland, 1989). The side effects of cancer treatment that result in alopecia, fatigue, nausea, and decreased libido can affect the young couple's need for intimacy. The effects of cancer treatment on childbearing will also be faced by the young couple. Chemotherapy can have toxic effects on the patient's reproductive system, and radiation therapy for the pelvic area can render the patient unable to have children. These long-term side effects can greatly alter the patient's and the newly forming system's future plans. Interventions can be focused on the assessment of the patient's potential for recovery and the development of a balanced and flexible system, which promotes the discussion of intimacy, plans for children, the allocation of roles, and the flexibility of boundaries, particularly as the system adapts to the daily demands of cancer treatment.

CASE EXAMPLE 2 (Continued). Brenda's Treatment Protocol and Side Effects

Brenda and Bob had tremendous decisions to make regarding Brenda's treatment for early-stage breast cancer. Brenda commented, "Choosing which type of treatment to get for my cancer was one of the biggest decisions I have ever had to make, and I had to make it over the course of a weekend! That wasn't nearly enough time for Bob and I to come to a decision, especially when both of us would rather just not talk about a problem. I guess having to make this decision made us change how we tackle our life problems together." Brenda and Bob decided not to inform Brenda's family of origin until after their decision had been made. "My family would all become 'experts' and would have tried to tell me what to do. I decided to leave them out while we made our decision. Bob and I needed all the time we could get to come to some agreement just between the two of us."

Because of the couple's indecision, a problem-solving intervention was used to assist them in clearly defining the problem, while generating alternatives and implementing a decision. The couple defined the problem as, "How can we make a medical decision that will effectively treat Brenda's cancer while also maintaining her quality of life?" Brenda and Bob began to generate alternatives, which varied from not having any type of treatment to brainstorming about several different surgical and nonsurgical treatments. To have an adequate level of knowledge regarding medical options, both Brenda and Bob reported doing extensive research to gain all the information they could regarding treatment for early-stage breast cancer. They reported that women now have a choice between getting a modified radical mastectomy or a lumpectomy, which is perhaps followed by radiation therapy (Oktay & Walter, 1991). Following this brainstorming stage, Brenda and Bob continued in the decision-making process by considering the different consequences that may come from implementing each of the solutions. Brenda commented, "In some ways, we just wish the doctor would say, 'This is what you have to do.' Instead, we found that we had to work it out for ourselves. We began to look at the consequences of some of our options. If we decided to go with the mastectomy, then I would lose my breast and have to deal with that the rest of my life. But if we decided to go with the lumpectomy, I wouldn't know if we had done all we could to prevent recurrence. It was a choice between quality of life and quantity of life, and it was almost impossible to make."

Through the decision-making process, Brenda and Bob both decided upon getting the lumpectomy followed by radiation therapy. Brenda stated that it was a difficult decision, but that her "sexuality and feelings about becoming a new wife and future mother were all tied up in her body image right now." Further, Brenda had read accounts of women losing their sex drive as a result of breast cancer treatment. "I want to minimize the impact this illness is going to have on me. Sometimes I just think, "Hey cancer, I am not going to give you any power over me!" Brenda and Bob decided to tell Brenda' family of origin about the diagnosis and treatment decisions the day before Brenda's surgery. They decided to tell the family one member at a time in order to have more control over the information that was given. "At first my mother was furious with us. She felt betrayed and left out. Then she felt guilty that it wasn't her that was diagnosed instead of me. It was then that I told her, "See, this is why I couldn't come to you in the first place. I can't deal with all of your emotions and mine too!'" Brenda and her mother came to a compromise, with Brenda's mother having several announced and scheduled visits each week, but allowing Brenda and Bob to go through the treatment phase on their own. "My brothers were asked not to interfere too. I love my family, but it is time they let me grow up and do things on my own. I told them that I understand how much they must be hurting too, but that I needed to get through this first." The rest of Brenda's family was encouraged to help support one another and to determine the ways in which they could help Brenda and Bob without crossing the boundaries of their newly forming system. To minimize the potential intrusiveness of Brenda's family and to give each family member a sense of purpose, Brenda and Bob were prepared with a list of ways that the family could help the couple during the treatment phase. For example, Brenda asked if her mother could come and vacuum her house once a week since Brenda's arm was going to be sore from the surgery, and Brenda's brothers were asked to do the yardwork so that Bob could spend more time with Brenda.

Brenda's surgery was much like a surgical biopsy, except that a portion of the surrounding tissue was also removed (Oktay & Walter, 1991). In addition, axillary node dissection was performed, revealing that 1 out of 14 nodes was positive. Thus, Brenda reported that she had minimal lymph node involvement but that the results of the surgical procedure to remove the lymph nodes were worse than the lumpectomy itself. "I only have a little scar where the lumpectomy was performed, but I have a small hole where the lymph nodes were removed." Brenda reported that she was also experiencing some swelling of her arm (lymphedema). "I have to do specific exercises and I am already beginning to see improvement. Still, I wasn't really counting on this problem. I wish someone could have given me more information about it." Since Brenda did have some lymph node involvement, her oncologist recommended chemotherapy to treat possible distant micrometastases followed by radiation treatment. Brenda reported that since she was undergoing chemotherapy, she had lost most of her hair. "The worst part of it is the fatigue, though. I am so irritable and tired I don't really even know myself. Bob has been terrific, he has so much patience with me, but that makes me feel even more guilty. It's like I have brought on all these problems to our marriage. Even our future plans may need to change, because the chemotherapy and radiation may leave me infertile. I feel like Bob has gotten robbed of married life—the woman he married no longer exists, and I don't know if I will ever be the same again."

During the course of treatment, Brenda experienced some nausea, fatigue, confusion, and loss of sex drive. Bob accompanied her to most of her chemotherapy sessions, but at times Brenda preferred to go alone. "Sometimes, I felt like Bob was carrying too much. I already had to take time off from work and I was a burden at home, being so tired all the time. So I would go to chemotherapy alone and feel like I had accomplished something. I could gain a sense of independence and strength that way." Brenda continued her treatment and moved into radiation therapy. "Radiation hasn't been so bad. I have to go almost every day, but the side effects aren't nearly what they were with chemotherapy. I still get a little bit worn out, and some changes have occurred to my breast. It has changed slightly in size and has become a bit firmer. Still, I have lost some sensation and that makes me feel angry. It's like I am doing all that I can to keep this illness from affecting me, us, but it keeps on causing problems anyway." To further complicate Brenda's treatment, it was recommended that she take Tamoxifen (antiestrogen that inhibits tumor growth) for five years. Brenda reported having mixed feelings about the recommendation of long-term chemotherapy. "I guess I am glad I can continue to do something to fight my cancer. But, sometimes I wish that I could just forget about it once my treatment is done. Now I will be constantly reminded of how I have cancer."

Psychosocial Considerations: The Nature of Family Work during the Long Haul

Brenda and Bob are in the early stages of forming their new family system. In addition, Brenda comes from an enmeshed family that has made it difficult for her to differentiate from the family of origin and to create her own family system. The centripetal pull of the diagnosis and the treatment phases of the illness acted on the new system, resulting in Brenda and Bob pulling inward and forming a rigid boundary between their newly forming system and Brenda's family of origin. Brenda's family was able to recognize the needs of the new couple and to respect the boundaries that Brenda and Bob had given them. Brenda's mother would call and ask if it was a good time before coming over to the house, and Bob found that Brenda's brothers were including him in more family discussions. Through the boundaries that the new couple set, the extended family was beginning to include Bob as a member of the family and respect the new couple as a separate, yet connected family entity.

Through counseling, Brenda and Bob also had to learn to cope with and adapt to several changes in functioning including (1) finding new meaning in Brenda's work, (2) letting go of the idea of a "just world," and (3) sexual functioning and childbearing (Oktay & Walter, 1991). Brenda remarked, "I have decided to go back to work, although I am going back a different and in some ways, a wiser woman now. I guess I have a different type of respect for the health care field. I know that we do know a great deal about how to help people with serious illnesses, but we don't know everything. I am letting my profession have its faults. I am accepting life as it comes now, one day at a time." Both Brenda and Bob also talked about getting through their existential crisis and the treatment phase: "We used to think that our life would just naturally flow one way—we met, we fell in love, we got married, and then we were going to have children and a family of our own. Now we see that God can have very different plans in mind. We are learning to let go of our ideas of a 'just world.' Bad things can happen even if you don't really deserve it. You can be the best person in the world, and still bad things can happen. Now, we are just trying to make the best of a terrible situation."

The effects of chemotherapy and radiation treatment may have also had an impact on Brenda's ability to have children.

> I am not sure if I can have children, nor do I think I want to have any biological children of our own. We discussed the process of ovum banking due to the possibility of early menopause caused by the treatment. But I was so overwhelmed that I couldn't go through one more thing. Bob and I have talked about the ramifications of cancer treatment and infertility, and at first I was just devastated. Because of the cancer and its treatment, we have decided not to try and have our own children. I think I would be too worried about passing breast cancer along to my daughters. Now, I need time to mourn our decision not to have our own children. I sometimes feel angry at what was taken away from us, and sometimes I feel very sad about the opportunities that have been lost. I guess you could say that I am grieving; my plans in life have definitely changed. But on good days I think maybe it is God's plan. Maybe I am supposed to adopt children and give them a great home. Then both of us get really excited about adoption. It has given our life a depth we didn't have before.

Although Brenda and Bob talked about their enthusiasm for adopting children, they were hesitant to discuss their sexual relationship. "It is hard for us to know how to go about having sex right now. I am still finishing up my treatment and I feel so tired all the time. Its hard to know how we are going to rebuild our sex life." Brenda reported the need to "get to know herself again" after her treatments have ended. She stated that she is just beginning to get her energy back. Bob added, "We still know that we love each other very much. It is just going to take some time to adjust to cancer treatment. Even though Brenda chose the lumpectomy, we have still gone through a lot and we can't lose sight of the big picture and that it is all about patience, love, kindness, and communication. Because of this, we feel we can talk about and get through anything."

Outcome of the Treatment Phase for the Newly Forming Family

As a result of the diagnosis and the treatment phase for the newly forming couple, Brenda and Bob have learned to communicate more effectively and to make sure that both of their opinions, desires, and needs are heard. Bob was becoming increasingly vocal in stating his opinions and needs, and Brenda was responding by listening to and validating those needs and holding them separate from her family of origin. By pulling inward into their relationship during a time of crisis, and by stating clearly the boundaries of their new system, Bob and Brenda were able to fortify their newly forming family and to create a new system of their own. Brenda is still close to her family of origin, but now her parents and her brothers accept Bob as a part of the family system as well.

Meaning in life and meaning for life changed for Brenda and Bob. During the treatment phase, they were able to alter their meaning in life by accepting an "unjust world" and by growing past their normal assumptions about how life would unfold. Moreover, Brenda was beginning to alter her more childish beliefs in an unfailing medical system. She commented that her newly found wisdom had made her a more realistic and compassionate nurse. Their meaning for life had also changed. While they still continue to go to their church, they report how their lives have been changed because of going through treatment for cancer. Now, important aspects of life, health, fertility, and a long life span are no longer taken for granted. Thus, the treatment phase had deepened Brenda and Bob personally and interpersonally.

☐ The Family with Young Children during Treatment

Families with young children encounter unique disruptions to the family system during the treatment phase. For example, mothers and fathers going through cancer treatment may have difficulty with carrying out child-rearing tasks, meeting financial responsibilities, meeting the challenges of work, and in maintaining intimate relationships with their partners. Meeting achievement needs during the treatment phase may also be disrupted, as patients and their partners must often struggle with the responsibilities of work and finances and may encounter increased difficulties regarding employment status and financial commitments (Rowland, 1989). Goals that include sending the children to college, taking family vacations, and meeting mortgage obligations may need to be altered in order to meet the financial demands of cancer treatment. The balance between dependence and independence may center on the patient's ability to return to work, or on how treatment regimens can be arranged according to demands of work and family schedules (Rolland, 1994).

Young children of cancer patients may also encounter psychosocial difficulties as they witness their parents undergoing cancer treatment and its side effects. Knowing what and how much to tell young children is a normal concern for cancer patients. The family's overriding set of values, beliefs, and social circumstances help to frame how the family will approach discussing cancer with young children (Babcock, 1997). The family system's rules and boundaries will also help determine communication patterns between the sub-systems in the family. Rules regarding communication take the form of (1) who can talk to whom, (2) the particulars of what can be said about the illness and to whom, (3) how often the illness can be discussed, and (4) how readily divergent interpretations of cancer's effect on the system are tolerated in the family system.

CASE EXAMPLE 3 (Continued). Sally's Treatment Protocol and Side Effects

Sally and Sam discussed Sally's illness and her treatment options with their oncologist. They found out that Sally was diagnosed with stage IIa cancer of the cervix, which in-volves portions of the vagina, but has no evidence of parametrial (tissue surrounding the cervix) involvement. Sally and Sam, under the direction of their oncologist, decided upon radical hysterectomy with the removal of the pelvic lymph nodes. "Having the surgery was one of the most difficult things I have ever had to go through. Thank God Sam was there for me. I felt like my whole future, my whole reason for being, was ripped out of me. Recovery has been a bit difficult too. At first it was difficult for me to go to the bathroom. I couldn't feel it if I had to go. . . . It was very strange and uncomfortable. I am still strug-gling with constipation and I am on a special diet." Sally's hysterectomy also involved shortening of the vagina, resulting in sexual dysfunction. "It is very difficult for me to even think about sex right now. I am grieving over my inability to have children, and I am experiencing too much pain, physically and emotionally, to just jump into having sex. It has only been a couple of weeks since my surgery." Sam agreed that it was difficult to even discuss their sexual difficulties at this point in Sally's treatment and recovery. "Right now, we are dealing with intense loss. I have such strong feelings and they are all mixed up. On one hand, we feel that Sally's chances of survival are really good, around 75%–80%. So, about that, I feel like we just got a huge break and I could dance for joy! But on the other hand, I feel we just lost our future children. We both feel so sad about having our family just stopped in its tracks like that." Through counseling, the couple learned to use a grief ritual to begin to deal with their heartache over the loss of having more children. The ritual consisted of writing their lost future children a letter and tying it to a balloon and releasing the letter with the balloon. In this way, Sally and Sam were able to experience some closure and resolution in dealing with their grief.

Since Sally had just been released from the hospital, she was still experiencing the side effects of the surgery, including difficulties with bowel and bladder elimination. Sally learned that her difficulties with constipation were a result of denervation of the rectum and that she is expected to recover within a few months (Averette & Nguyen, 1995). Al-though she and Sam have begun the process of grieving for the loss of Sally's fertility, they have not yet faced their sexual difficulties that are a result of the illness and its treatment.

Psychosocial Considerations: The Nature of Family Work during the Long Haul

During the treatment planning and treatment implementation phases of the illness, Sally and Sam were both attempting to maintain their household and to continue to focus on parenting their young children, Sara and Sean. In addition, Sally was concerned with her and Sam's own feelings of grief, as well as those of her mother. In essence, three genera-tions were being affected by cancer: Sally and Sam's marital dyad (the "sandwich genera-tion"), Sally's mother, and Sally and Sam's children. For the multigenerational system, the nature of family work during the treatment phase includes (1) facilitating effective communication within and between generational subsystems, (2) helping Sally and Sam to continue their developmental tasks of raising a family and bonding as a marital subsystem during cancer treatment, (3) assisting Sally's mother in her own grief as well as helping her to provide care for her daughter, son-in-law, and grandchildren, and (4) continuing to help the family communicate with their young children about sensitive subjects such as cancer and its treatment and their ramifications for the family system.

Sally and Sam discussed the difficulties they were having communicating about the illness and its treatment, particularly with family members outside of the marital subsystem. "I don't know who is harder to talk to, my children or my mother. I guess I thought I could tell them all just one time about the cancer and its treatment and be done with it. I didn't realize that I would have to continue to talk about it over and over again." To begin to contain the amount of time that Sally was having to spend discussing her medical condition with her family, it was suggested to her that she have family meetings one to two times a week, where all interested parties could be present to ask questions and hear about Sally's course of treatment. If a family member had a question that they wanted answered outside of this meeting time, they were encouraged to write it down on a notepad in the kitchen. In this way, Sally's children and mother would have their needs be met, as well as Sally's need for a more regulated discussion around her condition.

Sally and Sam were primarily occupied with their own feelings of grief. Within their subsystem, through the speaker–listener techniques (for more information on this technique, see Chapter two, case conceptualization of the newly forming couple), Sally and Sam had to learn to discuss their feelings on a deeper level and not to assume they understood how the other felt (Babcock, 1997). Sally and Sam are now in the process of learning to be more flexible and accepting of each other's emotional ups and downs. Sam stated, "We are trying to give each other support without being overly sensitive. Too, we are trying to keep a sense of humor, although much of the time one or the other of us is either sad or angry. Now, we notice all the little things that are really so important—the stuff we used to take for granted. Like having dinner together, or watching television with the kids, or tucking them in at night. When Sally was in the hospital, she used to cry at night in her hospital bed when she knew her mother, instead of her, was tucking the kids into bed."

Sally experienced both physical and emotional difficulties during her stay in the hospital following her surgery. Although her mother was able to fill much of Sally's role as family caregiver in the household, Sally still worried about her children and what they were experiencing. Sally's mother was aware of how Sally must be worrying and missing her children. As a result, she had the children make cards for their mother and tape recordings of songs and messages they wanted to share with her. Sally's mother made short visits to Sally in the hospital and was able to give her the pictures, cards, and tape recorded messages from the children. Sally remembered, "Those wonderful gifts got me through the surgery and afterward. I realized how much I already have and how much I have to be thankful for. It was hard having a hysterectomy, and I am still sad. But I have my children and the love of my family to keep me going."

Sally's mother was also experiencing some difficulties adapting to Sally's treatment. Upon her request, she came in for an individual counseling session during Sally's stay in the hospital. Sally's mother, Sue, is 59 years old and has been married to Rick for more than 36 years. Sue discussed her husband, who she described as "emotionally distant and unable to help her through this." Sue also made note that Sally was her only child and that they have been very close since her birth. "We didn't even go through a bad time when she was a teenager. We have always been close. We always thought that she would have a large family—especially since she was an only child. I go around all day thinking, 'Why couldn't this have been me?' Sally isn't yet done with her family. Why would God take that away from her? From any woman?" Sue discussed her feelings of guilt and isolation. Her emotionally disengaged relationship with her husband had resulted in an overidentification with her daughter and her daughter's family. Thus, the news of her daughter's illness and infertility left her emotionally devastated, even though she understood that Sally's chances of survival were very good. Sue wanted to discuss ways in which she could help her daughter without crossing the boundaries into Sally and Sam's own family system. Sue was able to identify her own abilities and ways that she could help the family. Sue remarked how she loved to cook, so she suggested that at least for a while she would cook the evening meals and bring them over for the family to reheat and to share. Sue also stated that she was helping out with the grocery shopping and the household chores. "Still, sometimes I feel like I am interfering, especially since Sally has returned home from the hospital. I guess I shouldn't assume they want me to help. Perhaps I should ask them more often what they need." During the counseling session, it was discussed how the treatment phase consists of many cycles. Renegotiating boundaries and power structures as well as reallocating roles, rules, and responsibilities was an ongoing task of this phase. Thus, the treatment phase marks a time of flexibility with regard to family functioning. This is an important time for ongoing and open communication between Sue and her daughter. Sue remarked how it may be time to reevaluate her role in helping her daughter and her family.

Sally, Sam, and their two children also came in for a follow-up consultation a few weeks after Sally's surgery. Their primary concern at this point in the treatment process was the effects cancer was having on the children. Sally started the session, "We told them both that I was very sick, and we thought that would be enough. Both of them are beginning to act really badly at home. They don't want to go to bed. They want to hang all over me. They throw fits when we don't do the things they want to do, like go to the park, or color, or just play. But neither of us seems to have the energy right now."

First, we discussed the importance of ongoing communication about cancer, its treatment, and its effects on the future of the family (Babcock, 1997). "Sean just wants to sit on my lap all the time and hang on me. He has also started to want his old blanket back, and he won't go to sleep without his bottle. I know he is too old for these things, but I can't seem to take them away from him. I guess I feel guilty for leaving them while I was in the hospital." Children Sean's age cannot understand the complexities of the illness, but they do experience feelings of separation that are a result of the illness and its treatment (Jennings, 1986; Rowland, 1989). Sean needed to have an established routine and consistent caretaking in order to make him feel safe. Sally was experiencing the difficulties in continuing her developmental tasks of childrearing due to her physical rehabilitation and the guilt placed on her by the illness. She was encouraged to offer Sean comfort and assurance that he would be taken care of, even though she is sick right now. Both she and Sam could offer Sean comfort and safety by establishing a routine for meals, playtime, nap time, family time, and bedtime.

Sara, age six, was able to talk a bit more readily about her mother's illness: "I love my Grandma, but I don't want her to be my Mommy. I want my Mommy to do things for us like she used to." During Sally's hospital stay, Sara believed that her grandmother was now going to live in the home and become the primary caregiver. Sara was experiencing confusion over the roles that her mother and her grandmother were performing during the treatment phase of the illness. Sally was comforted by knowing that her mother was going to continue to be her mother, and her grandmother was going to be her grandmother. Moreover, children Sara's age are beginning to expand their understanding of the world, to learn basic skills, and to achieve a sense of industry by reaching small, attainable goals (Rittenberg, 1996). Sara's sense of competence and mastery over the effects of the illness could be facilitated by having her help with small chores around the house, and by having her help with her mother's needs.

At the end of the session, Sara surprised us all by asking, "Where is the baby, though?" At first, neither Sally nor Sam could understand what Sara was asking. They had to ask Sara for more information. Sara continued, "You said that we are going to have another baby in our family and that you and Daddy are planning it. You said that I am going to be a big sister to a new baby someday. Mommy, you went to the hospital and that's where people get babies, like when you got Sean. So, where is the baby now?" Sally and Sam had not addressed Sally's infertility and changes in family planning with Sara. With tears in her eyes, Sally said, "I forgot that I told Sara that she was going to be able to help out with another baby someday. I told her those things when I was going to see the doctor about discontinuing birth control and to discuss pregnancy. I never dreamed this would happen." Although it was difficult, Sally and Sam had to explain to Sara that, because of cancer, Mommy could not have anymore children. Sam told Sara, "Mommy was in the hospital to get the cancer out so that she could live and be your Mommy for a long time. But, because she was so sick, we cannot have a little baby brother or sister. But we still need you to help out at home with Sean and with Mommy while she is sick." Because of this conversation, it became clearer to both Sally and Sam how easy it is for young children to become confused regarding changes in (1) primary caregiving roles, (2) the integrity and safety of the system, (3) daily family functioning in the form of routines and rituals, and (4) family system development and plans for additional children.

Outcome of the Treatment Phase for the Family with Young Children

The treatment phase for this family with young children was marked by joy in the discovery that Sally's chances of survival were high, but also by the realization that the family system would have to grieve the loss of unborn children as a result of infertility. Issues of body image and sexual dysfunction were not yet ready to be addressed by Sally and Sam. During the treatment phase, the demands of the illness necessitated a focus on daily functioning, role reallocation, boundary setting, and, most importantly, maintaining flexible and open communication within the marital subsystem and between generational systems. After the crisis of surgery and Sally's hospital stay, the family had to renegotiate the responsibilities and roles within the family. To help during the initial period of the treatment phase, Sally's mother had taken on Sally's role during hospitalization. However, to prevent the illness from becoming embedded in the family system, Sue was encouraged to discuss her role in her daughter's family system and to renegotiate her responsibilities in response to the family's needs as they transitioned into a more chronic phase of the illness (Rolland, 1994). In addition, Sally began to have "Mommy time" with each of her children during the day. Even though she was fatigued through her treatment and rehabilitation, she began to have reading time with Sara and storytelling time with Sam before his daily naps. This renegotiation of roles and responsibilities helped Sally and Sue to regain their own roles in the multigenerational structure of the family system. In turn, this helped the children to know that their mother was becoming active in the "role of mother" once again. This provided a sense of safety for the children.

Sean and Sara's confusion regarding the illness and its treatment also needed to be reevaluated during this phase of the clinical course of cancer. Sally and Sam were able to begin to provide their children with a daily routine and family rituals that helped Sean and Sara to feel increasingly secure within their family system. Daily routines and family rituals, such as meal times together and a story before bed, replaced Sean's need for his blanket and bottle at bedtime. Sara began to take over small chores at home. Although Sally remarked that it was often easier just to do these herself, she allowed Sara to do small chores and thus to gain a sense of mastery, participation in the family system, and to fulfill her promised role as "helper in the family." By learning to communicate effectively during the many cycles of the treatment phase, and by taking the time to reallocate roles and responsibilities when needed, the family system was prepared to make a transition into the rehabilitation phase of the illness.

☐ The Family with Adolescents during Treatment

Families with adolescents will have different challenges than families with young children. While it may be difficult to assure young children of their basic safety needs, adolescents will have difficulties negotiating the balance between independence from and dependence upon the family system (Nelson et al., 1994). During the treatment phase, adolescents may need to adjust to new roles in which they must care for their younger siblings, prepare meals, help care for the ill parent, and perform otherwise more "adult" activities and responsibilities. Role strain and the blurring of boundaries may need to be carefully assessed, particularly during the initial, centripetal phase of early treatment (Rolland, 1994).

Relationships with friends may also undergo shifts during this phase of the illness, as the adolescent is often pulled inward to care for the family and to assume the functions of the ill parent (Nelson et al., 1994). When the inward pull of the treatment phase relaxes, roles and responsibilities can be reevaluated and reassigned to ensure that the relationship and achievement needs of the adolescent, and of the family system, are being met.

CASE EXAMPLE 4 (Continued). Frank's Treatment Protocol and Side Effects

Frank was diagnosed with stage II Hodgkin's disease and was scheduled to receive radiation treatment. First, it was recommended that he undergo a staging laparotomy (exploratory abdominal surgery) to evaluate the spleen, liver, and abdominal lymph nodes. Frank's condition was considered "favorable" since he had no large masses and no symptoms. Since the hospital where Frank was being treated had modern radiotherapy equipment and radiation oncologists with extensive experience, it was recommended that Frank receive total lymphoid irradiation. This means that Frank received radiation to three treatment fields: (1) the mantle field near the lungs, vocal cords, heart, and thyroid; (2) the paraaortic field, which extends from the diaphragm to the spleen; and (3) the pelvic or inverted Y field, which encompasses the pelvic region and a large area of bone marrow (Rosenthal & Eyre, 1995). Frank was to receive radiation treatment over the course of about six weeks and was told that he may experience side effects from the radiation treatment, which include hypothyroidism and myelosuppression (a reduction in bone marrow functioning). In addition, he was also to receive multiple cycles of MOPP (nitrogen mustard, vincristine, procarbazine, and Prednisone). Side effects from MOPP can include nausea, alopecia, and mood changes.

Psychosocial Considerations: The Nature of Family Work during the Long Haul

Although Frank's family was adapting well to the treatment phase of the illness, the adolescents in the family were having some difficulties adjusting to their father's illness and the ramifications of his treatment. Adolescents can be deeply influenced by cancer in at least four different aspects of development: (1) developmentally normal conflicts with parents, (2) intellectual mastery, (3) emotional intensity and mood swings, and (4) concerns with social life outside of the family system (Adams-Greenly, Beldoch, & Moynihan, 1986). Frank Jr. was having particular difficulties in each of these areas.

It was difficult for Frank Jr. to discuss his intense emotions during a follow-up counseling session. He said, "It is so hard for me to talk in front of everyone. I guess I feel so many things at once, and I am afraid everyone will laugh at me." After much reassurance from his family, especially from his siblings, who "promised not to laugh or make fun of him," Frank began to open up and to discuss his perceptions and problems with his father's illness. "At first I was really scared and I couldn't even come in to the first session. I thought that I had caused my father's illness. You see, when Grandpa died of cancer, I kept wishing it had been Dad instead of Grandpa. Dad and I were fighting about all kinds of stuff and Grandpa was just this really cool, laid back person." In essence, Frank Jr. had idealized his grandfather, especially during his illness and after his death. During adolescence, some children may idealize a family member and devalue another, particularly if they are in direct conflict with the devalued family member (Adams-Greenly et al., 1986). Frank Jr. was feeling guilty over idealizing his grandfather and causing a potential threat to his father's health and well-being. The family was able to discuss Frank Jr.'s guilt and to reassure him that he did not cause his father's illness.

Frank Jr. was also having difficulty understanding the nature of his father's illness, its treatment, and the side effects of the treatment from an intellectual standpoint because he was missing the weekly family meetings. "No one tells me anything around here, and I don't want to go to those stupid meetings. All I know is that Dad has cancer, just like Grandpa, and that he is being treated with drugs and radiation. I see him feeling really tired and losing weight. So what am I supposed to think? That he is going to die soon, just like Grandpa." Adolescents at Frank Jr.'s age are able to use well-developed abstract reasoning capabilities. Thus, adolescents often use intellectual mastery as a coping mechanism in the adaptation to threatening situations (Adams-Greenly et al., 1986). Frank Jr. needed to become more informed regarding his father's type of cancer, its treatment, and its long-term prognosis, and the family meetings may have become too threatening or vulnerable of an environment Therefore, it was encouraged that Frank Jr. have an individual meeting with his parents to clarify his father's illness and course of treatment. During this meeting he expressed some confusion; he thought that his father's exploratory surgery was an operation for stomach cancer, and said, "I saw the scar where Dad had his operation, so I looked up stomach cancer in a book at school. Stomach cancer can be fatal and I was sure my father was going to die soon, just like Grandpa." During this meeting with his parents, and because of Frank Jr.'s developmental stage and need for information, both Frank Jr. and his parents were encouraged to read about Hodgkin's disease, its treatment, and its rate of survival.

Frank Jr. was also experiencing intense emotions both due to his developmental age and his father's illness. As a result of these strong feelings, Frank Jr. had been getting into fights at school. He explained, "I get so scared and upset sometimes. I feel like the stress from helping with the business is getting to me and I don't know what else to do but yell and get into fights at school. I just seem to snap at little things, and I can't help it." In addition, Frank Jr. had not been turning in his schoolwork. Notes were being sent home from his teachers inquiring about Frank Jr.'s increasingly disturbing behavior at school. Frank Jr. commented, "I feel so overwhelmed by it all, work, school, my friends, my Dad's illness. I just feel as if I am going to blow up at any minute and I can't concentrate on anything." It was recommended that Frank and Anne meet with the principal at Frank Jr.'s school to discuss the temporary upheaval in their family. Frank Jr.'s parents agreed that the burden of the treatment phase had been placed primarily on Frank Jr.

Outcome of the Treatment Phase for the Family with Adolescents

Since the crisis period of the treatment phase had transitioned into the chronic, long haul of daily treatment, it was recommended that the family's rules, roles, and responsibilities be reevaluated at this time. Frank Jr.'s parents discussed ways in which Frank Jr. could begin to feel comfortable at the family meetings and to join the family in discussing family issues. Frank stated that he would come if it was not going to be "all emotional." Frank's parents agreed to monitor the level of emotion in the meeting, yet they also normalized that emotion was common and appropriate during this time. At the next family meeting, the family discussed ways that Frank could take some time off from the family business to have more time to concentrate on his schoolwork and on his own personal social needs. Frank Jr. was relieved when his parents agreed that his social activities were particularly important at this stage of his development. "I have been doing so much to help out with the family business, that I don't have much time for school or my friends. I get angry about that and then I feel guilty that I should want to help my family more." By receiving permission to resume his activities with his friends at school, Frank remarked that much of the tension he had been feeling was released. By helping Frank Jr. to resume his appropriate life cycle tasks, his schoolwork began to improve and his mood swings were less volatile and troublesome. Thus, the family system was enriched because of Frank Jr.'s ability to regain his developmental momentum.

☐ The Family Launching Children during Treatment

Families launching their older children during the treatment phase will encounter challenges similar to those of families with adolescents, albeit with greater complexity. The centrifugal momentum of this family life cycle is generally at its peak when older children leave the home to assume various degrees of independence from the family. Older children who have already established themselves as independent from their families of origin will often have less difficulty balancing independence and dependence than will those children who are in the beginning stages of leaving the family of origin (Rolland, 1994). Older children who have just left the family system in order to establish themselves in outside relationships and in their careers are more likely to be the ones called back into the family system to help care for the family during treatment (Rolland, 1994). The struggle to find a delicate balance of interdependence with the family may be difficult for the adult child during this time of need. But again, as the initial demands of treatment begin to decrease, the needs of the older child and the family system in the launching stage of development must be reevaluated so that the family can regain developmental momentum. In so doing, cancer does not permanently impede family systems development, and successful adaptation for the entire family system can take place during treatment and subsequent phases of the disease (Rolland, 1994).

CASE EXAMPLE 5 (Continued). Claire's Treatment Protocol and Side Effects

Claire and Greg went to a follow-up consultation with Claire's oncologist to discuss Claire's diagnosis, prognosis, treatment options, and long-term rehabilitation needs. They reported that Claire has stage II breast cancer with a tumor less than 5 centimeters in dimension. Claire's prognosis was considered "good," especially since the tumor had a high degree of differentiation and that test results indicated the presence of estrogen and progesterone receptor proteins (indicative that the regulatory controls of the mammary epithelium are functioning; Dow, 1997). However, there is a history of breast cancer in Claire's family, which could complicated her long-term prognosis. Since Claire's mother died of breast cancer seven years ago, Claire and Greg decided that Claire would undergo a modified radical mastectomy. Claire reported that a modified radical mastectomy involves the excision of the tumor, the entire breast, and axillary lymph nodes. Both she and Greg decided to wait about six months postsurgery to discuss possible breast reconstruction. Claire was also scheduled to go for systemic treatment for her cancer in the form of chemotherapy treatments. She was experiencing some anxiety regarding chemotherapy and reported being nervous about losing her hair, becoming nauseated, fatigued, and even gaining weight. "Now that I am starting to get my family life back together again, especially with my marriage, I am going to fall apart physically. I can't seem to get it together!" Greg quietly took Claire's hand and stated, "We'll get through the surgery, the chemotherapy, and the radiation treatments together. I'll write at home and take care of you." Claire also discussed radiation therapy. "I guess I have to have all forms of treatment. The surgery and the chemotherapy bother me more than getting radiation treatments. I don't think radiation will be painful, but I do wonder about being radioactive and all that." Claire was assured by her oncologist that she would not become radioactive. However, she may experience some pain in the breast, slight burning to the treated area, and fatigue.

Long-term side effects of the illness and its treatment were reported to be early menopause and possibly lymphedema. Claire was to do special exercises to increase her range of motion and to decrease tightness in her affected arm (Dow, 1997). Claire remarked that losing the ability to have children and going into early menopause made her feel sad and angry: "It isn't that I want to have more children; we don't want that at all. But it does make me feel sad and angry that I have to go into menopause because of cancer, and not because I am naturally aging and maturing. I feel cheated out of normal, healthy development."

Claire's surgery went well, although she did experience phantom breast pains and moderate symptoms of lymphedema. She had to stay in the hospital longer than is typically expected to care for an infection that developed as a result of her surgery. She was able to return home a few days later and began her exercises to help with her impaired arm and shoulder immobility. She also reported that her chest felt tight due to the disruption in lymphatic drainage. "I was focusing more on losing a breast and going through chemotherapy. I didn't really think about how the surgery would impair my movement and keep me from being able to do things. I can't hardly use my arm at all right now. But the doctor says that most of my mobility will return in time." Claire was scheduled to begin chemotherapy the following week. Following chemotherapy treatment, Claire would finish her treatment protocol with daily rounds of radiation therapy.

Psychosocial Considerations: The Nature of Family Work During the Long Haul

After the initial crisis period of the treatment phase had subsided, Claire and Greg fell into the routine of receiving chemotherapy treatments. At this time, Claire began to experience increased levels of depression and anxiety. She reported that her anxiety and depression were not only a result of the illness and its treatment, but that her relationship with Greg was not going as well as she had hoped. It was recommended that all the family members come to a follow-up counseling session. Greg, Claire, and Katherine were in attendance as Claire began to discuss her difficulties in adaptation to her illness: "At first, I thought the illness would change things, make things better for me in some ways. And in some ways it has. At least now Greg pays some attention to me and to our marriage. But I still feel as if I am alone in this struggle. I call Katherine, but I feel guilty for not talking to Greg. Now I know that when I talk to Katherine instead of Greg, I am just increasing the distance we have between us in our marriage."

Structural family therapy was used to help Claire, Greg, and Katherine in their adaptation to the launching stage of the family life cycle and to the demands of cancer treatment. Structural therapy provides a framework for viewing the family as a system of patterns of interactions (Kemenoff, Jachimczyk, & Fussner, 1999). With regard to family functioning, Claire is thus not regarded as the identified patient, but as the "symptom bearer" of the problematic patterns of interaction that are taking place in the family. This family has developed rules of interaction that have decreased the range of behaviors that can take place within the family system. Because of this, the subsystems within the family cannot carry out their primary functions. For example, Claire has limited range of communication with her husband. As a result of this limited communication, the marital subsystem cannot carry out the primary function of enhancing the marital bond (Kemenoff et al., 1999).

Additional concepts used in structural family therapy include (1) complementarity, or the mutual accommodations of the family members (e.g. for one to act like a parent, the other must act like a child); (2) alignments, or the emotional connections family members have with one another; and (3) boundaries, or the rules that govern the levels of contact between the various family members and subsystems. These concepts, which are central to structural family therapy, were used in conjunction with the demands of the treatment phase to help Claire's family to regain their developmental momentum during the launching stage of the family life cycle. First, observations of the familial patterns of interactions were made. Claire began the session, "I feel pretty alone, even though Greg does seem to care a bit more than he used to. I guess I was just expecting, . . . needing, a miracle." Greg remained silent as Claire shared her needs for greater intimacy, deeper conversations, and attention from Greg. Katherine reached over to hold her mother's hand and got tears in her own eyes as her mother kept talking about her depression and fear. Katherine stated, "I feel like I just want to move back home and protect her. And then again, I get frustrated because there are so many things going on in my own life right now. I am ready to graduate, ready to get a new job, and ready to travel to Europe next summer. But when I think of all these things, I feel guilty. My Mom needs me now and I shouldn't be so selfish." It was difficult for Greg to begin to share his feelings: "I don't know where to start. It seems like everyone else has such an easy time of talking about their feelings. I don't quite know how. I do know how to write my articles for the paper and for magazines, but other than that, I don't know how to tell my wife how much I love her and want her to be alright." Greg bowed his head and looked away.

From observing the family's interaction, it appeared that Claire and Katherine had formed a strong alignment based on the complementary interaction of Claire being in need and Katherine stepping in to rescue her. Since Greg was unable, at this time, to understand the ramifications of Claire and Katherine's strong alignment, he felt left alone to work and to enjoy his own sports and activities: "I feel alone, too. But I don't know how to rebuild my marriage. Now that we have all stared death in the face, life and our family seem too precious for me to just let them go to waste. Claire seems so depressed and stressed all the time, I don't know how to be around her."

During family therapy, the family used space to depict how their family is functioning currently and how they wish it could begin to function in the future. For example, it was suggested that Claire and Greg move closer to one another and join hands, signifying their new stronger marital alignment. In addition, Katherine moved her chair a bit farther away from her parents and let go of her mother's hand. This signified her need to move away from the family of origin and to resume her own developmental tasks of differentiation. Katherine was reassured, however, that she was still important and needed by her mother, just not as the sole support provider. In addition, special family tasks were assigned with the intention of creating a stronger bond within the marital dyad and forming more solid boundaries between the marital subsystem and the children's subsystem. The first tasks involved Greg taking the time each day to write his wife a note to encourage her and to communicate how he feels. The note could be about anything: his work, his thoughts, his feelings, or any wishes or fears he had regarding the illness. Greg readily agreed to this task since his primary way of communicating with others was through the written word.

Claire would benefit from receiving frequent meaningful communication from her husband. In order to increase the boundaries around the marital subsystem and to encourage communication between Claire and Greg, a speaker–listener exercise was used. The couple was encouraged to express their feelings through "I" statements and to listen to and empathize with their spouse. This intervention was conducted through reflecting the message that the speaker delivered to make sure that the message was fully understood. In the case of Claire and Greg, there was quite a bit of mind reading and assumption making, which made communication and reflection difficult. In order to decrease these communication patterns, the couple was coached to respond to their partner without judgment. Even though this was an unfamiliar and, at times, uncomfortable exercise for them, through practice they were able to come to a better understanding of each other's feelings without blame and withdrawal. Using these new communication tools, Greg would exchange his written messages for spoken communication with his wife. In turn, Claire's sense of loneliness and isolation would decrease. With the increase in communication, the couple was able to more freely engage in caring behaviors for each other. In fact, the couple had scheduled a date in order to have time together where they were not focused on Claire's cancer. They had planned to go to dinner and a play. This increase in caring behaviors was beginning to fortify the marital relationship. Claire was also assigned a special task. It was recommended that she limit the calls she made to her daughter to once or twice a week. During these calls she was to begin to monitor herself in regard to her role as "mother in need." Instead, she would focus on expressing the facts regarding her health and treatment progress. In response, Katherine was to monitor her reactions as the "rescuer." By making a conscious effort to notice their own complementary interactions, it was hypothesized that the boundaries between parent subsystem and child subsystem would be rectified. This, in turn, would reduce the unhealthy enmeshed interactions between mother and daughter, and thereby reduce guilt and ambivalent feelings in Katherine.

Outcome of the Treatment Phase for the Family Launching Children

Claire had difficulty adapting during the treatment phase of the illness, in terms of physical, emotional, and family functioning. Physically, Claire was not prepared for the results of the surgery and had to continue with her exercises to increase her range of motion and ability to use her arm. After a few months, she was able to resume normal activities within the limitations of the effects of her chemotherapy treatment. During her chemotherapy, she experienced bouts of nausea and fatigue. The demands of the illness and its treatment intensified her feelings of loneliness in her marriage. Through structural family therapy and behavioral marital therapy, Claire and Greg were able to strengthen their marital bond and to decrease Claire's dependency on her daughter Katherine. In short, Claire's family was able to become flexible enough to grow and to adapt during the treatment phase of the illness. Because of this, the family was prepared for the next phase of the clinical course of cancer.

☐ The Family in Later Life during Treatment

Patients in later life often will have disruptions in the form of altered relationships, interdependence, achievement, and body image. Older patients may become socially isolated and have few people to give them the care they need during the treatment phase. Older patients who have become accustomed to independence and autonomy may have difficulty adapting to their increased need for dependency. They may also feel "cheated" out of a healthy and long-anticipated retirement, especially when the financial burden of cancer treatment uses much, if not all, of their savings and potential income.

The side effects of cancer treatment are more likely to be of greater consequence to the older cancer patient. Issues surrounding the effects of aging and dependency may be accelerated due to cancer treatment. The aging process may become enhanced when the older patient experiences fatigue and is unable to carry out typical daily routines. If treatment is particularly debilitating, the older adult may feel shame at needing assistance with personal hygiene or incontinence (Rowland, 1989). Older patients may need to live with their adult children, particularly during the treatment phase, and face role reversals with their children that can result in dependency for the cancer patient and resentment for the adult caregiver.

Concerns regarding sexuality and body image for the older patient may become exacerbated by cancer treatment side effects. For example, prostate cancer therapy may lead to a loss of libido and breast enlargement in men, and some breast cancer therapies may result in a hirsute face, deepening of the voice, and altered libido in women (Rowland, 1989). Interventions for cancer patients at this developmental stage can focus on the changes in body image, the maintenance of personal integrity, and the balance between dependence and independence. Specific points of counseling can address the accelerated aging process, the practical management of treatment side effects, the effects of treatment on body image, the management of personal hygiene during treatment, and changes in sexual functioning due to cancer treatment.

CASE EXAMPLE 6 (Continued). Red's Treatment Protocol and Side Effects

Red recently went to the hospital for an outpatient procedure during which radioisotopes were implanted. Red remarked that he was nervous about receiving the implants, but the procedure was not too painful: "It only took about an hour, and I was able to resume my normal activities in about three days." With radiation treatment for prostatic cancer, some degree of urinary incontinence may occur. Red also commented that he was experiencing diarrhea and had decreased the fiber in his diet and was drinking plenty of fluids. He said, "For the most part, I feel like I am really lucky. The Doc caught my cancer at an early stage, and since I am in relatively good health to begin with, I am receiving the best treatment possible for a man my age."

Psychosocial Considerations: The Nature of Family Work during the Long Haul

Red experienced minimal side effects from prostatic cancer treatment. His outpatient surgery was unremarkable, and he was able to continue with his daily tasks within a few days following the implantation. He commented, "I knew that I needed to get back on my feet as soon as possible. Right after the day of my implants, Rachel got very sick. It really scared me. I know how much we depend on each other and her health is not the best. I think that she has more difficulty with her health right now than I do with mine." Red had to set limits on the effects of his illness in order to focus on the needs of his wife.

Cancer's impact on families in later life is complicated by concurrent illnesses and the potential for the occurrence of a "resource vacuum." Red continued, "I know that I can't die from this cancer. If I do, there will be no one around to take care of Rachel. We have kids and grandkids, but they all live so far away. Our friends and neighbors have been around to help us through the initial shock of the diagnosis, but now that things have settled down, they have all pretty much disappeared again." Rachel noted that they were close to their daughter Rene but "She needs us for support more than the other way around right now. If something should happen to Red, I don't know where I would go."

Outcome of the Treatment Phase for the Family in Later Life

Although Red's prostate cancer was caught at an early stage and his prognosis is favorable, the impact of the disease and its treatment was still felt by this couple. Soon after Red's treatment completion, the extended family visited. Red and Rachel commented on how they each experienced a greater depth in their relationships with their children and grandchildren: "Although many of them could only stay in town a few days, we had a bond that was greater than ever before. It felt like the threat of cancer just reverberated through the family, making us closer." Rachel and Red still worry about the loss of the other. Because of cancer, they began to reevaluate their external resource and to allow others into their subsystem. Rachel explained, "I know now that I could lose Red. I sometimes think of him as the strong one who can live and last forever. Now I know that we need to reach out to others for support. We can't do everything for each other forever." In realizing their need for outside help, Rachel and Red decided to call upon their son, who lives 30 miles from them. In doing so, they were able to ask for him to come several times a week to assist with chores around the house. By opening up the boundaries of their system and identifying their needs, Red and Rachel began to increase the amount of external support available to them and to prepare themselves for the next phase of the clinical course of cancer.

☐ Summary

In this chapter the focus was on the family during the treatment phase of the illness. Biomedical variables of importance and the major psychosocial issues of the "long haul" of daily living with cancer treatment were explained. Next, important considerations for the six family life cycles during the treatment phase were presented, followed by detailed case examples relevant to each of the six family life cycles. The importance of family flexibility and the recognition of developmental delays as *temporary* were emphasized. Intervention strategies and outcomes of the treatment phase were also presented.

The next chapter is about the important biomedical information and psychosocial considerations relevant to the remission/rehabilitation phase of the illness. This information will be followed by further elaboration of the six case examples, with an emphasis on transforming and reorganizing the family system.

☐ References

Adams-Greenly, M., Beldoch, N., & Moynihan, R. (1986). Helping adolescents whose parents have cancer. *Seminars in Oncology Nursing, 2*(2), 133–138.

Armitage, J. O. (1997). Bone marrow and blood stem cell transplantation. In M. Dollinger, E. H. Rosenbaum, & G. Cable (Eds.), *Everyone's guide to cancer therapy* (3rd ed., pp. 96–105). Kansas City, MO: Andrews McMeel Publishing.

Averette, H., & Nguyen, H. (1995). Gynecologic cancer. In G. Murphy, W. Lawrence, & R. Lenhard, Jr. (Eds.), *American Cancer Society textbook of clinical oncology* (2nd ed., pp. 352–579). Atlanta, GA: American Cancer Society.

Babcock, E. N. (1997). *When life becomes precious: A guide for loved ones and friends of cancer patients.* New York: Bantam Books.

Baider, L., & Kaplan De-Nour, A. (1988). Breast cancer—A family affair. In C. Cooper (Ed.), *Stress and breast cancer* (pp. 155–170). New York: John Wiley and Sons.

Baider, L., & Sarell, M. (1984). Couples in crisis: Patient-spouse differences in perception of interaction patterns and the illness situation. *Family Therapy, 9*(2), 115–122.

Blanchard, C., Albrecht, T., & Ruckdeschel, J. (1997). The crisis of cancer: Psychological impact on family caregivers. *Oncology, 11*(2), 189–202.

Bowers, B. (1987). Intergenerational caregiving: Adult caregivers and their aging parents. *Advanced Nursing Science, 9*, 20–31.

Broderick, C., & Smith, J. (1979). The general systems approach. In W. Burr, R. Hill, F. Nye, & I. Reiss (Eds.), *Contemporary theories about the family* (vol. 2, pp. 112–129). New York: Free Press.

Burish, T., Snyder, S., & Jenkins, R. (1991). Preparing patients for cancer chemotherapy: Effective coping preparation and relaxation interventions. *Journal of Consulting and Clinical Psychology, 59*(4), 518–525.

Burke, R., & Weir, T. (1982). Husband-wife helping relationships as moderators of experienced stress: The "mental hygiene" function in marriage. In H. I. McCubbin, A. E. Cauble, & J. M. Patterson (Eds.), *Family stress, coping and social support.* Springfield, IL: Charles C. Thomas.

Carter, E., & McGoldrick, M. (Eds.). (1989). *The changing family life cycle: A framework for family therapy* (2nd ed.). Needham Heights, MA: Allyn and Bacon.

Cassileth, B. (1997). Alternative and complementary therapies. In M. Dollinger, E. Rosenbaum, & G. Cable (Eds.), *Everyone's guide to cancer therapy: How cancer is diagnosed, treated, and managed day to day.* Toronto, Ontario, Canada: Sommerville House Books Limited.

Dollinger, M. & Rosenbaum, E. (1997). What happens in chemotherapy. In M. Dollinger, E. Rosenbaum, & G. Cable (Eds.), *Everyone's guide to cancer therapy: How cancer is diagnosed, treated, and managed day to day*. Toronto, Ontario, Canada: Sommerville House Books Limited.

Dow, K. (1997). Breast cancer. In C. Varicchio, M. Pierce, C. Walker, & T. Ades (Eds.), *A cancer source book for nurses*. Atlanta, GA: Jones and Bartlett Publishers.

Downey, G., & Coyne, J. (1990). Children of depressed parents: An integrative review. *Psychological Review, 108,* 50–76.

Germino, B., & Funk, S. (1993). Impact of a parent's cancer on adult children: Role and relationship issues. *Seminars in Oncology Nursing, 9*(2), 101–106.

Holland, J. C. (1989). Radiotherapy. In J. C. Holland & J. H. Rowland (Eds.), *Handbook of psychooncology: Psychological care of the patient with cancer* (pp. 134–145). New York: Oxford University Press.

Holland, J., Geary, N., & Furman, A. (1989). Alternative cancer therapies. In *Handbook of psychooncology: Psychological care of the patient with cancer* (pp. 508–515). New York: Oxford University Press.

Howes, M., Hoke, L, Winterbottom, M., & Delafield, D. (1994). Psychosocial effects of breast cancer on the patient's children. *Journal of Psychosocial Oncology, 12*(4), 1–21.

Jennings, C. (1986). Children's understanding of death and dying. *Focus on Critical Care, 13,* 41–45.

Keitel, M., Cramer, S., & Zevon, M. (1990). Spouses of cancer patients: A review of the literature. *Journal of Counseling and Development, 69,* 163–166.

Kemenoff, S., Jachimczyk, J., & Fussner, A. (1999). Structural family therapy. In D. Lawson & F. Prevatt (Eds.), *Casebook in family therapy*. Belmont, CA: Brooks/Cole, Wadsworth Publishing Company.

Kramer, S., Hanks, G., Diamond, J., & Maclean, C. (1984). The study of patterns of clinical care in radiation therapy in the United States. *Cancer, 34,* 75–85.

Kurtz, M., Kurtz, J., Given, C., & Given, B. (1995). Relationship of caregiver reactions and depression to cancer patients' symptoms, functional states, and depression—A longitudinal review. *Social Science Medicine, 40*(6), 837–846.

Laizner, A., Yost, L., Barg, F., & McCorkle, R. (1993). Needs of family caregivers of persons with cancer: A review. *Seminars in Oncology Nursing, 9*(2), 114–120.

Lederberg, M. S. (1998). The family of the cancer patient. In J. C. Holland (Ed.), *Psycho-oncology* (pp. 981–993). New York: Oxford University Press.

LeFebvre, K. (1978). The cancer patients and their spouses: A study by self-report (Doctoral dissertation, University of Tennessee, 1978). *Dissertation Abstracts International, 44,* 611B.

Lewis, F., Hammond, M., & Woods, N. (1993). The family's functioning with newly diagnosed breast cancer in the mother: The development of an explanatory model. *Journal of Behavioral Medicine, 16*(4), 351–370.

Lewis, F., Woods, N., Hough, E., & Bensley, L. (1989). The family's functioning with chronic illness in the mother: The spouse's perspective. *Social Science Medicine, 29*(11), 1261–1269.

Lynam, M. J. (1995). Supporting one another: The nature of family work when a young mother has cancer. *Journal of Advanced Nursing, 22*(1), 116–125.

Mitchell, M., & Catane, R. (1997). What happens in biological therapy. In M. Dollinger, E. Rosenbaum, & G. Cable (Eds.), *Everyone's guide to cancer therapy: How cancer is diagnosed, treated, and managed day to day*. Toronto, Ontario, Canada: Sommerville House Books Limited.

Montgomery, R., Gonyea, J., & Hooyman, N. (1985). Caregiving and the experience of subjective and objective burden. *Family Relations, 34,* 19–26.

Morrow, G. R., Roscoe, J. A., & Hickok, J. T. (1998). Nausea and vomiting. In J. C. Holland, W. Breitbart, & P. B. Jacobson (Eds.), *Pscyo-oncology*. New York: Oxford University Press.

Nelson, E., Sloper, P., Charlton, A., & While, D. (1994). Children who have a parent with cancer: A pilot study. *Journal of Cancer Education, 9*(1), 30–36.

Newsome, J., & Schulz, R. (1999). Caregiving from the recipient's perspective: Negative reactions to being helped. *Health Psychology, 17*(2), 172–181.

Northouse, L. (1995). The impact of cancer in women on the family. *Cancer Practice, 3*(3), 134–142.

Northouse, L., & Peters-Golden, H. (1993). Cancer and the family: Strategies to assist spouses. *Seminars in Oncology Nursing, 9*(2), 74–82.

Oberst, M., & James, R. (1985). Going home: Patient and spouse adjustment following cancer surgery. *Topics in Clinical Nursing, 7*(1), 46–57.

Oktay, J., & Walter, C. (1991). *Breast cancer in the life course: Women's experiences.* New York: Springer.

Ortho Biotech, Inc. (1994, February). *Dimensions of caring: Understanding and overcoming fatigue.* Raritan, NJ: Author.

Pellegrini, C., & Byrd, D. (1997). What happens in surgery (pp. 40–48). In M. Dollinger, E. Rosenbaum, & G. Cable (Eds.), *Everyone's guide to cancer therapy: How cancer is diagnosed, treated, and managed day to day.* Toronto, Ontario, Canada: Somerville House Books Limited.

Pellegrini, C., Rosenbaum, E., & Dollinger, M. (1997). Laser therapy. In M. Dollinger, E. Rosenbaum, & G. Cable (Eds.), *Everyone's guide to cancer therapy: How cancer is diagnosed, treated, and managed day to day.* Toronto, Ontario, Canada: Somerville House Books Limited.

Pickard-Holley, S. (1991). Fatigue in cancer patients: A descriptive study. *Cancer Nursing* [On-line serial] *14,* 13–19. Available: www.cancerjournals.com

Rait, D., & Lederberg, M. (1989). The family of the cancer patient. In J. C. Holland & J. H. Rowland, *Handbook of psychooncology: Psychological care of the patient with cancer* (pp. 585–597). New York: Oxford University Press.

Rigatos, G. (1992). Treatment nausea and vomiting in cancer patients: A conditioned reflex? In H. Schonoll, V. Tewis, & N. Plotnikoff (Eds.), *Psychoneuroimmunology.* Lewiston, NY: Hagrefe & Huber Publishers.

Rittenberg, C. (1996). Helping children cope when a family member has cancer. *Support Cancer Care, 4,* 196–199.

Rolland, J. S. (1994). *Families, illness, and disability.* New York: Basic Books.

Rosenbaum, E. H., Dollinger, M., Piper, B. F., & Rosenbaum, I. (1997). Coping with treatment side effects. In M. Dollinger, E. H. Rosenbaum, & G. Cable (Eds.), *Everyone's guide to cancer therapy: How cancer is diagnosed, treated and managed day to day* (3rd ed., pp. 136–151). Toronto: Somerville House Books Limited.

Rosenfeld, A., & Caplan, G. (1983). Adaptation of children of parents suffering from cancer: A preliminary study of a new field for primary prevention research. *Journal of Primary Prevention, 3,* 244–250.

Rosenthal, D., & Eyre, H. (1995). Hodgkin's disease and Non-Hodgkin's lymphomas. In G. Murphy, W. Lawrence, Jr., & R. Lenhard, Jr. (Eds.), *American Cancer Society textbook of clinical oncology* (2nd ed., pp. 451–469). Atlanta GA: American Cancer Society.

Rowland, J. (1989). Developmental stage and adaptation: Child and adolescent model. In J. Holland & J. Rowland (Eds.), *Handbook of psychooncology: Psychological care of the patient with cancer* (pp. 519–543). New York: Oxford University Press.

Schag, A., Ganz, P., Polinsky, M., Fred, C., Hirji, K., & Petersen, L. (1993). Characteristics of women at risk for psychosocial distress in the year after breast cancer. *Journal of Clinical Oncology, 11,* 783–793.

Sherman, A. C., & Simonton, S. (1999). Family therapy for cancer patients: Clinical issues and interventions. *The Family Journal: Counseling and Therapy for Couples and Families, 7*(1), 39–50.

Sneed, P. K. (1997). Hyperthermia. In M. Dollinger, E. H. Rosenbaum, & G. Cable (Eds.), *Everyone's guide to cancer therapy: How cancer is diagnosed, treated, and managed day to day.* Toronto, Ontario, Canada: Sommerville House Books Limited.

Stone, P., Richards, M., & Hardy, J. (1998). Fatigue in patients with cancer. *European Journal of Cancer* [On-line serial], *34,* 1670–1676. Available: www.cancerjournals.com

Vess, J., Moreland, J., & Schwebel, A. (1985). A follow-up study of role functioning and the psychological environment of families of cancer patients. *Journal of Psychosocial Oncology, 3,* 1–13.

Vogelzang, N. J., Breitbart, W., Cella, D., Curt, G. A., Groopman, J. E., Horning, S. J., Itri, L. M., Johnson, D. H., Scherr, S. L., & Portenoy, R. K. (1997). Patient, caregiver and oncologist perceptions of cancer-related fatigue: Results of a tripart assessment survey. The Fatigue Coalition. *Seminars in Hemotology, 34 (3 suppl. 2),* 4–12.

Welch-McCaffrey, D. (1989). Family issues in cancer care: Current dilemmas and future directions. *Journal of Psychosocial Oncology, 6*(1/2), 199–211.

Wellisch, D. (1979). Adolescent acting out when a parent has cancer. *International Journal of Family Therapy, 1,* 230–241.

Zemore, R., & Shepel, L. (1989). Effects of breast cancer and mastectomy on emotional support and adjustment. *Social Science and Medicine, 28*(1), 19–26.

CHAPTER

Rehabilitation and the Family Life Cycle: Living in Limbo

Cancer treatments have advanced significantly over the past few decades. Where previously cancer was a certain death sentence, new and more aggressive cancer treatments have resulted in increasing numbers of cancer survivors. However, while aggressive treatment can lead to extended life expectancy and ultimately survivorship, these new treatments are not without physical and emotional ramifications. At times, patients may even wonder if cancer treatment and its side effects are worse than the disease itself (Harpham, 1994). In addition, the length of hospital stays is on the decrease and the family has become responsible for administering more complex treatment to their sick family members at home (Barg, 1997). For these reasons, the rehabilitation phase for cancer patients and their families is often more difficult than undergoing actual cancer treatment (Harpham, 1994).

Life after cancer will never be the same, and thus rehabilitation is a time of physical, emotional, and family systems reorganization, often requiring a reinvention of the patient and the family. During the rehabilitation phase, the focus of coping shifts from the "long haul" of the treatment phase to the "life in limbo" of the rehabilitation phase (Halvorson-Boyd & Hunter, 1995). Patients and their families may begin to wonder if life will ever be "normal" again. While the lifestyle before cancer may never fully be regained, how the patient and the family system adapt during the rehabilitation phase is crucial to the formation of a new concept of "normalcy" (Harpham, 1994; Rolland, 1994).

☐ Medical Variables during the Rehabilitation Phase

Overview of Rehabilitation

Rehabilitation is the process by which patients and families are helped to recover their functional status while maintaining a high quality of life (Barg, 1997; Gunn, 1984; McKenna, Wellisch, & Fawzy, 1995). Rehabilitation also has been defined as "a process by which individuals within their environments are assisted to achieve optimal functioning within the limits imposed by cancer" (Mayer & O'Connor-Kelleher, 1993, p. 433). The rehabilitation process begins at the time of diagnosis, includes cancer treatment, and extends through the recovery phase, preparing the patient for survivorship (Watson, 1996). Successful physical rehabilitation is not enough; quality of life during recovery is equally important.

Four objectives for cancer rehabilitation have been outlined by the National Cancer Institute (NCI). They are (1) the provision of psychological support upon diagnosis; (2) the facilitation of optimal physical functioning after treatment; (3) the provision of vocational counseling when needed; and (4) the facilitation of optimal social functioning (McKenna et al., 1995). To this end, a team approach is often taken toward helping the patient and the family recover from cancer (Barg, 1997; Gunn, Dickison, & McBride, 1984). During rehabilitation, oncologists, physiatrists, psychiatrists, psychologists, social workers, chaplains, physical therapists, occupational therapists, nurses, and many others begin to help the patient and the family recover from, and rebuild life after, cancer.

Because cancer is not one disease, but more than 200 different diseases, the impact of cancer and its treatment can be vastly different for each patient. Some patients will undergo only minor surgery (i.e., the successful removal of a cancerous mole), while others will undergo intensive chemotherapy treatments, radiation treatments, and even disfiguring surgeries, leaving them physically and emotionally altered. For these patients and their families, life will be permanently, and often profoundly, changed. Recovery and rehabilitation bring a "life of limbo" for the survivors of cancer. Creating a new, "normal" life after cancer begins with a reevaluation of the medical, emotional, and social variables of the illness.

The Rehabilitation Process

Cancerous tumors can have varying responses to treatment, including a complete response leading to no detectable signs of cancer, a partial response, and no response to treatment. When there has been a response to treatment, resulting in no evidence of disease, the patient is said to be in "partial remission" (Harpham, 1994). Further, even though there may be no detectable signs of cancer, it usually takes at least one year, and more often five years, to be considered "cured."

Because cancer diagnosis and treatment involves such varied outcomes, at least three different pathways to optimal functioning are possible. First, rehabilitative cancer care includes the development of a treatment plan with quick return to optimal functioning as the goal. This form of rehabilitation is used for patients with uncomplicated cancer treatment and typically does not involve extensive physical rehabilitation. Second, comprehensive rehabilitation includes a more extensive treatment plan that utilizes a variety of rehabilitation services for specific impairments (e.g., bowel or bladder dysfunction, uncontrolled pain, self-care limitations). Finally, conservative or subacute rehabilitation involves a treatment plan that considers necessary adjustments for optimal functioning and length of life, typically due to advanced disease (Salcido & Jenkins, 1994; Watson, 1996).

Specific areas for possible rehabilitation are evaluated by the treatment team at the time of diagnosis and after treatment has been completed. Rehabilitation procedures can be preventative, restorative, supportive, or palliative (McKenna et al., 1995). Preventative rehabilitation is used when impairments are anticipated, and interventions are utilized to avert future disabilities. For example, teaching a woman specific exercises to avoid the swelling, pain, and decreased functioning of the arm, following a mastectomy, is designed to prevent lymphedema. Restorative rehabilitation is designed to restore the patient's functioning to as near a pretreatment state as possible. For instance, a breast reconstruction following mastectomy. Supportive rehabilitation is focused on long-term, more permanent impairments that could result in specific disabilities. In supportive rehabilitation, the goal is to maximize functional capacity. Finally, palliative rehabilitation involves efforts to decrease a patient's dependence on others for help with activities of daily living, while also providing physical comfort and emotional support (McKenna et al., 1995).

Biopsychosocial Concerns of Rehabilitation.

Biopsychosocial Concerns of Rehabilitation.   A wide range of rehabilitation concerns must be assessed during this phase of the clinical course of cancer. Both the obvious (e.g., prostheses or ostomy) and the subtle (e.g., spiritual or existential) concerns have been noted to be important during rehabilitation planning (Barg, 1997). Toward the end of treatment, planning for patient follow-up care and identifying patients' available resources should take place. Some important rehabilitation needs include (1) nutritional information, (2) symptom management, (3) bowel and bladder retraining/management, (4) swallowing and speech, and (5) a variety of psychosocial needs such as vocational/ financial rehabilitation, relationships issues, and spiritual/existential concerns. Nutritional information should include (1) how to ensure the patient is receiving a proper diet, (2) how to avoid anorexia and cachexia, and (3) how to assess and overcome physical barriers such as swallowing difficulties. Knowledge regarding symptom management is crucial to successful rehabilitation and recovery. Symptoms such as fatigue, weakness, nausea, sensory alterations, constipation, diarrhea, lymphedema, mucositis (inflammation of membranes in mouth), dyspnea (difficulty breathing), and depression may continue to be experienced by the patient weeks to months after treatment completion (Barg, 1997). With some types of cancers requiring ostomies (an artificial opening to help drain bodily wastes), bowel and bladder management must also be understood by both the patient and the family before treatment completion.

Psychosocial needs are also taken into consideration by the treatment team. Some patients will need speech and language rehabilitation to increase effective communication. Relationships with family members may also be altered due to changes in body image, sexual functioning, role reversals, and overall family functioning and expectations. Vocational and financial considerations must also be evaluated during rehabilitation. The rehabilitation process often focuses on helping the patient to resume productive functioning with regard to work and functional status to increase the patient's sense of mastery, control, self-esteem, and developmental momentum (Barg, 1997; Watson, 1996). Finally, spiritual issues and existential dilemmas resurface during the rehabilitation phase, as the patient and the family begin to re-create their lives during a time of uncertainty (Halvorson-Boyd & Hunter, 1995).

Antitumor Effects and the Aftereffects of Cancer Treatments

Antitumor effects are a variety of processes that result in the continued elimination of cancer cells after the completion of a full course of treatment. This process can continue for weeks to months following the completion of active cancer treatments (Barg, 1997; Harpham, 1994). For example, chemotherapy remains active for weeks after the final dose is administered. The duration of its antitumor effect is dependent upon the types of drugs used, dose intensity, and the patient's physical response to the drugs. Immunotherapy can also have long-lasting effects if self-perpetuating changes in the immune system have occurred due to immunotherapy (Harpham, 1994).

Antitumor effects are generally positive effects of cancer treatment. With antitumor effects, the cancer cells are continuing to be destroyed days to weeks after the last treatment. However, there are adverse side effects of cancer treatment referred to as "aftereffects." Aftereffects of cancer treatment are complications and side effects that can take place relatively soon after the completion of treatment. These "delayed effects" are regarded as expected changes that occur as a result of cancer treatment (Harpham, 1994). "Delayed complications" can also occur soon after the completion of treatment. Such complications are less common aftereffects that are related to cancer treatment. Some include a type of lung inflammation following radiation treatments (i.e., radiation pneumonitis), infection due to low blood counts, and severe anxiety that is directly related to the stress of cancer treatment (Harpham, 1994). Other aftereffects of cancer treatment can occur months to years after treatment completion.

"Late effects" are the expected changes that can take place long after cancer treatment has been completed. Some expected late effects include skin changes as a result of radiation therapy, or early menopause caused by chemotherapy (Harpham, 1994). "Late complications" can also occur months to years following cancer treatment. These unexpected occurrences include such developments as a second type of cancer due to bone marrow transplantation or other forms of cancer treatment (Harpham, 1994). The aftereffects of cancer treatment are presented in Table 4.1.

There are specific aftereffects caused by surgery, chemotherapy, and radiation therapy. The aftereffects of surgery are usually experienced immediately or within weeks following the procedure and are due to (1) the effects of the anesthesia, (2) the increased energy needed to heal the incisional wound and assist in overall recovery, (3) the physical and emotional reaction to the surgical process, and (4) hormonal changes that are a result of specific types of surgeries (i.e., castration or the removal of parathyroid glands). These aftereffects of surgery can lead to immediate loss of energy and activity, emotional distress, and changes in sleeping and eating patterns. However, except for more extreme surgical cases (i.e., amputations), the aftereffects of surgery are usually resolved relatively quickly when compared with some of the aftereffects of chemotherapy or radiation treatment (Barg, 1997; Harpham, 1994).

Chemotherapy can cause aftereffects such as changes in the blood resulting in anemia (low red cell counts) or in neutropenia, an increased risk of infection (low white cell counts). Drugs used in chemotherapy can also affect hormone-producing organs such as the ovaries and gonads, resulting in sexual dysfunctions such as infertility and impotence (Harpham, 1994). Late effects from chemotherapy can occur months to years after chemotherapy treatment due to changes in normal cell functioning leading to leukemia or a solid tumor, changes in the reproductive organs, and changes in hormone-secreting organs such as the adrenal glands (Harpham, 1994; Moosa et al., 1991). Radiation therapy can cause late effects that are specific to the areas that were irradiated. Late effects can result from changes in the body's circulation that cause scarring, narrowing, or a loss of normal cells from the target organ (Harpham, 1994). Normal cells can also be affected, leading to possible leukemias or soft tissue cancers (sarcomas; Harpham, 1994; Moosa et al., 1991).

The aftereffects of cancer treatment can result in damage to the gastrointestinal tract, the nervous system, the circulatory system, the endocrine system, the skin, the lungs, and the head and neck. Aftereffects involving the gastrointestinal system can result in a poor appetite, difficulties in swallowing, diarrhea, constipation, and a stricture of the esophagus. Aftereffects involving the nervous system can result in numbness (due to a vitamin deficiency or nerve damage), headaches (due to hormonal changes, sinus problems, or emotional stress), and vision or hearing problems. Difficulties with the nervous system can also lead to changes in memory and mental clarity and difficulties with balance. Changes to the circulatory system can result in generalized swelling or swelling of the extremities. This can be due to a blockage of a vein or of the lymph system of that particular area, or to kidney, liver, or heart problems. Other aftereffects involving the circulatory system include faintness, which can be due to anemia, deconditioning, damage to the

TABLE 4.1. The Aftereffects of Cancer Treatment

	When do they occur?	What are they?	How?
Antitumor Effects	Weeks or months following cancer treatment	Positive effects from chemotherapy, radiation therapy, or other forms of treatment	By remaining active in the system after treatment completion; chemotherapy drugs remaining active in the system, working to eliminate cancer cells
Aftereffects			
Delayed Effects	Soon after treatment completion	Common or expected changes that are a result of treatment	Fatigue Weight loss Changes in diet Redness/burning
Delayed Complications	Soon after treatment completion	Less common changes that are a result of treatment	Lung inflammation; infection due to low blood counts
Late Effects	Long after treatment completion	Common or expected changes that are a result of treatment	Skin changes resulting from radiation therapy; early menopause resulting from chemotherapy
Late Complications	Months to years following treatment	Unexpected occurrences due to treatment	Development of a second cancer due to bone marrow transplantation
Treatment-Specific Aftereffects			
Surgery	Immediately or within weeks following surgery	Changes resulting from surgical procedure	Effects from anesthesia; Incisional healing; Hormonal changes; Psychosocial or emotional reactions
Chemotherapy	Can result in both delayed and late effects or complications	Both common and less common changes due to chemotherapy	Anemia Infertility/impotence Leukemia
Radiation	Can result in both delayed and late effects or complications	Both common and less common changes due to irradiation	Scarring; Loss of normal cells to target organ; Soft tissue cancers (i.e., sarcomas)

(Continued)

TABLE 4.1. Continued

	When do they occur?	What are they?	How?
Site-Specific Aftereffects			
Gastro-intestinal	Delayed or late effects	Ramifications of illness and its treatment	Poor appetite; Difficulties with swallowing; Diarrhea or constipation; Stricture of the esophagus
Nervous System	Delayed or late effects	Ramifications of illness and its treatment	Numbness; Headaches; Vision/hearing problems
Circulatory System	Delayed or late effects	Ramifications of illness and its treatment	Faintness (anemia); General or localized swelling
Endocrine System	Delayed or late effects	Ramifications of illness and its treatment	Hypothyroidism
Skin	Delayed or late effects	Ramifications of illness and its treatment	Redness/burning Sensitivity Rashes/bruising Thinning of skin
Head and Neck	Delayed or late Effects	Ramifications of illness and its treatment	Disfigurement Dry mouth Cataracts Alteration in taste Difficulties with speech/swallowing

Note: Information from Harpham, 1994.

nervous system, heart rhythm difficulties, or to a hormonal imbalance. Changes to the endocrine system can lead to hypothyroidism, especially after receiving radiation treatment to the neck or pituitary gland, or after receiving interferon (Harpham, 1994). Changes to the skin include direct changes to skin cells and blood vessels due to chemotherapy or radiation therapy, resulting in redness, sensitivity, blisters, and general skin breakdown (Harpham, 1994). Since cancer treatment often weakens the immune system, additional changes to the skin can include rashes, sensitivity to medications and to the sun, and problems with bruising, tearing, and thinning of the skin. Aftereffects of cancer treatment can also lead to difficulties with the lungs, such as shortness of breath, allergies, infection, and chronic coughs (Harpham, 1994). Aftereffects involving the head and neck include dry mouth, difficulties with swallowing, cataracts (after radiation to the eye area), alterations in taste, and more serious aftereffects such as osteoradionecrosis of the jaw (a relatively rare bone infection caused by high-dose radiation to the jaw).

Rehabilitation of Specific Cancers

Lung.   Lung cancer patients may need to undergo preoperative rehabilitation emphasizing breathing retraining and pulmonary rehabilitation after radiation or surgery. They may also need to be instructed as to range of motion exercises, particularly on the side of the surgical incision (i.e., thoracotomy; Lind, 1992). Specific interventions to monitor disease progression must include (1) scheduling of follow-up care, usually at three-to-four-month intervals for the first three years, then four to six months for the rest of the patient's life (Faber, 1991); (2) monitoring for possible brain, bone, and liver metastases; and (3) teaching the patient and the family to watch for signs and symptoms of metastatic disease, including changes in personality, changes in respiratory status, bone pain, and jaundice (Lind, 1992).

Breast.   Breast cancer patients may have undergone disfiguring surgeries resulting in the need to reestablish new identities and self-images. The patient may have undergone a lumpectomy, which, in contrast to a mastectomy, removes only the tumor and a narrow margin of breast tissue (Entrekin, 1992). Physical alterations of the lumpectomy, or partial mastectomy, can include minimal breast disfigurement and disruptions to the skin and lymphatic system (Entrekin, 1992). The breast cancer patient undergoing a modified radical mastectomy (removal of the entire breast) may face different rehabilitation needs. These include the loss of a breast as well as disruptions to the integrity of the skin and the drainage in the lymphatic system (Entrekin, 1992). During rehabilitation, breast cancer patients may suffer from lymphedema, an accumulation of lymph, which results in feelings of heaviness or fullness of the arm. Since lymphedema is easier to treat and to cure when it is detected early, patients and their families are encouraged to watch for signs such as feelings of tightness in the extremity; enlargement of fingers, so that rings no longer fit; decrease in strength; pain; aches; or redness, swelling, or signs of infection. Additional rehabilitation issues include (1) physical restoration of the affected arm; (2) cosmetic rehabilitation, which may include prosthesis or reconstruction for mastectomy patients; and (3) psychosocial rehabilitation focusing on body image, loss and grief, and sexuality (Barg, 1997).

Cancers of the Reproductive System.   Cancers that damage patients' reproductive systems may leave them with sexual dysfunctions that can greatly alter plans regarding children and family. Patients with cervical, endometrial, and ovarian cancers can be left with changes in body image, sexual dysfunction, altered bowl elimination, and altered urinary elimination (Flannery, 1992). Patients with testicular, penile, and prostate cancers can also be left with changes in sexual functioning, altered sexuality, body image disturbances, and ineffective family coping (Flannery, 1992).

Colorectal and Bladder.   Patients with colorectal and bladder cancers may be left with permanent ostomies that can cause many difficulties long after formal cancer treatment has ended. Rehabilitation issues include elimination control, care and adjustment of the ostomy, and psychosocial rehabilitation focusing on self-concept, potential sexual dysfunction, and body image disruptions (Barg, 1997; Strohl, 1992). Management of colostomies, ileostomies, and urostomies include (1) the control and elimination of odor caused by food, oral medicines, poor hygiene, infection, or active disease (Lind, 1992); (2) the management of skin irritation caused by leaks in the ostomy appliance, a bad or improper fit, or an allergic reaction; and (3) hyperkeratosis (a growth on the skin) caused by overexposure to urine (Lind, 1992).

Head and Neck.   Cancers of the head and neck can often leave patients with permanent disfigurements, with difficulties swallowing and speaking, and even with difficulties in cognitive and personality functioning. Rehabilitation issues include (1) the maintenance of optimal nutrition, (2) shoulder and neck dysfunction rehabilitation, (3) speech and communication rehabilitation, (4) restoring acceptable appearance and function, and (5) self-care considerations (Barg, 1997).

Other Cancers.   Patients with cancers of the bone and soft tissue and patients with cancers of the central nervous system will also be left with many rehabilitation needs. Patients with soft tissue malignancies may need to undergo extensive psychosocial and vocational rehabilitation after a restoration of function via prostheses, appliances, and ambulatory aids (Barg, 1997). Patients suffering from cancers to the central nervous system may suffer from a loss of bowel and bladder control, decreases in cognitive functioning, and modifications in mobility resulting in a substantial decrease in quality of life (Barg, 1997).

Fatigue during Rehabilitation.   Fatigue is a very common complaint of cancer patients, both during and after treatment (Cella, Passik, Jacobsen, & Breitbart, 1998). Studies have reported that as many as 78%–96% of cancer patients report fatigue, and yet it has been difficult to define and understand (Physician's Desk Query [PDQ], 1999). Fatigue has been described by a variety of terms such as tired, weak, exhausted, weary, worn out, heavy, or slow, and it can be exhibited as a physical, mental, or emotional experience. Acute fatigue has been defined as normal and expected tiredness that comes on quickly, lasts a short time, and is improved by rest. Chronic fatigue is long-term, persistent tiredness that does not improve with rest and can interfere with a person's daily functioning.

The exact cause of cancer-related fatigue is unknown. It is likely that there are many different causes that include (a) cancer treatments, (b) the disease itself, (c) anemia, (d) nutritional deficiencies, and (e) a variety of psychological factors. Thus, there is no agreed-upon, standard treatment for fatigue, but rather there are a variety of fatigue management strategies.

Medical management of fatigue typically begins with an attempt to identify and treat any underlying causal factors (Miaskowski & Portenoy, 1998). For example, if a patient is found to be anemic, the direct treatment of anemia should follow. When there are no identifiable medical causes, a variety of energy conservation measures are recommended. These include self-regulation strategies designed to identify patterns of energy use and to conserve needed energy. In addition, judicial use of exercise and a variety of patient education strategies have proven helpful.

Fatigue can be a very debilitating and distressing symptom for patients eager to recover during the rehabilitation phase of the illness; and yet a variety of barriers to treatment of have been identified (Cella et al., 1998). These include an attitude that fatigue is an expected part of the disease and its treatment. Some patients report they want to be "a good patient" and are afraid they may distract their oncologist from his primary role if they complain of fatigue. Thus, it is significantly underreported and undertreated. Family members can play an important role in helping patients identify, track, and report chronic fatigue that becomes debilitating and distressing.

Other Difficulties during the Rehabilitation Phase.   There are several other difficulties that may arise during the rehabilitation phase that may impede the rehabilitation process. Some cancer patients may experience nutritional and related difficulties, sleep disturbances, acute or chronic pain, and sexual dysfunctions.

Nutrition during cancer treatment and rehabilitation is essential to successful recovery. Cancer patients may experience cancer cachexia, which is characterized by weight loss, early satiety, and loss of appetite resulting in a decrease in caloric intake and a depletion of essential nutrients (McKenna, 1991). Some patients, especially those with esophageal or oral cancers (McKenna, 1991), have prior histories of poor nutritional practices, often due to excessive alcohol and drug use. Patients will differ in their ability to ingest food. Some patients will be able to eat normally with only mild aversions to some foods (e.g., meat), while others will have great difficulty swallowing (dysphagia) and may need to liquefy their food. Others, such as patients with bowel obstructions, will need intravenous feeding (McKenna, 1991). However, repeated use of central veins can lead to difficulties in finding usable veins. Catheters can be permanently inserted to decrease the irritation, complications, and pain of repeated needle sticks.

When cancer patients develop infections, the presence of the infection can delay the rehabilitation process and tumor management (McKenna, 1991). Since many cancer patients are immunocompromised either because of the disease or its treatment, they are more vulnerable to infection.

Other problems that can impede the rehabilitation process include difficulties such as anxiety, sleep deprivation, acute or chronic pain, and sexual difficulties. Many patients also suffer from depressive-like symptoms, such as anhedonia, feelings of guilt/worthlessness, feelings of hopelessness, and disruptions in their appetite and/or sleep habits. For many patients, disruptions in their activities of daily living, such as early retirement due to their cancer, can cause patients to feel worthless because their activity was a large part of their identity. Patients can be treated with cognitive behavioral and supportive-expressive psychotherapy techniques as a means of reducing depressive symptomology. Some amount of anxiety and fear is experienced by almost all cancer patients during rehabilitation (Harpham, 1994). High levels of anxiety can affect sleep patterns and increase feelings of pain. Anxiety can be managed by patient education; stress reduction therapies such as relaxation, biofeedback, hypnosis, and visualization; and cognitive therapies. Difficulties receiving adequate relaxation and restful sleep could also be due to medications, changes in daily schedules, and uncontrolled pain (Harpham, 1994; McKenna, 1991).

Pain is often the most feared component of cancer (McKenna, 1991). With current pharmacologic and nonpharmacologic knowledge of pain management, pain can most often be controlled and even eliminated. Nonnarcotic analgesics are the first-line agents for mild to moderate cancer pain, followed by narcotic analgesics for more severe pain. Adjuvant analgesics, which include anticonvulsants, phenothiazines, butyrophenones, tricyclic antidepressants, antihistamines, amphetamines, and steroids, can also be given when pain proves difficult to control (McKenna, 1991).

Many adult cancer patients will experience some form of sexual dysfunction or difficulty following cancer treatment (Anderson & Lamb, 1995; Anderson & Schmuch, 1991). Males recovering from prostate, testicular, and penile cancers will more than likely encounter sexual difficulties. Young males recovering from testicular cancer can suffer from retrograde ejaculation, decreased pleasure from orgasm, and erectile dysfunction (McKenna et al., 1995). Females recovering from breast, cervical, ovarian, or vulvar cancer can also experience sexual difficulties. Colorectal and bladder cancers, as well as many types of chemotherapy, can also lead to difficulties with body image and sexual functioning.

While many patients undergoing cancer rehabilitation will suffer from sexual difficulties as a result of cancer and its treatment, 75% are reported to be reluctant to bring up the subject of sexual functioning (McKenna et al., 1995). Masters and Johnson (1966) and Kaplan (1979) have provided useful frameworks for understanding human sexual functioning in healthy men and women. Sexuality can be viewed from a multidimensional framework, which encompasses the phases of the sexual response cycle: sexual desire, sexual excitement, orgasm, and resolution. Since the experience of cancer can effect both the psychological and physical aspects of sexuality, cancer patients can have difficulties in any of the phases of the sexual response cycle.

A model for the assessment of sexual functioning in cancer patients has been proposed, using the acronym ALARM (which stands for activity, libido, arousal, resolution, and medical history, as described below; Anderson & Lamb, 1995). The assessment begins with a focus on the frequency of sexual activity: "Prior to the appearance of any signs of your illness, how frequently were you engaging in intercourse?" Next, the patient's libido/desire for sexual activity is examined: "Prior to the appearance of your illness, would you have described yourself as generally interested in having sex?" Then, the patient's arousal and orgasmic functioning are discussed: "When you are interested in having sexual activity, do you have any difficulty in becoming emotionally and physically aroused?" Following the examination of the phases of sexual functioning, the patient's feelings of resolution are assessed: "Following sexual activity, do you feel that there has been a release of tension? Do you have any feelings of discomfort or pain? On a scale of 1 to 10, how would you rate your sex life?" Finally, the patient's medical history is obtained, including any concurrent medical illnesses (e.g., diabetes, hypertension), the patient's psychiatric history, and any history of substance abuse (Anderson & Lamb, 1995; Anderson & Schmuch, 1991).

Barriers to Effective Rehabilitation and the Receipt of Support Services

There are several barriers that could prevent the patient and the family system from completing successful cancer rehabilitation. First, patients and their families may erroneously perceive cancer as an acute illness, with expectations that when cancer treatment has ended, the patient can return automatically and easily to a "normal" level of functioning and daily lifestyle. This perception can lead to frustration and despondency when the patient is not able to return to the preillness level of functioning and physical, emotional, and functional abilities are not readily achieved. However, when cancer is perceived as a chronic illness with long-term ramifications, changes, and life alterations, the rehabilitation process is placed in a more realistic context, and adaptation to the aftereffects of cancer treatment becomes easier for both the patient and the family system (Harpham, 1994).

Caregivers may also encounter barriers to the receipt of support services during cancer rehabilitation. Barriers include financial constraints, lack of transportation, stigma regarding receiving outside support, and family resistance. Often, families are not aware of available support services, or services are overworked and unable to accommodate additional patient and family needs (Barg, 1997). Along these lines, there are very few cancer treatment centers that offer comprehensive cancer rehabilitation services for patients and their families. Thus, care after the completion of formal treatment is often fragmented, lacking in both physical and emotional support services (Barg, 1997). However, the rehabilitation needs of cancer patients and their families are being increasingly recognized. Knowledge about pain management, cancer-related fatigue, sexual functioning, psychosocial considerations, and family systems functioning after the crisis of cancer, is growing. As a result, more patients and their families are being assisted with the uncertainties of living in limbo after cancer treatment (Halvorson-Boyd & Hunter, 1995; Harpham, 1995).

☐ Rehabilitation and Psychosocial Considerations: Living in Limbo

Transition from the Long Haul to Living in Limbo

The completion of active treatment can be a time of great ambivalence for cancer patients and their families. On one hand, the end of treatment represents a milestone along the road to recovery, a time for celebration. On the other hand, it is a time of heightened distress due to the absence of the reassuring medical staff (Sherman & Simonton, 1999). Cancer patients often look forward to the completion of treatment and a reduction in treatment side effects, only to be left with underlying feelings of anxiety and uncertainty about the future. To add further complication, these conflicting emotional responses are in direct contrast with other family members who often interpret the completion of active treatment as a time to "get back to normal," and to resume daily life without the focus of cancer and its treatment (Spiegel, 1993). But for the patients, particularly those who have undergone extensive cancer treatment and need comprehensive rehabilitation therapies, life after the storm will never be the same again, and a new life with a heightened risk for cancer recurrence must be faced. For the patient, temporary changes must be dealt with during this phase (e.g., hair loss, fatigue) as well as permanent losses for some (e.g., loss of speech, loss of a breast, loss of functional abilities, loss of feeling that the world is a "safe" place followed by an increased feeling of vulnerability; Christ, 1991; Sherman & Simonton, 1999). The specific needs and tasks of the family system during the rehabilitation phase are presented in Table 4.2.

The patient and the family must now begin to shift from the long haul of incorporating active treatment into the daily routine, to living in a state of limbo where life is uncertain and the myth that life-threatening illnesses happen only to others is irrevocably lost (Rolland, 1994). During this shift, it is easy for families to become immobilized due to feelings of loss of control over daily functioning and future events. After going through the crisis of diagnosis and treatment, families must begin to reestablish a sense of control over their lives—even if this feeling of control is illusory (Rolland, 1994). The rehabilitation phase is a time of rebuilding and integrating the experience of cancer into personal and family functioning. Support groups and psychoeducational programs, which emphasize the ambivalent feelings patients and family members may be experiencing, often help to distinguish between the expected emotional roller coaster from feelings of going "crazy" in the aftermath of treatment for a serious illness (Rolland, 1994).

The patient and the family system can be left permanently paralyzed and developmentally stagnant if they are unable to move through this phase of rehabilitation and limbo, into a life with a new set of rules, expectations, and even existential beliefs (Harpham, 1994). This important shift from one phase of the clinical course of cancer to another is tantamount to family systems moving from one developmental stage to another, wherein different needs arise and new tasks demand second-order changes as seen by new behaviors, rules, roles, boundaries, and potentially modified beliefs (Rolland, 1994). Families who are flexible in meeting the role demands of the rehabilitation phase, rather than remain rigidly fixed in preillness roles, and families with more marital communication have been shown to experience less role conflict, less role strain, and less overall disruption to the family system (Vess, Moreland, & Schweble, 1985).

Assessment Questions.   Rolland (1994) has outlined several questions that help to assess family functioning during a time of illness-phase transition:

1. How has the family had to reorganize itself?
2. In what ways have pre-illness roles changed for each family member? (both functional and affective roles)
3. How much illness-related responsibility does the patient resume?
4. Are the illness-related responsibilities taken on by the ill family member congruent with family expectations?
5. Besides the ill family member, who has primary caregiving responsibilities for managing (rehabilitating) the illness?
6. How were the responsibilities decided upon and assigned?
7. How does everyone feel about the current caregiving arrangement?
8. Could other members share responsibilities to alleviate any burdens on the primary caregiver?
9. Does the family's organization seem realistic at this time?
10. Does the patient and family have accurate information regarding recovery and rehabilitation processes? (p. 67)

It is sometimes easier for families to want to forget about the severity of the illness and its treatment and to move too quickly back into "normal" life. In doing so, expectations of immediate recovery and standards of rehabilitation and functioning may be set too high, resulting in increased frustration, distress, and discrepancies between the needs of the patient and those of the other family members (Harpham, 1994). Using the above-listed assessment questions, the family is helped to rebuild its new system with thoughtfulness in their plans for long-term organization and congruency between the realistic demands of the illness and the emotional desires of the family members.

Cancer Patients Living in Limbo

The completion of active treatment and the rehabilitation phase is more than just physically surviving cancer, it is about the quality of life experienced by cancer patients and their families (Harpham, 1994). During the rehabilitation phase, cancer patients may experience the entire range of emotional reactions, from elation over the completion of treatment to deep depression because life still appears "unreal" and uncertain. Although emotional reactions during this phase of the illness will vary widely depending upon individual coping skills and styles, both physical and emotional responses will depend greatly upon the cancer patient's type of cancer and its severity, as well as his or her age and place in the family life cycle. Psychosocial considerations are thus dependent upon the extent to which physical rehabilitation is needed by the patient and the developmental tasks that may be delayed (temporarily or permanently) due to the illness (Rolland, 1994).

Grief and Loss.   Some cancer patients may experience feelings of grief and loss at critical points along the clinical course of cancer such as during the termination of treatment (Clark, McGee, & Preston, 1992). Most cancer patients experience some degree of grief, whether these feelings are due to the loss of existential myths regarding the assumptions of the "normal" unfolding of life events, or the loss of physical appearance, function, and abilities. Again, emotional responses to loss will differ according to age and developmental task requirements. Loss of the ability to have children will be very different for the young adult during cancer rehabilitation than for the patient who is raising or has finished raising a family. Physical difficulties such as fatigue and chronic pain can permeate every aspect of the patient's lifestyle, forcing changes in functioning, interpersonal rela-

Table 4.2. The Rehabilitation Phase and the Family Life Cycle: The Importance of Reorganization and Integration during "Life in Limbo"

	Life cycle tasks	Cancer's potential disruptions to the system	Psychosocial interventions	Specific topics of communication
Single young adult	Establishing self in the world of work; forming intimate relationships	Disruption to self-concept; disruption to confidence in forming deep, committed relationships; potential for isolation	Help to restore confidence in body image; help to decide upon prosthesis needs/wants or reconstructive surgery	Discuss sexuality, body image, future career and relationships; discuss difficulties with rehabilitation
Newly forming couple	Balancing power; negotiating roles; determining responsibilities; accepting new members into the family	Disruption to the boundaries of the system; disruption to the emotional dyadic bond; disruption to future family plans	Help to restore boundaries; help to create new organization within the system; help to clarify desires for family structure	Discuss roles and boundaries; discuss possible sexual concerns; discuss desires for future family planning
Families with young children	Changing structure of multigenerational system to allow for "parent" and "grandparent" roles	Disruption to new roles; skews between period of recovery for patient and for family; fears of recurrence for some or all members	Help to integrate illness into family structure; help to put limits on the illness in daily living; help parent and children subsystems to re-create healthy boundaries	Discuss hopes for the future; discuss values and reasons for living; discuss fears regarding recurrence and risk for other family members
Families with adolescents	Creating flexible boundaries; adapting to external influences on the system recovery	Disruption between adolescents needs for loosening of boundaries and the patient's need for assistance during rehabilitation	Help to address skews in patient recovery needs and developmental needs; assist family in reevaluating structure during rehabilitation to meet demands of a chronic illness	Discuss perceptions of recovery time; discuss family's developmental needs and patient's recovery needs

Families launching children	Creating new boundaries; addressing midlife concerns: generativity, life reassessment, and friendships	Disruption in the task of launching children; disruption to the need to maintain meaningful life work and contributions	Help to address needs for young adults to become independent during rehabilitation; facilitate patient's discovery of meaning in work and life	Discuss relational skews; discuss patient's need for physical, psychosocial, and emotional needs during recovery
Families in later life	Examining life in multigenerational context	Disrupt plans for retirement; disrupt meaningful tasks; disrupt sense of worth	Help patient to identify meaningful tasks that can be resumed during rehabilitation; help sandwich generation to adapt during rehabilitation	Discuss quality of life concerns; discuss feelings of worth and feelings of being a burden; discuss caregiver stressors

tionships, and self-definition via developmental tasks and accomplishments. For younger cancer patients, such as the single young adult, or for families raising and launching children, these changes can result in increased feelings of grief and loss. Whether these changes are temporary or permanent, developmental tasks such as having children, raising children, functioning at home or at work, and planning for the future are often put on hold during the rehabilitation phase, while the patient and the family reconstruct their life assumptions, worldviews, and self-images. Risk factors associated with grief during rehabilitation include a cancer diagnosis with a poor prognosis or likelihood of recurrence, perceived or actual changes in body structure, and changes in functioning due to cachexia, amputation, or cognitive dysfunction (Clark et al., 1992). Whether these risk factors are evident or not, the patient should be assessed routinely for feelings of grief and loss by monitoring changes in weight or changes in sleep, rest, or eating patterns, and by assessing for any decrease in physical or psychosocial functioning (Clark et al., 1992). Patients can be encouraged to discuss their perceptions of their losses and how they are coping with those losses. In addition, patients may begin to experience anticipatory loss as they look to an uncertain future with an elevated risk of cancer, both for the self and for other family members.

Anger.   Cancer patients may also experience intense feelings of anger, anxiety, and depression, particularly following the completion of treatment (Harpham, 1994). For the young adult, anger may be a result of the perception that "life is unfair." Anger, therefore, may be a normal reaction to the disruption of the assumptive world of the young cancer patient and his or her family. Although anger may be a result of the presence of the disease, it can become displaced onto other persons in the family, at work, or at school. It can be helpful for the patient to refocus on the illness and the patient's interpretation of the illness as the source of the anger rather than triangulating a person into the patient–disease relationship (Harpham, 1994).

Anxiety.   Anxiety can intensify during the rehabilitation phase, particularly at the time of routine checkups. Potential sequelae of anxiety includes psychosomatic illnesses, such as gastric ulcers or colitis; behavioral changes, such as acting out or eating disturbances; physical symptoms such as nausea, vomiting, and headaches; and cognitive disturbances, such as panic, loss of memory, or problems with concentration and decision making (Clark et al., 1992). Anxiety can be a result of fears that the checkup will (1) reveal recurrent cancer, (2) force a reentry into the role of "the patient," (3) cause emotional upheaval until the test results become available, (4) cause emotional strain in relationships with others, and (5) conjure feelings of being out of control and uncertain about the future (Harpham, 1994, pp. 236–237). It is important to normalize these feelings and fears for the patient so that the patient can continue to comply with routine medical assistance by receiving needed checkups and examinations. It may also be helpful to reframe doctor's appointments and annual checkups and exams as "investments" in the patient's future. If patients understand that early detection can improve rates of successful treatment and survivorship, then patients may view these visits as "allies" instead of "enemies."

Depression.   Although depression is commonly experienced by many cancer patients, it is often underdiagnosed and subsequently undertreated (Passik, 1996; Passik & Breitbart, 1996). Depression is often experienced by cancer patients after receiving prolonged or difficult treatment and at the termination of treatment (Clark et al., 1992). The sequelae of depression include somatic changes related to alterations in sleeping and eating, fatigue, loss of libido, loss of interest, loss of the ability to concentrate, and, in some cases, suicidal ideation (Clark et al., 1992; Harpham, 1994). Depression after the completion of active treatment can be exacerbated by chronic pain or fatigue, sleep deprivation, some types of medications, hormonal or chemical imbalances, and emotional stress (Harpham, 1994). Assessing for depression in cancer patients entails (1) investigating the presence of risk factors, (2) investigating the presence of the defining characteristics of depression, (3) noting the pattern of symptoms of depression (onset, frequency, severity, associated symptoms, and aggravating and alleviating factors), (4) assessing the meaning of the symptoms to the client and the family, and (5) assessing the impact of depression on the client and the family, including the perceived effectiveness of current strategies used to relieve the symptoms (Clark et al., 1992).

Patients who may be having particular difficulty adjusting to the rehabilitation phase and life in limbo may need further psychosocial assistance in dealing with grief, anxiety, anger, and depression. Interventions such as psychoeducation regarding emotional and physical ramifications of cancer and its treatment may help to minimize the risk of symptom occurrence or symptom severity. Assisting patients in focusing on short-term attainable goals and helping them to redefine goals, values, and self-perceptions in terms of realistic limitations set by the disease can also help to alleviate depression and anxiety. In addition, the monitoring of patient reactions to antidepressants, sedatives, or other drugs, as well as cautioning the patient against abrupt discontinuance of antidepressants or the use of alcohol while taking psychotropic medications is also important in the psychosocial care of the patient during rehabilitation (Clark et al., 1992).

Children of Cancer Patients Living in Limbo

Children of cancer patients must often deal with complex emotional responses that are characterized by overwhelming feelings of love, fear, irritability, insecurity, and anger (McKenna et al. 1995). Children's responses to cancer are often minimized or even ignored by the medical staff and by the parents during times of treatment and rehabilitation (Cancer Care Inc. and NCI, 1977). This minimization of children's needs can result in sleep disorders, eating disorders, mood/affect disorders, school problems, and acting-out behaviors (McKenna et al., 1995). The needs of children of cancer patients during the rehabilitation phase vary widely, from the young child who wants reassurance that his or her basic safety needs will be met, to the adult child of a cancer patient who is struggling with the demands of caregiving. However, children of all ages have reported low personal control over the disease and treatment outcome (Compas, Worsham, Ey, & Howell, 1996). As a result of feeling a lack of control, many children will demonstrate emotion-focused coping and high avoidance strategies (i.e., not thinking about or discussing the disease; Compas et al., 1996). Greater avoidance has been shown to lead to higher symptoms of anxiety and depression, and thus open communication about cancer, its treatment, and treatment outcome reduces avoidance and is important to healthy adaptation (Compas et al., 1996).

Continuing to Communicate with Children.   It remains necessary to continue to communicate with children throughout the clinical course of cancer. While it is important to speak truthfully about the success of the cancer treatment and hopes for the future, the amount of information will vary according to the child's age and desire to understand the details of treatment outcome (Harpham, 1994). However, all children will need to know some basic facts about cancer (1) cancer is not contagious, (2) there are different kinds of cancer, and (3) physical and behavioral changes are to be expected during and after cancer treatment (i.e., fatigue, loss of hair, difficulties with concentration). Still, many children remain confused about their parent's illness and report having little information about it (Nelson, Sloper, Charlton, & While, 1994) and being fearful that cancer is recurring when they witness their parent becoming fatigued and irritable (Harpham, 1994). Communicating facts about the success of cancer treatment and its ramifications will help reassure children that these are expected components of the cancer rehabilitation process (Harpham, 1994).

Children are usually concerned about safety needs, the ability of the family to stay together, and whether the well parent will become ill (Northouse, 1995). During the rehabilitation phase, these fears may resurface, particularly when the ill parent is (1) going for checkups, (2) undergoing extensive rehabilitation therapies, (3) experiencing chronic pain or fatigue, (4) adjusting to a poor prognosis, or (5) having emotional difficulties (Compas, Worsham, Epping-Jordan, Grant, Mireault, Howell, & Malcaren, 1994; Harpham, 1994; Northouse, 1995).

Spouses of Cancer Patients Living in Limbo

The rehabilitation process can upset the balance of intimacy in the marital dyad, especially during the rehabilitation phase and in response to a life crisis (Bolger, Foster, Vinokur, & Ng, 1996). Intimacy has been defined in several ways, including (1) exposing the self in verbal and nonverbal ways with trust that the partner will be understanding and not betray that trust (Wynne & Wynne, 1986), (2) entering into areas of concern or interest for the other partner so that shared meanings can be created (Weingarten, 1991), and (3) maintaining autonomy with clear boundaries while having the capacity to bring the "self" into the relationship (Lerner, 1989). The process of rehabilitation can affect intimacy in all of these areas beginning with exposing the true self via communication (Rolland, 1994). Cancer patients and their spouses can experience shameful thoughts and feelings that can impede the communication process, thus leaving both partners feeling isolated (Rolland, 1994). It is often very difficult to acknowledge negative feelings toward a loved one who is ill, or toward a loved one who is attempting to help in the best manner possible. Acknowledging these negative reactions openly can lead to feelings of guilt and to questions regarding a positive self-image (Oberst & James, 1985). Moreover, these feelings of guilt can lead to overcompensating behaviors such as excessive helping with functions and tasks that the patient does not welcome (Newsome & Schulz, 1998). Often family members will be plagued with fear and as a result will overcompensate by interacting with an optimistic and cheerful façade with the patient. Taylor, Wood, and Lichtman (1983) refer to this phenomenon as "secondary victimization" of the cancer patient. This victimization can take many forms, such as guarded communication, unrealistic hopefulness, and physical avoidance by support persons. These strategies may leave a patient feeling abandoned, uncared for, or rejected. While not all thoughts and feelings need be communicated, normalizing in advance emotional responses such as anger, death wishes, and ambivalence can help to counteract shame, secrecy, and subsequent isolation (Rolland, 1994). Those who are dissatisfied with the level of support from family members or who are socially isolated may find their needs better met through different means, such as remaining in close contact with professional health care services.

During the rehabilitation phase, couples have the opportunity to redefine their relationships and to rebuild their shared lives. Due to the impact of the illness and its intense recovery process, they have the added opportunity to reconsider the important qualities of their partnership while weeding out what is trivial (Rolland, 1994). Couples can create shared meaning from the illness by viewing the disease and the recovery process as "our illness," rather than as "his illness" or "her illness." By joining in the recovery process together, the needs of both the patient and the caregiver can be brought to the foreground, and the beliefs about the boundaries, rules, and roles governing the illness can be discussed in terms of a shared experience.

When partners can retain or achieve intimacy through communication and through shared experiences, and if the disease can be framed as a conjoint issue, then boundary setting is easier to accomplish, and limits are set on the power the disease has to control levels of intimacy within the partnership (Keitel, Cramer, & Zevon, 1990; Rolland, 1994). There are several simple strategies that couples can use to keep the disease "in its place" and to maintain optimal levels of intimacy despite the demands of rehabilitation. These strategies include (1) arranging times that are only for caregiving- and illness-related activities and other times that are preserved for other activities and discussions; (2) appointing areas of the home that are designated as "off limits" to illness-related activities; and (3) encouraging friends and neighbors to visit the home, so that the home can remain connected to pleasurable activities and memories (Rolland, 1994).

Setting these boundaries and encouraging the incorporation of "normal" family and social functioning can help to reduce isolation and disruptive emotional patterns that are often experienced during rehabilitation (Harpham, 1994). A disruptive pattern is characterized by the patient's need for continuing physical and emotional recovery and rehabilitation that is often counter to the spouse's need to "move on" and to "get back to normal." Other, more specific, patterns of interaction can become imbedded in the partnership if boundaries are not placed on the illness. These patterns include (1) ill partner versus healthy partner, (2) disabled versus abled, (3) in pain versus pain-free, (4) dependent versus independent, and (5) confined versus out in the world (Rolland, 1994, p. 247). Defining limits to caregiving, and setting boundaries on the illness can help to decrease long-term partnership dysfunction and to reduce survivor guilt that may occur later in the clinical course of cancer (Rolland, 1994).

☐ The Six Family Life Cycles during the Rehabilitation Phase: The Importance of Transformation and Reorganization

Most cancer patients and their families will need to undergo some form of rehabilitation, whether it be to reduce anxiety and fear responses or to help promote optimal functional abilities. However, the ramifications of cancer treatment and its side effects will have very different outcomes for persons in each of the life cycle stages. For example, cancer- and treatment-related infertility will be very different for the single young adult than for the cancer patient in later life. Thus, the rehabilitation phase will have a different impact on the various family life cycles. Families in different life cycles will need to transform their families and to integrate the cancer experience into their lives. A new sense of "normalcy" must be created, resulting in changed family systems. The following are continuations of the family case examples.

☐ The Single Young Adult during Rehabilitation

Long after treatment has been completed, young females and males with cancer will undergo changes that necessitate physical and psychosocial adjustment. Unmarried females have unique rehabilitation concerns that are just beginning to be examined in the literature (Gluhoski, Siegel, & Gorey, 1997). For example, unmarried females with breast cancer often can be pessimistic regarding future relationships and fears about disclosing their illness (Gluhoski et al., 1997). Unmarried women may believe that they are unable to attain a long-term committed relationship due to the disease and its treatment. Moreover, they may become more selective of the type of partner they desire, knowing that the illness necessitates a partner who is willing to remain committed to the relationship even if cancer should reoccur (Gluhoski et al., 1997).

Single young males recovering from cancer and its treatment can also encounter both physical and psychosocial difficulties. Males with testicular cancer often undergo the removal of the affected testicle (i.e., an orchiectomy), resulting in disfigurement. If metastasis was suspected, an additional operation known as a lymph node dissection may have been performed, resulting in a large abdominal scar and severed nerves that were used to control ejaculation. Males may thus be left with "dry" ejaculation (ejaculation with no semen or fluid) and subsequent concerns regarding sexuality and masculinity.

During the rehabilitation phase and beyond, single cancer patients may struggle with when to tell new partners about their experience. Fear of rejection after sharing the news may result in a prevailing reluctance to begin new relationships at all (Gluhoski et al., 1997). Single cancer patients can also experience profound loneliness and isolation if they are unable to share the experience of cancer with someone who deeply cares for them. Making important rehabilitation decisions, such as decisions regarding breast reconstruction, breast or testis prostheses, or meeting the daily demands of rehabilitation, can be more difficult when attempting to "go it alone" (Cella, 1987).

CASE EXAMPLE 1 (Continued). Mark's Rehabilitation Needs

Since Mark's testicular cancer was diagnosed in its early stages, Mark did not have to undergo a lymph node dissection. Thus, Mark was able to continue to experience normal ejaculations after his orchiectomy. Although Mark, his family, and a few of his friends were able to adapt well during the treatment phase of the illness, Mark began to experience some difficulty during the rehabilitation phase. Mark and his girlfriend Marie requested a follow-up consultation six months after his surgery. Mark began, "It feels as though I have come a long way since the diagnosis. I mean at first I was scared to death and then I decided to take a semester off and move back with my parents during my surgery. Now, I guess, the reality of it has sunk in. I am returning back to school and I have made some major changes in my life. I am now going into architecture instead of going for my mechanical engineering degree. It seems I can use my interest in art a bit more with a degree in architecture. I don't have difficulties with my own personal decisions, but I am having difficulty with my decisions regarding dating and marriage." Mark and Marie both agreed that cancer had greatly altered their relationship. While they were both happy that Mark had come to some new decisions regarding his career plans, and thus was beginning to successfully differentiate from his family of origin and their expectations, they were concerned about the long-term effects cancer may have on their relationship. Thus, they were currently going through a transition phase precipitated by Mark's rehabilitation concerns. Mark and Marie's subsystem needed to be reevaluated in terms of Mark's physical and emotional rehabilitation.

Assessing Psychosocial Considerations: The Effects of Living in Limbo

As a single young adult, Mark was experiencing distress regarding the nature of forming intimate relationships with women, particularly Marie, at this point in his life. Thus, Mark and Marie's subsystem has had to reorganize itself to meet the demands of the rehabilitation phase. Mark commented, "I am not sure if it is fair to continue a serious relationship with Marie. It doesn't seem fair to her. I mean I feel as if I am not really attractive. And what if the cancer comes back? What if I pass on cancer to my children? How is that fair to my family?" Because of these uncertainties, Mark requested that their relationship "slow down" for the time being. "Slowing down" included casually dating other people. Marie did not like this decision and stated, "We are just going through a transition. We need to talk about this more." Marie commented that their roles with each other were changing now that Mark was physically and emotionally rehabilitating from his surgery. "It used to be that I was the one he counted on—just as if I were part of his family. Now that he feels better about himself, he doesn't need me anymore. I can't take care of him like I used to." Mark realized that was part of the problem: "I don't want you to care for me like you did when I was just getting over my surgery. I need to feel well and to feel like a partner, not like a patient." It became readily apparent that Mark wanted to take more responsibility for his physical and emotional rehabilitation needs. He expressed his desire to increase his independence from both his family of origin and from Marie.

Outcome of the Rehabilitation Phase for the Single Young Adult

Mark was beginning to successfully adapt physically to the rehabilitation phase of the illness. He discussed the prospect of getting a prosthesis to replace the removed testicle: "I guess I am going to have one because I want to look and feel normal. Plus, it will make me feel more in control about who I want to tell about cancer." Emotionally and psychosocially, Mark had greater difficulties during the rehabilitation phase: "Cancer really changed me. In some ways it was for the better. I know now more about who I am, what I want from my life, and how to be independent." Although the rehabilitation phase presented some transitional difficulties for Mark and Marie, both agreed to attempt to change their roles with one another. Marie was required to give up her role as caregiver" and Mark was required to take more responsibility for his emotional rehabilitation needs.

☐ The Newly Forming Couple during Rehabilitation

The newly forming couple is usually in the midst of negotiating the balance of power within the relationship when cancer strikes. In addition, rules, roles, and boundaries are being established to form the structure of the new family system. During treatment, the couple's new structure may need to be put on hold while the couple incorporates the demands of the illness into their daily functioning. However, when the treatment phase transitions into the rehabilitation phase, the couple must reorganize their new system and reestablish the rules of the relationship. Roles such as "patient" and "caregiver" may need to be reevaluated, and rehabilitation concerns such as body image, sexual functioning, family planning, and overall psychosocial adaptation may need to be addressed.

CASE EXAMPLE 2 (Continued). Brenda's Rehabilitation Needs

Brenda was diagnosed with early-stage breast cancer and was treated with surgery (lumpectomy), chemotherapy, and radiation treatments. In addition, she was to continue to take long-term chemotherapy (Tamoxifen) for the next five years. Although Brenda reported substantial recovery from her lymphedema, she also reported experiencing increasing levels of depression and anxiety well into the rehabilitation phase of the illness.

The depression and anxiety were causing a strain on her new marriage and affecting her sexual functioning. She said, "I am just so depressed and tired all the time. I worry about cancer recurring and I don't feel like myself. I know I will never be the same again, but I don't know how to adapt to the illness . . . to integrate it into my new life. I feel stuck and unable to build a life with Bob." It was recommended that Brenda take part in a breast cancer recovery group for her depression and anxiety. It was also recommended that an antidepressant medication be considered. Later, she and Bob would attend couples counseling for their sexual difficulties.

Assessing Psychosocial Considerations: The Effects of Living in Limbo

During the group session, Brenda learned that she was not alone in her recovery. She realized that women her age typically have difficulties in their adaptation to breast cancer in several areas: (1) emotional, including anger or depression regarding the nature of a "just world" or the "normal, assumptive world"; (2) sexual, including body image and sexual functioning; and (3) relational, including relationships with their spouses and their mothers (Oktay & Walter, 1991).

The women shared their feelings of depression and anger. Many were angry that they had taken care of themselves their whole lives, only to be diagnosed with breast cancer. Some of the participants turned this anger outward and focused on the medical staff or on their families. Brenda commented, "Now I understand that I can't blame myself or anyone else for this illness. My anger is only serving to keep me distant from my husband and the people I work with. But now I don't know what to do with my emotions. It seems that my anger has turned inward and has become depression." One of the women in the group stated that she used her strong emotions to help other women with breast cancer. She commented, "Now I work with women at the American Cancer Society and in the I Can Cope group in my community. I feel like I can take my emotions and put them to some use. It is a way that I can regain a sense of control over myself and my actions. By helping others, I can integrate the illness as something positive in my life."

Other women discussed their difficulties with body image and sexuality. Many of the women had had mastectomies and commented on the difficulties in wearing a prosthesis, in finding comfortable clothing, and wearing bathing suits. Brenda sat and listened as they shared their stories of breast reconstruction and body image. One woman commented, "Now I know that I am much more than my body. It is the total me that makes me attractive. . . . I have to keep my focus on the 'real me,' the person who is a loving wife, daughter, and mother." Other women discussed the effects chemotherapy had on their sexual functioning. "Chemotherapy just zapped me. I couldn't even think about sex for months during chemotherapy and afterward. Now, I finally have the energy to initiate sex and to enjoy it again. But it has taken me some time."

Finally, the women discussed their relationships with their spouses and their mothers. Many of the women talked about how kind and giving their husbands had become, while others told stories of loneliness and isolation. One woman decided to get a divorce during her chemotherapy treatments. She said, "I knew my marriage was bad, but when he refused to come to the hospital with me and when he told me to 'get over it already,' I knew I had had enough. It was time to start living. I may not have a lot of time left. The divorce was rough, right in the middle of my treatments, but I had to do it. Now I am rebuilding my life after a divorce and after cancer."

The women also had stories to share about their relationships with their mothers during cancer rehabilitation. At least four different mother–daughter relationship patterns can occur when daughters are in young adulthood: (1) responsible mother, dependent daughter; (2) role reversal to responsible daughter, dependent mother; (3) peerlike; and (4) mutual mothering. Brenda stated that she was trying to establish herself as responsible in her relationship with her mother so that Brenda would be viewed as an equal or a friend: "I want to be more like her friend now, but she keeps trying to take over and to 'mother' me. I have to keep putting my foot down. Now I can hardly talk to her. I have to keep things from her and it feels like I am shutting her out. I try and talk to Bob about my feelings, but it overwhelms him and he doesn't know what to do. So now I can't really talk to anyone."

Outcome of the Rehabilitation Phase and the Newly Forming Couple

The group sessions helped Brenda to integrate the illness and its treatment into a new life for herself and for her marriage. Comparisons with others through cancer support groups are used during times of threat because people have a need to evaluate their resources and emotional responses (Festinger, 1954, as summarized in Wood, 1989). Therefore, when under threat, people are motivated to engage in social comparison to gain information about themselves and to determine the appropriateness, intensity, and nature of their emotional reactions (Gibbons & Gerrard, 1991; Taylor & Lobel, 1989). Through upward comparison, which is the comparison with better-off others, cancer groups offer the "instillation of hope, . . . the imparting of information and advice, the giving of support and help, or altruism" (Cella & Yellen, 1993, p. 59). Better-off others can serve as "models of possibility" in cancer support groups, representing to other members the ability to successfully cope with cancer (Adams, 1979). Downward comparison, which is the comparison to worse-off others, serves to protect or boost one's self-esteem to make oneself feel better (Wills, 1981). Knowing that you are better off than others and that your situation is not as bad as it could be can increase one's self-esteem and improve psychological well-being.

During the months that followed, Brenda became an active member of the group as well as a volunteer for various community services. These activities lifted her depression and decreased her levels of anxiety. After successfully adapting to the psychosocial and emotional demands of the rehabilitation phase, Brenda and Bob began couples counseling to address their sexual difficulties. Cancer's impact on their marital relationship, their sexual functioning, and their family planning continued well into the survival phase of the illness and is discussed in the next chapter.

☐ The Family with Young Children during Rehabilitation

The rehabilitation phase is a time of both celebration and sadness. The family may feel joyous due to the termination of treatment and their ability to see the "light at the end of the tunnel" during the patient's rehabilitation. However, the patient and the rest of the family system may have very different recovery time frames, with the patient needing more time to adapt to the physical and emotional scars left by the experience of cancer. Moreover, the rehabilitation phase can mark a time of recognizing physical limits and confronting the death of prior dreams and plans.

The life cycle of having and raising young children can be particularly difficult to navigate when it is complicated by the demands of cancer rehabilitation. Grandparents who may have been filling in as surrogate "parent" during the treatment phase may need to readjust their roles in the family system. Moreover, both the well and the sick parent may need to readjust their places in the family system, slowly taking on more and more responsibilities with the children and the home during this transitional phase. At times it may be difficult to discern when and how to reestablish boundaries, rules, and roles. Much of the young family's new structure will depend upon the severity of the disease, the aggressiveness of the treatment received, and the patient's rehabilitation needs.

CASE EXAMPLE 3 (Continued). Sally's Rehabilitation Needs

Sally needed both physical and psychosocial assistance during her rehabilitation. Physically, Sally reported suffering from continued depression, anxiety, and fatigue. In addition, she was also diagnosed with dyspareunia (vaginal pain during intercourse) due to the results of her hysterectomy. Sally reported that she experienced a lot of pain during intercourse: "I have been hesitant to talk to Sam about my pain until now. I was afraid he'd think that I was making it up, or that I was just making an excuse not to have sex. It was so difficult for me to have sex during my treatment, and I know that he wants to get back to normal, whatever that is, as soon as possible."

Sally and Sam were not experiencing the same needs, at the same time, during the rehabilitation phase. They were "at different places" along the path of recovery during rehabilitation. During a follow-up session that took place a few weeks after Sally completed treatment, she discussed her continuing depression, anxiety, and fatigue, which were a result of the illness and its treatment: "I am so tired and depressed all the time. It seems that I never really feel well, and because I am so run down, I can't be a good wife and mother. It makes me feel just terrible." Sam responded by reflecting and validating her feelings yet offering her support by saying, "I understand that you feel like you are not able to do the things that you would like to do at home, and that makes you feel bad about yourself. I think you are a wonderful wife and mother; we just need to put cancer behind us and move on. I can't understand why we don't just start living again and being a family like we used to." Sally and Sam continued to express their differing needs, with Sally needing to concentrate on her emotional and physical recovery, and Sam needing to "have his family back." In addition, they were both unsure of Sally's mother's role in the family. Sally commented, "There are times when I am so thankful to have her near. She has helped us so much, I don't know what we would have done without her. Then I feel guilty because I want her to go away and leave us alone for awhile." Sally and Sam both wanted to continue to reorganize the structure of their family system during this transitional phase of the illness.

Assessing Psychosocial Considerations:
The Effects of Living in Limbo

Sally's family was having difficulty making the transition between the treatment phase and the rehabilitation phase of the illness. Sally and her mother were confused in terms of defining the boundaries between their subsystems, and Sally and Sam reported conflicting differences in their needs during the rehabilitation process. Because of this, the children were also having difficulties adapting to this phase of the illness. It was reported that Sara was demonstrating a regression in age by asking for her old blanket, teddy bears, and even a bottle. Sally said, "She hasn't wanted these things for a long time! What is happening to us? Even little Sean is having difficulty with bowel and bladder control, especially at night. We are all falling apart!" For this family, limits had not been placed on the illness, and cancer was becoming embedded in the structure of their family system, impeding the process of normal individual and family development.

Sally's physical needs were addressed first. Sally's high levels of depression and anxiety were reported to her oncologist and oncology nurse. It was recommended that Sally begin taking antidepressant medication in conjunction with couples counseling to help her adapt more successfully during this phase of the illness. She said, "I can't get over the fact that I can't have anymore children. I feel as though I have aged 30 years in the past few months. I know that Sam hears me when I talk about my grief, but he can never totally understand how I feel." It was also recommended that Sally and Sam talk with Sally's gynecologist and attend sex therapy to better understand the changes brought about by Sally's surgery and treatment. In addition, Sally wanted to bring the children to family counseling to see if they could begin to unravel the fears and concerns the children were experiencing.

Outcome of the Rehabilitation Phase and the Family with Young Children

During individual counseling Sally was able to address her deep sadness over her inability to have more children: "I know I should be happy that Sam and I have two wonderful children already—everyone keeps telling me that. But it doesn't work that way. I feel devastated. The person I was is gone forever. My dreams and plans for my family have been destroyed. I can't seem to move forward." Sally decided to write a poem to her unborn children, expressing her grief over "losing" them:

> We have never met, yet
> > I know you.
> We have never shared a home, yet
> > I can feel your presence here.
> We have never talked or laughed, yet
> > I hear your voice and
> > I rise to answer your every need.
> We have never been close, yet
> > I smell your sweet smell and my arms ache
> > because you are not in them.
> We have never met, yet
> > I have to say good-by.

Sally was encouraged to share her poem with Sam so that he could better understand her grief. Sam was so moved by Sally's poem, he had it framed for her. It hangs in their hallway at home, paying homage to the children they would never have. After writing and hanging the poem, Sally and Sam were ready to place some limits on the disease. Both of them decided that there would only be certain times when they would participate in illness-related activities as a way to compartmentalize the salience of the cancer. Sally commented, "Right now, I guess I use every minute of every day thinking about the illness and trying to manage my fatigue and depression. The antidepressants and the therapy are helping, so I think I can just use a bit of each morning to tend to my own needs. Then I will feel refreshed and better able to help my children with their needs." Sally and Sam also wanted to put spatial limits on the illness by designating special areas of the home that are "off limits" to disease-related activities. According to Sam, "The illness permeates every wall of every room. Now that the treatment phase is over and we are beginning to move on, I think that our bedroom and the kitchen should be off limits." Sally added, "And the kids' rooms too. I am tired of thinking about my infertility in their rooms." Sally and Sam were also encouraged to invite good friends and neighbors over to the home. Sally stated, "I think that we can plan a small open house for our families and friends. It will be an open house held in celebration of our new life and all that we already have. We are ready to begin creating new, good memories in our home."

Sally, Sam, and Sally's mother, Sue, also discussed the new limits and boundaries to be put on the subsystems: "Mom understands that we want more privacy now that Sally is recovering. But I think that she is lonely and bored without us to care for." Despite Sue's desire to be needed as a caretaker, Sally stated that her mother was receptive to communicating about new roles in the family. In order for Sally to regain a sense of control over her household, they decided that Sue would begin calling Sally and asking if it was okay to come to the home. In addition, since Sally's depression and anxiety were lifting, and limits had been placed on the illness, the children also began responding to their healthier environment. Sally reported, "I think they are doing better, but Sara still seems sad over not having a baby brother or sister. But, she is seeing me get better and stronger every day. I think that really helps her to feel better too."

Sally and Sam began to address the difficulties with their sex life. Sam understood that Sally's physical pain was the result of her hysterectomy, and that the pain was not his fault. The sex therapist was able to recommend appropriate polyglycol-based, water-soluble lubricants to help reduce Sally's physical pain and discomfort. The sex therapist discussed different techniques to increase the couple's intimacy without having intercourse. Both nongenital and genital touching was explored through the sensate focus technique (Kaplan, 1987). It was also recommended that different sexual positions be used in order to decrease pain from intercourse. By addressing their physical, emotional, psychosocial, and family systems difficulties during the rehabilitation phase of the illness, Sally's family was able to integrate the experience of cancer into their lives and to transform their family into a healthier functioning system. Rather than let cancer become a permanent focal point of their existence, the family was beginning to put limits on cancer and to create new dreams and plans for their family system.

☐ The Family with Adolescents during Rehabilitation

The rehabilitation phase is a time that is often marked by differences in needs, concerns, and worries of the patient and the other family members. As such, it is can be a time of upheaval and confusion. This phase can be further complicated by the ever-changing boundaries of the family system with adolescents. When the family with adolescents enters the rehabilitation phase, problems in (a) family relationships, (b) external boundaries, and (c) role confusion can make for a turbulent time. Adolescents, in particular, may display a broad range of behaviors during the rehabilitation phase, from overfunctioning to irresponsibility (Ackerman, 1980). Adolescents who were overly responsible during the diagnosis and treatment phases of the illness may suddenly shift in the other direction and become absent and disengaged during the rehabilitation phase. This behavior can create problems between the patient who still needs care and the adolescent who desires freedom, growth, and independence from the family of origin.

CASE EXAMPLE 4 (Continued). Frank's Rehabilitation Needs

Since Frank was diagnosed with stage II Hodgkin's disease, he had been treated with radiation therapy alone. During the treatment phase and on into the rehabilitation phase, Frank was experiencing some weight loss, skin reactions, and myelosuppression (i.e., "a reduction in bone marrow function, resulting in a reduced release of leukocytes and platelets into the peripheral circulation," Varricchio, Pierce, Walker, & Ades, 1997, p. 467). Because of Frank's disease and its treatment, he reported that he was suffering from fatigue and that it was now affecting every aspect of his life. Frank stated that he had been experiencing fatigue for several months, but was hesitant to bring it up. Frank's symptomatology included significant fatigue with the need to rest, generalized weakness, poor concentration, decreased motivation to work, and marked emotional reactivity. Frank commented, "I was afraid to discuss my fatigue with anyone, because I thought that it meant the treatment wasn't working or that I was depressed. I wanted the treatment to work, and I wanted to be a good patient, a successful patient. I didn't want anything to interfere with my treatments or my rehabilitation." Anne added, "We also didn't want Frank to have to be on any more medication. The radiation was bad enough." In essence, Frank was reporting several barriers to receiving treatment for fatigue.

Assessing Psychosocial Considerations: The Effects of Living in Limbo

The rehabilitation phase brought about difficulties for Frank and his family. Frank reported that he wanted to ignore the side effects of radiation treatment and "get back to normal." Anne stated, "I know that he is trying to do too much and that he hasn't fully recovered. But since Frank Jr. decided to return to his sports and life with his friends, Frank really doesn't have much help at work. I have been thinking about increasing my workload at the catering shop so that Frank can take it easy for awhile. But he doesn't really like that idea." Frank was looking at cancer as an acute illness that would quickly subside after treatment. Through the course of the session, Frank was helped to understand that cancer should be regarded as a chronic illness, one from which he can recover, but one with long-term effects. By framing his disease as a chronic illness, Frank was ready to address the fatigue and to alter his daily routine.

A thorough assessment of Frank's fatigue was conducted. The above-mentioned barriers to the treatment of cancer-related fatigue were noted. Onset, course, duration, and the daily pattern of Frank's fatigue were examined (Cella et al., 1998). Frank reported that his fatigue began during the course of treatment and had been steadily increasing over the last few months. Frank noted that he woke up each morning feeling exhausted. He reported experiencing headaches and muscle aches throughout most of the day. He also stated that he would gain some energy during the midafternoon, but that this would last for only a couple of hours. Exacerbating factors included long hours at his work, poor nutrition, and insomnia. Frank reported that his experience of fatigue lead him to feel depressed and anxious. Frank ended the assessment by stating, "It seems like this exhaustion is worse than the disease itself! It effects my whole life; I can't seem to do anything I used to. I am not the same person I was a year ago."

Family functioning was also reassessed during the rehabilitation phase. Anne commented, "Frank Jr. was so responsible while Frank was receiving his treatment. Frank Jr. filled in for Frank at work and helped with the chores at home. I know that it really got to him after awhile, but now it seems that none of the kids want to help out at all. We regularly had the family meetings, and they helped, but we have since stopped because we no longer felt that we needed them. The kids have all gone their separate ways and they can't see that Frank and I still need help." It was recommended that the family reallocate their roles and responsibilities to fit this phase of the illness. The family was experiencing a skew in needs, between the children's need to continue with their adolescent development and Frank's need for assistance during the rehabilitation phase. Like Frank, his family was behaving as if Frank's disease was an acute disease that ended at the time of treatment completion. The family had resumed its developmental momentum at the cost of the patient's need for recovery time.

Outcome of the Rehabilitation Phase and the Family with Adolescents

Frank's physical needs were treated first. Frank's fatigue was treated using a three-stage hierarchical strategy (Cella et al., 1998). The first tier involved the identification of underlying causes of Frank's fatigue. It was recommended that Frank be treated for mild dehydration and that he consult with a nutritionist to ensure he was getting proper nutrition. In addition, Frank was also examined and treated for any underlying infections. Next, Frank's fatigue was treated directly (Cella et al., 1998). It was recommended that he conserve his energy during the morning hours and only work during the afternoon when he felt his fatigue lift. He was also taught specific relaxation techniques that would help him conserve his energy during the day and to sleep more restfully at night. Last, it was recommended that Frank and the family begin to perceive cancer as a chronic illness rather than as an acute disease. Thus, Frank and his family were encouraged to modify their expectations of Frank's recovery time frame and to devise more realistic plans and short-term goals.

Frank's family came in for a follow-up family therapy session to discuss their difficulties with normal developmental adaptation during the rehabilitation phase. Frank, Anne, their daughter Alexis, and their son Fred were present during this session. Frank explained, "Frank Jr. has a game tonight and he didn't want to miss it. He doesn't want to talk much about the illness these days. He is off doing his own thing for the most part." The family members each wanted to discuss their needs during this phase of the illness. Alexis began, "I guess I saw Frank Jr. helping out so much these past few months. I don't blame him for moving on and being with his friends more. Somehow, I think that it is my turn now to help out. I've been off doing my own thing with my friends and I feel kind of guilty about that. Maybe I can help a little bit more." Fred understood what his sister was saying and offered, "I can be of more help too. I am not sure how, though." The family needed to discuss their changing roles and responsibilities. Temporary and appropriate rules, roles, and boundaries would help reduce the gap between the family's developmental needs and Frank's need for recovery time. Anne reassured them, "These changes won't last forever, you know. After Dad recovers and gets his strength back, we'll change again. We can be flexible." After much discussion, it was decided that the family would begin to have bimonthly family meetings in order to increase the communication regarding member needs in the family. In addition, during the counseling session, Alexis agreed that she would help out more with the catering business so that Anne could accept more work. Fred began to help Frank out more in his work, and Frank was allowed more rest periods and time to recover. The family agreed that Frank Jr. should stay on his ball team and be allowed to remain relatively disengaged from the system. Frank commented, "At first I was really mad and hurt that Frank Jr. wasn't helping out more. It's as if he just stopped caring. Now I know it is his responsibility, of sorts, to become independent. Soon he will be going away to college and I want him to be ready for that." With the family in agreement of the temporary rules, roles, responsibilities, and boundaries governing the family system, they were better able to meet the demands of the rehabilitation phase. Although the process of recovery took longer than expected, Frank was able to resume most of his normal activities during the months of his rehabilitation. The family's structure would be reevaluated during the survival phase.

☐ The Family Launching Children during Rehabilitation

The rehabilitation phase of the illness can create difficulties for both the older children leaving home and for the parents who are adjusting to midlife tasks. Children who have left home and have established independent lives of their own may not be readily available to assist the patient during the recovery period. Conversely, adult children who have not been fully launched from the system may be pulled inward to help during the rehabilitation phase. Again, their developmental tasks of achieving independence from the family of origin may be delayed during this phase of the illness.

It is important to note, however, the parents' struggles with midlife concerns during the cancer rehabilitation. As parents advance in age, and as their children leave home, they are faced with the realistic perception of a finite lifespan and the idea that "Whatever we are going to do, we must do now" (Oktay & Walter, 1991, p. 147). In addition to the growing awareness of a finite lifespan, midlife also brings about the reassessment of one's life, the need for feelings of generativity, and changes in the need for intimate friendships (Oktay & Walter, 1991). The awareness of a finite lifespan and the reassessment of one's life are processes that can be compounded by cancer. Fear of cancer recurrence may serve to enforce the necessity to quickly evaluate the course of one's life and to make changes "before it's too late." Cancer patients in midlife may also discover the need to generate meaning in their lives by "giving back" during the rehabilitation phase. Many cancer patients in midlife may discover new ways to utilize their time. For example, some cancer patients may decide to donate some of their time to volunteer work and helping others recover from cancer. Thus, the need for meaningful work during midlife can be magnified by the experience of cancer. Friendships may become more important during this life cycle and during this phase of the illness. During earlier stages of development, parents must focus on family needs and the needs of their children (Oktay & Walter, 1991). However, as the demands of the family and the demands of the illness wane in their intensity, patients during this life cycle can focus more on cultivating and relying upon close friendships.

CASE EXAMPLE 5 (Continued). Claire's Rehabilitation Needs

Claire came in for follow-up consultation during the rehabilitation phase of her illness. Greg did not accompany her to the session. Claire began, "Greg and I have come a long way, but I still feel that something is missing. I know I ask a lot from him, maybe more than he can give me right now. He just wants to move on, as if I never got sick. But I feel differently. There are still so many things I need to work through." Claire discussed the difficulties she was experiencing adjusting to her prosthesis: "I can't get used to it. So I have decided to go in for breast reconstruction. I don't really know what to expect, but it can't be worse than this prosthesis." Claire reported that the swelling in her arm had gone and that she regained most of her range of motion. She said, "That arm still feels funny though. I get numb in my arm and fingers. The nurse called it 'peripheral neuropathy' and said that it was a result of the chemotherapy." Claire was also going through menopause as a result of her cancer treatment. She relayed, "I guess I am learning to adjust to all these changes. I have my good days and my bad days." Claire stated that she believed her physical rehabilitation needs were being met by the treatment team. She also reported feeling positive about breast reconstructive surgery.

Assessing Psychosocial Considerations: The Effects of Living in Limbo

Claire also wanted to discuss the psychosocial and emotional aspects of cancer rehabilitation. She said, "I feel like I am living in limbo. I keep thinking, do I have cancer still? Is it gone? Did they get all of it? Will it come back? I especially feel nervous when I have to go in for my checkups. I decided to take my fears in my own hands and I am learning about complementary therapies. Right now, I am using a combination of herbs, meditation, and exercise to help me feel in control."

Claire was also reassessing her marriage and her personal life. "This seems to be a time of in-betweens for me. I know that I love Greg, but now I know that we may not ever have the marriage I truly think we could have. I am starting to concentrate on my own life and what I need. I am going back to school next week and I am really excited about that. I couldn't go during the treatment phase, but now it is time I start doing something worthwhile in my life. I have also started to volunteer at the hospital. I work one night a week on the intensive care unit. I talk to families who may need information, or who may need to talk about their fears. Because of cancer, I can relate to them. It has made me a deeper, better person."

Claire discussed the effects that "living in limbo" had on her and her family: "For me, I am using this time to take care of myself. I am going in for breast reconstruction and I am seeking additional ways to look after my health. The relaxation techniques and the new diet I am on make me feel really good. My family and I have grown a bit distant, though. They seem to want to move on, and I guess I am letting them." Claire reported that she had made new friends at the hospital and in her classes: "There are these two women who are terrific! They have gone through so much in their lives. I feel I can really talk to them about my illness and what I am going through. It also takes some of the pressure off of Katherine and Greg. I can just let them do what they need to do, at least for right now."

Outcome of the Rehabilitation Phase and the Family Launching Children

During rehabilitation, Claire was attempting to take care of both her physical and psychosocial needs. Her family was experiencing an extreme skew between the recovery needs of the patient and the needs of the other family members. Claire had decided to allow the skew to take place. She was beginning to address her own developmental, midlife needs during the rehabilitation phase. Claire's focus on support outside of her family was assisting her in coping with the rehabilitation process. Studies have shown that social isolation can increase the risk of illness becoming terminal (Spiegel, 1995). From this conclusion, it could be hypothesized that those with social support have better coping resources and receive more help in managing their lives during their illness, which increases their longevity. Studies by Reynolds and Kaplan (1990) found that women who were the least socially connected were more than twice as likely to die from cancer as compared with those who were the most socially connected. Therefore, Claire's new social support may alter the risk factors from isolation, producing buffering effects for the patient and allowing her to more adequately cope with the illness (Taylor, Falke, Shoptaw, & Lichtman, 1986).

Claire later reported that she "loved the breast reconstruction. It isn't like my old breast,

I mean I don't have any feeling in it and it is kind of hard, but it looks great and I couldn't be more pleased with the results." Claire's physical recovery from breast reconstructive surgery was unremarkable. She was able to continue with her college classes and her volunteer work. Because she was able to address her developmental needs during this phase of the illness, she reported an increased feeling of generativity in her life: "My life has so much more meaning than it ever has. I found great meaning in raising Katherine, but I need something to make me feel worthwhile now. My work and my school helps me feel like I still matter . . . like I still have something to contribute to this world. And, it is interesting that as I feel better about myself, I am feeling better about my marriage. My self-worth is no longer based only on what my family thinks of me, but rather how I view myself. This has enabled me to start viewing my relationships in a different way. Instead of needing these relationships as a way to define who I am, I now want to participate in relationships with my husband and my daughter Katherine." As a result of these new feelings of self-esteem, Claire was beginning to act on caring behaviors for Greg, without expecting anything in return. Claire began to realize that her cancer may have served a greater purpose in her life by forcing her to reevaluate her own worth as well as the relationships around her. Claire summed up her feelings by stating, "I am beginning to realize that breast cancer is not about dying, but it is about learning how to live."

☐ The Family in Later Life during Rehabilitation

Older patients may face unique difficulties during the rehabilitation phase of the illness. For many patients in later life, the aging process may be accelerated due to the disease and its treatment. For these patients, dreams and plans for an enjoyable retirement may be thwarted by threat of cancer, its treatment, and its recovery time period. The losses encountered during later life may be compounded by the losses faced during rehabilitation, as the older patient learns to deal with loss of energy and the potential loss of physical functioning. After the crises of the diagnostic and treatment phases have died down, the patient in later life can take time to reassess the impact cancer has had on his or her life and to adapt to the losses brought about by the illness (Oktay & Walter, 1991).

CASE EXAMPLE 6 (Continued). Red's Rehabilitation Needs

Red and his wife Rachel attended a follow-up counseling session a few months after Red's treatment completion. Red began the session, "I went to a men's cancer group meeting in the community last week. I wanted to make sure that I was adjusting to cancer, at least as well as everyone else. I found out that I didn't have it nearly as bad as other guys my age do. Because of their cancer treatment, some of them had lost their ability to have erections. I guess these guys had to have their prostates removed and their lymph nodes worked on. [Red is referring to a prostatectomy with lymph node dissection.] These guys had difficulty urinating and were really struggling with the effects of cancer. Some of them had been treated with hormones and had experienced breast enlargement too." Red reported having few rehabilitation needs of his own; however, he was worried about his wife's health, which had been a source of concern for some time. "Like I said before, I feel really lucky. I didn't have to go through surgery or hormone therapy. Some of the men in the group were really suffering. They have to struggle with impotence, incontinence, and the fear of recurrence. I really don't feel I have to struggle at all with my own needs right now. I am just more concerned about Rachel and how she is getting along, and I don't know what I would do without her."

Assessing Psychosocial Considerations: The Effects of Living in Limbo

Red and Rachel were adapting to the losses brought about by Red's cancer. Although Red reported few physical rehabilitation needs, both of them discussed their fears of losing one another. Red commented, "We have both faced the death of many family members and the death of our friends. Our children live far away and it seems like we only have each other. For us, the most frightening thought is losing each other. We don't know how we could adapt to that."

Red and Rachel were facing their own mortality during the rehabilitation phase of the illness. While they were beginning to reach out to others, first by opening up their system to new friends and to family members, and second by Red attending the community cancer group, they were also pulling inward in order to help each other with sickness and other later life concerns. Since Red reported minimal rehabilitation needs, they became focused on Rachel's declining health. Red stated, "It may seem like I am the one who needs help—because I have cancer and all. But truly, I believe that Rachel needs more help right now than I do. She is tired and in pain all the time." Thus, living in limbo for Red and Rachel meant the double threat of losing either partner. The threat of loss was suspended over them in the form of possible recurrent cancer or another unrelated illness.

Because of the couple's level of fear, during the follow-up session, the "living, just in case" philosophy was presented (Babcock, 1997). This philosophy presents a way of looking at life with no assurances or guarantees. Because none of us know when our last day will be, we must prepare for death "just in case" by taking care of funeral preplanning, advanced directives, a living will, and increasing communication with family and social support systems. The couple was encouraged to discuss their final wishes with their spouse and their children. These tasks are a way to prepare "just in case" something was to happen to Red or Rachel. Many patients state that they have experienced a sense of relief after having made arrangements for death, while others have stated that they felt as if it was an admission of defeat. Red and Rachel stated that they saw it as an opportunity to take some of the fear out of the dying process and to regain some control over their future. After the couple discussed taking care of the "just in case" necessities, then the discussion focused on how they can enjoy the "living" part of the philosophy. Red and Rachel stated that they wanted to do more of their favorite activities, which included traveling and golf. In addition, Rachel stated that she would like to spend more time with her children and grandchildren. Red and Rachel agreed that they would make arrangements to visit their children in the next few months rather than waiting for the family get-together at the holidays.

Outcome of the Rehabilitation Phase and the Family in Later Life

Because of the structure of their relatively closed system and their potential for a "resource vacuum," Rachel and Red looked into the cost of nursing home facilities and in-home care nursing, "just in case." Rachel explained, "We probably can't afford much, but we need to know all of our options in case one of us is left alone." They also began to discuss the possibility of moving closer to some of their children and grandchildren to help them prepare for future needs. "I guess this illness brought home the realities of sickness, old age, and death for us. Before cancer, we were just content to focus on ourselves and our trip to visit the kids every year. Now we know we need more support and we need to make some changes," reflected Rachel. Both Red and Rachel were also worried about becoming a burden to their families if they should get seriously ill: "We have decided to update our wills and to make plans for our own funerals and burials so we won't be a burden to our family."

Although the illness brought many lifespan realities into focus for Red and Rachel, they also noted some positive changes that had occurred. Red commented, "Cancer made me realize how precious life is. My wife and my family are so important to me, more important than retirement funds, vacations, and trips across country. I will do anything I can to make life easier for Rachel, my kids, and my grandkids." Thus, Rachel and Red wanted to minimize the burden placed on their family members and to maximize their own usefulness in later life. Rachel finished, "No matter how old you are, no matter how sick a person gets, you are still important. You can still perform worthwhile activities and give to others."

☐ Summary

In this chapter the focus was on the family during the remission/rehabilitation phase of the illness. Biomedical variables of importance during the rehabilitation phase and the major psychosocial issues of "living in limbo" and reorganizing the family system to adapt to cancer rehabilitation were explained. Next, important considerations for the six family life cycles during the rehabilitation phase were presented, followed by a detailed case example relevant to each family life cycle. In each case example, the importance of adapting to life "in limbo," or the uncertainty of life, was emphasized.

The next chapter will explain the biomedical information and psychosocial considerations relevant to the survival phase of the illness. This information will be followed by further elaboration of the six case examples, with an emphasis on the importance of using rituals to adapt to cancer.

☐ References

Ackerman, N. (1980). The family with adolescents. In E. Carter & M. McGoldrick (Eds.), *The family life cycle: A framework for family therapy* (pp. 147–169). New York: Gardner Press, Inc.

Adams, J. (1979). Mutual-help groups: Enhancing the coping ability of oncology clients. *Cancer Nursing, 1*, 95–98.

American Psychological Association. (1994). *Diagnostic and statistical manual of mental disorders* (4th ed.). Washington, DC: Author.

Anderson, B., & Lamb, M. (1995). Sexuality and cancer. In G. Murphy, W. Lawrence, Jr., & R. Lenhard, Jr. (Eds.), *American Cancer Society textbook of clinical oncology* (pp. 699–713). Atlanta, GA: American Cancer Society.

Anderson, B. & Schmuch, G. (1991). Sexuality and cancer. In A. Holleb, D. Fink, & G. Murphy (Eds.), *American Cancer Society textbook of clinical oncology* (pp. 606–616) Atlanta, GA: American Cancer Society.

Babcock, E. N. (1997). *When life becomes precious: A guide for loved ones and friends of cancer patients.* New York: Bantam Books.

Barg, F. (1997). Rehabilitation. In C. Varricchio (Ed.), *A cancer source book for nurses.* Atlanta GA: American Cancer Society.

Bolger, N., Foster, M., Vinokur, A., & Ng, R. (1996). Close relationships and adjustment to a life crisis: The case of breast cancer. *Journal of Personality and Social Psychology, 70*(2), 283–294.

Cancer Care, Inc. and National Cancer Foundation (NCI). (1977). *Listen to the children: A study of the impact on the mental health of children of a parent's catastrophic illness.* New York: Cancer Care Inc.

Cella, D. (1987). Cancer survival: Psychosocial and public issues. *Cancer Investigations, 5*, 59–67.

Cella, D., Passik, S., Jacobsen, P., & Breitbart, W. (1998). Progress toward guidelines for the management of fatigue. *Oncology, 12*(11a), 369–377.

Cella, D., & Yellen, S. (1993). Cancer support groups: The state of the art. *Cancer Practice, 1,* 56–61.

Christ, G. (1991). Principles of oncology social work. In A. Holleb, D. Fink, & G. Murphy (Eds.), *American Cancer Society textbook of clinical oncology* (pp. 594–605). Atlanta, GA: American Cancer Society.

Clark, J., McGee, R., & Preston, R. (1992). Nursing management of responses to the cancer experience. In J. Clark & R. McGee (Eds.), *Core curriculum for oncology nursing* (2nd ed., pp. 67–155). Philadelphia: W.B. Saunders Company.

Compas, B., Worsham, N., Epping-Jordan, J., Grant, K., Mireault, G., Howell, D., & Malcaren, V. (1994). When Mom or Dad has cancer: Markers of psychological distress in cancer patients, spouses, and children. *Health Psychology, 13*(6), 507–515.

Compas, B., Worsham, N., Ey, S., & Howell, D. (1996). When Mom or Dad has cancer: II. Coping, cognitive appraisals, and psychological distress in children of cancer patients. *Health Psychology, 15*(3), 167–175.

Entrekin, N. (1992). Breast cancer. In J. Clark & R. McGee (Eds.), *Core curriculum for oncology nursing* (2nd ed., pp. 413–427). Philadelphia: W.B. Saunders Company.

Faber, L. (1991). Lung cancer. In A. Holleb, D. Fink, & G. Murphy (Eds.), *American Cancer Society textbook of clinical oncology* (pp. 194–212). Atlanta, GA: American Cancer Society.

Festinger, L. (1954). A theory of social comparison processes. *Human Relations, 7,* 117–140.

Flannery, M. (1992). Reproductive cancers. In J. Clark & R. McGee (Eds.), *Core curriculum for oncology nursing* (2nd ed., pp. 451–469). Philadelphia: W.B. Saunders Company.

Gibbons, F., & Gerrard, M. (1991). Downward comparison under threat. In J. Suls & T. A. Wills (Eds.), *Social comparison: Contemporary theory and research* (pp. 317–345). Hillsdale, NJ: Lawrence Erlbaum Associates.

Gluhoski, V., Siegel, K., & Gorey, E. (1997). Unique stressors experienced by unmarried women with breast cancer. *Journal of Psychosocial Oncology, 15,* 173–183.

Gunn, A. (1984). Cancer rehabilitation: An overview. In A Gunn (Ed.) *Rehabilitation* (pp. 1–27). New York: Raven Press.

Gunn, A., Dickison, E., & McBride, C. (1984). Physical rehabilitation. In A. Gunn (Ed.), *Rehabilitation* (pp. 23–40). New York: Raven Press.

Halvorson-Boyd, G., & Hunter, L. (1955). *Living in limbo.* San Francisco: Jossey-Bass Publishers.

Harpham, W. (1994). *After cancer: A guide to your new life.* New York: Norton & Company Ltd.

Kaplan, H. (1979). *Disorders of sexual desire.* New York: Brunner/Mazel.

Kaplan, H. (1987). *The illustrated manual of sex therapy* (2nd ed.). New York: Brunner/Mazel.

Keitel, M., Cramer, S., & Zevon, M. (1990). Spouses of cancer patients: A review of the literature. *Journal of Counseling and Development, 69,* 163–166.

Lerner, H. (1989). *The dance of intimacy: A woman's guide to courageous acts of change in key relationships.* New York: Harper and Row.

Lind, J. (1992). Lung cancer. In J. Clark & R. McGee (Eds.), *Core curriculum for oncology nursing* (2nd ed., pp. 403–412). Philadelphia: W.B. Saunders Company.

Masters, W., & Johnson, V. (1966). *Human sexual response.* Boston: Little, Brown.

Mayer, D., & O'Connor-Kelleher, L. (1993). *Rehabilitation of people with cancer: An oncology nursing society position statement.* Pittsburgh, PA: Oncology Nursing Society.

McKenna, R. J. (1991). Supportive care and rehabilitation of the cancer patient. In A. Holleb, D. Fink, & G. Murphy (Eds.), *American Cancer Society textbook of clinical oncology* (pp. 615–634). Atlanta, GA: American Cancer Society.

McKenna, R., Wellisch, D., & Fawzy, F. (1995). Rehabilitation and supportive care of the cancer patient. In G. Murphy, W. Lawrence, Jr., & R. Lenhard, Jr. (Eds.), *American Cancer Society textbook of clinical oncology* (pp. 635–654). Atlanta, GA: American Cancer Society.

Miaskowski, C., & Portenoy, R. (1998). Update on the assessment and management of cancer-related fatigue (pp. 1–10). In A. Berger, B. Portenoy, & D. Weissman (Eds.), *Principles and practice of supportive oncology.* Philadelphia: Lippincott-Raven Publishers.

Moosa, A. et al. (1991). *Comprehensive textbook of oncology* (2nd ed.). Baltimore: Williams and Wilkins.

Nelson, E., Sloper, P., Charlton, A., & While, D. (1994). Children who have a parent with cancer: A pilot study. *Journal of Cancer Education, 9*(1), 30–36.

Newsome, J., & Schulz, R. (1998). Caregiving from the recipient's perspective: Negative reactions to being helped. *Health Psychology, 17*(2), 172–181.

Northouse, L. (1995). The impact of cancer in women on the family. *Cancer Practice, 3*(3), 134–142.

Oberst, M., & James, R. (1985). Going home: Patient and spouse adjustment following cancer surgery. *Topics in Clinical Nursing, 7,* 46–57.

Oktay, J., & Walter, C. (1991). *Breast cancer in the life course: Women's experiences.* New York: Springer.

Passik, S. (1996). Supportive care of the patient with pancreatic cancer: Role of the psycho-oncologist. *Oncology,* 33–34.

Passik, S., & Breitbart, W. (1996). Depression in patients with pancreatic carcinoma. *Cancer, 78,* 615–626.

Physician's Desk Query (PDQ). (1999). Update [On-line]. Available: http://cancernet.nci.nih.gov/coping.html

Reynolds, P., & Kaplan, G. (1990). Social connections and risk for cancer: Prospective evidence from the Alameda County Study. *Behavioral Medicine, 16,* 101–110.

Rolland, J. S. (1994). *Families, illness, and disability: An integrative treatment model.* New York: Basic Books.

Salcido, R., & Jenkins, S. (1994). The subacute rehabilitation boom. *Journal of Subacute Care, 1*(1), 3–6.

Sherman, A., & Simonton, S. (1999). Family therapy for cancer patients: Clinical issues and interventions. *The Family Journal: Counseling and Therapy for Couples and Families, 7*(1), 39–50.

Spiegel, D. (1993). *Living beyond limits: New hope and help for facing life-threatening illnesses.* New York: Basic Books.

Spiegel, D. (1995). Social support in cancer. In N.R.S. Hall & F. Altman (Eds.), *Mind-body interactions and disease: Proceedings of a conference on stress, immunity and health* (pp. 73–83). Washington, DC: National Institutes of Health, Health Dateline Press.

Strohl, R. (1992). Colorectal cancers. In J. Clark & R. McGee (Eds.), *Core curriculum for oncology nursing* (2nd ed., pp. 470–479). Philadelphia: W.B. Saunders Company.

Taylor, S., Falke, R., Shoptaw, S., & Lichtman, R. (1986). Social support, support groups, and the cancer patient. *Journal of Consulting and Clinical Psychology, 54,* 608–615.

Taylor, S., & Lobel, M. (1989). Social comparison activity under threat: Downward evaluation and upward contacts. *Psychological Review, 96,* 569–575.

Taylor, S., Wood, J., & Lichtman, R. (1983). It could be worse: Selective evaluation as a response to victimization. *Journal of Social Issues, 39,* 19–40.

Varricchio, C., Pierce, M., Walker, C., & Ades, T. (1997). *A cancer source book for nurses* (7th ed.). Atlanta, GA: Jones and Bartlett Publishers.

Vess, J., Moreland, J., & Schwebel, A. (1985). A follow-up study of role functioning and the psychological environment of families of cancer patients. *Journal of Psychosocial Oncology, 3*(2), 1–15.

Watson, P. (1996). Rehabilitation services. In R. McCorkle, M. Grant, M. Frank-Stromborg, & S. Baird (Eds.), *Cancer nursing: A comprehensive textbook* (2nd ed., pp. 1300–1311). Philadelphia: W.B. Saunders Company.

Weingarten, K. (1991). The discoveries of intimacy: Adding a social constructionist and feminist view. *Family Process, 30,* 285–305.

Wills, T. (1981). Downward comparison principles in social psychology. *Psychological Bulletin, 90,* 245–271.

Wood, J. (1989). Theory and research concerning social comparison of personal attributes. *Psychological Bulletin, 106,* 213–248.

Wynne, L., & Wynne, A. (1986). The quest for intimacy. *Journal of Marital and Family Therapy, 12,* 383–394.

Survival and the Family Life Cycle: Living under the Sword of Damocles

☐ Definition and Meaning of Survival

The definition of survivorship is evolving within the field of psychooncology and oncology nursing (Ferszt & Waldman, 1997). Typically a cancer patient is considered a "survivor" if he or she is still living five years after diagnosis (American Cancer Society [ACS], 1998; Leigh, 1992). This can mean living disease-free, in remission, or even still receiving cancer treatment (ACS, 1998). Other definitions of survivorship have also been used, including being disease-free and off treatment for at least one year (Kornblith, 1998). A broader definition of survivorship has been proposed by the National Coalition for Cancer Survivorship (NCCS): "From the time of diagnosis and for the balance of life, a person diagnosed with cancer is a survivor." In addition, survivors also include any persons who have been affected by cancer other than the patient, such as all family members (Leigh, 1992). Although there are many definitions of survivorship, for the purposes of organization our definition begins after treatment completion and extends into the five-year survival period and beyond. In addition, issues of rehabilitation, recovery, and survivorship have many commonalities. However, the amount of time since diagnosis is the key factor, with recovery and rehabilitation taking place months after treatment and treatment completion, and survivorship beginning at least one year after treatment completion (Kornblith, 1998).

Survivorship has been described as living under the "sword of Damocles" (Harpham, 1994; Leigh, 1992). In the ancient Roman tale, a powerful ruler, Dionysius, had amassed great wealth and power. However, he lived in constant fear of assassination, which left him isolated and unable to trust anyone. Damocles, a lowly subject, was in awe of how much material wealth and power Dionysius had acquired and stated, "All this wealth must make you the happiest man alive!" Dionysius wanted to let Damocles understand first hand how truly "happy" all the wealth had made him. He put Damocles on a golden couch near beautiful things and wonderful food. Then Dionysius ordered a large sword to be put above Damocles's head suspended only by the hair of a horse. With the looming threat of the sword hanging over his head (much like the threat of assassination for Dionysius), Damocles could not enjoy any of the riches before him. Soon, Damocles begged to be released from the threat of the sword and to return to his "normal" life. So it is with many survivors of cancer. Although the goal of becoming a cancer "survivor" has become realized, the threat of cancer recurrence still looms, making even survivorship a difficult phase to navigate (Harpham, 1994). To ease the difficulties of survivorship, the NCCS has been advocating for quality cancer care for all survivors (NCI, 1995).

New advances in early detection and cancer treatment have resulted in notable changes in survival rates. For example, the five-year survival rate of Hodgkin's disease has increased from 5% to about 80% due to the MOPP chemotherapy regimen (DeVita, 1981; Urba & Longo, 1992). The five-year survival rates of acute myeloid and lymphoblastic leukemia have increased from 5% to around 40% to 70% due to the practice of allogeneic bone marrow transplantation (BMT; ACS, 1987; Kornblith, 1998); and the five-year survival rate for testicular seminoma has increased from less than 10% to more than 90% due to multidrug chemotherapy treatment (Einhorn, Richie, & Shipley, 1993). In 1999 (ACS, 1999) the overall five-year relative survival rate for all cancers was 60%. Thus, it is important for cancer survivors to remain informed about a variety of relevant medical advances. A number of accessible resources now exist, helping the survivor remain well informed. Two of most importance include the NCCS, which publishes *The Networker* and *Facing Forward,* newsletters for cancer survivors (NCCS, 1010 Wayne Avenue, Fifth Floor, Silver Spring, MD 20910; 301-650-8868) and CancerNet (www.nci.nih.gov) an on-line information service of the NCI.

Survivorship and Maintaining Health

During the early seasons of the survivor phase, patients will remain in contact with their oncologists for regular follow-up appointments. During these regularly scheduled appointments, patients will undergo follow-up tests and procedures. They may receive treatment for cancer-related complications and side effects of medications. In addition, survivors will also need to be monitored closely for recurrence, metastases, or the development of a second malignancy. Some will require ongoing rehabilitation, and others may need home health care. Patients and their families should also be supplied with information about ongoing psychosocial support services (Ferszt & Waldman, 1997). In this way, comprehensive cancer care can be provided for the patient long into the survival phase. Finally, all survivors will want to follow closely the general recommendations for health screenings for all persons their age.

Survivorship and Complementary/Alternative Medicine (CAM)

During the survival phase, patients and families may choose to be involved in complementary or alternative forms of treatment for a variety of reasons. These might include the need to remain actively involved in a plan to combat cancer, to remain in tune with the body's need for continued care, and/or to find comfort, support, and hope (Gray, Greenberg, Fitch, Parry, Douglas, & Labrecque, 1997; Harpham, 1994). Estimates suggest that as many as 80% of cancer patients show interest in CAM (Lerner & Kennedy, 1992; Montbriand, 1993), and yet few physicians are aware of the various CAM approaches available (Gray et al., 1997). Cassileth and Chapman (1996) have organized the variety of CAM approaches into the following categories: (a) dietary and herbal remedies (e.g., macrobiotics, dietary supplements, fasting/juice therapies), (b) biological treatments (e.g., chelation, shark/bovine cartilage), (c) use of the mind for emotional relief (e.g., imagery/

visualization, biofeedback, meditation), (d) reducing pain/stress through bodywork (e.g., acupressure, massage, yoga), (e) enhancing well-being through the senses (e.g., aromatherapy, music therapy, art therapy, humor), and (f) restoring health via spirituality and external energy forces (e.g., prayer/spirituality, therapeutic touch, faith healing). Currently, there are a few helpful guides to CAM (Cassileth & Chapman, 1996; Gray et al., 1997).

Physiologic Long-Term and Late Effects of Treatment

Little systematic and longitudinal research has been done on the long-term and late effects of cancer treatments, although the NCSS (www.CancerNet.nci.nih.gov) has identified examples of some specific physical systems affected by some cancer treatments. These include such problems as cardiomyopathy, bladder damage, renal insufficiency, and muscle atrophy, as well as the increased risks of future disease from compromised immune systems. In addition, related problems include a variety of functional changes (e.g., lymphedema, pain, fatigue, sleep disturbances), cosmetic changes (e.g., amputation, ostomies, skin/hair changes), and the psychosocial consequences of living with these physiologic effects (e.g., anxiety, mood changes, insurability, employment issues, stigma). Two specific functional changes warrant further discussion: impaired sexuality and chronic fatigue.

Survivorship and Impaired Sexuality

The most common type of sexual problems are loss of desire for sexual activity, erectile dysfunction in men, and pain during intercourse (dyspareunia) in women. Causal factors are complex and include a combination of both physical and psychological variables. Physical factors include direct organ damage secondary to cancer treatment, as well as fatigue and pain. Psychological factors include guilt, depression, disturbances in body image, and changes that occur in relationships secondary to cancer and its treatment.

Although many types of cancer and their treatments will lead to sexual dysfunctions, some will have more permanent effects on fertility (Anderson & Lamb, 1995; Barton Burke, 1997). Cancers of the cervix, uterus, ovaries, and breast can result in infertility. With cervical cancer, treatment of in situ cancer with cone biopsy will not usually result in infertility; however, a radical hysterectomy or cervical cancer or both treated with radiation therapy will result in infertility. Long-term discomfort during intercourse is also common, and modification of sexual positioning and the use of polyglycol-based, water-soluble lubricants are recommended (Barton Burke, 1997). Uterine cancer that has been treated with a total abdominal hysterectomy or radiation treatment will also leave female patients infertile. In addition, early menopause with sudden onset may be experienced (Anderson & Lamb, 1995). Patients with ovarian cancer who have undergone the removal of both ovaries (i.e., bilateral oophorectomy) will also experience menopausal symptoms and infertility. In cases of unilateral oophorectomies, patients may still have the ability to have children. For women who have been treated for breast cancer, infertility is dependent upon the type of cancer treatment used (Barton Burke, 1997).

Males who have been diagnosed and treated with prostate and testicular cancer may become impotent. Total prostatectomy may result in impotence and urinary incontinence. Males who have been treated for testicular cancer and who have undergone lymph node dissection may experience retrograde ejaculation from nerve damage. Bilateral treatment always results in impotence, and suggestions for the utilization of a sperm bank prior to chemotherapy is recommended for males wanting to have children. High doses of radiation can cause erectile and orgasmic difficulties, as well as reduced semen volume from radiation scatter to the prostate and seminal vesicles (Barton Burke, 1997).

Survivors of bladder, colorectal cancer, and leukemia may also suffer from infertility. Patients with bladder cancer, a common type of cancer for older males, who have been treated using radiation therapy are usually left infertile (Barton Burke, 1997). While survivors of colorectal cancer will not usually suffer from infertility (except in some cases where certain types of chemotherapy have been used), they can suffer long-term psychological dysfunctions due to the need for ostomies. Nerve damage for male survivors of colorectal cancer can also negatively affect erectile capabilities (Barton Burke, 1997). For survivors of Hodgkin's and non-Hodgkin's lymphoma, chemotherapy can effect sperm counts and ova maturation. Radiation to the testicles and chemotherapy may decrease sperm counts and ova maturation (Anderson & Lamb, 1995). Survivors from leukemia and its treatment may have short- or long-term effects on sperm count, sexual drive, and body image. However, sperm counts and ova maturation may rebound after treatment completion, leaving survivors with functional ability to have children (Barton Burke, 1997).

Survivorship and Fatigue

Fatigue is a common complaint of people with cancer, both during and after treatment. Estimates suggest that as many as 90% of cancer patients experience fatigue, particularly *during* treatment (Miaskowsi & Portenoy, 1998). Chronic, long-term fatigue is described as persistent, unremitting, or relapsing and has been reported to have significant negative effects on quality of life.

During long-term survival, fatigue continues to be a concern for many patients and their families, and yet little is known about specific causes or treatments. Causal mechanisms are complex and poorly understood, but are thought to include a variety of factors such as the late effects of treatment, nutritional, psychological (e.g., depression), and cognitive factors, as well as the side effects of multiple medications. There is no agreed-upon standard of care for fatigue, but management approaches should first treat any specific physiologic abnormalities (e.g., anemia, dehydration, electrolyte imbalance, dyspnea), and then include a variety of energy conservation techniques, combined with patient education, moderate exercise, and an adequate mix of rest and activity. Family members can have an important role in assisting patients with monitoring the intensity of fatigue and the variety of efforts to balance energy conservation with adequate exercise and physical activity.

☐ Survivorship and Psychosocial Considerations: Living under the Sword of Damocles

Transition from Living in Limbo to Living under the Sword of Damocles

During the previous rehabilitation phase, cancer patients and their families transform and reorganize their systems to integrate the illness into their daily routines, overall existential meaning, and plans for the future (Harpham, 1994). This integration of the illness into family functioning deepens during the survivorship phase as families resume either long-standing or modified personal, family, and social rituals. Four types of family rituals have been identified: (1) rituals that are a part of the daily routine such as at mealtimes and bedtime and during evening and weekend activities; (2) family traditions such as birthdays, anniversaries, and annual vacations; (3) celebrations such as those during religious holidays, national holidays, and New Years Eve; and (4) life cycle rituals such as births, retirements, weddings, and funerals (Imber-Black, Roberts, & Whiting, 1988; Rolland, 1994; Wolin & Bennett, 1984).

The assessment of family rituals can provide a window into family identity and stability and can be used to assess adaptation to chronic illness (Rolland, 1994). During the earlier phases of the clinical course of cancer, family rituals can be discontinued or interrupted due to the demands of the illness (Rolland, 1994). The long-term survivorship phase provides an opportunity for the family to resume, modify, or to create new rituals in order to maintain and convey family identity and shared beliefs (Rolland, 1994). When family rituals are not resumed, this could be an indication of family grief, fear for the future, or an inability to modify existing rituals to include the realities of the illness. Families that are able to transition easily into the long-term survival phase of cancer are able to incorporate new rituals into their lives and to begin to celebrate past family rituals that may have been pushed aside during the previous phases of the illness (e.g., an anniversary that was overlooked during treatment, or a family vacation that was postponed during rehabilitation). Since a serious illness can shatter the illusions of "infinite time together" (Rolland, 1994, p. 160), the emotional climate may be heightened during times of family tradition and celebration. Family members may now share a recognition that each family gathering may be the last. This awareness may be used to create positive change in family system communication, levels of family cohesiveness, and overall family functioning (Rolland, 1994).

Patients as Cancer Survivors

For survivors, the nonmedical effects of cancer and its treatment have been organized into three primary categories: (1) overall psychosocial effects, (2) economic and legal aspects, and (3) existential issues. Thus, in addition to treating the medical needs of cancer survivors, a follow-up regimen should be established to see that the psychosocial, legal, and existential concerns of cancer survivors are addressed.

Psychosocial Effects.   The overall psychosocial effects of survivorship include fear of recurrence, an increased sense of vulnerability and anxiety, changes in body image, inconsistent perceptions regarding the health of the survivor between the patient and the family, and social stigma (Leigh, 1992). Fear of recurrence is highly prevalent among cancer survivors, ranging from about 40% to 90% (Kornblith, 1998; Polinsky, 1994). This fear has been shown to be a correlate of psychological distress and overall adjustment and thus can serve as an indicator of overall survivor adaptation (Kornblith, 1998). Closely associated with fear of recurrence is an increase in a sense of vulnerability and anxiety coupled with a decreased sense of survival time. Psychosocial interventions with cancer survivors have been shown to facilitate emotional and functional adjustment and to have beneficial effects on disease- or treatment-related symptoms and even medical status (Kornblith, 1998). While psychosocial treatment has been demonstrated to have a significant effect on increased survival time for breast cancer patients (Spiegel, Bloom, Kraemer, & Gottheil, 1989), the effect of psychosocial interventions on survival time is still unclear (Fawzy, Fawzy, Hyun, Elashoff, Guthrie, Fahey, & Morton, 1993; Kornblith, 1998; Spiegel, 1992). However, there are several socioeconomic correlates of length of survival now noted in the literature, such as high socioeconomic status, private heath insurance, and involvement in social networks (Cwikel, Behar, & Zabora, 1997).

Psychosocial effects of survivorship also include changes in body image, differences in perceptions of the illness between the patient and the family, and social stigma (Leigh,

1992). For example, most studies on body image have focused on women with breast cancer and have shown that by 18 months posttreatment, women who have had breast-conserving surgery coupled with radiation therapy have a better body image and better sexual functioning than women who had mastectomies (Kornblith, 1998). However, psychological distress, fear of recurrence, and overall psychosocial adaptation remain equivalent for both groups of women (Kornblith, 1998). Adaptation of head and neck cancer survivors is more likely to be associated with physical dysfunctions such as difficulties with swallowing and eating than with facial disfigurement and thus body image (Baker, 1992; Kornblith, 1998). These long-lasting emotional and physical difficulties often remain a focal point for cancer survivors, long after their families have emotionally "moved on" (Rolland, 1994). As a result, wide differences in the perceptions of the illness can occur between the patient and the other family members. During this phase patients may feel isolated from their families and may be unable to meet the high emotional and functional expectations of family members, friends, and society (Harpham, 1994). This sense of distress may be exacerbated if augmented by social stigma, difficulties with employment, and economic problems.

Economic and Legal Concerns.   The economic and legal aspects of cancer survival involve job discrimination, insurance problems, and financial repercussions of having had a serious illness (Kornblith, 1998; Leigh, 1992). Myths such as (1) cancer is a death sentence, (2) productivity of cancer patients is low due to their continued illness, and (3) cancer is contagious are still prevalent in some work areas and could lead to job discrimination and difficulties for cancer survivors (Hoffman, 1989). A small subset of cancer survivors (2% to 6%) have reportedly experienced gross job discrimination such as being encouraged to quit their jobs, being transferred to less desirable jobs, and being denied deserved promotions (Kornblith, 1998). Cancer survivors searching for work have also experienced job discrimination such as not being offered a job and having difficulty finding a job due to their medical history (Hoffman, 1991; Kornblith, 1998). Some cancer survivors (38% to 45%) have reported experiencing hostile actions at the workplace (Feldman, 1989). Job discrimination in the workplace is illegal. Survivors are protected in federally funded workplaces through the Federal Rehabilitation Act of 1973 (Leigh, 1992). Survivors not working in a federally funded workplace are protected under the Americans with Disabilities Act (ADA) of 1990 (Leigh, 1992) or by state laws that prohibit cancer-related employment discrimination (Kornblith, 1998; Leigh, 1992).

Insurance Concerns.   Cancer survivors can also face insurance problems, which range from undergoing extended waiting periods for reimbursement to being denied insurance coverage (Leigh, 1992). After receiving treatment for a serious illness such as cancer, families can also experience increases in life and health insurance premiums, difficulties in moving from a group plan to individual coverage, and difficulties in supplementing inadequate insurance copayments (Kornblith, 1998). Further, at least 10% of cancer survivors have no insurance and can suffer financial devastation due to the illness and its treatment (Feldman, 1978). Legal protection for survivors experiencing insurance difficulties includes Consolidated Omnibus Budget Reconciliation Act (COBRA) of 1986, which rules that group coverage must be given to employees and their dependents if the employee loses the job or needs to work fewer hours (Leigh, 1992). The Employee Retirement and Income Security Act of 1974 (ERISA) also protects survivors who are denied full participation in employment benefit plans (Kornblith, 1998).

The economic effects of cancer can have lasting impact on survivors, effecting quality of life, psychosocial adjustment, and decision making regarding possible future medical treatment. The financial and psychosocial needs of cancer survivors are recognized by the American Cancer Society's "Cancer Survivors' Bill of Rights," which states that survivors are entitled to (1) the right to lifelong medical care, (2) the right to the pursuit of happiness, (3) the right to equal job opportunities, and (4) the right to receive adequate health care insurance (see Leigh, 1992, and Silverberg & Lubera, 1988; for details regarding "The Cancer Survivors' Bill of Rights").

Spiritual and Existential Concerns.   The spiritual and existential issues of survivorship include changes in life priorities and values, a deepening of meaning and sense of spirituality, and an increased passion for life (Leigh, 1992). Human beings have the impressive quality of transforming tragic events, such as cancer, into positive life-altering events that can result in better psychological functioning, improved emotional status, and renewed spiritual or religious strength (Kornblith, 1998; O'Connor & Wicker, 1995; Polinsky, 1994). With regard to psychological functioning, survivors often report that the experience of cancer changed their values, priorities, and overall approach to life (Belec, 1992). Many survivors have reported that they have been given a "second chance" on life (Kornblith, 1998). This second chance often affords survivors an opportunity to reassess priorities and to discover deeper meaning in their lives. Life is viewed as more precious, and thus cancer survivors will often report a greater appreciation for life (Cella & Tross, 1986). O'Connor and Wicker (1995) have suggested some specific questions that may help survivors clarify their thoughts and attitudes toward newly found meaning in life: "What helps you to live with the cancer (or having had cancer)? What is important in your life? What gives your life value and what gives you hope?" (p. 69).

Along with increased psychological functioning, survivors also note improved emotional states (Kornblith, 1998) and renewed spiritual faith (O'Connor & Wicker, 1995). Specifically, survivors will often express a more positive outlook for the future coupled with a diminished fear of death (Kornblith, 1998). Keith (1991) has offered some useful questions to help survivors to assess personal meaning and to create a sense of balance in their lives:

> Physically. Am I taking care of myself, eating well, and exercising to manage stress? Am I attuned to my body?

> Emotionally. Am I aware of and expressing my feelings? Am I in touch with my emotions?

> Intellectually. Is my mind stimulated, productive, challenged? Am I reading, thinking, or am I slipping into workaholic patterns?

> Socially. Am I having fun, playing? Have I laughed or made someone laugh today? Are my relationships strong? Do I have time for non-work related activities?

> Spiritually. Is my internal balance intact? Do I have precious moments of inner peace? Am I remembering to view my life as a gift? (p. 114)

Cancer survivors may also desire to give to other patients by participating in support groups or by volunteering their time to be of service to newly diagnosed patients (O'Connor & Wicker, 1995). By sharing their stories and by providing support to other cancer patients, survivors can instill hope in others while adding purpose and meaning to their own lives (O'Connor & Wicker, 1995).

Families of Cancer Survivors

While most families (74%) report high satisfaction with family functioning and the strengthening of family bonds during survivorship (Kornblith, 1998), children and spouses of survivors may report very different interpretations of the cancer experience (O'Connor &

Wicker, 1995). In some instances, families of survivors may wish to "move on with their lives" and put all thoughts of cancer from their minds completely (Sherman & Simonton, 1999). Conversely, their brush with serious illness and possible death of a loved one may leave them in a state of limbo, unable to plan for the future or to regain developmental momentum (Halvorson-Boyd & Hunter, 1995; Sherman & Simonton, 1999). In the first case, survivors and other family members may grow distant from each other, each having very different needs. The survivor may still need time to physically and emotionally adjust, and the family may need to begin to focus on daily functioning and planning for the future. In the second case, families can remain focused on the illness, with anniversary dates (i.e., date of diagnosis) acting as intense reminders of a traumatic experience (Harpham, 1994; Rolland, 1994). The importance of rituals can come into play during such anniversary dates. For example, families can make special plans by either distracting themselves from distressing memories on specific days or by celebrating happier occasions such as the anniversary date of treatment completion or newly created family traditions (Harpham, 1994).

Most studies also show that married couples who have had cancer usually remain married and oftentimes are even strengthened by the experience (Kornblith, 1998). Only a minority of couples have been shown to separate or divorce as a result of cancer (Kornblith, 1998). However, subtle differences have been noted to occur in a few marriages (11% to 28%) that have survived cancer. For example, survivors and their spouses have reported difficulties with communication regarding their fears and plans for the future, receiving needed emotional support, and maintaining sexual functioning (Kornblith, 1998).

Clinical Recommendations for Working with Cancer Survivors

Although the optimal time for intervention regarding survivorship is still unclear, it appears that psychosocial interventions are best applied early during the clinical course of cancer, such as during treatment or soon after treatment completion (Fawzy, Fawzy, Arndt, & Pasnau, 1995). In a comprehensive overview of the psychosocial adaptation of cancer survivors, Kornblith (1998) provides several clinical recommendations when working with families during the survivorship phase. First, psychosocial programs addressing the needs of cancer survivors should be comprehensive and include an educational component and either individual or group counseling opportunities. Sensitive areas of concern such as sexual functioning and financial ramifications of the illness should be addressed given the prevalence of infertility and body disfigurement associated with cancer and cancer treatment (Kornblith, 1998). Second, psychosocial morbidity factors such as extent of the disease, type of treatment, posttreatment health problems, unavailable medical treatment for health problems, and premorbid personality variables can be used to identify which survivors need to be targeted for intervention during the survival phase (Anderson, 1994). Patients who have psychosocial morbidity symptoms can be identified by the health care team and referred for appropriate mental health treatment (Kornblith, 1998). Continued mental health treatment during the survivorship phase can help to decrease psychosocial distress and anxiety and to reduce emotional and social isolation (Cwikel et al., 1997; Kornblith, 1998).

☐ The Six Family Life Cycles during Survivorship: The Importance of Rituals

Cancer can impact the family system well beyond the five-year survival period. For many families, the diagnosis, treatment, and rehabilitation phases of the clinical course of cancer mark a rite of passage into a new world where the family system is forever changed. Rituals can be used to help the family as they transition from the rehabilitation phase to survivorship. Rather than specific behavioral tasks, rituals are special tasks that are designed to address the cognitive and affective levels of family functioning (Imber-Black, 1993). In general, rituals should be tailored to fit the family's special structure, circumstances, and needs. Further, rituals in family therapy should rely on the symbolic actions that can result in a multiplicity of meanings (Imber-Black, 1993). Rituals can be used to celebrate milestones along the way, such as the date of treatment completion, or the date of good news regarding treatment outcome. New rituals can be created to celebrate the deepening of familial bonds and to recognize important anniversary dates. Although the experience of cancer is fraught with fear, anxiety, anger, and depression, it can also bring positive changes to the family system. Often, families in every life cycle report having an increased appreciation for life and relationships. The threat of cancer also shatters the illusions of infinite time and can act as a catalyst for revitalizing relationships and re-creating healthier family systems (Rolland, 1994). Thus, the survival phase can be a time of deepening family bonds and reveling in the gift of life. The effects of cancer survival on the family life cycle are organized in Table 5.1.

☐ The Single Young Adult during Survivorship

The single young adult who has survived cancer has gone through a rite of passage where death has been faced and life has become more precious. Since cancer is relatively rare in young adults (compared with the incidence of cancer in later life), the young adult may either feel damaged in preparation for subsequent life cycles or strengthened and ready to make the best of the life cycles ahead. Regardless of these feelings, the young adult's life will be forever altered by the experience of cancer. Decisions regarding the formation of intimate relationships, career, and future children will be difficult to make without taking into consideration the impact of cancer. Thus, cancer and its treatment will be woven into each subsequent life cycle the young adult encounters. The use of rituals can help to clarify the effects of the illness and thus help the young adult to make well-informed decisions during each life cycle stage.

CASE EXAMPLE 1 (Continued).
Mark's Long-Term Survival Concerns

Mark and his girlfriend, Marie, came in for a follow-up consultation almost one year following his surgery. Mark began the session by discussing his personal journey in adapting to cancer during the last year. He related, "I remember when I was first diagnosed. I was scared to death. I thought, 'Oh my, they are going to cut everything off and I am either going to die or live my life castrated!' Then I realized that I was not going to die and that I was only going to have one testicle removed. I guess compared with what I originally thought, that wasn't so bad! I did feel like I was a little boy again though, when I decided to move back home." Mark remembered that after his surgery he tried to play sports right away: "I wanted to show everyone that I was still tough, that I was still a man." Like Mark, males with testicular cancer are usually able to resume normal activities soon after cancer treatment. This early return to work and leisure activities promotes independence and helps them to return to a more masculine role, rather than remaining in the role of the "dependent patient." Mark commented on how returning to school and to his sports activities helped him to feel like his "old self again."

Mark also revealed that, in some ways, having testicular cancer made him feel more masculine than he had felt prior to his illness: "Before I got cancer, I was following in my brother's footsteps, just doing what he had always done and making sure my family always approved of me. When I got cancer, I decided that I was going to 'tough it out' and make it through the surgery and losing a testicle. I feel as if I faced death and castration and have become stronger because of it. I have since changed the course of my life and have become my own man, so to speak." Mark went on to say that for a while, he attempted to downplay the illness and the ramifications of treatment. He wanted to "be a man and just deal with it, move on, and get on with his life." Marie commented, "When he was denying the impact of the illness, he was difficult to talk to. He kept things all bottled up inside and I felt like I had to do all the talking and crying for him." Mark soon decided to examine the effect the illness and its treatment were having on his relationships with others. He said, "I don't feel less masculine or less in charge of my life, but I do feel more connected to others now. I guess I have learned that relationships are the most important things in life. Too, I can understand other people's pain better now that I have suffered a bit. I am thinking about becoming a Big Brother and helping other people." Marie remarked, "Our relationship has changed. I used to be the one who was always emotional and giving in our relationship. Now Mark seems more compassionate and caring. He has softened a little and at the same time has become more mature and independent from his family."

Marie and Mark decided upon a ritual to recognize the importance of the date of Mark's surgery. He said, "It will be the one year anniversary of my surgery in a couple of weeks. I know that this was a big day for me. I used to think the surgery would be the day my masculinity would be taken from me—now I know the opposite is true. It is the day I became my own person, the day I began thinking for myself, planning my own life, and becoming independent from my brother's influence and from my family's expectations. I still love them, but I know now that I must live my own life. To celebrate that day, Marie and I decided it had to have two components. The first is to celebrate my masculinity. To do this, I am planning on playing ball with the guys for a couple of hours. Then, I want to celebrate my new appreciation for relationships and intimacy. Marie and I are going to go to a nice dinner and celebrate all that we have gone through together. It may not be much, but we both want to recognize the impact that testicular cancer has had on our lives."

☐ The Newly Forming Couple during Survivorship

During the survival phase, the newly forming couple can return to the tasks of creating their new family, which encompasses the many dimensions of the dyadic relationship, including (1) economic concerns, (2) emotional connections, (3) power arrangements, (4) boundaries of the couple in relation to all external systems, (5) sexuality and intimacy, (6) views on childrearing, and (7) chores and leisure activities (Almeida, Woods, Messineo, & Font, 1998). Each of these dimensions will be affected by the experience of cancer and must be renegotiated during the survival phase. Economically, the newly forming couple may have become financially devastated due to the high costs of treatment, insurance premiums, or insurance deductibles. The new couple may need to rely on families of origin or others to help with their unexpected bills. Plans for buying their own home, having children, or other important life goals may need to be put on hold until well into the survival phase of the illness.

The couple may also have difficulties negotiating the emotional dimension of their new

(*text continued on page 164*)

TABLE 5.1. The Survival Phase and the Family Life Cycle: The Importance of Ritual while under the "Sword of Damocles"

	Life cycle tasks	Cancer's potential disruption to the system	Psychosocial interventions	Specific topics of communication
Single young adult	Forming intimate peer relationships; differentiating from the family of origin	Disruption can take place if developmental tasks are not resumed; disruption can take place if illness is not integrated into plans for future life cycles	Help to integrate illness into future plans; help to formulate rituals that commemorate the impact of the illness	Discuss how cancer affected all aspects of life; how cancer has affected plans for the future; address fears of recurrence
Newly forming couple	Negotiating economic issues and emotional connections; negotiating balance of power and levels of intimacy	Disruptions to communication, power arrangements, and boundaries; skews in recovery needs between patient and family may occur	Help to reestablish healthy boundaries between systems; help to transform system with new goals, plans, and dreams for future family structure	Discuss recovery skews; discuss physical, emotional, and psychosocial recovery needs for both patient and family members
Families with young children	Integrating new roles and subsystems into the multigenerational life cycle; nurturing young children	Family may have differing recovery times and needs; children may not adapt well, particularly if parents are experiencing grief, loss, and difficulty integrating the illness into a transformed system	Help family to grieve losses such as infertility, loss of energy, loss of assumptive world, and loss of dreams and plans; help family to transform system with new rules, roles, and dreams for future family functioning	Discuss boundary setting; discuss losses and grief; discuss impact of illness on all family members; discuss needs of all members; discuss ways to successfully integrate the illness into the family system

Families with adolescents	Loosening boundaries to allow for development of adolescents; allowing influence of external input	Disruption may occur to family development; disease may become embedded if family rules and roles do not remain flexible	Help family to identify rituals that were overlooked during previous phases of the illness; help family to create new rituals that address the changes in the family's system	Discuss the impact of the illness on each family member; discuss new rules, roles, and boundaries for the continuation of healthy adolescent development
Families launching children	Allowing for multiple exits and entries; renegotiating structure of the marital dyad	Long-lasing effects of cancer can impede launching of children; disease can become triangulated with the partners in the marital dyad	Help to set limits on the lasting effects of the illness; help marital dyad to address the new structure of the marriage	Discuss lingering effects of the illness; address skews in relationships that may be a lasting result of the illness; discuss the needs of marital subsystem
Families in later life	Preparing for retirement; adjusting to loss; reviewing life in multi-generational context	Long-lasting effects of cancer may bring about changes in living arrangements; older adults may need to leave their homes; single older adults may have fewer resources	Help adults in later life determine their future health needs and their available resources; help older adults to make life-style changes if necessary	Discuss available resources and the lasting effects cancer has had on the system in later life: discuss effects of necessary life-style changes

relationship. Communication, intimacy, interdependency and other aspects of the emotional dimension may have become more difficult to navigate due to the emotional complexities of cancer. In addition, power arrangements for the couple may have become skewed during prior phases of the illness, particularly since one partner was pushed into the "dependent patient role," and the other needed to become the "strong caretaker." During the survivorship phase, these roles and power arrangements should be renegotiated in order to prevent the illness from remaining central to the couples' relationship. Boundaries and limits must therefore be set on the illness, as well as on families of origin, friends, work, and other external connections. During the survivorship phase, these boundaries may need to be reassessed. Caring family and friends that were once let into the core of the system during prior phases may need to have new limits set on their involvement in the couple's system. New boundaries can help to solidify the newly forming couple's relationship and need for privacy and intimacy during the survivorship phase. Within these new boundaries, the couple can once again renegotiate their chores and leisure activities. During this phase, the couple may need to reallocate the activities associated with home care, work, food and meal preparation, and priorities regarding vacations and leisure time. Finally, the couple may need to reassess their shared views on sexual intimacy, childbearing, and child rearing. The cancer experience may have greatly altered the couple's previously shared views, plans, and goals in these important areas.

CASE EXAMPLE 2 (Continued).
Brenda's Long-Term Survival Concerns

During the initial months after Brenda's rehabilitation, she was able to address personal areas of concern such as body image, depression, and anxiety, which were ramifications of cancer and its treatment. Brenda and Bob began to attended couples counseling to address their current level of intimacy and sexual difficulties. Bob began, "In some ways the illness has changed our relationship for the better. Now I know that I am accepted as a part of the family. We have all weathered a pretty rough storm together. Brenda and I can talk about anything and I feel as if my opinion matters. Even her brothers and I are getting along better. Still, I feel like Brenda and I can be closer, especially sexually. Her surgery and chemotherapy treatments left her pretty depressed for a while. But now she seems much better, happier, and more like herself. We're ready to move on to the next phase of recovery and get some help with our sex life."

Before beginning sex therapy, Brenda and Bob decided to use a ritual to help them adjust to the changes cancer brought about in their lives. Brenda wanted to recognize the loss of their plans and dreams as well as to celebrate the preciousness of life and new beginnings. Brenda and Bob decided to plant a small, circular-shaped garden signifying the continuity of life and death. In their garden they planted spring bulbs of tulips and daffodils. Brenda and Bob wanted to witness the rebirth of the flowers each spring in order to gain a sense of life, beauty, and hope for the future. Each spring, Brenda and Bob wanted to plant a different type of flower to represent the unexpected changes that life brings. The ritual of planting the flower bed helped Brenda to feel understood by Bob. Thus, the ritual helped them to reduce any differences in their recovery time frames. After addressing her emotional needs, Brenda and Bob were ready to attend their first sex therapy session.

Using the ALARM method, the therapist assessed Brenda and Bob's current level of sexual functioning (Anderson & Lamb, 1995). First, Brenda and Bob's prior sexual activity was examined. Prior to the illness, Brenda and Bob were engaging in sexual activity an average of two times a week. Brenda commented, "But after I was diagnosed, all our sexual activity seemed to come to a complete halt. I just couldn't handle it, emotionally or physically." Brenda's personal interpretation of her libido was also assessed. Brenda said that prior to the illness she had "good libido," and actively desired sexual activity with Bob: "I was very interested in sex and in Bob as my partner. I also equated sex with becoming a mother, with having children, and with becoming a family. That seems as if it all has been taken away now. I no longer get aroused during sexual activity either. I guess I believe that sex will make the cancer come back. I don't know . . . that maybe sex will mess with my hormones and cause the cancer to come back. . . . It's kind of silly, I know. I just feel kind of dead inside. The chemotherapy made it difficult for me to get aroused, and now I just don't know how to relax." Brenda's feelings during the resolution phase or the final phase of sexual activity was assessed. Brenda stated that she did not feel a release of tension during the resolution phase of their sexual activity: "In fact, I feel more tense, more stressed, and like I am a failure. I am fortunate that I do not experience any pain, but I just get mad and depressed because I am not a good wife." The last segment of the ALARM assessment procedure entailed a recap of Brenda's medical history. Brenda reported that she has recovered from breast cancer and regards herself as a "survivor." She has regained almost full functioning to her arm, and she reports minimal change to her breast where the lumpectomy was performed.

Brenda was experiencing hypoactive sexual desire disorder in combination with difficulties with sexual arousal due to a precipitating medical condition. Brenda and Bob participated in behavioral sex therapy and set the following goals (Kelly, 1995): (1) to gain a sense of permission to value sexuality, (2) to make sexual activity a priority, (3) to eliminate barriers to a full sexual response, (4) to reduce performance pressures, and (5) to use specific sexual exercises to increase sexual enjoyment. Brenda was having difficulty giving herself permission to enjoy sexual activity again. She was equating sex with becoming a mother and having a family. Since this important aspect of sexual activity had been disrupted for Brenda, it was difficult for her to focus on creating an intimate, physical bond with her husband: "I was always taught that sex was for having children. Now that we are pretty sure we are going to adopt children instead of having our own, I guess I must believe that I shouldn't have sex." Brenda and Bob also noted that they had not made sex a priority during the treatment and rehabilitation phases of the illness. Bob commented, "We were focused on getting Brenda well. I wanted to make sure that she got through her chemotherapy and did her rehabilitation exercises. We just didn't make sex a priority then." By helping Brenda to reduce her depression and anxiety, and by giving herself permission to enjoy sex with her husband, some of the barriers to sexual enjoyment were eliminated. Further, they were going to set aside several times each week to make sex a priority. This way, there was more flexibility and less pressure to "perform" at any one time. Physiological barriers were also assessed. Brenda reported being unable to become aroused easily, and she believed this was in part due to the chemotherapy treatments. The use of special lubricants and sexual positioning to increase Brenda's ability to become sexually aroused was discussed.

Last, Brenda and Bob decided to reduce all performance pressures and to use specific exercises that would help them to increase sexual enjoyment. By using the phases of "sensate focus" exercises, Brenda and Bob were able to (1) use nonsexual massage in order to become relaxed and intimate, (2) provide sexual pleasure without the pressure to respond with arousal, and (3) learn more about how to communicate physically in order to direct each other toward effective stimulation (Kelly, 1995; Wincze & Carey, 1991). By working through both emotional and physical barriers, Brenda and Bob were able to increase their level of physical intimacy during the survivorship phase of the illness.

☐ The Family with Young Children during Survivorship

The survival phase can bring about difficulties for multigenerational family functioning, particularly when there are children in the home. The patient may worry about "passing on" cancer to his or her children, and thus issues of genetic testing and increased risk are often of concern during this phase. Once the demands of the diagnosis and treatment phases have passed, the lasting effects of the disease on the system can be addressed. For example, patients and their families may worry about cancer recurrence. Fears and worries can reverberate through the family system, causing young children to become fearful for their safety and the safety of their family. Living under the "sword of Damocles" is particularly difficult for young families who may also worry about the care of their children should cancer recur.

Conversely, for patients and their young families the survival phase can also be a time of great joy and deepened appreciation. The use of rituals can help to symbolize the transformation the family system has undergone and crystallize the new family structure. Birthdays, holidays, graduations, and other celebratory occasions that may have been bypassed during prior phases of the illness can now be enjoyed. In addition, new rituals can be created to recognize positive changes in the family system.

CASE EXAMPLE 3 (Continued).
Sally's Long-Term Survival Concerns

Sally and her family were able to adapt during the rehabilitation phase by first addressing Sally's depression, anxiety, and fatigue. Sally and Sam were also able to work through their sexual difficulties with a trained sex therapist. Sally reported that, since she was beginning to adapt better to the long-term ramifications of the illness, her children were doing better also. They began to place limits on the illness and to create boundaries between the family's subsystems. Sally's mother still was able to visit, but now she came over as "Grandma," and not as "caregiver-surrogate mother." Sally commented on her continued sense of loss: "Even Sara seems kind of sad still about not having a new baby in the home." It was recommended that the family decide upon a ritual that would address the sense of loss still being felt by Sally and Sara.

Sally and Sara both wanted to talk about their sadness over Sally's infertility. Sally stated, "I am sad because I can't care for more children. I can't give to them, help them grow, see them develop and mature." Sara stated, "I like to be a big sister to babies that need me." Sally and Sara were assigned the ritual called "the giving of gifts" (Imber-Black, 1993). For this ritual, Sally and Sara were to think of special gifts that they could give to the family or to friends as tokens of both their sense of loss and their appreciation for the family they do have. Rather than being bought, the gifts were either to be made or found within the home. Thus, Sara and Sally were to be creative in the gifts they chose. In turn, the creativity would serve to heighten the symbolism behind their giving.

The following week the entire family returned to discuss the ritual Sally and Sara had implemented. The whole family was smiling as Sally pulled out a large bag and began to hurriedly recant the events of the past week: "At first we just couldn't think of what to give and who to give to! It was so fun just talking to Sara about ideas of giving. It really made her feel included and grown up. We are closer now than we have been in a long time. She got a real kick out of thinking about gifts and the giving process." Sara chimed in, "I thought that we could color pictures together and put them on the wall, but Mommy came up with a better idea!" Sally and Sara had decided to make baby Afghans to give to the sick children at the community hospital. "I love to crotchet and I decided to put all the love I have for children into small, baby-sized Afghans. Look at them!" Sally pulled out three small Afghans from the large bag. Sara's face was beaming. "Mommy is going to let me go to the hospital with her when she gets some more of them done. And, I can help put the fringe on all of them too!" Sally and Sara decided to make the gifts for children diagnosed with cancer. "It will be my way of giving something to the children who are suffering. I can use my grief to create something precious for a child in need."

Through the use of rituals, Sally and her family were able to transform their grief into something positive. The process of thinking about and planning the ritual had many lasting effects on the family system. Sally and Sara were able to bond once again as mother and daughter. Sally described the Afghans as being something symbolic in themselves. "They represent my love and need to nurture children. The kids can wrap up in them and know that someone cares about how they are feeling, physically and emotionally." The ritual helped to channel Sally's grief and to transform her ideas of motherhood. Sally finished, "Now I know that I can give to children no matter what my life's circumstances are. There are countless ways one can be a mother, and there are countless children in need of special mothering."

☐ The Family with Adolescents during Survivorship

For families with adolescents, the survival phase is a time of renegotiating rules and roles and loosening external boundaries to allow for adolescent growth. Developmental tasks can be resumed during this phase. Thus, it is important to consider the ways in which cancer has affected the family system. For example, have the demands of the disease interrupted normal adolescent development? Are there any long-lasting effects that impede the family from regaining developmental momentum, resuming daily routines, or celebrating anniversaries, birthdays, and holidays with the usual rituals? Are any family members experiencing debilitating fears about cancer recurrence that may be keeping them from their developmental tasks? Is the experience of cancer preventing the family from creating healthy boundaries? In sum, the family with adolescents can begin again to address the developmental needs of the family system and to move forward in both the clinical course of cancer and the family life cycle.

CASE EXAMPLE 4 (Continued).
Frank's Long-Term Survival Concerns

Frank and his family attended a follow-up family therapy session one year after treatment completion. Frank began the session, "I just saw the oncologist and everything looks fine. Anne and I were both nervous about going to see the doctor today. We were kind of scared that something might be wrong again. It seems as if the fear of cancer will never go away. I mean when is it safe to say, 'I had cancer' rather than 'I have cancer'? Still, the doctor was reassuring today and I don't have to come back for awhile." Anne and the children also reported their fears. Anne stated, "I guess we are all just beginning to realize how much Hodgkin's disease affected us all. There were so many ups and downs and challenges to go through. At first, we all pulled together as a family. It was as if the diagnosis just pulled us together for awhile. Then during Frank's treatment everything seemed out of balance. Frank Jr. had to carry so much of the responsibility of the family business. It really took its toll on him. I guess he became the 'man' of the family during Frank's treatment." Frank Jr. commented, "Yeah, that was a really difficult time for me. I felt like I had to grow up really fast and I was mad about that. There were so many things I missed out on. I had to leave the team for awhile, and my birthday was pretty rotten too. Remember that? I had to work at the shop after school. It seemed like no one really cared about my birthday or anything." Alexis added, "Christmas was kind of different too. Dad was still so tired and we didn't have much money because of the cost of doctor bills and everything. We all missed out on a lot last year." The family discussed the losses of the past year and decided to plan a new ritual that would help to make up for lost family celebrations. In keeping with the assigning of rituals, the family was encouraged to make the ritual a meaningful one. It was suggested that the new ritual include the unique contributions of each family member.

The family came in the following week to share their new family ritual. Frank began the session, "First, I wanted to do something special for Frank Jr. since he helped out so much during the long haul of treatment. Frank, I was going to give this to you when you graduated from college, but it seems that you have successfully 'graduated' from something even more important. You were there for the family when we needed you the most. Your mother and I will never forget that. Too, we missed your birthday and now I want to say, 'Happy birthday, son.' I am truly glad you were born. I want to give you your grandfather's watch and to tell you to always remember to take time for your family and for yourself. You are a remarkable young man and your grandfather would be proud of you." Frank Jr. stood to receive the watch and he hugged his father in appreciation.

Anne began to discuss their family's plans for a new holiday ritual. "We talked last week about how bad Christmas was last year too. We wanted to do something special that would help us to come together as a family and to celebrate a cherished ritual that was missed during Frank's cancer treatment and rehabilitation. Even though it is July, we all decided that we would celebrate Christmas. But, instead of giving gifts, we each wanted to make something for the Christmas tree that would be symbolic of our family unity during a time of crisis." Fred was first to present his contribution, "I took a family picture and put it in a frame. We can hang it on the tree this year and remember how we all came together to fight Dad's illness." Alexis added, "I strung beads together to symbolize how we all hung together as a family during a time of need. Each bead is separate and unique, but we are all unified by the 'chain' of the family." Next, Anne shared her contribution, "I made fabric hearts to hang on the tree to signify the love we have for each other. Each is made from some of our old clothes. See, Alexis this is your dress material from when you were still a toddler. Fred, this is your old pajama material from when you were little, and Frank Jr., this is a heart made from the material of your first little league shirt. Frank, this is heart is made from an old shirt I used to love to see you wear, and this last one is from one of my old dresses I used to wear to church all the time." Frank Jr. spoke next: "I have something too. It's not done yet, but I am making a wooden toy train from some of the scrap materials in Dad's shop. We can put it under the tree this year. I guess it symbolizes the hard work and energy it takes to pull a family through a crisis. It also represents a time of going away and returning, just like our family right now." Finally, it was Frank's turn: "I wanted to make something special for all of us to enjoy year after year. After I thought about it a bit, I decided that I would make something from some scrap shop materials too. I decided to make a tree stand for our Christmas tree. It symbolizes the importance of the tree's trunk and its stability in holding our family tree's branches together. It symbolizes strength and the provision of a firm foundation. It is where it receives the water to keep it green and fresh. I will put each of our names on it and I will date it. Each Christmas we'll be reminded of how we all pulled together. We can all remember to be forever grateful for life and for our family."

☐ The Family Launching Children during Survivorship

Families launching their children are already experiencing a multiplicity of shifts in the structure of the family system. The system must remain prepared to accept the many changes occurring as young adults move out of the system and back in again as the need arises. Cancer can have lasting effects as family members renegotiate their roles, rules, and boundaries during this life cycle. For example, the older child who wishes to move out of the home may feel the need to remain at home due to the lasting effects of the illness. Plans for college, moving away from home, starting a new job, and otherwise making a life independent from the family of origin may be more difficult because of the threat of cancer recurrence.

For parents, relationship skews may arise apart from the normal developmental difficulties of renegotiating the structure of the marital dyad while launching children. Specifically, the illness may have become triangulated into the new structure of the marital subsystem (Rolland, 1994). The partners may have negotiated responsibilities that are contingent upon the nature of the illness. For example, the ill partner may have needed deeper, more effective communication during the crisis of the diagnosis phase and the long haul of the treatment phase. However, if deeper communication was based solely on the triangulation of the illness with the marital system, then "surviving" and "getting well" for the patient means losing needed communication. Thus, it remains important that changes for the family launching children occur without the interference of the disease (Rolland, 1994). Limits should be placed on cancer that allow the couple to directly address their changing subsystem. These limits include: (1) refraining from making changes contingent upon the disease, (2) maintaining the perception of cancer as "our problem" rather than as "my problem" or "your problem," and (3) continuing to reevaluate the family system's functional patterns throughout the course of the illness (Rolland, 1994).

CASE EXAMPLE 5 (Continued).
Claire's Long-Term Survival Concerns

Claire came in for a follow-up consultation one year after treatment completion. She said, "Greg didn't feel it was necessary for him to come today. He told me that he knew my checkup would be fine. The doctor did say that I am doing well and I am glad about that. But I am disappointed that Greg did not come with me. For awhile things were going better. We were talking more and he was writing me letters and notes all the time. I felt that we were getting closer than ever before. Now that I have had breast reconstruction and things seem to be going well for me, he has gone back to being his old self." Claire and Greg had allowed cancer to become triangulated in their relationship. As they were renegotiating their marital dyad after the launching of their children, many of their changing roles and rules had been predicated on the demands of the illness. Now that Claire was considered a "survivor," the new rules governing communication no longer applied. She exclaimed, "I wish that we could communicate without the threat of cancer! Now, I guess I have a choice—be sick and need Greg to help me, or get well and lose my new bond with him. Neither one of these alternatives is particularly appealing." Claire was helped to understand how the illness had become triangulated with her relationship with Greg. She was encouraged to begin to take care of her own needs during the survival phase of the illness, while at the same time addressing the needs of the marital dyad. "Physically, I am taking care of myself by participating in the complementary treatments I told you about. I am learning a lot about meditation, diet, and herbs. I have planted my own herb garden so that I can grow some of them myself. It makes me feel as if I have some kind of control over cancer recurrence when I drink my herbal tea and practice my meditation. I know that I feel more at peace with myself and my life since I began those treatments." Claire also reflected on her emotional self-care practices: "Meditation helps, but I guess I feel kind of sad and lonely much of the time. I have my friends to help me, but that is not the same as being close to your husband. I am not really in touch with my emotions where Greg is concerned. It is too sad. It hurts too much to think about. I just want to deny that anything is wrong and just keep our marriage as it is. I mean, it could be worse." Intellectually, Claire was continuing her classes and reported feeling challenged and alive: "I have goals and plans that keep me intellectually stimulated. I should be done with school in a couple short years. I feel productive and motivated to be of service to my community." Socially, Claire remarked that she had made several friends over the course of the year. She reported having new friends from the hospital staff, from school, and from her volunteer job. Claire stated, "Socially things are going great." Last, Claire reported that her spiritual life had changed for the better during this past year: "It's funny, but at first I was really mad at God and the world. Now, I see that cancer has helped me to realize how precious life is. I feel connected to God and life like never before. My meditation time has been really helpful because I have gotten to know God more. I just wish that I could share these new feelings with Greg."

In sum, Claire was successfully adapting to the survivorship phase in many aspects of her life. However, her marital relationship had become triangulated with her illness. Claire was encouraged to continue to care for her personal needs, while at the same time confronting her own emotional distancing from Greg. Her communication needs were to be addressed without making them contingent upon her health—but rather on her needs to be close to her husband. Claire was encouraged to schedule "talk times" with Greg, where they would discuss topics of interest and activities in their day outside of the cancer. When schedules became hectic and "talk times" were not feasible, Claire was encouraged to write her feelings and activities in a journal and share them with her husband. Greg was then encouraged to respond to Claire's journal with his own thoughts and feelings, therefore allowing him to express himself through words. This way, communication in the marriage was restructured by placing cancer outside of the marital system.

At a follow-up session, Claire reported that communication within the marital dyad was getting better: "Katherine is busy planning her trip to Europe and I have had a couple of weeks of vacation from classes. I have used this time off to try and get closer to Greg. He told me he has seen all the positive changes that I am going through. I told him that I want him to join me in those changes. I told him directly that I wanted us to talk more, and to share our lives more. Our marriage isn't perfect, but he is responding to my requests. Still, I have learned that marriage is a two-way street, and I am going fishing with him more often and even writing him more notes now in my journal!"

☐ The Family in Later Life and Survivorship

Like with the other life cycles, cancer can impede the developmental process of the family in later life. Moreover, the long-term effects of cancer in later life can have a distinct rippling effect, as the adult children in the extended family system are usually involved as well. Adult women in the "sandwich generation" can end up taking care of both their own children and their ill parents long into the survival phase, particularly if the illness has become embedded in the family system. Thus, the patient's needs and the needs of the members of the extended family system must be renegotiated during the survival phase.

For married couples in later life, cancer may have served as a catalyst for change. Aging couples faced with a serious illness may decide to move closer to their adult children or to legalize the distribution of their belongings after death. For single older adults, the effects of cancer may be more severe. The single adult in later life may decide to leave a long cherished home for the safety of a nursing home, or may decide to move in with adult children. Thus, the survival phase can bring about many changes that can have long-term ramifications for the entire family system.

CASE EXAMPLE 6 (Continued).
Red's Long-Term Survival Concerns

Red and Rachel were unable to come in for their one-year follow-up counseling session because they had moved out of the state to be near their oldest son and his family. However, Red did write a letter reporting their current health status and how cancer had changed their lives:

> I just wanted to write you a quick note letting you all know how things are going with Rachel and me. I just got back from seeing an oncologist here in Florida. He says I am doing just fine and that I'll probably be around for awhile. So he says to me, "Yeah Red, you can buy green bananas." That just means that I'll be around when they're ready to eat! So both of us were really glad about my health report.
>
> The bad news is Rachel was just diagnosed with breast cancer a few weeks ago. It really hit us hard. She begins her treatments next week. I knew I needed to worry more about her than about myself. She isn't as strong as I am, and her health has never been the best. The cancer has also started to spread to her bones, so I guess that was why she was in so much pain all the time. Right now we need all the help we can get. We're glad we moved out here to be with our oldest son and his wife, but we sure are sad to be away from home and all of our friends and the people we got to know so well during my treatment. Too, it feels as if we are becoming a burden to our son and his family. We are trying to cope with the news as best we can on our own, but our son and daughter-in-law keep wanting to help and I can't say "no" when I need them so much.
>
> I think about losing Rachel all the time. It just doesn't seem fair, working all our lives to enjoy our retirement days together and then we get one blow after another. First my cancer, which is really under control, and now Rachel. But I didn't write to complain. We have a lot of family support down here and we have found a new church we love. With God's guidance we'll get through this like we have all the other difficulties in life. Thanks for all your help.
>
> Keep in touch,
>
> Red

A year later, Red came in to see the treatment team during a brief visit from Florida. He told us that Rachel had died a few months ago. Her death was very sudden and very difficult for him. He reported how he had cared for her during her last few months of life. He said, "I needed this visit. I just wanted to see my old friends and neighbors again and to see the home Rachel and I had lived in and loved for so many years." A few days later, Red returned to Florida and the support of his extended family.

☐ Summary

In this chapter the focus was on the family during the survival phase of the illness. Biomedical information on topics such as remaining informed, using unconventional cancer therapies, and adapting to infertility/impotence were addressed. Psychosocial issues associated with long-term survival were presented, followed by a continuation of the case examples for each of the six family life cycles. A family systems approach toward intervention was emphasized.

The next chapter will explain important biomedical information and psychosocial considerations relevant to the recurrence phase of the illness. This will be followed by further elaboration of some of the previous case examples and an introduction to new families with recurrent cancer.

☐ References

Almeida, R., Woods, R., Messineo, R., & Font, R. (1998). The contextual model. In M. McGoldrick (Ed.), *Revisioning family therapy: Race, gender, and culture in clinical practice*. New York: The Guilford Press.

American Cancer Society (ACS). (1987). *Cancer facts and figures—1987*. New York: Author.

American Cancer Society (ACS). (1999). *Cancer facts and figures—1998*. New York: Author.

Anderson, B. (1994). Surviving cancer. *Cancer, 74*, 1484–1495.

Anderson, B., & Lamb, M. (1995). Sexuality and cancer. In G. Murphy, W. Lawrence, Jr., & R. Lenhard, Jr. (Eds.), *American Cancer Society textbook of clinical oncology* (2nd ed.). Atlanta, GA: American Cancer Society.

Baker, C. (1992). Factors associated with rehabilitation in head and neck cancer. *Cancer Nursing, 15*, 395–400.

Barton Burke, M. (1997). Sexuality, sexual dysfunction, and cancer. In C. Varricchio, M. Pierce, C. Walker, & T. Ades (Eds.), *A cancer source book for nurses* (7th ed.). Atlanta, GA: The American Cancer Society: Jones and Bartlett Publishers.

Belec, R. (1992). Quality of life: Perceptions of long-term survivors of bone marrow transplantation. *Oncology Nursing Forum, 19*(1), 31–37.

Cassileth, B., & Chapman, C. (1996). Alternative and complementary cancer therapies. *Cancer, 15*, 1026–1034.

Cella, D., & Tross, S. (1986). Psychological adjustment to survival from Hodgkin's disease. *Journal of Consulting and Clinical Psychology, 54*, 612–622.

Cwikel, J., Behar, L., & Zabora, J. (1997). Psychosocial factors that affect the survival of adult cancer patients: A review of research. *Journal of Psychosocial Oncology, 15*(3/4), 1–34.

DeVita Jr., V. (1981). The consequences of the chemotherapy of Hodgkin's disease: The 10th David A. Karnofsky Memorial Lecture. *Cancer, 47*, 1–3.

Einhorn, L., Richie, J., & Shipley, W. (1993). Cancer of the testis. In V. DeVita, S. Hellman, & S. Rosenberg (Eds.), *Cancer: Principles and practice of oncology* (4th ed.). Philadelphia, PA: JB Lippincott.

Fawzy, F., Fawzy, N., Arndt, L., & Pasnau, R. (1995). Critical review of psychosocial interventions in cancer care. *Archives of General Psychiatry, 52*, 100–113.

Fawzy, F., Fawzy, N., Hyun, C., Elashoff, R., Guthrie, D., Fahey, J., & Morton, D. (1993). Malignant melanoma: Effects of an early structured psychiatric intervention, coping, and affective state on recurrence and survival 6 years later. *Archives of General Psychiatry, 50*, 681–689.

Feldman, F. (1989). Inquiries into work experiences of recovered cancer patients: The California experience. In I. Barofsky (Ed.), *Work and illness: The cancer patient* (pp. 25–47). New York: Praeger.

Feldman, F. (1978). *Work and cancer health histories: Study of experiences of recovered blue-collar workers*. Oakland, CA: American Cancer Society, California Division.

Ferszt, G., & Waldman, R. (1997). Psychosocial responses to disease and treatment. In C. Varricchio, M. Pierce, C. Walker, & T. Ades (Eds.), *A cancer source book for nurses* (7th ed., pp. 245–252). Atlanta, GA: American Cancer Society.

Gray, R., Greenberg, M., Fitch, M., Parry, N., Douglas, M., & Labrecque, M. (1997). Perspectives of cancer survivors interested in unconventional therapies. *Journal of Psychosocial Oncology, 15*(3/4), 149–171.

Halvorson-Boyd, G., & Hunter, L. (1995). *Dancing in limbo*. San Francisco, CA: Jossey Bass Publishers.

Harpham, W. (1994). *After cancer: A guide to your new life.* New York: W.W. Norton and Company.

Hoffman, B. (1989). Employment discrimination against cancer survivors: Multidisciplinary interventions. *Health Matrix, 7*(1), 2–10.

Hoffman, B. (1991). Employment discrimination: Another hurdle for cancer survivors. *Cancer Investigation, 9*(5), 589–595.

Imber-Black, E. (1993). The giving of gifts—A therapeutic ritual. In T. Nelson & T. Trepper (Eds.), *101 interventions in family therapy* (pp. 120–125). Binghamton, NY: The Haworth Press.

Imber-Black, R., Roberts, J., & Whiting, R. (Eds.). (1988). *Rituals in families and family therapy.* New York: Norton.

Keith, S. (1991). Surviving survivorship: Creating a balance. *Journal of Psychosocial Oncology, 9*(3), 109–115.

Kelly, G. (1995). *Sexuality today: The human perspective* (4th ed.). Guilford, CT: The Dushkin Publishing Group.

Kornblith, A. B. (1998). Psychosocial adaptation of cancer survivors. In J. Holland (Ed.), *Psycho-oncology* (pp. 223–254). New York: Oxford University Press.

Leigh, S. (1992). Cancer survivorship issues. In J. Clark & R. McGee (Eds.), *Core curriculum for oncology nursing* (pp. 257–264). Philadelphia: W.B. Saunders Company.

Lerner, I., & Kennedy, B. (1992). The prevalence of questionable methods of cancer treatment in the United States. *CA-A Journal for Clinicians, 42,* 181–191.

Miaskowsi, C., & Portenoy, R. (1998). Update on the assessment and management of cancer-related fatigue. In A. Berger, B. Portenoy, & D. Weissman (Eds.), *Principles and practice of supportive oncology* (pp. 1–10). Philadelphia: Lippincott–Raven Publishing.

Montbriand, M. (1993). Freedom of choice: An issue concerning alternate therapies by patients with cancer. *Oncology Nursing Forum, 20,* 1195–1201.

National Cancer Institute (NCI). (1995). *Imperative for Quality Cancer Care.* [On-line]. Available: www.cancernet.nci.nih.gov

O'Connor, A., & Wicker, C. (1995). Clinical commentary: Promoting meaning in the lives of cancer survivors. *Seminars in Oncology Nursing, 11*(1), 68–72.

Polinsky, M. (1994). Functional status of long-term breast cancer survivors: Demonstrating chronicity. *Health Social Work, 19,* 165–173.

Rolland, J. S. (1994). *Families, illness, and disability: An integrative treatment model.* New York: Basic Books.

Sherman, A., & Simonton, S. (1999). Family therapy for cancer patients: Clinical issues and interventions. *The Family Journal: Counseling and Therapy for Couples and Families, 7*(1), 39–50.

Silverberg, E., & Lubera, J. (1988). Cancer survivors' bill of rights. *Cancer, 3,* 32.

Spiegel, D. (1992). Effects of psychosocial support on patients with metastatic breast cancer. *Journal of Psychosocial Oncology, 10*(2), 113–120.

Spiegel, D., Bloom, J., Kraemer, H., & Gottheil, E. (1989). Effect of psychosocial treatment on survival of patients with metastatic breast cancer. *The Lancet, October,* 888–891.

Urba, W., & Longo, D. (1992). Hodgkin's disease. *New England Journal of Medicine, 326,* 678–687.

Wincze, J., & Carey, M. (1991). *Sexual dysfunction: A guide for assessment and treatment.* New York: Guilford Press.

Wolin, S., & Bennett, L. (1984). Family rituals. *Family Process, 23,* 401–420.

6

Recurrence/Advanced Disease and the Family Life Cycle: Life in the Balance

While many cancer patients will survive cancer, others will experience relatively brief periods of remission followed by cancer progression, metastasis, or development of a second primary cancer. Still others who have been initially diagnosed with advanced stages of cancer will experience either a controlling of cancer growth and spread or a rapid advancing of the disease. The medical and emotional demands of the recurrent/advanced disease phase are similar to the crisis of the initial diagnosis (Gotay, 1984; Loscalzo & Brintzenhofescoz, 1998), with the centripetal pull of this phase necessitating greater family cohesion. However, unlike during the initial diagnosis phase, medical treatment goals often shift from an attempt to cure the disease to an attempt to merely control the disease or to improve the patient's quality of life (Loscalzo & Brintzenhofescoz, 1998; Schmale, 1976). Cancer treatment can be used to slow the progress of the disease or to provide palliative care. During the recurrent/advancing disease phase, patients and their families often struggle to create a balance between maintaining optimal quality of life and preparing for death and loss.

☐ Medical Variables during the Recurrent Phase

Recurrent, Second Primary, and Metastasis/Advancing Disease

Patients may experience a recurrence of their cancer. Recurrence is the "reappearance of a disease after treatment had caused it to apparently disappear" (Dollinger, Rosenbaum, & Cable, 1997a, p. 768). Recurrent cancer can occur months to years after the initial diagnosis and treatment. Moreover, many cancer survivors are at an increased risk for developing a second primary type of cancer (Harpham, 1994). For example, some courses of radiation treatment and chemotherapies are associated with an increased chance of developing leukemia (Harpham, 1994). Some behaviors also put cancer survivors at an increased risk for developing second cancers. Cancer patients who continue to smoke after being treated for such cancers as the throat, head and neck, and tongue are at a much higher risk for developing a second smoking-related cancer.

Some cancer patients will have tumors that do not respond to treatment. Advancing disease is often characterized by an increase in somatic symptoms such as pain, nausea, anorexia, stomatitis, or skin excoriation (Ferszt & Waldman, 1997). Patients may also suffer from impaired mobility, disfigurement, and loss of energy, which may leave them and their families feeling helpless and, once again, out of control (Ferszt & Waldman, 1997).

During advanced disease, the tumor may continue to grow and to spread (metastasize) throughout the body (Volker, 1992). Cancer can also metastasize or "spread from one part of the body to another by way of the lymph system or bloodstream" (Dollinger et al., 1997a, p. 762). Cancer metastasis is "the ability of transformed cells to relocate from their original populations by direct extension, invasion, and/or establishment of remote sites" (Ellerhorst-Ryan, 1997, p. 31). All primary cancers have a potential for metastasizing, yet some kinds of cancer are more likely than others to spread. In the case of cellular division, tumor cells will travel elsewhere in the body due to changes with the extracellular matrix (American Cancer Society [ACS], 1998). This matrix acts as "tissue cement" that holds the cells that form organs together. When mutations in the cells occur, enzymes can be produced that break down the extracellular matrix and free the cancerous material to travel to distal parts of the body. Cancer metastasis is not a random survival and dissemination of cells, but a selective growth process determined in part by host immune defenses and the number of cells that are released by the primary tumor. For example, a patient with lung cancer may develop a metastasis to the skeleton or liver. There are various ways in which cancer can spread throughout the body. For example, cancer cells can be disseminated by the lymphatic system if the cancerous cells have invaded nearby lymph nodes (Volker, 1992). However, most cancers metastasize via the bloodstream (Volker, 1992). When the tumor does not respond to proven standard medical treatments, clinical trials of new agents or alternative treatments can be explored (Loscalzo & Brintzenhofescoz, 1998).

Inheritability, Predisposition, and Familial Clustering

When the disease advances, fears that other family members may be at an increased risk for developing cancer may arise. Often there is a misunderstanding between inherited cancers, inherited predisposition to cancer, and familial clustering or aggregation. Only about 1% to 2% of all malignant cancers are truly inherited cancers (Ellerhorst-Ryan, 1997). Inherited cancers occur at conception and require that only one parent pass on the defective gene (Ellerhorst-Ryan, 1997). Examples of inherited cancers include retinoblastoma (an intraocular malignancy in children), Wilm's tumor (childhood cancer of the kidney), and familial adenomatous polyposis (FAP), which leads to inherited colorectal cancer (Ellerhorst-Ryan, 1997). While these types of cancers are more likely to be inherited (up to 40% of these types of cancers are due to heredity factors), only about 8% of breast and ovarian cancer cases are truly hereditary in nature (Ellerhorst-Ryan, 1997).

Although only one parent must pass on a defective gene in inherited cancers, both parents must contribute altered genes for an inherited predisposition to occur (Ellerhorst-Ryan, 1992). When both parents pass on altered genes, this can lead to faulty DNA repair, pigmentosa, immune deficiencies, higher incidence of leukemia, non-Hodgkin's lymphoma, and breast, ovarian, stomach, and pancreatic tumors (Ellerhorst-Ryan, 1997).

Last, familial clustering is evidence of a pattern of cancer within the family system. However, with familial clustering the interplay of heredity, diet, and environmental factors is unclear (Ellerhorst-Ryan, 1997). For example, in most families where a pattern of breast cancer has occurred, it is due to familial clustering, and thus to a combination of physiological, environmental, and behavioral components, rather than to exclusively hereditary factors (Ellerhorst-Ryan, 1997).

Palliative Care during the Recurrent Phase

Palliative care has been defined as the "active total care of patients whose disease is not responsive to curative treatment" (World Health Organization [WHO], 1990, p. 804). Palliative care begins with the recognition that, while curative treatment is not a realistic expectation, there are still innumerable ways to enhance quality of life during the advancing of the disease (Pace, 1997). By addressing the multifaceted needs of the patient and the family, palliative care seeks to affirm life and to view dying as a normal process of life, neither hastening nor postponing death (Schachter & Coyle, 1998; WHO, 1990). There are several key elements of palliative care. First, palliative care is best provided by an interdisciplinary team that can help the patient and the family in all areas of functioning such as physical, informational, emotional, social, and spiritual (Schachter & Coyle, 1998). Second, palliative care provides relief from physical signs and symptoms of advanced disease, which include pain, nausea, confusion, constipation, and loss of physical functioning (Pace, 1997; Schachter & Coyle, 1998). In addition, the informational needs of the patient and the family must also be met. The patient and family must (1) understand the patient's physical, emotional, and mental condition and how to participate in daily care; (2) know the truth about the patient's physical condition and realistic prognosis; (3) correct any misconceptions about the disease and its progression, including what signs and symptoms to expect; and (4) be in touch with available resources for continuing care (Pace, 1997). Third, palliative care encompasses the facilitation of emotional, social, and spiritual adaptation during advanced stages of the disease. These include coping with fears of death, managing increased levels of anxiety, dealing with disruptions to familial and social relationships, and questioning the meaning and purpose of life (Pace, 1997; Schachter & Coyle, 1998; WHO, 1990).

Since most patients will be cared for in the home during advanced stages of the disease, families are on the "front lines" of patient care during this phase and must cope with both the emotional demands of the illness as well as the management of physical symptoms (Schachter & Coyle, 1998). Therefore, it is important that the health care team and the family have periodic meetings in which to determine the best plan of care for the patient during this phase of the disease (Schachter & Coyle, 1998; Walsh, 1990). Thus, palliative care also includes the provision of a support system for the family during disease advancement (Schachter & Coyle, 1998).

Depression, Anxiety, and Cognitive Impairment in Advancing Disease

During the advancement of the disease, the interaction between the physical and emotional components of cancer becomes increasingly blurred. As the disease begins to progress, physical symptomatology increases, accompanied by intense emotional responses and oftentimes cognitive impairment (Breitbart & Passik, 1993a). Symptoms of depression, anxiety, and cognitive dysfunction often increase dramatically during advanced stages of the illness (Breitbart & Passik, 1993a). For example, the prevalence of depressive symptoms has been shown to increase from 25% to more than 75% in patients during the advanced stages of cancer (Bukberg, Penman, & Holland, 1984). Moreover, the prevalence of organic mental disorders, such as delirium, has been reported to be as high as 85% in terminally ill patients (Breitbart & Passik, 1993a; Massie, Holland, & Glass, 1983). Fear of death, pain, and suffering, particularly during the advanced stages of the disease, often bring about increased levels of anxiety for both the patient and the family. These psychiatric responses during this phase of cancer are difficult to diagnose and treat due to the intense interaction between the disease, its treatment, and psychosocial responses.

Depression in advanced cancer patients can be a result of several factors, including the disease itself, cancer treatments, uncontrolled pain, and hopelessness (Breitbart & Passik, 1993a). Somatic signs and symptoms generally used to assess for depression (i.e., insomnia, fatigue, change in diet) cannot be relied upon when working with advanced cancer patients since these symptoms are more than likely a result of the disease and its treatment. Rather, the psychological symptoms used in the assessment of depression are of greater value (i.e., the assessment of hopelessness, worthlessness, dysphoric mood, and suicidal ideation; Breitbart & Passik, 1993a; Bukberg et al., 1984). For advanced cancer patients, depression is best managed using a combination of antidepressant medications and psychotherapy (Breitbart & Passik, 1993a).

Anxiety must also be assessed during the recurrent phase of cancer. Although many advanced-stage cancer patients will suffer from some anxiety, it should not be assumed that a high level of anxiety is an inevitable factor in advanced-stage disease (Breitbart & Passik, 1993a). Patients are often fearful of uncontrolled pain, isolation, death, and of the unknown. Anxiety is also difficult to discern due to confounding disease, treatment, and psychosocial variables (Breitbart & Passik, 1993a). Anxiety can therefore be a result of medical complications or due to psychological factors associated with death and dying. When assessing for anxiety and deciding upon treatment, it is best to consider the patient's subjective level of distress (Breitbart & Passik, 1993a) and to examine any medications that may be resulting in increased levels of anxiety and cognitive impairment. High levels of anxiety can be controlled by using a combination of anxiolytic medications in conjunction with psychotherapy and supportive care (Breitbart & Passik, 1993a).

Many advanced-stage cancer patients will experience cognitive dysfunctions such as delirium, dementia, organic mood, and organic anxiety disorders (Breitbart & Passik, 1993a). In one study, more than 75% of advanced-stage patients were diagnosed with delirium (Massie et al., 1983). Once again, cognitive disorders are difficult to diagnose due to the complexity of the interactions between cancer-related variables and its treatment and the psychosocial responses to the illness. Moreover, once a patient has been diagnosed as having a cognitive disorder, it may be difficult to determine the specific type of impairment and its etiology. For example, delirium and dementia are particularly difficult to differentiate due to their shared clinical features of impaired memory, judgment, and disorientation (Breitbart & Passik, 1993a). However, this differentiation can be crucial to the patient's and the family's quality of life, since delirium is characterized as a process that can often be reversed with the reduction or discontinuation of identified medications (Stiefel, Breitbart, & Holland, 1989). The assessment and treatment of delirium is, at best, a complicated process involving an exploration and correction of its underlying causes, which could include direct causes (i.e., primary brain tumors or metastasis to the central nervous system) or indirect causes (i.e., organ failure, electrolyte imbalance, chemotherapeutic agents, steroids, opioids, infections, and nutritional deficiencies; Breitbart & Passik, 1993a; Fleishman & Lesko, 1989). After organic causes have been either ruled out or appropriately treated, other supportive interventions can include (1) a quiet room with familiar objects, (2) a visible clock and calendar, and (3) the presence of familiar family members (Breitbart & Passik, 1993a).

Pain Management during the Recurrent Phase

Pain is one of the most feared consequences of cancer (Breitbart & Passik, 1993b). It has been estimated that more than 70% of cancer patients will experience significant pain at some point during the clinical course of cancer, particularly with the advancing of the disease (Breitbart & Passik, 1993b; Portenoy & Foley, 1989). Moreover, some 25% of cancer patients will die without having received adequate pain relief (Portenoy & Foley, 1989). Levels of pain intensity have been reported to differ according to cancer type. For example, only 5% of leukemia patients report pain during the course of the illness compared with 50% to 75% of patients with lung, colon, and gastrointestinal tract cancer, or 85% of patients with bone or cervical cancer (Portenoy & Foley, 1989).

Pain can be classified as either acute or chronic. Acute cancer-related pain is generally associated with the first symptoms of cancer or the first signs of cancer recurrence (Portenoy & Foley, 1989). In addition, acute pain may be a result of cancer treatment (e.g., postoperative pain), and thus (1) the cause of pain may be readily identifiable, (2) the course of pain may be predictable, and (3) the controllability of pain may be more manageable (Portenoy & Foley, 1989). Chronic pain is often associated with cancer progression. As the disease progresses, the pain may escalate in its intensity (Portenoy & Foley, 1989).

Pain is viewed as a subjective and personal experience consisting of the presence of a noxious stimulus resulting in a somatic (nociception) response in combination with an affective response (i.e., the meaning of the pain, the environmental context, prior experience with pain, and the perception of pain controllability; Breitbart & Passik, 1993b; Breitbart, Passik, & Rosenfeld, 1994). The interplay between the psychological and the physiological aspects of pain is complex. Negative somatic response has been shown to lead to increased emotional distress, anxiety, and depression (Ahles, Blanchard, & Ruckdeschel, 1983). Conversely, high levels of anxiety and the subjective meaning attributed to pain have been reported to increase the perception of physiological pain (Portenoy & Foley, 1989). Thus, pain is regarded as more than a somatic event, but also a multidimensional phenomenon consisting of nociception, perception, and expression (Breitbart & Passik, 1993b).

In the assessment of pain, it is important to address both the physical and the psychosocial components of the patient's unique experience. A multidimensional approach should be used in the assessment of cancer-related pain (Breitbart & Passik, 1993b). Often, the high levels of pain that patients may be experiencing are passed off as psychogenic in nature and are not treated with appropriate pain medication (Breitbart & Passik, 1993b; Portenoy & Foley, 1989). Further, it has been demonstrated that while hospital staff and caregivers are usually in accordance with patients' ratings of pain at low to moderate levels, this concordance does not hold up when patients report higher (7+ on a scale of 0 to 10) levels of pain (Grossman, Sheidler, Sweden, Mucenski, & Piantadosi, 1991). Therefore, it may be that the medical staff and family cannot readily assess, empathize with, and thus help manage pain at higher levels of intensity. Other barriers to proper pain assessment include "1) lack of knowledge of current pharmacological or psychotherapeutic approaches, 2) a focus on prolonging life rather than alleviating suffering, 3) lack of communication between doctor and patient, 4) limited expectations of patients to achieve pain relief, and 5) doctors' fear of amplifying addiction and substance abuse" (Breitbart & Passik, 1993b, p. 246). Cancer-related pain is best managed using a multimodal approach consisting of pharmacological, anesthetic, neurostimulatory, and psychotherapeutic methods (Breitbart & Passik, 1993b).

Since many patients who are experiencing pain also report increased levels of anxiety and depression (Ahles & Martin, 1992), it is important to continue with psychotherapeutic interventions, such as cognitive-behavioral therapies, even after medication for somatic complaints has been prescribed (Breitbart & Passik, 1993b). Some patients who are experiencing pain may be suffering from such high levels of anxiety and depression that their ability to comply with treatment or to function independently is severely compromised (Breitbart, Passik, & Rosenfeld, 1994). Since pain, mood, and behavior are interconnected, it may be necessary to evaluate the patient's psychosocial adaptation and functional capabilities only after successfully managing cancer pain (Breitbart & Passik, 1993b).

☐ Recurrence/Advanced Disease and Psychosocial Considerations: Life in the Balance

Transition: From under the Sword of Damocles to Life in the Balance

Cancer survivors often report fear of recurrence, and yet this phenomenon is discussed relatively little in the psychooncology literature (Germino & O'Rourke, 1996; Sales, 1992). When cancer recurs, the proverbial sword of Damocles has dropped, and the family's fears have become a reality. While death and loss may have been more easily denied during earlier phases of the clinical course of cancer, cancer recurrence and advanced disease brings the family closer to the endpoints of medical knowledge in terms of curative treatment and thus to the reality of terminal illness (Sales, 1992). Because of this, the transition from living under the sword of Damocles to one of living in a state of precarious balance is difficult. Both the patient and the family are faced once again with treatment decision-making options, the availability of clinical trials, and maintaining hope and psychological well-being while living under the direct threat of death and loss.

The recurrent/advanced disease phase brings about a new crisis for the family system, one that is as difficult, if not moreso, to navigate as the initial diagnosis (Chekryn, 1984; Given & Given, 1992). The centripetal force of the crisis pulls the family inward once again to respond to the high demands of the illness (Rolland, 1994). Families that are able to adapt more readily to the recurrence phase are those that have been strengthened during earlier phases of the clinical course of cancer, and thus early intervention may have provided lasting effects on family functioning throughout subsequent phases of the clinical course of cancer (Sales, 1992). Moreover, the recurrent phase is epitomized by the acceptance that expectations regarding curative treatment are usually unrealistic (Loscalzo & Brintzenhofescoz, 1998). Therefore, families must refocus their efforts toward comfort, care, and open communication about sensitive subjects such as death, loss, and the surviving family system without a beloved family member (Loscalzo & Brintzenhofescoz, 1998). If the family remains too rigidly fixed on the search for cure, panic and increased levels of anxiety are more likely to occur due to the added stress of unrealistic expectations (Loscalzo & Brintzenhofescoz, 1998).

Advanced-Stage Cancer Patients Living in the Balance

Patients with recurrent or advanced disease often encounter similar psychosocial difficulties that are associated with the initial diagnostic phase such as adjusting to changes in roles and life styles, living with uncertainty, and communicating about fears (Northouse, 1995; Sales, 1992). However, patients during the recurrent phase of the illness must also face feelings of isolation, helplessness, and hopelessness (Sales, 1992). When cancer treatment has failed at curing or controlling the disease, faith in the medical field may decrease, and effective communication between the patient, the family, and the hospital staff may become strained (Sales, 1992). Because of decreased curative options, hope for prolonged survival is diminished, and both patients and their families must make decisions about a new course of treatment and the reality of probable death from cancer (Loscalzo & Brintzenhofescoz, 1998). Often, for advanced cancer patients, treatment decision making must take place when the family's emotional and financial resources have been depleted.

Most patients with advanced-stage cancer (around 70%) report needing ancillary care services (Schulz, Williamson, Knapp, Bookwala, Lave, & Fello, 1995). These additional services include (1) help with activities of daily living, (2) assistance with emotional difficulties, (3) help with housekeeping services, and (4) help with medical transportation (Schulz et al., 1995). Financial difficulty has also been shown to be a predictor of poor psychological adaptation during advanced stages of the disease (Schulz et al., 1995). It has been estimated that families with advanced-stage cancer typically spend more than $200 per month on health-related expenses (Schulz et al., 1995). This added monthly expenditure is particularly difficult to manage when key family members are on a fixed income or must either quit or substantially miss work due to sickness or to caregiving responsibilities (Schulz et al., 1995). Thus, worries regarding health care expenses, overall financial concerns, and sacrifices made because of medical costs are directly related to psychological well-being during this phase of cancer (Schulz et al., 1995; Williamson & Schulz, 1992). Thus, financial difficulties as well as the health status of the patient including level of pain (Breitbart & Passik, 1993a) can all be regarded as predictors of patient psychological adaptation to advanced disease.

As Gotay (1984) has noted, there are some differences in coping strategies between patients in the early stages of cancer and those with advanced cancer. One of these differences is in the use of denial. During the initial diagnostic phase, denial of the seriousness of the illness can be used as a protective blanket shielding the patient and the family from the frightening diagnosis and its possible ramifications. Conversely, during advanced stages of cancer, patients rarely report using denial as a coping mechanism. Most patients report being fully aware of the severity of the new prognosis and the advancement of the disease. Moreover, patients and their families are less likely to use information seeking as a coping strategy during advanced stages of cancer (Gotay, 1984). Medical information regarding the patient's specific type of cancer and any potential treatments may become sparse, thus leaving the patient and the family with little comfort in information-seeking coping strategies. During later stages, patients and their families are more likely to seek comfort in prayer and in their religious practices or spiritual beliefs. Daily functioning concerns also differ for the two groups. Specifically, cancer patients early in the clinical course are usually most concerned about fulfilling work obligations and modifying their roles within the family system, whereas advanced-stage cancer patients are usually concerned about functioning in all areas of their lives (Gotay, 1984). The inability of advanced cancer patients to function in any area of daily life can lead to anger, fear, and a loss of trust and hope (Loscalzo & Brintzenhofescoz, 1998). Advanced cancer patients, particularly those with increased levels of pain and suffering, can also experience significant levels of depression, anxiety, and overall mood disturbance (Breitbart & Passik, 1993a), as well as feelings of blame and guilt (Loscalzo & Brintzenhofescoz, 1998). The advanced-stage cancer patient may wonder, "What did I do wrong? Was it my negative attitude? Was I foolish to hope this was over forever?" (Loscalzo & Brintzenhofescoz, 1998, p. 666). Questions such as these can leave the patient feeling as if he or she were to blame for the illness and its recurrence and in a state of hopelessness (Bunston, Mings, Mackie, & Jones, 1995; Ringdal, 1995).

Hope is often regarded as a true "vital sign," a direct indication of how the advanced cancer patient is adapting during this crisis phase (Nowotny, 1991). Patients who have lost all sense of hope are thrown off balance and left feeling overwhelmed by cancer recurrence and progression. They are no longer able to live in a state of balance between hope for the future (i.e., decreased pain, safety and well-being of the family) and preparedness (i.e., beliefs in God, religiosity, meaning in and for life). A complete loss of hope can mean a decrease in quality of life for both the patient and the family system (Nowotny, 1991). Hope has also been linked to immune system functioning and thus even to issues of survival (Eysenck, 1987); however, these conclusions are being debated (Ringdal, 1995). Social support, internal locus of control, and adaptive coping all have been associated with the concept of hope (Lazarus & Folkman, 1984; O'Connor, Wicker, & Germino, 1990; Raleigh, 1992).

Although hope is illusively defined, it is often regarded by professionals as crucial in the assessment of overall adaptation to crisis (Beck, Lester, Trexler, & Weissman, 1974; Menninger, 1959). There are many components, or dimensions, of hope, each that can be used to assess specific areas of hope in patients with advanced cancer. Nowotny (1991, 1989) has identified six components of hope: (1) a hopeful confidence in future outcomes, (2) hopefulness that future relationships with others can be maintained, (3) hopeful beliefs about the possibility of a future, (4) spiritual beliefs that help sustain hope, (5) hope as it affects a patient's ability to maintain an active involvement in life, and (6) hope as it helps prepare a patient to be ready to encounter future uncertainties. Advanced cancer patients can have confidence in their own inner strength and in the expertise of their caregivers to achieve desired outcomes, particularly if these outcomes are within realistic expectations. The cancer patients who have confidence that pain and suffering can be decreased will have increased hope for their own future and for their present quality of life. Patients that have hope in their relationships with others will have a sense of trust that they will be cared for and loved for the remainder of their lives. Strengthening advanced cancer patients' hope in relationships with others will enhance their abilities to seek and to receive help from others and to decrease feelings of isolation and despair.

Patients with a low sense of hope for the future tend to be unable to envision a future for themselves (Nowotny, 1991). Small yet worthwhile goals can create a sense of control over the future and hope for a life beyond the pain and suffering of advanced disease. Along these lines, religious or spiritual beliefs are an important component of hope (Nowotny, 1989, 1991). Advanced cancer patients may need to reassess their relationships with God and to reevaluate the meaning of and in their lives. Providing a safe and comfortable environment in which to discuss such sensitive issues can do much in helping the patient to gain a sense of hope through careful life review and an examination of personal spiritual beliefs.

Active involvement and inner readiness are two additional components of hope (Nowotny, 1991). Advanced cancer patients, particularly those suffering from pain and fatigue, may succumb to inactive and passive life styles, with few personal goals and little gratification from their roles and relationships with others (Nowotny, 1991). Helping patients to devise and revise their goals according to their abilities will facilitate a sense of mastery and hope. During the advanced stages of cancer, many patients can still make choices, participate in decision making, and discuss their own desires and goals (Nowotny, 1991). By helping advanced cancer patients to identify and to achieve small attainable goals, their inner readiness to be an active participant in the remainder of their lives can be enhanced (Nowotny, 1991). By strengthening the advanced cancer patient's sense of hope, the balance between hope and preparedness can be more readily sustained.

Families of Recurrent/Advanced-Stage Cancer Patients Living in the Balance

Both children and spouses of patients in the advanced stages of the disease have difficulties coping with the daily care of the patient, increased hospital stays, the responsibilities of day-to-day living, and facing impending loss. During this stage, children of all ages begin to experience difficulties with disruptions to their own age-appropriate developmental tasks (Siegel, Palamara Mesagno, Karus, Christ, Banks, & Moynihan, 1992). Children of advanced-stage cancer patients will often experience distress and anticipatory grief responses due to (1) loss and separation from the ill parent due to frequent hospitalizations and overall deterioration in health, (2) loss of both parents' abilities to be emotionally and physically available, (3) loss of family routine and familiar patterns of role functioning, and (4) loss of family financial resources (Siegel et al., 1992).

Coping strategies will differ between younger and older children (Christ, Siegel, & Sperber, 1994). Adolescents are typically very aware of their parents' deterioration in health and are not likely to be able to use denial or assertive optimism to cope at this time (Christ et al., 1994). Instead, adolescents must begin to use more intellectual defenses, to search for meaning and deeper understanding, and to seek help when needed (Christ et al., 1994). Younger children who are more physically and emotionally dependent upon their parents may identify closely with the ill parent and develop somatic symptoms that mimic the parent's physical distress (Christ et al., 1994). Somatic responses in young children can be a result of misunderstandings and miscommunication about the advancing of the illness and its treatment (Christ et al., 1994).

Spouses of the sick partner will also experience increased levels of distress as the illness advances, particularly if the patient reports higher levels of distress (Kaye & Gracely, 1993), or if the patient and the family system is young (Mor, Allen, & Malin, 1994). Spouses and patients experiencing advanced stages of the disease must balance their lives with the demands of the illness in several domains: (1) managing the illness, (2) learning to live with the realities of the illness and maintaining a sense of control, (3) healing and keeping distress at a minimum, and (4) preparing for death (Lewis & Deal, 1995). All of these demands must be juggled, balanced, compartmentalized, as well as actively faced during the advanced stages of cancer. In managing the illness, couples often set limits on the amount of focus the illness has in their lives (Lewis & Deal, 1995). Although the couples must educate themselves and discuss the details of the disease and its treatment, many couples put limits on their time talking about the disease, focusing on the illness only during times of treatment or increased disease-related symptomatology (Lewis & Deal, 1995). Many become empowered and maintain a sense of control by learning all they can about their disease and any treatments or clinical trials that may be available. In addition, couples manage the illness by "checking in" with each other on a daily basis regarding both physical and emotional distress levels (Lewis & Deal, 1995). Couples attempt to live and to cope with the advancing illness by being thankful for the gift of life and for the support and comfort they find in each other. Couples can heal, even during advanced stages of the illness, by recognizing the seriousness of the disease while at the same time maintaining a sense of optimism for the future (Lewis & Deal, 1995). Finally, couples must balance the realties of the illness by preparing for death. This is often the most difficult domain for spousal subsystems to address, especially when treatment options have dwindled (Lewis & Deal, 1995). During this phase of the illness, patients and their spouses can begin to plan "as if" death were a real possibility and to begin planning for the future after the death of a spouse. These plans may include shopping for a casket, making funeral plans, and discussing life without a spouse or partner (i.e., taking care of the children and the family, insurance policies, marriage after the death of a spouse; Lewis & Deal, 1995). Although these topics are often painful to discuss, if they are not addressed the surviving spouse can be left with additional burdens during the final phase of cancer and during bereavement (Lewis & Deal, 1995).

Special Considerations: Caregiving during the Recurrence Phase

Family caregiver burden and distress should be assessed during this phase, particularly if the advanced cancer patient is experiencing a longer dying trajectory (i.e., terminal illness that lingers for many months or even years), greater overall health deterioration, pain, and immobility (Buehler & Lee, 1992; Given & Given, 1998). Caregiver burden has been defined as "a multidimensional biopsychosocial reaction resulting from an imbalance of care demands and requirements relative to physical, social, emotional, and financial resources available to the individual providing care and support to a family member with cancer" (Given & Given, 1998, p. 95). The characteristics of the caregiver (age, gender, marital status, living arrangements), the characteristics of the patient and the illness trajectory, as well as the past relationship between the caregiver and the patient, should all be taken into consideration (Given & Given, 1998). Caregivers are usually women, over the age of 55, taking care of either a spouse or another family member (Given & Given, 1998). Older females are usually taken care of by their adult children, whereas older males are usually cared for by their spouses. This is in large part due to the longevity of women (Given & Given, 1998). Spousal caregivers, as well as caregivers who live with the patient, have been shown to be at a higher risk for distress and burnout (Given & Given, 1998; Stommel & Kingry, 1991), and wives and daughters who act as caregivers are at the highest risk for depression resulting from caregiving obligations (Stommel, Given, & Given, 1990).

Patient characteristics and the disease trajectory are also variables to consider when assessing caregiver burden. Patients with recurrent disease can cause caregiver burnout and distress (Wright, Clipp, & George, 1993). However, even more than recurrent cancer, patient immobility has been shown to lead to increased caregiver distress (Given & Given, 1998). Patient characteristics such as severity of functional impairment and severity of symptoms have also been shown to be correlates of increased caregiver depression (Clipp & George, 1990). And caring for patients with severe cognitive deficits often leads to high sustained levels of caregiver burnout and distress (Carey, Oberst, McCubbin, & Hughes, 1991; Given & Given, 1998). It is thus important to note that patients with physical impairment and overall health deterioration may be more readily cared for than patients with severe cognitive deficits. This could be due, in part, to a decreased sense of "mutuality" within the caregiver–patient relationship. Given and Given note, "Mutuality is the gratification in the relationship and meaning in the care situation and the caregiver's ability to perceive the patient as reciprocating by virtue of existence" (1998, p. 96). When the patient has severe cognitive impairment, perceived levels of mutuality may decrease, leaving the caregiver without the buffers of a sense of competency and feelings of reciprocity in the caregiving relationship. In addition to cognitive impairment, an illness trajectory that is marked by constant change in patient status (i.e., deterioration in health, functioning, mobility) that necessitates constant changes in family roles, responsibilities, and emotional responses is also indicative of higher levels of distress for the caregiver and the family system (Lloyd & Coggles, 1990).

The contextual and historical relationship between the primary caregiver and the patient in conjunction with the stage of family development should also be taken into consideration when assessing for caregiver burden (Given & Given, 1998). Although there are many family members, friends, and professional health care workers who care for advanced cancer patients, usually there is only one primary caregiver (Given & Given, 1998). The past relationship between caregiver and patient can have a direct influence on the quality of patient care and on the amount of caregiver distress (Given & Given, 1998). The previous dyadic relationship must be considered in terms of both type and quality (Given & Given, 1998). For example, for spouses (an intragenerational type), the caregiving process can be enhanced if the relationship has a history of emotional bonding, shared memories, and a mutual commitment to the spousal subsystem. Conversely, caregivers who are more distant relatives (intergenerational), who have little emotional ties with the patient, or have established maladaptive patterns of interaction, are more likely to show increased distress and a greater likelihood of institutionalization for the patient (Given & Given, 1998). Intragenerational caregiving relationships (e.g., spouse to spouse) are more likely to result in entrenchment and possible isolation, whereas intergenerational caregiving relationships (e.g., adult child to parent) are more likely to lead to multiple role strain and overload (Given & Given, 1998).

While emotional strain, lack of information, and lack of available resources may lead to negative responses in connection with the caregiving process (Carey et al., 1991), others have noted positive reactions to caregiving (Lawton, Moss, Kleban, Glicksman, & Rovine, 1991). It appears that when caregivers have sufficient internal and external resources, they gain a sense of competency and are able to derive meaning and satisfaction from being able to perform much needed duties (Archbold, Stewart, Greenlick, & Harvath, 1990). Thus, predictors of less role strain and decreased caregiver burden include (1) increased levels of perceived mastery and competence in the provision of care, (2) a sense of meaning associated with the task of caregiving, and (3) confidence in perceived ability to provide future patient care (Given & Given, 1998).

There are several strategies that can be used to assist family caregivers and to reduce caregiver distress (Given & Given, 1998). First, the health care providers should consider the primary caregiver as a part of the cancer care team. As such, caregivers must be provided with ongoing assistance and accurate and dependable information regarding patient daily care, possible changes in symptomatology and medication, as well as the expected illness trajectory (Stiles, 1990). The reports on patient functioning need to be taken seriously by the health care providers, and any modifications in patient care should be made after careful examination of the patient's physical and emotional needs, level of caregiver burden, and family functioning and adaptation (Given & Given, 1998). Caregivers can experience guilt, anger, and resentment toward siblings or other family members who may not be helping as much as the primary caregiver would like. Thus, any possible conflicts that might arise within the family system should also be carefully examined. Informational needs as well as both the positive and negative aspects of caregiving should be closely monitored by the health care team (Given & Given, 1998; Rolland, 1994).

During this phase of cancer, families are caring for their sick family member and are consequently an integral part of the cancer care team (Given & Given, 1998). Families must become involved in complex decision-making processes including (1) managing pain with pharmacologic and nonpharmacologic interventions, (2) administering specific doses and types of medication, (3) watching for infection and subtle changes in symptomatology, and (4) providing comfort and emotional support to the patient and to other family members (Given & Given, 1998). Thus, it remains important that the health care team work with the primary caregiver and the family system in order to provide appropriate and well-timed interventions, which result in optimal patient care, comfort, and overall health and well-being.

☐ The Six Family Life Cycles during the Recurrence Phase: The Importance of Balance

This phase of the clinical course of cancer is marked by a time of cancer progression, recurrence, metastasis, or the development of a second primary cancer. In any one of these scenarios, cancer can be serious and life threatening. Thus, for all the family life cycles, adaptation during the recurrent phase is often more difficult than the initial diagnostic phase (Given & Given, 1992). The patient's prognosis is usually poor, and the goals of treatment shift from one of cure to one of palliation and disease control (Loscalzo & Brintzenhofeszoc, 1998). A poorer prognosis can mean substantial difficulty with psychosocial adaptation during this phase. Increased levels of anxiety, depression, hopelessness, and helplessness are more likely to occur, often leading to withdrawal and isolation from family and other support systems. Thus, like during the diagnostic phase, a multifaceted assessment procedure is necessary. It is important to consider variables such as (1) the patient's medical context, including treatment planning and prognosis; (2) the family's life cycle and preillness structure; (3) the patient and the family system's current level of functioning; and (4) treatment goals and interventions. The effects of recurrence on the family life cycle are organized in Table 6.1.

☐ The Single Young Adult during Recurrence

Since cancer incidence increases with age, it is relatively rare that a single young adult be diagnosed with a life threatening type of cancer. When a young adult is diagnosed with advanced-stage cancer or metastatic cancer, severe disruption to our collective normal assumptive world takes place. The news of a young adult being diagnosed with a serious disease is usually surprising, and can cause a rippling effect, which extends from the immediate family system to the community at large. The young adult's school, the sports team on which he or she may play, and the hospital staff are generally hit hard by the unusual occurrence of a life threatening disease in young adulthood.

The following is a case example of a young woman recently diagnosed with melanoma. While most skin cancers are not necessarily dangerous or life threatening, malignant melanoma (i.e., the malignant mole) is a notable exception (Mitchell, 1997). Melanoma, or the "black tumor," is not only the most malignant of all skin cancers, it is also one of the most malignant types of all cancers (Mitchell, 1997). The incidence rate of melanoma is rising faster worldwide than any other type of cancer, and excessive exposure to ultraviolet light is a suspected cause for this increase (Mitchell, 1997). Although melanoma is more likely to be diagnosed in middle to later adulthood, an increasing number of young adults are being diagnosed with melanoma, particularly young adults who have experienced intense sunburn in their childhood (Mitchell, 1997).

CASE EXAMPLE 7. Jenny's Medical Context

Jerry and Janet Wachtel came in for a psychosocial consultation to discuss their 20-year-old daughter, Jenny. Jenny and her parents were recently told that Jenny's malignant melanoma was out of remission. Mrs. Wachtel began the session: "This has been the most devastating year of our lives—at least so far. And we know it is only going to get worse. . . . "

(text continued on page 188)

Table 6.1. The Recurrence Phase and the Family Life Cycle: The Importance of Balance

	Life cycle tasks	Potential disruptions	Psychosocial interventions	Topics of communication
Single young adult	Differentiate from family of origin	Can cause permanent delays	Facilitate developmental growth in spite of a life threatening illness; help young adult to achieve small, attainable goals	Discuss gamut of emotions—anger, guilt, isolation, fear
Newly forming couple	Create new system; balance power; negotiate roles, rules, and responsibilities	Recurrence can result in permanent upset in balance of the newly forming system; emotional, legal, and developmental disruptions can occur	Help couple to crystalize their union by setting appropriate boundaries on external influences on the illness; redefine future plans and goals	Discuss multigenerational impact; discuss the limits of the illness; discuss needs of the family of origin
Families with young children	Raise children; incorporate roles of parents and grandparents into the system	Recurrence can disrupt parenting roles; upset balance in marital dyad; emotional disruptions to parents, children, and grandparents	Help young family to organize system to meet the high demands of recurrence; mobilize external resources; help couple to set limits on illness; help children to feel safe	Discuss effects on children, marital dyad, and future generations; discuss fears for future, care of the children; discuss needs of patient, family members

Families with adolescents	Accept external influences on the family system; loosen boundaries for adolescent	Recurrence can delay the developmental momentum of adolescent; cause additional strain between parents and adolescents	Help system to define all responsibilities of recurrence phase; help system to assign tasks; help system to balance needs of illness with the needs of adolescents	Discuss effects of recurrence on all family members; identify temporary developmental delays; discuss fears and hopes for future
Families launching children	Accept multiple exits and entries; redefine rules, roles; create intimacy in marital dyad	Recurrence can disrupt redefinition of marital dyad; disrupt launching of age-appropriate children; permanently alter goals and plans for both patient and spouse	Help system to identify specific demands of recurrence and its effect on developmental tasks and goals; to create new, attainable goals and plans	Discuss death; discuss potential sources of hope; discuss future wishes; discuss individual family members' needs
Families in later life	Adjust to retirement; maintain a sense of generativity	Recurrence can bring despair to older patient and spouse; may necessitate a change in living arrangements	Help system to assess resources; help system to determine best site of care; help patient set attainable goals; assess burnout	Discuss needs of patient, caregiver; discuss death; discuss home, hospice, hospital care

Jenny's mother stopped a moment to compose herself. "Let me start at the beginning," she continued. About a year ago, Jenny noticed a mole on her neck that began to change in shape and color. We went to see a dermatologist who immediately sent us to an oncologist. We were in a state of shock. Jenny was diagnosed with Clark's level III malignant melanoma. We further learned that Jenny's tumor had invaded the layers of the skin by about 2.4 millimeters. You see, the severity of melanoma is characterized by the depth of its invasion. You can bet that my husband and I did quite a bit of reading this past year about melanoma."

Jenny's father went on to discuss Jenny's initial treatment for malignant melanoma: "At first the treatment team was very positive about Jenny's chances for remission. We thought that maybe we had caught it early enough and that surgery may even cure her. Then Jenny was put on chemotherapy, and the oncologist reported a 50 percent shrinkage. We were thrilled and we thought the treatment was going to work." Both parents were silent for a few moments before Jenny's father continued: "But now the cancer is back and her chances for survival are very low. The doctor wants to use an investigational procedure. We have read about the new interleukins that are being tested. We think the doctor wants her to try one of the interleukins in combination with interferon-alpha." Again, Jenny's parents sat quietly for a moment to gain their composure. Jenny's mother related, "The first time she was diagnosed with cancer was bad enough. Our hopes were much higher than they are now, and we thought we had a fighting chance. Now we don't think Jenny has long to live at all. But . . . I don't think she is accepting that. At this point, she thinks it is like the first time—surgery to remove the tumor followed by chemotherapy. And, physically, she does not feel sick, so I think that she is still hoping that her cancer will be cured. It is hard to discuss our fears with her that there probably is no cure for the kind of cancer she has." Both parents described how Jenny still feels well and healthy: "She doesn't show any signs or symptoms usually associated with cancer. Jenny seems to be in perfect health. That could be another reason we don't want to talk with her about our fears."

Jenny's Family: Preillness Structure and Current Level of Family Functioning

Jenny's parents discussed their family structure and the affects cancer was having on their family system. Their family genogram is illustrated in Figure 6.1. Jenny is an only child and was on vacation during spring break when she first noticed the changes in the mole. When Jenny got home from her vacation, she showed her mother the mole. Jenny did not return to school but was treated for malignant melanoma via surgery and chemotherapy treatments. Jenny was described as being a "happy, well-adjusted young adult, full of life and plans for her future." Jenny's mother stated, "We three have been a very close family. We moved to the Midwest from California about 15 years ago when Jenny was still young. So, much of our extended family is out west." Jenny's parents went on to describe their small family system as very close: "It was very hard for us to let go of Jenny when she

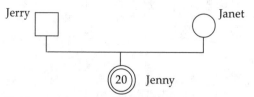

FIGURE 6.1. The single young adult during recurrence genogram.

decided to go to college. We were hoping she would stay near home and go to a campus close by home, but she decided to go to a larger university and room with two of her friends. We are all so close. But I am glad that she did go away for a while now. That one semester at school made her so independent! It was a real challenge for her to come back home to be cared for during her treatment. Now she seems like a small child and we want to protect her from all pain and fear, yet at the same time respect her new independence." Jenny's mother continued, "I feel so responsible for her illness. She got so many sunburns as a little girl when we were in California. From all that we have read, exposure to ultraviolet light, which results in sunburns in childhood, is linked with malignant melanoma. I don't think that I can ever forgive myself for what has happened. I just didn't protect my daughter better."

Case Conceptualization

The Wachtel family is currently experiencing the devastation of cancer recurrence. For them, the recurrence phase is even more difficult than the initial diagnosis of cancer. For Jenny's parents, the realization of the severity of the illness is all too clear. However, this realization has created communication difficulties between them and their daughter, who believes that the possibility of a cure is still attainable. Jenny's mother was also experiencing an existential crisis. Primarily, her belief that she is responsible for her daughter's illness precludes her from having open discussions regarding the severity of the illness. The mother's existential crisis and Jenny's asymptomatic responses to the disease all keep the family from addressing the realities of the disease and its treatment. In addition, the lack of communication intensifies Jenny's role as the "child" in the family and thus impedes any developmental growth that could take place during the remainder of her lifespan.

Jenny's developmental tasks of creating an identity apart from her family of origin, of developing intimate peer relationships, and exploring her career interests will probably be prematurely and permanently delayed due to the severity of her illness. Enchancing her quality of life, facilitating open communication, and assisting all family members in their adaptation to Jenny's illness is paramount. The family's tasks at this time are to begin to communicate their knowledge about Jenny's diagnosis as well as their interpretations for the reasons behind the illness, and to create the optimum quality of life for all family members.

Psychosocial Recommendations

Psychosocial recommendations for the Wachtel family include helping them to maintain an optimal quality of life while at the same time addressing the severity of the illness. However, it should be emphasized that each patient and family member adapts to the crisis of cancer recurrence in his or her own way. Patients such as Jenny may not want to understand the severity of their illnesses. Although using denial as a coping mechanism is more rare during advanced-stage illness (Gotay, 1984), patients' protective coping responses are important for them to maintain and must be respected. Thus, it was recommended that both the parents and Jenny take part in a consultation to determine each person's view of the illness.

Jenny reported that she feels fine: "I really don't feel sick at all. I know that I can beat this thing. I am young and in good health, except for the skin cancer. I went through treatment once and I can do it again. In fact, this time I don't have to have surgery, so it will probably be easier. I also realize that there are no guarantees in life and this illness may cut my life short, but I am not going to go through life like I am already dead. I realize what the doctors have told me, but I am young, so I think that I may be able to beat the odds. I love life right now and want to enjoy it, regardless of what the future holds." Jenny's father stated, "Your mother and I are both very worried about you, though. We think this is very serious and we just want you to know how concerned we are." Jenny replied, "I know how much you care and how you always worry about me. But I am not a little girl anymore, and I do wish that you would stop trying to protect me from everything. I mean, now that I am living back at home, I feel like a kid. I have to ask your permission to do everything. Then, on top of it, you treat me as if I am made of glass. Just respect me and let me grow up and live my life."

During the session, the family decided to put limits on the disease for now. They did this by limiting their conversation about it. In addition, Jenny's parents were encouraged to put limits on the disease by allowing Jenny to have time with her friends, by maintaining a set of responsibilities in the home, and by continuing her education through home studies. Jenny and her parents also decided on new roles and responsibilities that each person would have in the home. Jenny's father stated, "I guess we have to recognize that you are a grown woman. Still, we should always tell each other where we are and when we'll be home. Further, each of us will have our own responsibilities around the house, and we'll hold you to those responsibilities. We want to respect your wishes of not being treated like you're made of glass!" It was difficult for Jenny's mother to agree to hold Jenny to her responsibilities and to treat her like an adult. She said, "I feel so responsible for her illness. I just want her to be happy every second of every day. I am not sure I can make her do chores or do things for us around the house." Jenny interrupted, "But Mom, I need to help. And, I want to go to my chemo treatments alone sometimes. I need to feel well. I need to feel responsible and adult-like. Please help me to feel that way." Due to Jenny's need to continue with her personal development, Jenny's parents allowed Jenny to seek emotional support from her many friends. Jenny's parents loosened their boundaries with their daughter's friends and allowed them to take part in many family activities such as mealtimes and watching videos together. Jenny's mother was helped to place limits on the impact of her personal existential crisis in order to help her daughter regain developmental momentum in spite of a life threatening disease. Rather than allow her guilt to interfere with her communication with Jenny, she began to attend a support group for women with children suffering from severe illness. In this way, she could share her guilt and grief with others, yet not allow these feelings of deep regret to completely consume her valuable time with her daughter.

☐ The Newly Forming Couple during Recurrence

The impact of advanced or metastatic disease on the newly forming couple is devastating to the new system. Couples who are just beginning this stage of family development may never get the chance to establish their own system as a separate entity from their families of origin. The normal life cycle tasks of negotiating the balance of power and establishing the structure within the new system will more than likely be directed by the demands of cancer. Dreams and plans may need to be permanently set aside so that the newly forming couple can focus on their remaining time together. Couples who are not yet married may struggle over if and when to legalize their relationship. Knowing the severity of the illness, the couple must learn to balance the daily goal of maintaining optimal quality of life with the realties of eventual loss.

The following is a case example of a newly forming couple recently diagnosed with small cell lung cancer. Each year there are more than 175,000 new cases of lung cancer in the United States (Glassberg, Cornett, & Jahan, 1997). Small cell lung cancer, or "oat cell carcinoma of the lung," composes about one-fourth of all lung cancer cases (Glassberg et al., 1997). Small cell lung cancer has a rapid clinical course, with an average survival time, without treatment, of only several months (Glassberg et al., 1997). Cigarette smoking is a major contributing factor in the development of lung cancer. Other risk factors include exposure to asbestos, nickel, chromium compounds, and air pollutants (Glassberg et al., 1997).

CASE EXAMPLE 8. Dan's Medical Context

Dan, age 34, his finance, Holly, his two sisters, Phylis and Janet, and his mother, Jane, attended the initial psychosocial consultation. Their family genogram is illustrated in Figure 6.2. Phylis, the oldest sibling, began the session, "We all know that it is Dan who is the patient, but we are all really hurting too." All of the family members knew that Dan was diagnosed with inoperable, small cell lung cancer and that the cancer had begun to metastasize to Dan's bones. Dan was to receive chemotherapy with adjuvant radiotherapy for palliative purposes. Phylis stated, "Dan was coughing all the time and he lost a lot of weight. We knew that he was really sick, but we had no idea that it was lung cancer! We are all in a state of shock." Dan's family is currently experiencing the initial existential crisis phase of the clinical course of cancer. This was the family's first time dealing with cancer, so they have not had the "preparation time" of the diagnostic, treatment, and rehabilitation phases. In essence, Dan's family had just walked into a jungle without a map to guide them (Lerner, 1994). The family system was faced with the diagnosis of cancer, the news of inoperability, and the understanding that Dan would probably live only about 6 to 12 months (Glassberg, Cornett, & Jahan, 1997). Thus, each family member was experiencing an existential crisis and attempting to adapt to the devastating news in his or her own way.

Dan's Family: Preillness Structure and Current Level of Family Functioning

Phylis did most of the talking for the family: "Dan is the only male in the family. Our Dad left us years ago, so Dan if very special to us. I feel so badly about this, I can't tell you. It should have been me for one thing. I am the oldest in the family. Why wasn't it me instead of my baby brother? The family always comes to me with their problems, and I should be able to help! I can't do anything about this! There is nothing to do but pray and cry." Dan's mother added, "God is very important to our family. We all believe in His healing power.

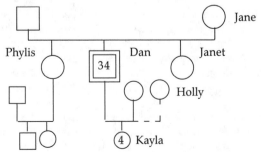

FIGURE 6.2. The newly forming couples during recurrence genogram.

There is nothing He can't cure if that is His will. We must not give up hope that Dan can survive." The women all nodded in agreement. When asked, Holly commented on her relationship with Dan: "We are very close. The whole family is so close that I feel as if I am a member of the family already. Dan and I were going to get married next month, but we have decided to postpone the wedding until after his chemotherapy." The women all agreed that Holly was, indeed, a part of the family. When encouraged, Holly talked more about her relationship with Dan: "Dan and I have known each other for about two years. He has a daughter, Kayla, who is four years old, from a previous marriage. We all get along, and I love Kayla with all of my heart. . . . I guess the only bad thing is that Dan sometimes throws these fits. I mean even on our way over here, Dan got all mad and slammed the trunk down and started yelling at all of us. We get kind of scared of him when he gets like that." Phylis added, "He has always been like that though. Janet and I would usually just tell him what to do and he would do it. Then, all of a sudden he would just throw one of his fits. He is usually really easy to get along with."

Dan had been sitting quietly in a wheelchair listening to the women discuss him. When asked about his perception of his illness and his views on the family he replied, "I don't know. For the most part I agree with what they are saying . . . but really I want them to hear me now. I guess I want them to know that I know that I am going to die soon. The doctor said that they can't operate and remove the lung and that the treatment is for palliation—which just means that they are helping to relieve my pain, right?" Dan's mother interrupted, "but we can't question God's power and His plan. You can still survive this, Dan." Dan just shook his head and looked at the floor. Breaking the silence, Dan stated, "Phylis, you can help me by not helping me so much. Getting lung cancer right now is so unfair. I just got a new job and I was beginning to feel like a man. Then I get sick, I have to be in this stupid wheelchair, and I feel like a baby all over again. Stop helping me! Just listen to me and then leave me alone." This was the first time Dan had ever told his family what he needed from them.

Case Conceptualization

Dan's family has beliefs that underlie the way they cope with stress. Existential themes such as "having an unquestioning faith in the healing power of God" is the primary coping mechanism for the family. However, the maintenance of this theme kept them from hearing Dan's beliefs regarding his prognosis and potential death. Thus, this family theme was preventing important communication from taking place. Moreover, the women in Dan's family are quite verbal and tend to talk a great deal for Dan. Hence, his "blowing up" was in reaction to needing to feel heard. They have kept him in the role of "baby" in the family, which hinders the ability for the family to hear his needs. These dynamics do not allow Dan time, space, or reason to create or to express his own opinions and ideas. The family noted that Dan's usually passive nature can become aggressive at times. This is because the patterns of family interaction preclude Dan from openly expressing his thoughts and emotions. Subsequently, Dan occasionally throws "fits" to make sure he is heard once in awhile, again reinforcing his "baby" of the family role. It appears that these fits are a means of attempting to regain some power and control in a chaotic situation. Unfortunately, this is a means of pseudoindependence that will compromise the effectiveness of his coping.

Although Holly is emotionally accepted as a family member, her relationship with Dan has not been legalized. She and Dan may need to discuss the pros and cons of marriage, particularly since Dan has only a short time to live and has a young daughter to raise.

Legal decisions could vastly alter Holly's future and her role in this family and other future family systems. In addition, Holly and Dan's subsystem appears to be having difficulty maintaining boundaries between their subsystem and Dan's family. Holly and Dan's sisters are very close, and their bond may be having a direct influence on the power negotiations in Dan and Holly's newly forming relationship. Dan's aggressive outbursts can be regarded as his attempt to regain some of his power and independence, which is being thwarted by both the disease and his family system.

Psychosocial Recommendations

All of the family members were in agreement regarding Dan's diagnosis and medical prognosis. However, there is a large discrepancy between Dan's acceptance of his prognosis and his family's need to hold onto the belief that Dan could survive. It was recommended that Dan be allowed to speak his own thoughts and feelings without being judged. The family, including Dan, was encouraged to respect differing perceptions of Dan's prognosis, no matter how scary it may be to hear, and to refrain from using punitive words or behaviors when there is disagreement. Dan and Holly also discussed the boundaries they needed to maintain, particularly while Dan was receiving his chemotherapy treatment. Dan suggested to his sisters that they "give us a break for a couple of weeks while we get adjusted to this news." Dan and Holly also requested time to discuss their plans for marriage. By taking time for themselves, Dan and Holly's developmental momentum was regained for their newly forming system.

For the next two weeks, the family agreed to listen to each other without passing judgment, and to let Holly and Dan work on their own system. Phylis commented, "I guess I can give you a break for a couple of weeks. Maybe I need these two weeks for myself, too. We all need time to adjust to this news. Just know that I love you enough to let you be." Through the course of his illness, Phylis and the other sisters began to ask Dan about his feelings and beliefs more often. In addition, they also began to listen to Dan's responses and to validate them. Each of the sisters took time to just be present with Dan without attempting to "fix" his problems or to change his personal beliefs. In this way, Dan's individual developmental momentum could be regained, even at the time of advanced disease and impending death. In addition, Dan's sisters' needs were addressed. The sisters were encouraged to take care of their spiritual needs through prayer, meditation on the Bible, and attending a church support group for caregivers of cancer patients, but to do these activities in ways that were not intrusive to Dan or Holly. In this way, both the needs of the patient and the family were addressed and met.

☐ The Family with Young Children during Recurrence

A life threatening illness is particularly difficult to handle when there are young children to raise. The ramifications of the potential loss of a parent during this life cycle are long-lasting and far reaching. The patient's health status may change rapidly during this phase of cancer, and well thought out communication between the adult subsystem and the children is needed. Whether there is detailed communication about the ill parent's recurrence or advanced status, both parents and children are well aware of the deterioration in health of the sick parent at this time (Siegel et al., 1992). Usually, the family witnesses the patient's more rapid weight loss, increased fatigue, and the general inability to perform previous role functioning in the family system (Siegel et al., 1992). Although both the well and the sick parent are under much stress due to the demands of the advancing disease, most parents have been shown to be aware of the impact of the illness on their children (Siegel et al., 1992). Children of advanced-stage cancer patients have been shown to exhibit increased depressive symptomatology and anxiety, as well as increased externalizing behaviors such as acting out and aggressive behaviors (Siegel et al., 1992). Moreover, the demands of the illness can developmentally delay the academic and social achievement of school-aged children, thus leaving them with diminished self-esteem, deficits in social competence, and fewer resources to help them cope with the loss of a parent (Seigel et al., 1992). Thus, the distress of advancing illness can have long-lasting ramifications for children who can become unable to forge their own social networks or to perform their own achievements outside of the family system (Christ et al., 1994).

The following is a case example of a woman recently diagnosed with colorectal cancer. One out of every 17 Americans will be diagnosed with colorectal cancer (Rosenbaum & Dollinger, 1997). When this type of cancer is detected early and when it is still localized to the large bowel (i.e., the colon and rectum), it is highly curable (Rosenbaum & Dollinger, 1997). However, when the tumor has invaded through the bowel wall, or if it has spread to nearby lymph nodes, chances for cure are reduced (Rosenbaum & Dollinger, 1997). Risk factors include advancing age, family history of colorectal cancer, relatives with benign polyps, previous polyps of the colon and rectum, inflammatory bowel disease (e.g., ulcerative colitis or Crohn's disease), and diets high in fat and low in fiber (Rosenbaum & Dollinger, 1997).

CASE EXAMPLE 9. Cindy's Medical Context

Cindy and her mother, Caren, came in for a psychosocial consultation. Cindy had recently been diagnosed with stage IV (Dukes' D) colon cancer. Her cancer has spread from the wall of the colon into her liver. Cindy was in both physical and emotional pain as she discussed her medical context: "It all started last summer when I began experiencing severe constipation and blood in my stool. I was in a lot of pain, but I wasn't scared for my life. I have always had problems with my digestive system, including polyps on my colon and colitis, just like my Dad. So, I just thought, 'Here we go again, back to the doctor.' But this time wasn't like the other times. I went in for extensive diagnostic testing and the doctor did a full workup on me. I had blood tests, imaging tests, and then I had to have a colonoscopy. The doctor found a large mass on the left side of my colon. I was told that it is a large malignant mass." Cindy paused and her mother continued for her: "She has to have the tumor and over a third of her colon removed next week. She'll have to have a colostomy. Since her tumor is in the left side of the colon, the doctor said her colostomy will more than likely be a permanent one. Reconnection of her bowel will not be possible because too much stool contamination is in that area of the bowel. However, the doctor said that much of her pain should be decreased as a result of the operation. Next, she'll have to go through chemotherapy to try and keep the liver metastasis under control. The nurse said that they can put in an infusion pump after surgery and she can receive her chemotherapy on an outpatient basis after she recovers from surgery." Cindy and her mother both went on to describe Cindy's poor prognosis. The tumor has penetrated the bowel wall, Cindy's pelvic nodes are involved, there is a large obstruction in her bowel, and the tumor cells are poorly differentiated. All of these signs are indicative of a poor prognosis (Rosenbaum & Dollinger, 1997).

Cindy's Family: Preillness Family Structure and Current Level of Family Functioning

Cindy, age 36, and Caren, age 56, discussed their family system. Their family genogram is shown in Figure 6.3. Cindy's father, Eric, died almost 15 years ago from colon cancer. Cindy has two brothers: Cameron, age 38, and Zachary, age 40. Caren was Eric's primary caregiver during the last few months of life. The three children were away at college and their new jobs during their father's illness. Caren explained, "I took care of my husband until the day he died of colon cancer. I have gone through that tragedy already. I can't believe I am going to have to go through it all over again with my daughter."

Cindy has been divorced from Jack for more than four years. Cindy went through the divorce when she was pregnant with her third child: "I had to move in with my mother to make ends meet. Mom had been living alone for so long that it was a real change for her, but everything was working out pretty well until now. Mom stays at home with the kids while I work at the factory here in town. The kids are great. Jimmy is four, Jana is six, and Jeremy is eight. We all get along pretty well, although it is hectic sometimes. Jack sees the kids every other weekend, and he has them for two months in the summer. He just got remarried about six months ago, and his wife Jennifer and I get along pretty well." Caren added, "Now that Cindy has been diagnosed with cancer, our whole lives are turned upside down. We were just working everything out, and now this. Cindy makes the money in the family, and she can get some disability money and receives some child support from Jack, but we don't really know how we are going to make it emotionally or financially. Then, I think, what am I going to do if she dies? What will happen to the kids? What will happen to our family and to me?" Cindy interrupted, "We can't think about that now, Mom. We have to take one day at a time. For now, I can get some money and my insurance can help pay some of the doctor bills. Let's just concentrate on getting me through surgery, adjusting to a colostomy, and getting to my chemotherapy treatments. That's enough for me to handle right now."

Case Conceptualization

Cindy's family has had to learn to be flexible in order to meet the demands of a divorce, raise three young children, and function effectively with three generations in the household. Cindy has been able to change her role from one of "daughter" to one of "adult and

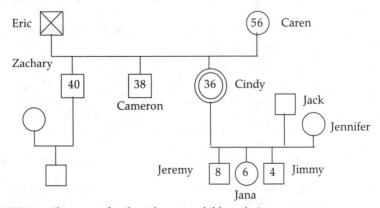

FIGURE 6.3. The young family with young children during recurrence genogram.

wage earner." Moreover, Caren reports her ability to successfully navigate between the roles of "grandmother" when Cindy is home from work, to primary "caregiver and mother" when Cindy is at work. Thus, the family system is constantly switching roles to meet the needs of their system, demonstrating much flexibility with regard to generational and functional roles. Further, Cindy reported that when Jack has visitation with the kids, her and her mother's roles and have been able to find equality in their mother–daughter relationship.

The illness will necessitate further role changes. In addition to the roles of "grandmother," "mother," and "mutual partner," Caren is anticipating the need to become Cindy's primary "caregiver." These multiple demanding roles will potentially result in role strain and excessive caregiver burden for Caren, particularly as the disease progresses. Cindy will also need to shift roles. She is used to being the wage earner in the family. This role, as well as the role of "mother" to her three children, has given her a sense of power and differentiation from the structure of her original family of origin, even though she lives with her mother. Now she is faced with (1) losing her independence by becoming a patient, (2) dealing with issues of body image as a result of her colostomy, (3) diminishing her status as wage earner for the family, (4) reducing her role as an active "mother" in the lives of her three children, (5) facing the possibility of increased physical and emotional pain during the advancing of the disease, and (6) dealing with her own death at an early age.

Psychosocial Recommendations

Cindy was already attempting to adapt to advanced cancer. She wanted only to cope with the immediate future, which entails her surgery, the adjustment to her colostomy, and chemotherapy. Before going in for surgery, Cindy and her mother decided to discuss the details of Cindy's medical benefits with her boss at the factory. They also decided to make a list of the kinds of ancillary care services they may need in the future. Caren stated, "I may need some help taking care of Cindy, the kids, and the house. When I took care of my husband, I didn't have three little children to care for at the same time, and it was difficult enough. I think that both of us will need some emotional assistance too. This is all going to be very hard on us. The situation looks so hopeless."

Both Cindy and her mother were experiencing an existential crisis that was a result of their changing roles. Cindy's meaning in life centers around the need to care for her children and to provide for her family. Because of her changing roles and her poor prognosis, she could potentially experience increased depression, anxiety, and even suicidal ideation. These psychosocial responses must be carefully monitored throughout the clinical course of her disease. She may need to take antidepressant or antianxiety medication, particularly if the disease continues to progress.

Caren mentioned the "hopelessness" that she was experiencing. Although she continued to feel hopeless regarding future outcomes, she was able to find hope that her relationships with her daughter and grandchildren could be successfully maintained. However, Caren continues to struggle with hope for her own future and her hope in maintaining an active involvement in life. Both Caren and Cindy stated that they were beginning to think about joining a church so that they could generate hope from new spiritual or religious beliefs and practices.

Following Cindy's surgery, Jack took the children for a few weeks in order to let Cindy have some time to recover from her surgery and to adjust to her colostomy. The children were told that "Mommy is really sick," and they were allowed to visit Cindy for an hour in the evenings and for a couple of hours on the weekend. The children were aware of Cindy's deteriorating health. Caren reported that they "constantly need to be reassured that they will be cared for and loved."

During a follow-up individual session, Caren reported that she was overwhelmed with the responsibility of caring for her daughter: "It is just so emotionally devastating to see your daughter die away right before your eyes. I watched as the same thing happened to my husband years ago, and it is like reliving a nightmare. Both her and the kids need for me to be strong, but I am falling apart inside. I don't have the energy I had 15 years ago, and I am scared of losing my daughter and my grandkids at the same time. Cindy and Jack have already discussed Jack taking the kids after she dies. I know it is the best thing for the children, but how am I going to cope with the loss of my daughter and my grandchildren at the same time? All I see ahead of me is loneliness and sadness." It was recommended that Caren concentrate on small attainable goals that help her to envision a slightly brighter future for herself. Jack was encouraged to spend some time over at the house with the kids and Cindy, while Caren takes some time for herself. Caren was able to use a few hours each week to begin to cultivate new relationships at a support group for caregivers and at the church she had begun to attend. Moreover, Caren's potential for caregiver burnout was carefully monitored over the next several months. Caren was helped to gain a sense of mastery in the caregiving process, a sense of meaning associated with caregiving tasks, and a sense of confidence in providing future patient and self-care.

☐ The Family with Adolescents during Recurrence

Adolescents can have a particularly difficult time during the advanced stages of cancer in a parent (Christ et al., 1994). The normal developmental tasks of separating from the family system and identifying with peers and social networks outside of the family environment are often delayed due to the centripetal force of this phase of cancer (Rolland, 1994). The adolescent's developmental needs are thus in direct opposition to the needs of the family with an advanced cancer patient. Often adolescents are required to fill in for the sick family member by helping to raise younger siblings, do more household chores, and to provide nursing care for the sick parent (Christ et al., 1994). When one parent is taken out of the cohesive executive parental subsystem, the oldest child is often placed in the role of the parental assistant (Nichols & Schwartz, 1991). Because of the demands of the illness, adolescents can often miss out on important developmental tasks that take the form of participating in sports, forming close peer relationships, performing optimally academically, and participating in other extracurricular activities (Christ et al., 1994). Adolescents should thus be helped to balance their needs to be of service to the family with their own developmental needs outside of the family system.

The following is a continuation of the case example illustrating Frank's family system. Although Frank had recovered from Hodgkin's disease, he was recently diagnosed with a second type of cancer, leukemia. Leukemia is a systemic cancer affecting the cells in the blood and thus is found wherever blood travels (e.g., bone marrow, lymph nodes, spleen; Gee, 1997). Although leukemia is often regarded as a childhood disease, it occurs in many more adults than children (Gee, 1997). Incidence rates have not changed over the last 50 years, but survival rates have increased, particularly for children (Gee, 1997). Treatment goals for leukemia focus on remission rather than cure. Remission rates are inversely related to the patient's age, with older patients being at an increased risk for treatment complications and death (Gee, 1997). Risk factors include exposure to significant doses of radiation and toxic organic chemical compounds.

CASE EXAMPLE 4 (Continued). Frank's Medical Context

Frank and Anne came in for a psychosocial consultation a few days following Frank's diagnosis of acute myeloblastic leukemia. Frank began the session, "I never did feel like I recovered fully from Hodgkin's disease. I am fatigued and really worn out, not like my old self at all. I guess it didn't surprise me when the doctor told me that I have leukemia. I knew something was really wrong with me. This second cancer is probably a result of the treatments I received for my first cancer." Frank had gone in for a follow-up consultation with his doctor with the symptoms of fever, enlarged lymph nodes, swollen gums, and bruises on his skin. The doctor also discovered that Frank has an enlarged liver and spleen. All of these signs are indicative of leukemia. A definitive diagnosis of leukemia was made via a bone marrow aspiration and biopsy.

Frank and Anne reported the decisions regarding treatment. Frank's treatment is to be divided into two phases, the first being an "induction" phase, which includes chemotherapy treatment with the goal of obtaining remission. The next is a "consolidation" phase, which involves the continuation of treatment, even though Frank would be in remission. The consolidation phase is carried out because residual disease is suspected. Frank understood that the drugs he would receive were likely to cause significant nausea and vomiting, so he will be prescribed medication to help diminish or control these side effects (Rosenbaum & Dollinger, 1997). Frank was also aware that he would experience a reduction in his normal white blood cells and platelets. This would leave him vulnerable to infection. Because of this, Frank would need to stay in the hospital for approximately four to six weeks. In the hospital, Frank would be able to receive blood and platelet transfusions and intravenous antibiotic treatment to control potential infection.

Frank's Family: Preillness Family Structure and Current Level of Family Functioning

Frank and Anne discussed how their family had been doing over the last several months. Anne remarked, "It seems like things never really got back to a normal routine. Frank still feels so sick, and the kids are all out doing their own thing. Frank Jr. is away at college and he rarely comes home for a visit. I think that everything has been too difficult for him. He is taking the time to establish a life for himself away from us." Frank added, "Yeah, everything is out of control. We haven't even seen the kids long enough to tell them about the diagnosis of leukemia. I guess I don't have the energy. I don't even have the energy to enforce the normal rules at home. Alexis and Fred just do what they want. I think Anne feels sorry for them, for all of us, and tries to do everything herself. We need to pull our family back together and deal with this as a family again. It seems like we keep coming together and then growing apart. It's all so confusing."

Anne and Frank also discussed their financial difficulties. Frank stated, "Ever since I was diagnosed with Hodgkin's disease we have had to struggle with our finances. We only have small businesses, and we can barely meet our usual bills, let alone the costs of my health care. Anne works at her job full time now, and she is thinking about asking Alexis to take a year off from high school to help her. I know that Alexis would love to do that, she loves spending time with her Mom, but I think that it is a ridiculous idea. Alexis has her own life and her own needs. I don't want to stop the family in its tracks again."

Case Conceptualization

Frank's family has become disengaged, partly because of their current life cycle, and partly because of the severity of the disease. Thus, Frank and Anne report feeling "out of control" and separated from their children. Changing roles and boundaries need to be addressed within the limitations of Frank's disease. The developmental tasks of loosening boundaries and opening the system to external influences need to be continued, taking Frank's deteriorating health into consideration. To successfully adapt during this phase, the family must learn to balance the needs of the adolescents with Frank's needs for treatment and recuperation. None of the children are aware of the severity of Frank's disease. Anne and Frank have begun to form a rigid communication boundary between their subsystem and the children as a means of gaining some control over the situation. However, this rigid boundary prevents them from discussing the news of Frank's second type of cancer, their need for assistance, and the family's need to "pull together."

Psychosocial Recommendations

It was recommended that Frank and his family come in for a family therapy session. Frank Jr. was away at college, she did not attend. Frank and Anne were able to tell Alexis and Fred about Frank's diagnosis of acute leukemia. They discussed Frank's treatment and the possibility of achieving remission. They went on to address the family's need to develop new rules and roles during this phase of the illness. Anne commented, "Just like the last time, this is going to be hard, but we need to pull together and get through it. Again, these roles and rules are only temporary. We can change them as we go." Because the family may need to remain flexible in terms of rules and roles during the course of Frank's illness, the family decided to implement family meetings again. Family meetings can help the family make decisions about daily task allocation as well as help them to become more integrated as a system (Visher & Visher, 1993).

During the meeting, the family was encouraged to write down all the things that need to be done in order to keep the household running smoothly. To increase his sense of contribution to the family, Frank wrote down the list for the family. Next, the family was asked to decide who will perform certain tasks. They were able to decide who would take care of the household chores and who would help out in the businesses. Anne was relieved of many of the household chores. They would be handled by Alexis and Fred after school. Anne agreed to work a few more hours at the catering business with the help of her sisters. Finally, the family agreed there should be consequences if responsibilities were not carried out as assigned. Alexis and Fred were asked to determine the type and extent of consequences needed if they did not take care of their responsibilities. By having predetermined consequences, it was easier for Frank and Anne to set limits on their children's behavior and to enforce the agreed-upon consequences when necessary. The family was able to use their family meeting time to address the family's changing needs as Frank's illness progressed.

☐ The Family Launching Children during Recurrence

The recurrence phase of cancer brings about difficulties for families launching their children. For the parent with advanced-stage cancer, the complexities of launching children may be compounded by the severity of the illness. The seriously ill parent may attempt to set goals of seeing his or her children go to college, witnessing the marriages of his or her children, or making sure the older children have established themselves in their own careers and lives. In these cases, the developmental process may actually be accelerated so that the parent can be a part of the accomplishments achieved by their adult children. The older children may be expected to accelerate the developmental process by increasing their independence and their responsibilities toward the family. In a sense, they may be pulled inward relationally toward the family system but required to gain independence and responsibilities earlier due to the advancing of the disease. On the other hand, developmental growth may be delayed by the illness in some cases, as both the older children and the parents pull the system inward to once again meet the demands of cancer treatment. Children in the launching stage may postpone going to college, push back wedding dates, and delay seeking their own careers in order to stay home and care for the sick parent. Thus, the recurrent phase of the clinical course of cancer is in direct odds with the developmental needs of this family life cycle.

The following case example is a continuation of Claire's family. Claire was recently diagnosed with recurrent breast cancer. Recurrent breast cancer can be found in the area of the original breast surgery, within the chest wall, or it may be metastatic disease found anywhere in the body (Dollinger et al., 1997b). Most patients with recurrent breast cancer will develop other areas of metastasis (Dollinger et al., 1997b). Patients who develop chest wall recurrence after modified radical mastectomies generally have a poorer prognosis than patients who received conservative surgery followed by radiation therapy (Dollinger et al., 1997b).

CASE EXAMPLE 5 (Continued). Claire's Medical Context

Claire was recently diagnosed with recurrent breast cancer. Claire had been going in for her regular checkups at about four-month intervals. She knew that something was wrong when she discovered some changes in her incisional scar. She also reported experiencing pain in her shoulder, hip, and lower back. Claire understood that her breast cancer had metastasized to her bones. She was to begin receiving chemotherapy treatments next week.

Claire's Family: Preillness Family Structure and Current Level of Family Functioning

Claire and her husband, Greg, came in for a consultation shortly after receiving the news of Claire's cancer recurrence. Claire stated, "I am so scared. I can't believe that this is happening to us again. Katherine is in Europe and I don't want to upset her with the news. I'll just have to wait until she gets back to tell her. Peter is busy at the pharmaceutical company and is thinking about getting married, so I am fearful of telling him too. I don't want to burden him with my problems now. I am just so mad! I want to finish my degree, see my kids get married and have their own families. I want to watch my grandchildren grow up! Why is this happening again? Did I do something wrong? I went to all my checkups. I have been taking care of myself by watching what I eat, by meditating every day, and by drinking my herbal teas. What else could I have done to prevent this? I am so torn between just giving up and throwing in the towel, and trying to fight cancer with all that I've got. I am just not sure I can go through chemotherapy again. I am really afraid that I can't do it again." Greg was also emotionally distraught: "I let Claire down last time. I know that I wasn't really there for her and now she is sick again. I feel like I am to blame for all of this. I'm sure I could have done something more to help her. I am so afraid I'll make the same mistakes again."

Case Conceptualization

Claire and Greg have successfully launched their children. Katherine and Peter are both establishing themselves as single young adults in their worlds of work and intimate relationships. However, communication within the marital subsystem has been a challenge. Claire reported "doing her own thing" both at school and in her volunteer work. She said, "I guess I got my support from my friends. I mean, I know that Greg and I love each other, but without a crisis to deal with, we have nothing to talk about." Greg agreed, "I have never been much of a social person or much of a talker. But I do wish that I could be closer to Claire. I am so scared that I am going to lose her. Now I see all the time I have wasted. I want to try and make it up to her and to our marriage." The centripetal momentum of earlier crisis phases of the illness seemed to pull Greg and Claire together. It appears that during the chronic phases of treatment and remission, Greg and Claire had lapsed back into their old patterns of relating to one another. Now that the crisis of recurrence has occurred, Greg and Claire are challenged once again to reexamine their communication patterns.

Communication between the marital subsystem and the children has been cut off as well. Claire reported, "I just couldn't bother Katherine with my fears of cancer recurrence any longer. She was finishing school and getting ready to go to Europe. She had so much to do and so many things on her mind. Every time I talked to her, I felt like I upset her. I tried to keep our conversations light, but then it just got easier to stay away from her too." During the prior phases of the clinical course of cancer, Claire had begun to slowly isolate herself from her family and loved ones. She stated that it had become easier just to focus on her work: "I guess I became more like Greg. I couldn't deal with thinking about my fears and cancer, and I couldn't deal with trying to make my family work by myself. Instead, I learned to focus on my own needs. Now, it seems like I am alone and helpless. I don't think I can do it all alone anymore." The family's rules and boundaries had become maladaptive, in large part due to the demands of the illness. Communication patterns would need to be examined and new ones put into effect. Rigid boundaries would need to be replaced by more flexible ones, and overall patterns of family interaction would need to be changed.

Psychosocial Recommendations

It was recommended that Claire and Greg continue to put limits on the disease in their lives. At first Claire was hesitant: "How can I put limits on cancer? I think about it all the time, and the pain reminds me that I am still sick." Claire chose to set limits on her illness by compartmentalizing her thoughts. She was assigned to take 30 minutes each day where she would just think about her illness. If worries or concerns came into her mind outside of that 30-minute period, she was instructed to write those thoughts down in order to deal with them during her scheduled time. In addition, Claire reinforced her new limits by taking time each day to focus on doing something for her family and for herself. This would help her to gain a sense of control over her life while at the same time minimizing her distress (Lewis & Deal, 1995). In turn, Greg was to check in with Claire every day to get an update on her health status and daily needs (Lewis & Deal, 1995). By checking in daily, Greg could help to monitor and to make sure that Claire was taking needed pain medication. In addition, her depression and anxiety could also be assessed and treated, if necessary. Greg's fears of losing Claire to cancer were also addressed. It was recommended that they begin to plan "as if" death for either of them were a real possibility. When both were in agreement, they could discuss insurance policies, funeral plans, and burial plots for both of them. It was also recommended that Greg take part in decision making regarding any clinical trials for which Claire may be a good candidate. Claire said, "I want your input, Greg. We need to discuss all of these things. We're each thinking about them anyway. So why not discuss them together? Don't be afraid you will scare me or upset me. I don't want to feel isolated and alone anymore. We are both afraid. So let's share our fears."

During a follow-up session, it was recommended that Greg and Claire write down all of their fears, putting each one on a separate index card. They were to put their fears in boxes that were symbolic of their personalities (Rediger, 1993). Claire stated, "My box is an old stationery box. I love it because it was given to me by my mother when I was just a girl. It is symbolic of how I still feel like child, especially since I got cancer." Then Greg shared his symbolic box: "Mine is an old shaving kit. I've had it for a long time and I never use it anymore. When I was looking around the house for a box, I found it and I couldn't believe how long it had been since I used it. Remember how I used to use it all the time when we first got married? I guess it is symbolic of how I don't appreciate the things that have been with me for a long time. I take them for granted. I just put them on the shelf and never appreciate their beauty and usefulness." It was recommended that they keep their boxes in special places and discuss their fears one by one, as the need arose. In this way, they could gain a sense of control over their fears and the illness, as well as enhance communication within the marital system.

Gradually, their communication patterns began to change. Greg and Claire decided to tell Katherine and Peter together about the news of the recurrence phase: "It was so hard telling them both. It was like we had to relive the news ourselves all over again. But once it was out, we all felt so close to one another and the support was overwhelming." At a follow-up session Claire reported how the "fear box" had helped her and how she has a "wish box" now, too: "The fear box really helped me through the initial crisis. Sometimes I felt so afraid of everything that I would take out all my cards at once and spread them on the floor around me. Then, one by one, Greg would place them back in the box with me. I felt so supported and loved when we did that together. Then, I made a wish box. Katherine brought me some wonderful perfume from Paris in a gold box. I decided to keep the box she wrapped it in and use it as my wish box. I have so many wishes and hopes for the future. Now, when I am feeling sad or out of control, I take out my wishes and focus on the smallest one. Sometimes I just wish for the pain to subside. Sometimes I wish to see the day of my children's weddings. No matter how small the wish is, it seems to give me a sense of hope, and it helps me to deal with the fear of death."

☐ The Family in Later Life during Recurrence

Although advanced stages of cancer and cancer metastasis are generally associated with aging, the effects of cancer on the family system can still be debilitating. Older adults with cancer may need to forego all retirement plans and dreams; move from their long-cherished homes into hospitals, nursing homes, or the homes of their children; and face the possibility of a painful death. Spouses and adult children may need to delay their own developmental needs in order to care for the sick family member. Older adults caring for their spouses may not have the strength, health, or stamina to see to all their ill spouse's needs. Thus, external resources are important to assess when intragenerational caregiving is being attempted by adults in later life. Similarly, adult children caring for their ill parent may become overwhelmed in their attempt to meet the needs of their own families and the needs of their ailing parent. External resources, such as extended family members, older grandchildren, and professional health care workers, may need to be enlisted to help when intergenerational responsibilities become too great.

The following case example depicts a male in later life who has recently been diagnosed with extensive-stage small cell lung cancer. The staging system of small cell lung cancer focuses on whether the disease is limited or extensive (Glassberg et al., 1997). Limited-stage small cell lung cancer is cancer that is confined to the site where it originated, whereas extensive-stage disease is widespread (Glassberg et al., 1997). With extensive-stage lung cancer, the average survival time is only about 6 to 12 months, even with current treatments (Glassberg et al., 1997).

CASE EXAMPLE 10. Carl's Medical Context

Carl, age 86, was recently diagnosed with recurrent metastatic small cell lung cancer. Lung cancer had metastasized to Carl's brain, and his cognitive functioning was rapidly declining. Carl was often disoriented and was suffering from dyspnea, anorexia, and pain. Currently, he was hospitalized in order to monitor his pulmonary functioning, to assess his level of cognitive impairment, and to control his pain. Carl had been a heavy smoker all of his adult life and had not complied with recommendations for smoking cessation.

Carl's Family: Preillness Family Structure and Current Level of Family Functioning

Carl's wife, Ruth, came in for a psychosocial consultation. "I have been with Carl for over 60 years and I have never seen him like this. He is not himself at all. His personality has changed so much that I don't even know him. Most of the time he barely recognizes me and he almost never recognizes our children." Carl and Ruth have four children and 10 grandchildren. All of them live in the same town and have been helping Ruth take care of Carl. Their family genogram is illustrated in Figure 6.4. Ruth explained, "My kids try and help out, especially Mary. But they don't know what it has been like these past few months, watching him waste away and lose his mind. He is in so much pain that sometimes I pray to the Lord to take him away and relieve him from his suffering. I feel so guilty, but I just can't take care of him anymore. He has difficulty controlling his bowel movements, and I am too weak to keep him clean. The last time I bathed him, we both almost fell as I tried to help him from the tub."

Case Conceptualization

Ruth was experiencing severe emotional distress even though she reported having much external support. Ruth's age, her own physical stamina, the immobility of her husband, and his cognitive impairment all contributed to her burnout and distress. Although Ruth reported loving her husband and having "countless wonderful memories together," there was no mutuality in the caregiver–patient relationship due to Carl's physical and cognitive impairment (Given & Given, 1998). Thus, Ruth was a prime candidate for burnout, in-

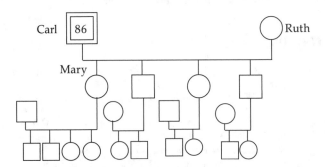

FIGURE 6.4. The family in later life during recurrence genogram.

creased anxiety, and severe depression. Ruth was also having difficulty deciding whether to permanently hospitalize her husband. She said, "He always said he wanted to die at home with me by his side. I just don't know if I can help him do that. I am afraid that I will end up hurting him and myself in the process."

Psychosocial Recommendations

It was recommended that Ruth discuss her concerns with the treatment team. Ruth also obtained information regarding in-home health care services, hospice care, and hospitalization. Her daughter, Mary, helped her to decide on Carl's care. Mary explained, "Mom and Dad had a great marriage. We are a close and loving family. But she is going to hurt herself and Dad if she keeps on caring for him at home. They both almost got hurt the last time she tried to bathe him. We talked to the oncologist and we have decided that Mom can no longer care for him alone. We are going to have help from home health care services. They can help both him and Mom maintain a higher quality of life until the day he dies. Mom, you shouldn't feel badly about getting help. It is for your own health and safety." Ruth nodded in agreement: "I know it is for the best. I can't administer his pain medication like he needs me to. I can't bathe him or help him to the bathroom either."

Ruth was considered a valuable member of the treatment team (Stiles, 1990). She was to report any changes in patient functioning, no matter how subtle. Specifically, she was to monitor any changes in pain medication needs, cognitive functioning, and pulmonary functioning. She was encouraged to talk with her husband, sing to him, touch him, and read to him. She was also encouraged to care for herself by maintaining adequate nutrition, getting plenty of breaks and rest, and visiting with her extended family. Ruth and her family were also encouraged to discuss the necessity of advanced directives with the staff social worker in order to prepare for the next phase of the clinical course of cancer.

☐ Summary

In this chapter, the focus was on the family during the recurrence phase of the illness. Important biomedical variables, such as understanding cancer metastasis, pain management, and ongoing cancer treatment, were discussed. In addition, the importance of maintaining a sense of "balance" in the family system was highlighted. During this phase of the clinical course of cancer, the family system must attempt to maintain a balance between sustaining hope for remission or cure while preparing for death and potential loss. New case examples were introduced, and previous case examples were continued. In the final chapter, family adaptation to terminal cancer will be addressed.

☐ References

Ahles, T., Blanchard, E., & Ruckdeschel, J. (1983). The multidimensional nature of cancer related pain. *Pain, 17,* 277–288.

Ahles, T., & Martin, J. (1992). Cancer pain: A multidimensional perspective. *Hospice Journal, 8,* 25–48.

American Cancer Society (ACS). (1998). *Metastatic cancer.* [Brochure]. Atlanta, GA: Author.

Archbold, P., Stewart, B., Greenlick, M., & Harvath, T. (1990). Mutuality and preparedness as predictors of caregiver role strain. *Research Nursing Health, 13,* 375–384.

Beck, A., Lester, D., Trexler, L., & Weissman, A. (1974). The measurement of pessimism: The hopelessness scale. *Journal of Consulting & Clinical Psychology, 42,* 861–865.

Breitbart, W., & Passik, S. (1993a). Psychiatric aspects of palliative care. In D. Doyle, G. Hands, & N. MacDonald (Eds.), *Oxford textbook of palliative medicine* (pp. 609–626). New York: Oxford University Press.

Breitbart, W., & Passik, S. (1993b). Psychological and psychiatric interventions in pain control. In D. Doyle, G. Hanks, & N. MacDonald (Eds.), *Oxford textbook of palliative medicine* (pp. 244–256). New York: Oxford University Press.

Breitbart, W., Passik, S., & Rosenfeld, B. (1994). Psychiatric and psychological aspects of cancer pain. In P. Wall & R. Melzack (Eds.), *Textbook of pain* (pp. 825–859). New York: Churchill Livingstone.

Buehler, J., & Lee, H. (1992). Exploration of home care resources for rural families. *Cancer Nursing, 15,* 299–308.

Bukberg, J., Penman, D., & Holland, J. (1984). Depression in hospitalized cancer patients. *Psychosomatic Medicine, 43,* 199–212.

Bunston, T., Mings, D., Mackie, A., & Jones, D. (1995). Facilitating hopefulness: The determinants of hope. *Journal of Psychosocial Oncology, 13*(4), 79–102.

Carey, P., Oberst, M., McCubbin, M., & Hughes, S. (1991). Appraisal and caregiving burden in family members caring for patients receiving chemotherapy. *Oncology Nursing Forum, 18,* 1341–1348.

Chekryn, J. (1984). Cancer recurrence: Personal meaning, communication and marital adjustment. *Cancer Nursing, 7,* 491–498.

Christ, G., Siegel, K., & Sperber, D. (1994). Impact of parental terminal cancer on adolescents. *American Journal of Orthopsychiatry, 64*(4), 604–613.

Clipp, E., George, L. (1990). Caregiver needs and patterns of social support. *Journal of Gerontology, 45,* S102–111.

Dollinger, M., Rosenbaum, E., & Cable, G. (Eds.). (1997a). *Everyone's guide to cancer therapy: How cancer is diagnosed, treated, and managed day to day* (3rd ed.). Toronto, Ontario, Canada: Somerville House Books Limited.

Dollinger, M., Rosenbaum, E., & Cable, G. (Eds.). (1997b). Breast. In M. Dollinger, E. Rosenbaum, & G. Cable (Eds.), *Everyone's guide to cancer therapy: How cancer is diagnosed, treated, and managed day to day* (3rd ed., pp. 356–384). Toronto, Ontario, Canada: Somerville House Books Limited.

Ellerhorst-Ryan, J. (1997). The nature of cancer. In C. Varricchio (Ed.). *A cancer source book for nurses* (7th ed., pp. 31–43). Atlanta, GA: Jones and Bartlett.

Eysenck, H. (1987). The place of anxiety and impulsivity in a dimensional framework. *Journal of Research in Personality, 21,* 489–493.

Ferszt, G., & Waldman, R. (1997). Psychosocial responses to disease and treatment. In C. Varricchio (Ed.), *A cancer source book for nurses* (7th ed.). Atlanta, GA: Jones and Bartlett.

Fleishman, S., & Lesko, L. (1989). Delirium and dementia. In J. Holland & J. Rowland (Eds.), *Handbook of psychooncology: Psychological care of the patient with cancer.* New York: Oxford University Press.

Gee, T. (1997). Leukemia. In M. Dollinger, E. Rosenbaum, & G. Cable (Eds.), *Everyone's guide to cancer therapy: How cancer is diagnosed, treated, and managed day to day* (3rd ed., pp. 512–524). Toronto, Ontario, Canada: Somerville House Books Limited.

Germino, B., & O'Rourke, M. (1996). Cancer and the family. In R. McCorkle, M. Grant, M. Frank-Stromborg, & S. Baird (Eds.), *Cancer nursing: A comprehensive textbook* (2nd ed.). Philadelphia: W.B. Saunders Company.

Given, G., & Given, C. (1992). Patient and family caregiver reaction to new and recurrent breast cancer. *Journal of the American Medical Women's Association, 47,* 206–210.

Given, G., & Given, C. (1998). Family caregiver burden from cancer care. In J. Holland & J. Rowland (Eds.), *Handbook of psychooncology: Psychological care of the patient with cancer* (pp. 93–109). New York: Oxford University Press.

Glassberg, A., Cornett, P., & Jahan, T. (1997). Lung: Small cell. In M. Dollinger, E. Rosenbaum & G. Cable (Eds.), *Everyone's guide to cancer therapy: How cancer is diagnosed, treated, and managed day to day* (3rd ed., pp. 540–544). Toronto, Ontario, Canada: Somerville House Books Limited.

Gotay, C. (1984). The experience of cancer during early and advanced stages: The views of patients and their mates. *Social Science and Medicine, 18*(7), 605–613.

Grossman, S., Sheidler, V., Sweden, K., Mucenski, J., & Piantadosi, S. (1991). Correlations of patient and caregiver ratings of cancer pain. *Journal of Pain and Symptom Management, 6,* 53–57.

Harpham, W. (1994). *After cancer: A guide to your new life.* New York: W.W. Norton & Company.

Kaye, J., & Gracely, E. (1993). Psychological distress in cancer patients and their spouses. *Journal of Cancer Education, 8*(1), 47–52.

Lawton, M., Moss, M., Kleban, M., Glicksman, A., & Rovine, M. (1991). A two-year factor model of caregiving appraisal and psychological well-being. *Journal of Gerontology, 46,* P181–189.

Lazarus, R., & Folkman, D. (1984). *Stress appraisal and coping.* New York: Springer-Verlag.

Lerner, M. (1994). Training for cancer: An interview with Michael Lerner. *The Journal of Mind-Body Health, 10*(2), 27–37.

Lewis, F., & Deal, L. (1995). Balancing our lives: A study of the married couple's experience with breast cancer recurrence. *Oncology Nursing Forum, 22*(6), 943–953.

Lloyd, C., & Coggles, L. (1990). Psychological issues for people with cancer and their families. *Cancer Journal of Occupational Therapy, 57,* 211–215.

Loscalzo, M., & Brintzenhofescoz, K. (1998). Brief crisis counseling. In J. Holland & J. Rowland (Eds.), *Handbook of psychooncology: Psychological care of the patient with cancer* (pp. 662–675). New York: Oxford University Press.

Massie, M., Holland, J., & Glass, E. (1983). Delirium in terminally ill cancer patients. *American Journal of Psychiatry, 140,* 1048–1050.

Menninger, K. (1959). Hope. *American Journal of Psychiatry, 116,* 481–491.

Mitchell, M. (1997). Melanoma. In M. Dollinger, E. Rosenbaum, & G. Cable (Eds.), *Everyone's guide to cancer therapy: How cancer is diagnosed, treated, and managed day to day* (3rd ed., pp. 568–578). Toronto, Ontario, Canada: Somerville House Books Limited.

Mor, V., Allen, S., & Malin, M. (1994). The psychosocial impact of cancer on older versus younger patients and their families. *Cancer Supplement, 74*(7), 2118–2126.

Nichols, M. P., & Schwartz, R. C. (1991). *Family therapy: Concepts and methods.* Needham Heights, MA: Allyn and Bacon.

Northouse, L. (1995). The impact of cancer in women on the family. *Cancer Practice, 3*(3), 134–142.

Nowotny, M. (1989). Assessment of hope in patients with cancer: Development of an instrument. *Oncology Nursing Forum, 16,* 57–61.

Nowotny, M. (1991). Every tomorrow, a vision of hope. *Journal of Psychosocial Oncology, 9*(3), 117–126.

O'Connor, A., Wicker, C., & Germino, C. (1990). Understanding the cancer patient's search for meaning. *Cancer Nursing, 13,* 167–175.

Pace, J. (1997). Palliative care. In C. Varricchio (Ed.), *A cancer source book for nurses* (7th ed.). Atlanta, GA: Jones and Bartlett.

Portenoy, R., & Foley, K. (1989). Management of cancer pain. In J. Holland & J. Rowland (Eds.), *Handbook of psychooncology: Psychological care of the patient with cancer.* New York: Oxford University Press.

Raleigh, E. (1992). Sources of hope in chronic illness. *Oncology Nursing Forum, 19,* 443–448.

Rediger, S. (1993). Putting away old loyalties in later life. In T. Nelson & T. Trepper (Eds.), *101 interventions in family therapy* (pp. 94–99). Binghamton, NY: The Haworth Press.

Ringdal, G. (1995). Correlates of hopelessness in cancer patients. *Journal of Psychosocial Oncology, 13*(3), 47–66.

Rolland, J. S. (1994). *Families, illness, and disability.* New York: Basic Books.

Rosenbaum, E., & Dollinger, M. (1997). Colon and rectum. In M. Dollinger, E. Rosenbaum, & G. Cable (Eds.), *Everyone's guide to cancer therapy: How cancer is diagnosed, treated, and managed day to day* (3rd ed., pp. 430–449). Toronto, Ontario Canada: Somerville House Books Limited.

Sales, E. (1992). Psychosocial impact of the phase of cancer on the family: An updated review. *Journal of Psychosocial Oncology, 9*(4), 1–18.

Schachter, S., & Coyle, N. (1998). Palliative home care—Impact on families. In J. Holland & J. Rowland, *Handbook of psychooncology: Psychological care of the patient with cancer.* New York: Oxford University Press.

Schmale, A. (1976). Psychological reactions to recurrent metastasis of dissemination cancer. *International Journal of Radiation Oncology Biology Physics, 1,* 515–520.

Schulz, R., Williamson, G., Knapp, J., Bookwala, J., Lave, J., & Fello, M. (1995). The psychological, social, and economic impact of illness among patients with recurrent cancer. *Journal of Psychosocial Oncology, 13*(3), 21–45.

Siegel, K., Palamara Mesagno, F., Karus, D., Christ, G., Banks, K., & Moynihan, R. (1992). Psychosocial adjustment of children with a terminally ill parent. *Journal of the American Academy of Child and Adolescent Psychiatry, 31*(2), 327–333.

Stiefel, F., Breitbart, W., & Holland, J. (1989). Corticosteroids in cancer: Neuropsychiatric complications. *Cancer Investigation, 7*, 479–491.

Stiles, M. (1990). The shining stranger: Nurse-family spiritual relationship. *Cancer Nursing, 13*, 235–245.

Stommel, M., Given, C., & Given, B. (1990). Depression as an overriding variable explaining caregiver burden. *Journal of Aging Health, 2*, 81–102.

Stommel, M., & Kingry, M. (1991). Support patterns for spouse-caregivers of cancer patients: The effect of the presence of minor children. *Cancer Nursing, 14*, 200–205.

Visher, E., & Visher, J. (1993). Family meetings: A tool for developing roles and rules. In T. Nelson & T. Trepper (Eds.), *101 interventions in family therapy* (pp. 177–183). Binghamton, NY: The Haworth Press.

Volker, D. (1992). Pathophysiology of cancer. In J. Clark & R. McGee (Eds)., *Core curriculum for oncology nursing* (2nd ed.). Philadelphia: W.B. Saunders Company.

Walsh, T. (1990). Continuing care in a medical center: The Cleveland Clinic Foundation Palliative Care Service. *Journal of Pain and Symptom Management, 5*, 273–278.

Williamson, G., & Schulz, R. (1992). Physical illness and symptoms of depression among elderly outpatients. *Psychology & Aging, 7*, 343–351.

World Health Organization (WHO). (1990). *Cancer pain relief and palliative care.* Geneva: Author.

Wright, L., Clipp, E., & George, L. (1993). Health consequences of caregiver stress. *Medicine, Exercise, Nutrition, and Health, 2*, 181–195.

Terminal Illness and the Family Life Cycle: In a Strange Land

This last phase of the clinical course of cancer is a time marked by important decision making regarding additional treatment, palliative care, and the appropriate setting for that care. In addition, cancer pain, which has been closely associated with increased psychiatric symptomatology (Breitbart, Passik, & Rosenfeld, 1994), and cancer symptom control must each be carefully monitored and treated. During the terminal illness phase, the family must begin to "live just in case" by preparing advanced directives (Emanuel, 1998), preparing for the dying process and death, and preparing for life without a cherished family member (Babcock, 1997).

☐ Medical Variables during the Terminal Illness Phase

Song of a Man About to Die in a Strange Land
(Ojibwa poem, circa 1400; also quoted in Forman, 1998, p. 735)

> If I die here in a strange land,
> If I die in a land not my own,
> Nevertheless, the thunder,
> The rolling thunder;
> Will take me home.
> If I die here, the wind,
> The wind rushing over the prairie,
> The wind will take me home.
> The wind and the thunder;
> They are the same everywhere,
> What does it matter; then,
> If I die in a strange land.

The dying process is a deeply personal experience, a process that is central to one's intimate life story (Cassel, 1982; Storey, 1998). While most patients wish to die at home, in a "familiar land" free from pain and suffering, they must often face death in the strange land of the hospital, nursing home, or hospice health care setting. During the terminal illness phase, it is important to assess and to reassess the oncology health care setting that is the most appropriate for end-of-life care. This decision-making process is both a systematic and dynamic one. It is systematic because specific criteria must be taken into consideration each time the patient's health care setting is evaluated. Specific criteria include: (1) the physiological needs of the patient, (2) the current knowledge and information needs of the patient and the family, and (3) coping strategies used by the patient and the family that affect the patient's health and well-being (Stephens Mills, 1992). The specific status of the patient's health, including the patient's degree of mobility, elimination patterns, and the patient's ventilation and current respiratory status, must also be evaluated by the medical team. The decision-making process is dynamic due to the constant change in the patient's physiological and psychosocial needs. As a dynamic process, decision making regarding the oncology setting should be collaborative (health care team, patient, family members, social workers, dietitian, chaplain and/or minister) and proactive, anticipating the future needs of the patient and the family system (Stephens Mills, 1992). Understanding the family's past experiences with illness and their strengths gained from past illness, or the past phases of the clinical course of cancer, can help to determine the proper setting for patients during the terminal illness phase (Stephens Mills, 1992). Determining where and why the patient is in the current health care setting, identifying the primary care provider, verifying the availability of support persons, evaluating the adequacy of finances, emotionally meeting the needs of the patient and the family, and considering if home is the preferred setting are all important in the determination of the appropriate health care setting (Stephens Mills, 1992).

Home health care for the patient can take the form of family caregiving, nursing agencies, and nursing home facilities (Stephens Mills, 1992). The Department of Health and Human Services defines home health care as "that component of a continuum of comprehensive health care whereby health services are provided to individuals and families in their places of residence for the purpose of promoting, maintaining, or restoring health, or of maximizing the level of independence, while minimizing the effects of disability and illness, including terminal illness." Families caring for their terminally ill family member may require the assistance of a home health care agency to (1) deal with managing pain, nutrition, elimination difficulties, and sleeplessness; (2) engage other family members in the caregiving process thereby extending patient care in the home; and (3) give the primary caregiver respite during periods of prolonged caregiving (Stephens Mills, 1992). Home care nurses, social workers, chaplains, pharmacists, respiratory therapists, mental health counselors, and dietitians can all help to provide in-home services for the terminally ill patient. Even patients who need intravenous therapy, ongoing chemotherapy, or antibiotic or analgesic infusion pump therapy can remain at home with the assistance of home nursing agencies. Advantages of home health care include the comfort and familiarity of the home setting, reduction in the risk of infection, and the maintenance of optimal daily living activities for both the patient and the family (Stephens Mills, 1992). The disadvantages of home health care include possible conflicting goals between the patient, the family, and the medical treatment team; high levels of stress and burnout for the primary caregiver; and possible financial complications involving insurance reimbursement.

Home Care

At times, either temporary or permanent nursing home placement may be required for patients who are in need of skilled nursing services. Often the decision to place the patient in a nursing home facility may be the result of a caregiving crisis, and come at great emotional cost to the patient's family (Stephens Mills, 1992). However, when the physical and emotional needs of the patient exceed the caregiver's ability to provide sufficient care at home, a nursing home or residential care setting may have the advantages of providing respite for the primary caregiver and providing care and resources that are not available in the home (Stephens Mills 1992).

Hospital Care

The hospital setting, including oncology units and general medical units, is another option for patient care during the terminal illness phase. An oncology unit is "a designated hospital area that facilitates the team approach to comprehensive cancer care by bringing into close proximity personnel and facilities necessary for such care; provides not only for the physical needs of the cancer client, but also for the ongoing emotional, social, and spiritual support of the client and his or her family or significant others" (Stephens Mills, 1992, p. 208). The advantages of an oncology unit include the ability to (1) meet the needs of patients with catastrophic and terminal illness, (2) provide technical knowledge and skilled interventions to terminal illness with readily available equipment, and (3) sustain a high degree of trust and cohesion between the medical team, the family, and the patient. However, the disadvantages of the hospital setting can include staffing shortages, increased family demands and frustrations, burnout, and psychological distress for members of the health care team and the family (Stephens Mills, 1992).

Hospice Care

The hospice setting has served to shape the current view of the process of death and dying (Forman, 1998). A frequently cited quote by Dr. Cicely Saunders, the founder and director of St. Christopher's Hospice, captures the intent and the mission of the modern hospice program: "You matter because you are you. You matter to the last moment of your life, and we will do all we can not only to help you die peacefully, but also to live until you die" (Pace, 1997, p. 260). The goals of hospice are to enhance patient quality of life, to provide medical and nursing care, to provide pain control, and to provide an alternative to acute care via a multidisciplinary care team (Pace, 1997). Professionals working in the hospice setting can also teach basic patient care to family members while lending emotional, social, and spiritual support (Pace, 1997). Hospice settings can be (1) community based (a community office of staff skilled to assist with home care), (2) hospital based (may be inpatient or a hospital-based home care program), or (3) hospital based with a hospice team (also referred to as the palliative care team working in a hospital setting), or (4) a freestanding hospice facility, such as a hospice house (Stephens Mills, 1992). In the freestanding hospice, the hospice team works with the family while the patient remains either in the home or in the hospice setting. The patient's and the family's biopsychosocial needs are met by the hospice team, which provides services aimed at reducing physical symptomatology (i.e., pain, nausea, confusion, dyspnea, constipation, and lack of physical functioning), meeting the patients and the family's intellectual needs (i.e., need to know the patients' prognosis, expected signs and symptoms, and available resources), and reducing emotional strain and social disruption (Pace, 1997). In addition, both the financial concerns and the spiritual needs of the patient and the family are addressed in the hospice setting (Pace, 1997). The advantages of the hospice setting include (1) around-the-clock care by skilled practitioners and caring individuals; (2) the identification of patient and the family as the unit of care; (3) an emphasis on the physical, emotional, psychosocial, and spiritual needs of the patient and the family; and (4) continuous and comprehensive care with the family after the patient's death (Stephens Mills, 1992).

Symptom Control during the Terminal Illness Phase

During the final phase of the disease, patients want their caretakers to know that they are more than just an amalgamation of cells, tissue, and organs (Storey, 1998). They want to be cared for in their totality and recognized as human beings with a rich history, present desires, and hopes for the future. Thus, symptom control during the terminal phase is more than just managing cancer-related pain. It is about addressing all of the needs of the patient and the family system: the physical, emotional, psychosocial, and spiritual components of life and death. Symptom control management begins with relaying honest information to the patient and to the family regarding the patient's health status, prognosis, and projected symptomatology (Storey, 1998). Following the provision of information, a careful examination of the patient's "medical intensity" and specific goals is needed. Examining the patient's "medical intensity" involves putting the patient into a developmental and personal context (Storey, 1998). For example, symptom control and treatment for an 89-year-old cancer patient with dementia will differ from the young adult who demonstrates no cognitive impairment and is both physically and mentally highly functioning (Storey, 1998).

Setting specific goals for symptom control management with terminally ill patients often encompasses (1) getting to know the person with the disease, his or her beliefs, desires, likes/dislikes, hopes, and fears; (2) gauging the medical intensity, his or her physical and medical context, prognosis, and overall health; (3) searching for treatable causes of the symptoms if possible (i.e., altering medication to reduce dementia or pain); and (4) treating the causes of the symptoms specifically by using multidisciplinary team efforts (Storey, 1998). Symptoms during the terminal illness phase usually involve crescendo pain (De Conno, Saita, Ripamonti, & Ventafridda, 1993; Storey, 1998), terminal restlessness (Breitbart, Bruera, Chochinov, & Lynch, 1995), rattling secretions (Storey, 1998), and the need for hope during the final weeks of life (Herth, 1990).

Crescendo pain is the "rapid escalation in the intensity of pain and anguish close to the end of life" (Storey, 1998, p. 742). Possible causes of severe crescendo pain can include physical distress, such as difficulties with swallowing, weakness, neuropathic pain, severe constipation, and ineffective pain medication (Storey, 1998). As with any degree of pain, crescendo pain can also be intensified by emotional and psychosocial responses such as anxiety, insomnia, interpersonal stress, anger, and hopelessness (Storey, 1998). A detailed evaluation of pain during the terminal phase of the disease is often difficult to obtain, particularly with patients experiencing dementia or delirium. Some components in the evaluation of pain include (1) identifying the specific type and stage of cancer, (2) knowing what medications have been prescribed and taken, (3) examining any changes that the patient has recently experienced (i.e., interpersonal distress, falls, advancing disease), and (4) recognizing who is caring for the patient and what the primary caregiver's views are on the patient's pain and meaning behind the pain (Storey, 1998). If the patient's pain cannot be controlled in the home setting, hospitalization may be required.

Terminal restlessness is a period of time, close to the end of life, during which a person experiences agitation and the inability to rest quietly and comfortably (Storey, 1998). It is often marked by delusions, hallucinations, and intense physical discomfort. Because of pain, discomfort, psychological distress, and cognitive impairment, many patients may suffer from fits of restlessness and agitation from which they can find no relief (Storey, 1998). An evaluation of terminal restlessness includes (1) examining any precipitating events (new medications, overdose of medication, new insults or injuries), (2) assessing for any urinary retention or severe constipation, (3) sorting out any analgesics or psychotropic medications that may be resulting in terminal restlessness, (4) looking for any metabolic imbalances, neurologic impairment, or possible infection, and (when all else is ruled out) (5) determining the potential efficacy of sedatives to relieve the patient from terminal restlessness symptomatology (Storey, 1998). Terminal restlessness and delirium are also primary reasons for patients to be hospitalized during the terminal illness phase (Storey, 1998).

In addition to terminal restlessness, advanced cancer patients may also experience rattling secretions, which is caused by difficulties in clearing their pulmonary secretions (Storey, 1998). These secretions could be due to pneumonia, bronchitis, or allergic rhinitis, all of which can be detected and controlled (Storey, 1998).

Of all the physical and psychosocial symptomatology experienced at the end of life, possibly the most distressing is a sense of hopelessness. Even during the final days of life, hope can be restored for the patient and the family by helping them to find meaning, beauty, and joy in their personal life stories (Cassel, 1982). Patients and their families can be helped to clarify their spiritual and religious beliefs and to recognize the unique roles and gifts they have given to the enduring multigenerational life cycle (Herth, 1990; Storey, 1998). With the provision of hope, ultimately the patient and the family may find peace and comfort during the final days of life.

Suicidal Ideation during the Terminal Illness Phase

During the terminal phase of the illness, cancer patients will frequently experience increases in pain and its subsequent psychiatric symptomatology such as anxiety and depression (Breitbart & Passik, 1993). Depression, particularly that associated with hopelessness, has been regarded as a predictor of suicidal ideation in terminally ill cancer patients (Breitbart & Passik, 1993). Hopelessness that is a result of feeling "like a burden" to the family, or that is accompanied by a sense of despair, regret, or worthlessness, is likely to lead to thoughts of suicide for the advanced cancer patient (Breitbart & Passik, 1993). Additional predictors of suicidal ideation in cancer patients include (1) delirium, (2) lack of perceived control, (3) preexisting psychopathology, (4) substance/alcohol abuse, (5) fatigue, and (6) social isolation (Breitbart, 1990).

Clinical accounts reveal that almost all terminally ill cancer patients entertain thoughts about suicide "as a way out" if cancer pain and suffering become too great (Breitbart & Passik, 1993). Terminally ill patients who experience fatigue, emotional distress, financial depletion, and spiritual exhaustion during the final phase of cancer are likely to contemplate suicide. Conversely, the presence of hope may act as an internal buffer against suicidal ideation. For example, patients who are able to maintain hope within the confines of the realities of their illness (i.e., pain can be controlled, there is meaning in their lives, their families will be taken care of, they have few regrets, they do not despair) are less likely to persist in suicidal ideation (Breitbart & Passik, 1993). Further, patients with strong relational and familial support systems are more likely to have an external control system, thus making them less likely to consider suicide as an optional "way out" (Breitbart & Passik, 1993).

However, inadequate pain control is probably the major factor in suicidal ideation (Breitbart, 1990). Ironically, patients with difficulty controlling pain and with thoughts of suicide can reach an impass in obtaining adequate pain medication because some medical professionals regard aggressive pain control as a form of euthanasia. This belief can deter the medical staff from providing their patients with more aggressive pain control medications such as opioid infusions (Breitbart, Passik, & Rosenfeld, 1994). Thus, both doctor and patient are left making the delicate decision between remaining in excessive pain with accompanied suicidal ideation, or prescribing aggressive pain control medications that could lead to terminal sedation (Storey, 1998) and ultimately death.

☐ Passive Euthanasia: Withholding and Withdrawing Treatment

It is important to note that in the process of crossing into the terminal phase of cancer, the relationship between the physician and the patient changes. Where once the physician was seen as possessing the ability to cure, now both the physician and the patient must recognize the limits of medicine and begin to bond in a different way (Barnard, 1998). In short, the new relationship must be forged on a shared and altered definition of hope. The focus of hope must shift from one of cure to one of comfort and enhanced quality of life. Indeed, both the physician and the patient must make this shift in focus in order to maintain a deepening bond during the end-of-life phase of the disease (Barnard, 1998). The professional staff can do much to promote hope for their dying patients, particularly when their own personal issues of life, death, and "the meaning of it all" are squarely addressed (Oratz, 1988). Terminally ill patients often hope to have loved ones around them, to be free from pain, to die a peaceful death, and to be able to use their talents even during their last days of life (Barnard, 1998; Herth, 1990; Kastenbaum, 1986). Conversely, patients often fear dying in isolation, dying with uncontrolled pain, and the depersonalization that can often occur during the terminal phase when all hope is lost (Barnard, 1998).

When hope for controlled pain is lost, and patients experience intractable physical and existential suffering, both the patient and the physician enter into a strange land of decision making where the rules are no longer clear cut. Passive euthanasia, or the withholding and withdrawing of life-sustaining treatment, has been distinguished from active, physician-assisted suicide, although the distinctions are still being debated (Barnard, 1998). Three differences have been made between active and passive forms of euthanasia. First, intentionality must be considered: Passive euthanasia is the withdrawing of treatment that can no longer accomplish its goal, and active euthanasia is the intentional act of ending the patient's life. Second, the right to be left alone must be considered: Passive euthanasia is regarded as the patient setting limits on the power others have over his or her life (a negative right), and active euthanasia is regarded as a positive request for intervention. Third, the possibility for continuing care must be considered: The discontinuation of care associated with passive euthanasia is a process that often can be reversed, and active euthanasia is a process that is irreversible (Weir, 1989).

The terminal illness phase brings the patient, the family, and the physician to crossroads with many delicate and sensitive decisions to be made. Many of these decisions will be based upon the patient's pain intensity, available treatments, the desires of the patient and the family, and the presence or absence of hope. Importantly, terminally ill cancer patients want to remain connected to family, friends, their personal God, and also to their physicians and health care providers. They do not want to become isolated and cut off from people who love them and from people who can comfort them (Barnard, 1998). Ultimately,

> the kinds of decisions that have to be taken with, and often on behalf of, the seriously ill are not purely technical. These decisions become an intrinsic component of the dying process. Depending on which decisions are taken, and on how they are reached, some people will have the chance to die well, as masters of their dying, not alone and not lonely. Others may die before their time, without a chance to live through their dying. Others may die too late, re-

duced to impersonal biological systems that have to be tended. (Roy, Williams, & Dickens, 1994, p. 381)

"Living Just in Case:" Understanding Advance Directives

None of us knows when we are going to die. And, in most cases, we do not know when or how our life will be taken. Often when a patient has advanced-stage cancer, we assume that the impending death will be due to the disease. However, we overlook the fact that an accident or misfortune may actually take a patient's life before the effects of the disease. With this uncertainty of the timing of death in mind, it is important that we are prepared for death at any moment . . . just in case. This preparation is especially important during the terminal illness phase, which can be a time of complex and sensitive decision making. It is helpful to prepare, well in advance, for life and death issues that may arise (Babcock, 1997). Addressing the importance of advance directives (e.g., living will, power of attorney, health care representation) early in this phase can help reduce tension, misunderstandings, and emotional turmoil if complications regarding the patient's wishes arise (Creagan, 1998). This includes the patient's determination of a "proxy," or one who will make decisions based on the patient's own wishes, the wishes of the family, or the wishes of the proxy himself or herself (Emanuel, 1998). To ensure that the patient's wishes are carried out, particularly during times of incoherence, coma, or other types of incapacitation, a written advance directive can be created. In general, there are five steps that should be followed in the creation of the advance directive (Emanuel, 1998). First, the topic must be raised clearly and sensitively. The topic of an advance directive can be addressed in this manner:

> Ms/r. X, I want to talk with you about planning for future medical care. Many now recommend that people make plans whether or not they have an illness, and that doctors discuss these issues routinely with patients. We should go through these issues together. It is a part of getting to know your values and helping to ensure that you are cared for the way you would want to be even in times of life-threatening illness. . . . There is nothing new about your health, and I am not hiding bad news that we have not already discussed; planning for the future simply is prudent. (Emanuel, 1998, p. 795)

Second, a structured discussion regarding the specifics of the directive can begin to take place. Different scenarios and how the patient would choose to respond to those scenarios can now be specifically discussed. For example, scenarios such as possible coma with small chance of recovery, possible waxing and waning consciousness, and possible chance of a persistent vegetative state, can all be addressed. In addition, there are several different interventions to consider: (1) resuscitation, (2) mechanical respiration, (3) renal dialysis, (4) artificial nutrition/hydration, and (5) pain control measures that may hasten the dying process (Emanuel, 1998). Third, after discussing these sensitive concerns, the patient can complete the advance directive document and finalize it after reviewing it with the doctor. Fourth, the advance directive should be reviewed periodically for any necessary changes (Emanuel, 1998). Finally, the advance directives must be made readily available and carried through according to the patient's wishes. Carrying through with the advance directive may become difficult if the patient was suffering from psychiatric disturbances at the time of the creation of the advance directive. Moreover, all relevant family members, as well as the attending physician, must be knowledgeable and respectful of the advance directive. If not, final decision making could become fractured and lead to intense differences of opinion and misunderstandings regarding the patient's wishes (Emanuel, 1998). However clear the advance directive may be, it is crucial that it not be activated before the patient reaches an incapacitated or "wishless" state. Direct communication with the patient should always take place whenever possible (Emanuel, 1998) .

☐ Terminal Illness and Psychosocial Considerations: In a Strange Land

Transition from Life in the Balance to the Terminal Illness Phase and Bereavement

Terminal Illness. The terminal illness phase is marked by the patient's deterioration in health status and a change of focus from one of curative treatment to one of palliative care (Barnard, 1998). If patients, physicians, or family members remain too rigidly fixed on the search for cure, panic and increased levels of anxiety are more likely to occur due to the added stress of unrealistic expectations (Barnard, 1998). Caring for the terminally ill will take the form of "healing" rather than of "cure." Healing represents the psychosocial, emotional, spiritual, and intrapersonal/interpersonal adaptation to the process of dying and to the acceptance of death. As such, there is still much that can be done in terms of healing for the patient and the family system. During this phase both the patient and the family can be assisted in (1) accepting the reality of the prognosis, (2) maintaining a meaningful quality of life, (3) adjusting to the patient's physical deterioration, (4) planning for the surviving family members, and (5) talking about feelings, hopes, fears, and wishes (Zabora & Loscalzo, 1998). While most patients and their families are able to adapt well during the terminal illness phase, some families during this emotionally intense time may exhibit maladaptive behaviors that may signify unusually high levels of distress or family systems dysfunctioning. These behaviors include direct interference with medical care, alliances with other family members against the health care team, encouragement of the patient to be noncompliant, and noncompliance with the advance directives (Zabora & Loscalzo, 1998, p. 535).

Adjustment during the terminal illness phase can take place over the course of many months or even years, when the patient experiences a longer dying trajectory. Conversely, the patient's health and physical status may deteriorate rapidly, giving both the patient and the surviving family members only a short time to adapt to the changes brought about by terminal illness and death (Bass & Bowman, 1990). Family members who care for terminally ill patients face the threats of physical exhaustion, isolation, depression, anxiety, insomnia, financial limitations, and hopelessness (Zabora & Loscalzo, 1998). They may become both physically and emotionally depleted and begin to cope with the overwhelming nature of the caregiving process by perceiving the dying patient as already deceased (Zabora & Loscalzo, 1998). "Anticipatory grief" was initially thought to be of benefit to the surviving family members in that they were able to engage in resolving relational conflicts with the patient, making funeral arrangements, and planning for the future in terms of finances and family functioning (Rando, 1983). However, there is minimal literature to support the benefits of anticipatory grief (Hill, Thompson, & Gallagher, 1988; Bass & Bowman, 1990). Instead, anticipatory grief and "premature emotional withdrawal from the dying patient creates confusion and a sense of terror in the patient. As a result, the family experiences guilt and shame because they are prepared for the loss, but the patient is still alive" (Zabora & Loscalzo, 1998, p. 539).

Bereavement. While the terms "bereavement" and "grief" are often used interchangeably (Lev, Robinson, & McCorkle, 1989), "bereavement" is used specifically for the loss of a person as a result of death, and "grief" is a process composed of changing feelings and behaviors resulting from that loss (Chochinov, Holland, & Katz, 1998). Additional concepts include "mourning," which is the social expression in response to loss and grief (i.e., the use of rituals, symbols, behaviors) and "complicated grief," which is "the failure to return to pre-loss levels of performance or states of emotional well-being" (Chochinov et al., 1998, p. 1017). Emotional and physical exhaustion during caregiving can lead to difficulties in family adaptation during bereavement (Bass & Bowman, 1990).

Bereavement marks the end of caregiving and the beginning of new emotional challenges for surviving family members (Zabora & Loscalzo, 1998). The central focus of the caregiver's and family's life—patient care—is now gone, and little can replace the meaningful demands of this activity (Zabora & Loscalzo, 1998). The family, and particularly the primary caregiver, must make the transition from one of caregiving to one of bereavement. Family members will often go through a period of intense grieving, which lasts for about six months (Zabora & Loscalzo, 1998). During this time, and beyond, family members will often report seeing the deceased in a crowd, hearing his or her voice, feeling his or her presence, and having dreams about being with the deceased (Zabora & Loscalzo, 1998). Family members may believe that their grief connects them with the memories of the deceased and that by moving through the grieving process they are somehow becoming disconnected from the deceased and their shared life together. However, family members can be reassured that their connection will remain and that nothing can take away "their memories and the life they shared" (Zabora & Loscalzo, 1998, p. 543).

Thus, the family must make many transitions during this phase of the illness. Terminal illness begins with a recognition that cure is no longer a realistic expectation, but that there is still much that can be done in terms of enhancing patient and family quality of life, managing pain and other physical symptoms, addressing relationship issues, and planning for the future. Following the death of the patient, the family must make the transition from one of caregiving to one of bereavement and facing intense loss. Last, the surviving family members must go through the final transition of moving beyond the period of intense grief and into a process of creating a new family system and new connections with the living. Throughout these transitions, the presence of hope can serve as the cornerstone to healing.

Comprehensive Care of Cancer Patients during the Terminal Illness Phase

Most patients (67%) report the desire to die at home (Ingham, 1998). However, due to difficulties with pain management, anorexia, nausea, and severe constipation, many patients die in institutions such as hospitals and nursing homes (Ingham, 1998). To provide comprehensive care for the terminally ill patient while optimizing the potential for end-of-life treatment in the home, we must consider a number of important variables. These include medical variables, psychosocial variables, financial variables, and the spiritual concerns of the patient, family, and community (Schachter & Coyle, 1998).

Medical Variables.   The patient's medical variables include his or her functional level (i.e., mobility versus immobility), ability to communicate, ability to participate in activities of daily living, and bowel and bladder functioning (from incontinence to self-care; Schachter & Coyle, 1998, p. 1006). The daily care of patients with minimal levels of functioning may be both physically and emotionally exhausting for the family. The family's knowledge regarding health care practices and previous experiences with illness should also be taken into consideration when planning for end-of-life home care. Further, there may be concurrent medical problems within the household that may compound the stress put on primary caregivers (Schachter & Coyle, 1998). Emotionally, it may be difficult for the family system to have a loved one die at home. The family system should be assessed for its ability to handle high levels of distress and emotional discomfort attached to the home environment. Conversely, caring for a terminally ill family member and helping him or her to heal emotionally during the dying process can be a profoundly meaningful experience (Schachter & Coyle, 1998). The community can help facilitate this meaningful process by providing agencies that specialize in home nursing care, visiting nurse services, end-of-life home care, and community support groups for family members (Schachter & Coyle, 1998).

Psychosocial Variables.   The psychosocial variables of the patient, family, and community should be assessed periodically. The psychosocial variables of the patient include the patient's (1) ability to integrate the dying experience and to create meaning; (2) need for control through the dying process as opposed to understanding death as beyond human control; (3) understanding of the disease process and personal prognosis; (4) developmental process and ability to maintain age-appropriate behavior; (5) mood, sensorium, and preexisting psychopathology; and (6) coping strategies (i.e., rationalizing, avoiding, denying; Schachter & Coyle, 1998). The family system should also be assessed with a focus on (1) psychosocial functioning, (2) preexisting family structure, (3) the presence of children in the home, (4) the impact that the death of a loved one will have on children, as well as (5) the family's ability to reconcile differences and to make treatment decisions (Coyle, Loscalzo, & Bailey, 1998; Schachter & Coyle, 1998). The family system should remain flexible enough so that roles and rules can be modified as needed, and maintain moderate levels of cohesion and bonding. The risk for family enmeshment and isolation during this phase is particularly great and could lead to difficulties both during the caregiving process and during bereavement (Bass & Bowman, 1990). For the community, the family's religious affiliation and friends and social networks and relationship with counselors, hospice teams, and volunteer groups should also be assessed as possible support systems for the family during end-of-life care (Schachter & Coyle, 1998).

Financial Variables.   Financial variables often weigh heavily on the family during the terminal illness phase. Financial concerns involve more than just difficulties with deciphering insurance policies, making claims, and filling out paperwork. They also include (1) assessing the patient's living arrangements and how to alter the environment to accommodate the needs of the patient, (2) examining the home finances and previous work status of the patient, (3) determining Medicare or Medicaid eligibility, and (4) assessing the patient's insurance coverage for hospital, home care, home health aides, private nurses, community nursing, and any equipment or medications the patient may need (Schachter & Coyle, 1998). The family's income and any financial help from the community can also be taken into consideration when assessing financial constraints (Schachter & Coyle, 1998).

Spiritual Concerns.   The spiritual care of the patient during the terminal illness phase is of particular importance (Bailey, 1998). To many, "Dying is more than a biological occurrence. It is a human, social, and spiritual event" (Bailey, 1998, p. 719). The concept of comprehensive spiritual care, especially for those with terminal illness, was generated from the modern hospice movement and addresses more than religious practices, but is the broader dimension of spirituality and a higher power that connects with something more than our physical selves (Bailey, 1998; Du Boulay, 1984):

Our destiny
is to run to the edge of the world and beyond,
off into the darkness:
sure in spite of all our helplessness,
strong in spite of all our weakness,
joyfully in love in spite of all
the pressures on our hearts
(Bailey, 1998, p. 730)

The International Work Group on Death, Dying, and Bereavement (IWG) has recently developed assumptions and principles of comprehensive spiritual care (see Bailey, 1998, p. 719). There are several general assumptions regarding the spiritual care of patients with serious or terminal illness. First, the principles of comprehensive spiritual care are based upon the perception that terminal illness, death, and bereavement can be a stimulus for spiritual growth. Consistent with this first principle, spirituality can be perceived as having many facets and forms of expression, including symbols, rituals, practices, patterns, gestures, and prayers or meditations. However, patients are not always aware of or need to discuss spiritual matters. Each patient's needs and perceptions of spirituality should be respected. Additionally, the environment can enhance or diminish one's spirituality, and appropriate action can be taken to ensure optimal surroundings. Joy is regarded as an important component of comprehensive spiritual care and is needed in times of despair. The clergy are generally regarded as having the primary responsibility for overseeing the spiritual care of the terminally ill (Bailey, 1998).

Terminally ill family members may struggle with their feelings of anger, fear, and despair, and with unanswerable questions of life, death, and the "meaning of it all." Thus, terminal illness can act as an impetus for spiritual development. To encourage spiritual growth, the caregiver can help the patient to direct anger constructively, to name fears specifically, and to understand that all questions in life are not able to be answered. The caregiver can facilitate spiritual growth and healing by listening, sharing, and helping the patient to engage in many forms of artistic, spiritual, and religious expression (poetry, drawing, painting, journal writing, meditating, praying, practicing religious rituals; Bailey, 1998). However, not all patients will want or need to explore spiritual or religious concerns. At times, the process of dying can paralyze patients emotionally and cognitively, leaving them with little to no energy with which to grapple with spiritual issues (Bailey, 1998). In cases such as this, it is wise for the caregiver or therapist or both to allow the patient to guide the discussion regarding spiritual needs.

The environment can either diminish or enhance the inner peace, safety, and spiritual growth of the terminally ill patient. Some institutions, such as hospitals, are designed primarily for the convenience and comfort of those who work in them, and not necessarily for the patients themselves (Bailey, 1998). However, this situation is changing. For example, the annual Symposium on Healthcare Design encourages the establishment of art departments, art exhibits, and performing arts in health care delivery (Bailey, 1998). Moreover, the landscape and architecture of health care settings are changing, with added gardens, atriums, and areas that provide sanctuary, privacy, and solitude for both patients and their families (Bailey, 1998). Soothing sounds and the blocking of aggravating noises (headphones for television watching) can also enhance the patient's environment (Bailey, 1998).

Although fear and despair are often associated with the dying process, joy and humor can also be found during end-of-life care. Joy can provide a sense of spiritual strength and foster hope during the terminal illness phase. It is thus important to discover what has brought the patient joy in the past. What practices can the patient still participate in that would bring him or her joy? Can any of these practices be modified in the future after the patient's health has deteriorated further? What can the family do to bring the patient and themselves joy? Much like religious or spiritual beliefs, the things that bring joy for some family members may be quite different for others. Promoting a spirit of openness, respect, and tolerance is thus important to facilitate personal and systems growth and enhance peace and safety for all patients, family members, and friends (Bailey, 1998).

Children and Spouses of Cancer Patients during the Terminal Illness Phase

The terminal illness phase can be the most difficult phase of the clinical course of cancer for the children and spouses of cancer patients. Children with a terminally ill parent are more likely to have higher levels of self-reported depression, anxiety, and lowered self-esteem (Siegel, Palamara Mesagno, Karus, Christ, Banks, & Moynihan, 1992). In addition, they can also exhibit a higher incidence of behavior problems and lower social competence (Siegel et al., 1992). When children experience a long dying trajectory of an ill parent, or if they are so young that all they have ever known is a chronically ill parent, adaptation to the death of that parent may be particularly difficult (Christ, Siegel, Freund, Langosch, Hendersen, Sperber, & Weinstein, 1993). Death may come as a shock to children who have repeatedly witnessed periods of remission (Christ et al., 1993). They come to expect that any deterioration in their parent's health status will be followed by periods of relatively good health and remission, not death. Still, the ways in which children adapt to their parent's death is largely determined by the relationship with the surviving parent (Christ, Siegel, Palamara Mesagno, & Langosch, 1991; Siegel, Palamara Mesagno, et al., 1990). Children who adapt more readily to the loss of a parent have usually had consistent and stable parental care during both the terminal illness phase and during the years following the death (Siegel, Raveis, Bettes, Palamara Mesagno, Christ, & Weinstein, 1990). During the terminal illness phase, children are likely to experience an increased sense of vulnerability and a heightened need for emotional support and physical care at a time when the well parent's emotional and physical resources are at their lowest. The developmental needs and tasks for the child, the well spouse, and thus for the child–parent relationship may be delayed or arrested altogether if these needs are not addressed during the terminal illness phase. Prevention strategies are being developed and refined in order to facilitate healthier adaptation to parental death during childhood (Christ et al., 1991; Siegel, Palamara Mesagno, et al., 1990). Prevention strategies to assist adaptation during terminal illness and on through the bereavement phase should begin at least six months prior to the patient's death (as estimated by the patient's physician; Siegel, Palamara Mesagno, et al., 1990). By addressing the needs of the parent–child relationship before the death of the patient, a parent can do much in terms of providing support, supplying pertinent information, and generating a needed focus on parent–child interactions (Siegel, Palamara Mesagno, et al., 1990). By providing support, the well parent can be helped to deal with intense grief issues and his or her feelings of loss, isolation, and depression. Further, the well parent's parenting skills can be supported and enhanced. In so doing, the parent–child relationship can be nurtured and helped to either create or maintain an environment that is safe to discuss fears and sadness and stable enough to provide consistency for the children. Bereaved children feel more safe and more willing to resume necessary developmental tasks when they are in a familiar and comfortable environment that provides consistency and stability (Siegel, Palamara Mesagno, et al., 1990). However, surviving parents must sometimes alter the child's familiar environment by moving to a new home, city, or state to be nearer to a support system, resulting in a change in the child's environment during a particularly vulnerable time. Although the death of a parent necessarily leads to some forms of change, children have been shown to demonstrate healthier adaptation when they are (1) informed about events and expected changes in the ill parent's health status; (2) prepared, as much as possible, for the ill parent's death; (3) encouraged to discuss their fears and concerns regarding the parent's illness and death; and (4) allowed to follow predictable daily routines (Bowlby, 1980; Siegel, Palamara Mesagno, et al., 1990).

Spouses of terminally ill patients are at an increased risk for depression, anxiety, isolation, and hopelessness (Given & Given, 1998). Moreover, many spouses may experience vicarious suffering from seeing the patient in pain (Dar, Beach, Barden, & Cleeland, 1992). When parenting responsibilities are necessary, spouses may also undergo decreased confidence in their parenting skills (Siegel, Raveis, et al., 1990). Spouses are thus pulled in several directions at once; they usually must tend to the care of the terminally ill patient and yet still be physically and emotionally available to their children (Siegel, Raveis, et al., 1990; Siegel, Palamara Mesagno, et al., 1990).

Regarding patient caregiving and pain management, patients and their spouses can have very different perceptions in terms of the patient's level of pain as well as the caregiver's level of distress. For example, Dar and colleagues (1992) found that spouses often are more concerned about pain management than are the patients themselves. Spouses have been shown to rate the patient's level of pain as more intense than the patient's own pain ratings. Further, while patient reports reveal that they are satisfied with the overall performance of spousal caregiving, patients often do not recognize the high levels of distress that their caregivers are experiencing, nor do they see that their spouses often feel inadequate as caregivers. However, some patients, knowing that their pain is causing severe discomfort to their spouses, will underreport their levels of pain intensity and wait unnecessarily for pain medication. Thus, it remains crucial for both the patient and the family to understand the importance of receiving pain medication at appropriate times, and for spouses to be considered at high risk for distress when patients are in pain.

While caring for a terminally ill family member, spouses must also maintain their role as parent when there are children in the home. Many parents will have particular difficulty remaining sensitive and responsive to their children's needs (Siegel, Raveis, et al., 1990). When a parent is caring for a terminally ill family member, they may become preoccupied with the needs of the patient and overwhelmed by his or her own emotional state, thus being rendered unable to be open to the needs of his or her children. Further, spouses have also demonstrated difficulty with setting standards and enforcing discipline for their children (Siegel, Raveis, et al., 1990). It takes energy and determination to set and to reinforce limits with children. The demands in this area of parenting may be too high for parents caring for a terminally ill family member. Thus, it is important to (1) determine possible role strain for the well parent; (2) ensure that the well parent receives needed behavioral and psychosocial support, especially when juggling the demands of caregiver and parenting; (3) bolster confidence in caregiving and parenting abilities; (4) facilitate the parent–child relationship during a time of intense focus on patient care; and (5) help generate a stable and consistent home environment during a time of upheaval and loss.

Caregiver Burden and Burnout during the Terminal Illness Phase

Caregivers working with terminally ill patients are at high risk for depression, anxiety, isolation, and general burnout (Bailey, 1998). It is thus important for caregivers to attend to their own physical, emotional, mental, and spiritual needs (Bailey, 1998). Besides the patient, professional caregivers, family members, and close friends are also susceptible to excessive burden and stress and should be watched for signs and symptoms of burnout

(Given & Given, 1998). Caregiver burden and burnout is "a reaction to chronic, job-related stress," and has been associated with higher rates of divorce, suicide, job turnover, and drug and alcohol abuse (McKenna, Wellisch, & Fawzy, 1995, p. 650).

A transactional model of burnout has been proposed as a useful framework for describing the burnout process (McKenna et al., 1995). The transactional model of burnout is delineated into three stages. In stage one, the caregiver begins to perceive the demands of caregiving as exceeding his or her current available resources. External factors (e.g., the environment, relationships, and goals) as well as internal factors (e.g., self-concept, identity, beliefs, and developmental concerns) can act as demands on the caregiver. When these perceived demands exceed the caregiver's resources, he or she is likely to become emotionally and physically imbalanced. This imbalance is expressed as physical exhaustion and emotional tension and anxiety (McKenna et al., 1995). In stage two, the caregiver attempts to regain a sense of physical and emotional balance by engaging in various coping behaviors or by drawing on additional available resources (McKenna et al., 1995). If the new coping behaviors are not enacted, or if they fail to reestablish needed balance, burnout occurs (McKenna et al., 1995). Thus, in stage three, multiple maladaptive coping behaviors can be seen including cynicism, withdrawal, isolation, altered work patterns, family conflicts, substance abuse, and uncontrolled crying (McKenna et al., 1995). These maladaptive coping behaviors can result in negative physical responses such as chronic fatigue, sleep disorders, and headaches, and negative emotional responses such as hopelessness, powerlessness, guilt, detachment, and depression (McKenna et al., 1995). The caregiver experiencing burnout can be directed toward more effective coping mechanisms and sources of support. These might include the utilization of stress management principles, support groups, substance abuse treatment, if appropriate, and family therapy, if indicated (McKenna et al., 1995).

Special Considerations: Life after Caregiving: The Bereavement Phase

Grief and the Individual Family Member.   The bereavement phase generally begins when the patient dies and caregiving tasks are no longer required. The bereavement period is a time of grieving. According to Bowlby's (1977) attachment theory, four phases of the grief process have been identified (Lev et al., 1989; Parkes, 1970, 1972, 1985, 1987). In the first phase, the surviving family member may experience panic attacks and significant anxiety alternating with periods of numbness (Lev et al., 1989). This acute phase of the grieving process lasts a relatively short period of time (some studies report a matter of days; Parkes, 1970) and is followed by feelings of yearning and protest (Lev et al., 1989). During this phase, survivors may experience feelings of anger and guilt coupled with a physiological response of restless energy (Lev et al., 1989). Although the yearning and protest phase lasts only a few weeks (Lev et al., 1989), restless energy and anger can become aimed at health care professionals and others, as surviving family members grapple with unanswerable questions such as, Was everything done that could have been done? Were there any mistakes made? Could the death have been prevented? (Chochinov et al., 1998). During this phase, surviving family members may need to be near places and things associated with the deceased. They may search for the deceased or feel as if the deceased were going to come home soon, and they may be preoccupied by thoughts and yearnings for the deceased (Chochinov et al., 1998). Care of the individual going through the yearning and protest phase includes (1) encouraging ventilation of feelings, including anger; (2) reassuring the family that searching and waiting behaviors are normal; (3) discouraging the family from discarding the loved one's belongings too early in the grieving process;

and (4) avoiding defensiveness when anger is directed toward the health care team and responding with understanding instead (Chochinov et al., 1998). The third phase is one of disorganization and is marked by apathy, hopelessness, depression, and social withdrawal (Chochinov et al., 1998). This phase of the grieving process can last well over a year, and surviving family members may need emotional and psychosocial support long after the patient's death has occurred (Parkes, 1970, 1972). If a surviving family member is experiencing a long period of disorganization and hopelessness, it may be necessary to monitor his or her physical status as well (e.g., sleep disturbances, substance abuse, nutritional intake, weight loss; Chochinov et al., 1998). The last phase is a time of recovery, when acute pangs of grief begin to subside and the surviving family member's appetite and interests return (Chochinov et al., 1998). Although these phases generally occur sequentially, there can be overlap between any one of the phases. Difficulties with recovery can take place when survivors do not expect to eventually regain preloss functional status. Then, the grieving process never fully ends, and anniversary reactions are expected (Chochinov et al., 1998).

While most survivors will go through the process of grieving and reach the final phase of recovery, others will have difficulty and encounter negative bereavement outcomes (Lev et al., 1989). Predictors of negative bereavement outcome include youth, low socioeconomic status, lack of preparation for death, anger, and self-reproach (Lev et al., 1989). A bereavement "Risk Index" consisting of eight items (age, occupation, length of preparation for patient's death, clinging/pining, anger, self-reproach, family support, and clinician's prognosis) can be used to identify survivors at high risk for negative bereavement outcome (Parkes & Weiss, 1983, p. 314). The Risk Index has also been used to predict spousal adjustment during the bereavement phase up to one year following the death of their spouse (Beckwith, Beckwith, Gray, Micsko, Holm, Plummer, & Flaa, 1990). Using the Risk Index, high-risk bereaved spouses were younger, had young children in the home, and had suffered a financial decrease in income during that year (Beckwith et al., 1990). Other predictors of poor bereavement outcome include lack of social support, prior psychiatric history, high initial distress with depressive symptoms, additional life stresses and losses, and prior high dependency on the deceased (Chochinov et al., 1998).

Grief and Children. Children are also deeply affected by the death of a parent or grandparent. The impact of a family member's death can have lasting ramifications on their individual development and on their future families (Weber & Fournier, 1985). In a unique study conducted to examine children's perceptions of a grandparent's death, it was found that children are more insightful and perceptive of the nature of death and dying than what parents would believe them to be (Irizarry, 1992). Children often notice subtle changes occurring in their parents and can remember in vivid detail the events of the day their grandparent died and how their parents dealt with death (Irizarry, 1992). Children often want more detail about how the grandparent died, what caused the death, and the exact moment of death (Irizarry, 1992). If the child is developmentally ready to face the death of a beloved family member, participating in family and community mourning rituals can help the child to learn more about the concept of death and how to cope with the uncertainties of life (Irizarry, 1992; Weber & Fournier, 1985).

Grief and the Family System.   The family system is the most intimate social system in which grief is experienced (Kissane & Bloch, 1994; Kissane, Bloch, Onghena, McKenzie, Snyder, & Dowe, 1996). Family systems that adapt more readily during the grieving process are more likely to be supportive, conflict resolving, and expressive (Kissane et al., 1996). Families at greater risk for difficulties with the grieving process are more likely to exhibit hostility and sullenness (Kissane et al., 1996), more extreme levels of cohesion (either enmeshed or disengaged), and more extreme levels of flexibility (either rigid or chaotic; Kissane & Bloch, 1994).

The avoidance of the grief process can also lead to family dysfunction (Kissane & Bloch, 1994). There are several patterns families may use in an attempt to side step the grieving process and to achieve a new, perhaps premature, equilibrium. These patterns of avoidance include (1) sealing off family boundaries and generating greater family enmeshment, (2) maintaining a family secret (e.g., death regarding passive or active euthanasia) at the expense of completing the grieving process, (3) assuming and maintaining inappropriate roles (e.g., the parentification of a child), (4) rekindling incomplete transgenerational mourning thereby amplifying the current grief intensity levels within the family system, and (5) accentuating differences in family members' individual mourning rituals, which can lead to isolation and family disintegration (Kissane & Bloch, 1994). Families that are more readily able to adapt during the bereavement phase are more likely to exhibit appropriate levels of cohesion, mutual support, clear and direct communication patterns, emotional expressiveness, and the ability to participate in conflict resolution with moderate levels of flexibility (Kissane & Bloch, 1994).

The loss of a family member will also vary in its impact on the family system according to its developmental stage (McGoldrick & Walsh, 1995). Families already dealing with multiple losses or experiencing life cycle transitions are more likely to have increased difficulties (McGoldrick & Walsh, 1995). Families who lose a young adult to cancer will often experience the excruciating pain of losing a loved one before "their time," out of the natural unfolding of the family life cycle. Further, siblings may be expected to fulfill the plans and dreams of the deceased, thus delaying their own unique path of development (McGoldrick & Walsh, 1995). Young married couples losing a spouse early in the marriage can become isolated or be pushed into a new relationship before the grieving process has been successfully navigated. For families with young children, the death of a spouse can lead to complications with the grief process due to the overwhelming demands of parenthood and financial caretaking obligations (McGoldrick & Walsh, 1995). Families with adolescents, or families that are in the launching stage of development, are at odds with the nature of bereavement, which tends to pull the family inward. Adolescents and young adults leaving the family system may be pulled in both directions simultaneously; their developmental needs to appropriately separate from the family of origin can be in stark contrast to the period of mourning, which requires increased family cohesion and emotional support (McGoldrick & Walsh, 1995). Families in later life will inevitably face the death of a spouse or loved one. Widowers are at a particularly high risk of suicide following the death of a wife and her caretaking functions (McGoldrick & Walsh, 1995). Widows may be left with financial difficulties and intense loneliness (McGoldrick & Walsh, 1995).

Family members can be helped to rely on one another for support and to regain developmental momentum even during the terminal illness and bereavement phase of cancer. The experience of terminal illness and death in the system will be woven into the family's transgenerational history, and how the current family system adapts—emotionally, psychosocially, and spiritually—to the illness and death of a loved one will determine the foundation for future family adaptation to terminal illness and, ultimately, to death and loss.

☐ The Six Family Life Cycles during the Terminal Illness Phase: The Importance of Caregiving and Grieving

This last phase of the clinical course of cancer is one of the most difficult to navigate. During the terminal phase, the patient's health begins to rapidly deteriorate, and thus both the emotional and physical demands of caregiving are high. Families can expect to experience a range of emotions, including shock, anger, fear, anxiety, loss of control, guilt, and grief (Babcock, 1997). Dreams, hopes, and visions for the future may need to be altered as the family prepares for the loss of a loved one. However, even in the midst of high levels of distress and despair, many family members may still feel a sense of hope—hope for a peaceful death without pain or fear, hope that the family system will be strengthened, hope from religious and spiritual beliefs, and hope for the patient's continued existence in some form of an afterlife. Family members will experience the terminal illness and bereavement phase in their own unique ways. Some will find solace in the family, close friends, or in prayer. Others will find diversion through work and social activities. Young children cope with death very differently from adults. They may not be able to understand the concept of death and may search for their lost mothers or fathers, waiting for their return (Cummock, 1996). They may wish for their own deaths so that they may "see Mommy or Daddy again in heaven." Older children may be able to understand more clearly the severity of this phase of the illness. However, their informational needs may require more direct conversation about the disease, the prognosis, and expectations for how the disease typically progresses. "One-shot" conversations about the terminal illness phase are not enough. Continued conversation about the illness and the "roller coaster ride" of this phase needs to occur for all children of any age.

When the death of a young adult occurs, shock will reverberate through the extended family system. Parents and grandparents may suffer from thoughts of survival guilt: "Why wasn't it me? I am supposed to die before my child or grandchild does." It is also difficult to anticipate the death of a loved one when there is little pain or adverse symptomatology involved. Thus, it may be more difficult to prepare for the death of a loved one when there are no apparent physical signs of sickness. Conversely, when there is much pain and suffering for the patient, caregivers and family members may feel a sense of relief mixed with their grief. However, relief is a response that can also be laden with guilt. It is thus important to allow and respect all emotional responses and unique ways of grieving (Babcock, 1997). The effects of the terminal illness phase on the family life cycle are organized in Table 7.1.

The Single Young Adult during Terminal Illness

CASE EXAMPLE 7 (Continued). Jenny's Family

Jenny's mother, Janet Wachtel, came for psychosocial assistance during the last months of her daughter's life. She related, "Jenny does not want to face the fact that she is dying. Since she says she doesn't feel sick, except from her treatment, she doesn't think she is going to die. But everything that I have read tells me that malignant melanoma is a serious form of cancer. I know that Jenny has fought long and hard. We have all had a very difficult time these last couple of years. But now I fear for the worst, and I can't seem to talk about my fears to anyone, not even my husband. I am supposed to be strong for the family, to help Jenny get to her appointments, to help with the side effects, and to pretend like we can beat the cancer. But in my heart, I don't feel that way. I am watching my daughter waste away before my eyes, and I can't deny it any longer."

During the course of a few months, Jenny's health did rapidly deteriorate. Her cancer had spread to her lungs and was making breathing difficult. Although the family had hoped that the clinical trial in which Jenny had taken part would be successful, the disease began to progress and she had to be admitted to the community hospital. Jenny's mother continued, "I at least wanted her to die at home in her own bed. I tried as long as I could to care for her at home. I just feel so helpless. I just try and keep focused on the small things. Her cancer hasn't spread to her brain, so she still recognizes me and we can talk for a bit each day. The nurses let me wash her hair and bathe her, and sometimes I read to her from her favorite books. Most of the time, she sleeps and I just hold her hand and stroke her hair and face. I pray that she will not be in any pain and I wish to God it were me in that hospital bed instead of her."

A few months later, Jenny died in her hospital bed of respiratory failure. Both her mother and her father were present at the time of her death. Jenny's mother remembered, "I was holding her hand, and her Dad was reading out loud to both of us. It was so strange. . . . Jenny looked at both of us right before she died. But she didn't have any fear or pain in her face. For that, I guess, I can be thankful. Then we just watched her go. The nurses called the doctor and they tried to resuscitate her. But now we almost wish they hadn't done that. We had decided beforehand that we would give intravenous nutrition for as long as Jenny was alive, and that we would resuscitate her if necessary. But she had looked so peaceful, so beautiful the day she died. I want to remember my little girl that way."

Over the course of the next several months, Jenny's mother discussed her experience with the process of grieving over the loss of a child: "At first I felt numb. Every day I would wake up and think, 'I've got to get to the hospital, Jenny needs me.' Then it would sink in all over again that Jenny is gone. With each day that went by I would get more and more numb. I don't even feel like getting out of bed. For so long, my days were filled with taking care of Jenny, exhausting visits to the hospital, discussions with the nurses and the staff. They were there to support me. Now I feel so alone and empty. It is like I have no purpose any longer. There is nothing worthwhile to fill my time and there is no one to talk to about my grief."

It was recognized that Janet was going through the beginning phase of grief, which is characterized by numbness and emptiness (Lev et al., 1989; Parkes, 1970). Moreover, Janet was relatively young, as was her daughter, she had little preparation for her daughter's death, and she was experiencing isolation, as she was not utilizing her family support. It appears that Janet may have attempted to control the pain of the loss of her daughter by pulling away slowly from the life she once knew and her former family system. All of these variables are indicative of negative bereavement outcome (Lev et al., 1989). In response to the presence of these negative predictor variables, it was necessary to reduce Janet's isolation and to increase her family support. In doing so, it was hoped that she would be able to move more readily through the process of grieving. It was recommended that her husband, Jerry, come to the next consultation.

Both of Jenny's parents came in for a follow-up consultation. Jerry began, "Janet and I are dealing with Jenny's death in very different ways. I try and keep busy and think of all the wonderful memories I have of her. I miss her so much—don't think I don't. But I don't know how to talk about it. I don't really know how to face her death. Sometimes I think that if I dwell on everything we have gone through over the last year or so, I'll fall apart. And then where would we be? We have to keep going, keep on living, even if our hearts are broken." During the course of the next several sessions, Janet and Jerry began to see how their grieving responses were very different from each other, keeping with traditional male–female gender role differences in coping. While they agreed to respect each other's different needs, they also began to realize they had several grief reactions in common. Jerry commented, "I was able to tell Janet how I thought I saw Jenny the other day. I was going to bed the other night, and I could have sworn I saw her at the computer working on one of her papers for school. I even heard her music playing. . . . Out of habit I

(*text continues on page 228*)

TABLE 7.1. The Terminal Illness Phase and the Family Life Cycle: The Importance of Caregiving and Grieving

	Life cycle tasks	Cancer's potential disruption to the system	Psychosocial interventions	Specific topics of communication
Single young adult	Differentiate from the family of origin	Terminal illness may permanently disrupt the process of differentiation from the family of origin; may permanently impede most developmental tasks	Facilitate development within the confines of the illness; identify ways in which the young adult can continue to develop during the terminal phase; help family prepare for untimely loss	Discuss needs for continued individual and family growth; discuss small, attainable goals; discuss emotional responses to terminal illness
Newly forming couple	Create new system; negotiate power, rules, roles, and boundaries	May permanently disrupt the creation of a new system; may permanently alter the balance of power within the new system; disrupt all plans, goals, dreams for the future	Help facilitate effective communication; help couple to re-create their plans for the future; help new couple to remain validated by their families of origin; help prepare all family members for loss	Discuss patient and family's fear; discuss altered plans and dreams; discuss continuing relationship between new partner and the patient's family
Families with young children	Raise and nurture small children; add new roles of "parent" and "grandparent"	Disrupt and overwhelm busy young family system; disrupt extended family systems as they help care for the ill parent; disrupt parenting skills; disrupt marital dyad	Help to mobilize available resources; assess for caregiver burnout and role strain; help patient and family to prepare for loss; help provide stability for children	Discuss emotional responses such as anger, fear, sadness; discuss the needs of both the patient and the family system; discuss care for children after death

Families with adolescents	Accept external influences on family system; loosen boundaries to allow for adolescent development	Disrupt centrifugal pull of the system delaying adolescent development; disrupt parenting skills; disrupt boundaries between marital subsystem and children's subsystems; disrupt normal role functioning	Facilitate flexible family system; determine how needs of the patient and the system will be met; prepare family system for death and loss; facilitate effective parenting skills; help to understand intense emotional responses of adolescents and all members	Discuss needs of patient and family system; help with advance directives; discuss emotional responses; discuss altered plans for the future; discuss relationship/spiritual concerns
Families launching children	Accept multiple exits from and entries back into the system; renegotiate intimacy of marital dyad	Disrupt launching of children; permanently delay or change family plans; disrupt new roles and rules of the system; terminal illness may result in role reversals and permanent shifts in family structure	Facilitate temporary changes in family structure; help family to maintain or to resume developmental momentum, when appropriate; help prepare partner and children for loss; help create shared memories and legacies	Discuss temporary shifts in roles; discuss fears; discuss altered plans for the future; discuss attainable goals; discuss small joys in life; discuss beliefs in death and afterlife
Families in later life	Maintain a sense of generativity; life review	Disrupt plans for later life; disrupt financial planning; may disrupt independent living	Promote proper setting for end of life care; assess caregiver burnout for spouse or adult caregiver	Discuss life review; discuss advance directives; discuss memories/legacies

went into her room to say goodnight. In a flash I realized what I had done. I was able, somehow, to find the strength to share all this with Janet." His wife responded, "I am glad you did. Now that we are talking a bit more about it, I don't feel so isolated. I don't tell you nearly all the thoughts and feelings I have, but I can share with you how guilty I feel about her death, and how much I yearn for her. I would give anything to have her here with us again. How can we rebuild our lives without her?"

During the months that followed, the Wachtels experienced yearning for their daughter coupled with feelings of anger and guilt regarding their daughter's death. They wondered if there was anything else they could have done. They questioned the health care team about possible treatments they could have tried or ways they could have prolonged their daughter's life. During this time, Janet reported feeling disorganized and out of control. She explained, "I just can't seem to do anything productive. I still feel empty inside and nothing really motivates me. I guess my numbness has turned into general apathy. I wonder if I will ever feel truly alive again." During the difficult months that followed, Janet agreed to be placed on an antidepressant and to attend weekly individual therapy sessions, during which she kept a journal of simple foundational behaviors she needed to accomplish each day, like getting out of bed, showering, and making sure she interacted with others. When she was ready, she joined a grief support group and began to share her grief with others who could deeply empathize with her.

Jenny's mother and father came in for a consultation one year after Jenny's death. They stated that they had moved beyond the "acute phase" of bereavement, but they were still going through the grief process. Janet stated, "Now I know that grief never really ends. But I have moved on from feeling apathetic and hopeless about my life. I am trying to focus on my marriage now. It has been hard for us to rebuild our marriage since Jenny has died, but we were already in the process of redefining our relationship when Jenny first moved back home from college. We are planning a brief vacation together, but first we have to say goodbye to Jenny in our own way. The memorial service was so formal and we were so numb." Jerry continued, "We don't even remember half of what happened. We do remember that all of her friends were there—it seemed like the whole school showed up for the funeral. So we have decided to say goodbye to her privately, and in our own way." Janet explained their plans: "We found some of Jenny's things that are representative of the different phases of her life. I picked out a baby gown she wore as an infant, a pair of overalls she wore as a toddler, and a toy horse she played with as a small child. We also found pictures and stories she wrote during her days in elementary school. We found old photographs of her and her friends at ball games and parties in high school. Last, we found poetry she wrote during her final days of life. We put all of these things in a special trunk to commemorate her life with us. This isn't much, and it won't bring her back to us, but we did this together, as a couple. We know that we need to lean on each other as we continue to feel intense grief and yearning for her. When the pain becomes too great, when her birthday or other special anniversary dates come around, or on the date of her death, we can pull out the trunk and feel closer to her. We know she will never leave us. She will always be a part of us."

The depth of their grief is apparent. The Wachtels are experiencing not only the loss of their child, but also the loss of their only child and their link to the future and to their future lineage. When a couple loses their only child, they also lose their hopes and dreams for grandchildren, plans for familial generativity, and giving of legacies.

The terminal illness phase was devastating for this small family and for the community in which they live. Although Jenny was able to continue with the developmental task of differentiating from her family of origin for as long as the disease would allow, to her mother and father she would always be "their little girl." The Wachtels worked with each other during the grieving process. Instead of giving in to the temptation of blaming each other for her illness and untimely death, they joined as partners in the grieving process. As a result, their marriage was strengthened in spite of their daughter's death.

Jenny's parents become involved in a crusade on Jenny's college campus where they helped to raise awareness of melanoma. They also started a scholarship fund in Jenny's name. As a testimony to both their marriage and the memory of their daughter, they worked together to take a proactive role in keeping their daughter's memory alive.

☐ The Newly Forming Couple during Terminal Illness

CASE EXAMPLE 8 (Continued). Dan's Family

Dan and his family continued to experience significant differences in their perceptions of the illness. Dan continued to try and speak to his family about his understanding of the seriousness of his disease, but his mother and sisters had difficulty listening. Due to their own needs for control, they focused on searching for miraculous cures and prayed for a cure for Dan's cancer. During the next few months, Dan's health began to rapidly deteriorate. His lung cancer metastasized to his brain. Consequently, he began to suffer from cognitive impairment, delirium, and confusion regarding his surroundings. His family came in for a consultation.

His sister, Phylis, began the session: "We had to admit Dan to the hospital last night. We are all drained and exhausted. He was living at home with Mom for most of these last few months. I came over and helped every day. It was horrible seeing him in so much pain. We had to keep giving him more and more medication, and our prayers to release him from his pain never seemed to be heard. Finally, we had to bring him in so that the medical staff could help monitor and control his pain." His mother continued, "It is my fault he is in such pain. I have doubted God's power during these last few weeks, and I believe that God may be punishing us because of my doubts." Phylis embraced her mother and tried to assuage her feelings of guilt. Both of them reported being devastated by seeing their loved one in so much pain and so close to death. Phylis continued, "The social worker asked us to prepare Dan's advance directives weeks ago when he was still coherent. Now, it is too late. None of us know what he wants during his final days of life."

Holly, Dan's fiancée, described the occurrences of the last couple of weeks: "Dan couldn't seem to get any relief from his pain. He always seemed to be out of it, just tossing and turning and crying out in pain. He would mumble about how he felt like a burden to us, how he wished for death. I think if he had had the strength to take his own life, he would have. Now that he is in the hospital, he is able to rest better. I think they are taking better care of him than we could at home. He is in too much pain."

Dan died within a couple of weeks after being admitted to the hospital. He was incoherent during the final days of his life and was unable to express his final wishes. Dan's sister stated, "I wish I had listened to him more. I was always just assuming he agreed with us. Now, looking back on it, all he ever wanted to do was be himself. I wish that I had stopped talking so much and let him alone—I wish that I had heard him." Throughout the grieving process the family began to realize how much they respected Dan as an individual and independent member of the family. His mother related, "I was always so busy making sure that everyone shared the same belief system I do. Now I can see that Dan had his own beliefs and desires for life. He struggled so hard to be independent from all of us women.

I wish we could have told him how much we loved him for who he was when he was still alive. I only hope that he knows our strange way of taking care of him was the only way we knew how to love him."

A few months following Dan's death, Holly requested a follow-up consultation. She began, "I wanted to come to a session by myself. There are so many things that I want to talk about to someone who cares—but who is not one of the family. Before Dan got really sick and was put in the hospital, we had conversations about our wedding, our future, the future of his daughter, and even our spiritual beliefs. Dan and I could talk when his family wasn't around. When his Mom or Phylis were with us, he just clammed up. I guess he figured that it was no use talking to them. They weren't going to listen to him anyway. I love Dan's family, but they are hard to deal with when you don't agree with them. They don't handle disagreements very well. I guess now that Dan is gone, I have been feeling increasingly distant from them. It seems like I remember Dan in one way; they remember him in another way. I just don't fit in anymore. Now, I am not only grieving the loss of my fiancé, but I am grieving over the loss of my future family. Everything has fallen apart."

She continued, "I think I could see all of this coming, though. It is kind of a confession that I am about to make. Dan and I discussed getting married before he died. I really wanted to make our relationship legal. But I knew that by getting married I would be a legal part of the family. I would be Kayla's step-Mom, and Dan's sisters' sister-in-law. I thought about this every day when Dan was alive. I know that he wanted to marry me, but I kept putting it off. In many ways I wish I would have married Dan. But now that I am becoming so distant with his family, I feel it is best that I didn't. But there is no way that I ever want to tell them that. It would hurt them too much. We keep telling each other that I am 'still family,' but I know that this isn't really the truth."

"Maybe that is what is driving us apart now—they want to keep holding on to worn out beliefs that aren't really true," she said. I am not really a family member. Dan was not really going to be cured. I wish that we could all face the truth and talk to one another about it. But we can't. We couldn't when Dan was alive, and we can't now. I know that Dan wanted three things. He wanted to marry me, he wanted to be heard by his family, and he wanted to die without pain. None of these wishes came true for him. Realizing this is what makes me the most sad. Now I have to handle this realization alone and begin to grieve in my own way. Slowly, I'll learn to say goodbye."

Holly worked with her counselor to construct a scrapbook full of the photos and memorabilia from her time together with Dan. She also made several small scrapbooks to give to Dan's family as a way of thanking them for the life she had shared with them. In that way, she could honor her memories with the family, keeping them all a treasured part of her life.

Although this family was able to address some long-standing maladaptive patterns of interaction, they were unable to successfully adapt to the terminal illness phase. The family continues to report having several regrets, having unresolved difficulties between them and the deceased, and having difficulty with communication patterns. While it was recommended that the family, including Holly, come in for a follow-up consultation to address the grieving process, they declined the invitation. Phylis explained, "Danny's dead and we believe that God must have wanted him to 'come home' at his own appointed time. There is nothing that we can do about that or about anything really." Even though the family declined treatment at this time, they were encouraged to consider counseling or pastoral guidance at a later date to assist with the emotional distress of the loss.

☐ The Family with Young Children during Terminal Illness

CASE EXAMPLE 9 (Continued). Cindy's Family

Caren, Cindy's mother, came in for a follow-up consultation. She said. "Cindy isn't doing very well lately. She seemed to be doing fine for a few months after the surgery. She even adjusted to the colostomy quickly. But she has grown so weak and so thin. It is difficult to get her to eat and all she wants to do is sleep. Sometimes even sleeping is hard for her since she is in so much pain. It has been so hard caring for her and for the children. Jack is with all of them right now. He tries to help, but he has no idea what it is like being the primary caregiver. I feel like my heart is broken and I don't have the energy to even walk anymore. I don't know how I get up in the morning. I guess it is just by sheer willpower." Caren was experiencing severe caregiver burnout in conjunction with the beginning stages of the grief process. She remarked how caring for Cindy was just like reliving the "nightmare" of caring for her husband when he died from colon cancer. She was anticipating Cindy's death and in some ways felt that Cindy had already left her. She related, "The strong Cindy that I raised and loved is gone. She is in so much pain that she doesn't seem to be herself at all. I get glimpses of the old Cindy every now and then, but it is very seldom these days." It was recommended that Caren be assessed for caregiver burnout and referred for an evaluation for an antidepressant medication. In addition, it was recommended that Cindy's pain medication be reevaluated.

Caren reported, "Weeks ago I knew that the demands of caregiving had exceeded my resources. Jack helps out with the children and it may be time for him to take them full time. It may help the children begin to transition to being at their father's house and foster a relationship with his new wife, Jennifer. I thought about asking Jennifer to help temporarily, but I don't know her and I feel awkward about going to her for assistance." Because of the excessive demands of caregiving and Caren's hesitancy with asking for help, she was experiencing an emotional and physical imbalance. Subsequently, she came in for a consultation to help regain her balance and to identify additional resources. It was recommended that Caren hold a family meeting with all available family members present.

During a follow-up family therapy session, Caren, her two sons, Zachary and Cameron; her former-son-in-law, Jack; and his new wife, Jennifer, were all present. Caren was able to list the specific demands of the illness, such as caring for the children, worrying about money, meeting Cindy's physical needs, and maintaining the household. The family agreed to help finance in-home nursing care that would help meet Cindy's physical needs. Jack and Jennifer agreed to care for the children three days each week. Jack commented, "We would take them full time, but we should let them adjust slowly to our home. We can take them permanently when it becomes necessary." Caren was also able to verbalize some of her needs, such as assistance with meals and family members to watch Cindy so that she could have time to take care of her personal business. Caren's sons also mentioned that it was important for Caren to have time to meet her emotional needs, such as breaks from caregiving in order to go to her Bible study and women's bingo night. Caren's sons volunteered to help out several hours a week. Jennifer also volunteered to make extra meals for Caren and the family. At the close of the family meeting Caren told everyone how much she appreciated the family coming to the session: "I don't know what we would do without all of you. This has been a real nightmare for us. The children need to have their family around them, to care for them and make them feel safe, healthy, and happy. All they see lately is me being sad and tired and their mother in pain and depressed. We need your help so badly." To prevent negative consequences on the children's capacity for intimate relationships in the future, directives to care for the children's emotional needs were also discussed. The adults in the family were encouraged to communicate clearly with the children about their mother's illness, her enduring love for them, and the lasting security from the surviving adult family members. In seeing to the informational and safety needs of the children, the family was able to combat significant regression behaviors in the children as well as prevent difficulties that may arise during later life cycles.

Cindy's physical and emotional status was also reevaluated. Cindy reported experiencing severe pain and periods of intense anxiety and depression. Cindy's pain medication was altered to help reduce her pain and to address her increased levels of anxiety. In addition, Cindy was treated with antidepressant medication to help alleviate her depressive symptoms. After careful examination of Cindy's response to her new medication, cognitive-behavioral techniques were employed to help further reduce her pain and anxiety. These techniques were recommended primarily to increase relaxation and reduce the distress associated with pain (Breitbart & Passik, 1993). Cindy was able to use several cognitive-behavioral techniques that helped her to reduce her pain and anxiety and to address her increased levels of depression, including (1) psychoeducation, (2) progressive muscle relaxation, (3) imagery/distraction, (4) meditation, (5) self-hypnosis, and (6) music/aroma therapies.

A few months later, Cindy died at home in the presence of her mother. Caren came in for a follow-up consultation six months following the death of her daughter. She said, "These last few months have been so hard. I have lost so many things that are so important to me. I watched my husband die from cancer, and now I have lost my daughter to cancer. I wish that God had taken me instead. In some ways, it would have been so much easier on all of us if it had been me. Now the children don't have their mother. Looking back on everything, I do feel like we did all that we could to help us get through this horrible tragedy. We all cared for the children and provided them with as much stability as we could. Since we worked out a regular routine with their father and stepmother, they have been more readily able to adjust to their new surroundings. Still, it is so hard on them. I go over and see them all the time, and I babysit for them whenever Jack and Jennifer need some time for themselves. It's funny how close Jack and I have become. Even Jennifer and I are talking more. Cindy's brothers are still pretty sad about their sister's death. But they have their own families and jobs to keep them busy. That's not true for me. But at least I have my new church and my new friends to help pass the time. I am even thinking about volunteering a few days a month at the American Cancer Center. I have a lot of experience caring for people with cancer, and they can probably use my help."

The caregiving and grieving process for this family was particularly difficult given the family's history of cancer and their family life cycle. The demands of the terminal illness phase necessitated an inward pull on the family system. Subsequently, in order to provide stability and care for the children, Caren was able to negotiate a working alliance with her former son-in-law and his new wife. In addition, because Caren received help before she reached the final stages of burnout, she was able to adapt more readily to the caregiving process. Further, since she was able to adapt more successfully during the caregiving process, she was also able to adapt during the grieving phase as well (Bass & Bowman, 1990). Thus timely and consistent therapeutic care helped to facilitate healthier family system adaptation during a very difficult phase of the clinical course of cancer.

☐ The Family with Adolescents during Terminal Illness

CASE EXAMPLE 4 (Continued). Frank's Family

Frank was experiencing nausea and vomiting as a result of his treatment for leukemia. He was released from the hospital several months ago, but was still at an elevated risk for infection. He and his family came in for a consultation regarding adaptation during the terminal illness phase. Frank began, "It seems like I have been sick for so long. Sometimes I am hopeful that I am still going to beat cancer and that, someday, everything will be back to normal, back to the way things were before I got cancer. But on days like today, I don't feel so hopeful. I feel like all the joy has gone out of my life and I am bringing my wife and my kids down with me. I know that a lot of my sadness is due to my treatment and its side effects, but that doesn't make things any easier." Frank's wife continued, "We are all going through a difficult time right now. We always thought that Frank would survive from cancer, but now we are not so sure. Franks' cancer is not in remission, it is progressing. There really isn't much more anyone can do for us." Frank's family was currently experiencing the transition from one of cure and remission to one of terminal illness and palliative care.

The family has been holding family council meetings every other week to check in with one another and to evaluate the family's changing roles, rules, and responsibilities. Last month, Frank Jr. decided to take a semester or two away from college to stay at home and help care for the family. Frank was currently unable to work, and Frank Jr. has temporarily taken over his father's business. Frank Jr. stated, "Alexis and Fred need to finish high school. That is really important to all of us. I was angry at first when Mom and Dad asked me to come home. But after I saw how weak my Dad had become, I was glad I came home." Frank Jr.'s family reassured him that this change was only temporary. Frank Jr. nodded his head in understanding and agreement.

The terminal illness phase was difficult for this family. Frank Jr. continued to support the family financially, and in essence he had taken over his father's role. However, the role reversal with his father made family interaction difficult, especially for Frank. Frank reported, "There is nothing for me to live for. Frank Jr. has taken over my role. I am still a husband to my wife, but some husband I am! We have little joy left in our marriage, now that I am so sick all the time. There is nothing for me now." It was recommended that Frank be evaluated for antidepressant medication and he and Anne come in for a brief consultation on a day when Frank was feeling relatively healthy.

After Frank had been taking antidepressants for a few weeks, he and Anne came in for a session, during which the mutuality of their marital relationship was addressed. Anne shared how she still turned to Frank for emotional comfort, intimacy, and help with decision making. Frank was encouraged to take more part in making family decisions, particularly with the future of the family business. Frank also wanted to address the sacrifices Frank Jr. was currently making. After reflecting on his concerns for his son, Frank expressed the desire to have deeper conversations with him. "I want to help him plan for his future, to decide on his role in the family after I'm gone, and to talk about marriage, and what it takes to be a good man, husband, and father. I guess I have been taking the easy way out by not talking with him much and avoiding important life lessons I could share with him. I have been taking a back seat as a father figure. It's time to jump back in and share the knowledge that I have gained in this life with all of my children while I still can."

The discussion during the session also focused on the things that continue to bring joy to their relationship and in their lives. At first, Frank commented on the things that had brought him joy in the past—his work, watching sports, making furniture for the home, and going on trips with the family. Frank and Anne were asked to think about what brings them joy now, since the illness. Frank was able to discover that there are several things that still bring him joy in his life: "I like it when we all just sit together as a family and watch movies on television. I can rest comfortably and see all my family around me. It's great when we watch a comedy and we all start laughing together. I love it when Alexis and Fred tell me about their days at school. I love it when I am awake early in the morning and I can see the sun come up. The house is so quiet and peaceful, I feel rested and calm during those times. I love it when the house doesn't smell like heavy foods, but when the wind blows through the windows, all fresh and clean. Those heavy smells make me feel so sick. . . . I didn't want to say anything about that though. I mean, my family has a right to eat hamburgers if they want to." Anne told Frank that she would be more careful about the types of foods and smells in the home. She said, "We can sacrifice hamburgers for you, dear!" They also decided to get up about half an hour before the children to enjoy the quiet morning hours together: "If we just sit on the back porch together and listen to the sounds of the morning, I know I can have a few minutes of joy with you each day." Frank also talked about his dreams of building a home for them someday: "Now I know that I will never be able to build our own home. But maybe the kids and I can build a dollhouse for our future grandchildren. You can all tell them that Grandpa Frank made it."

During the next few months, Frank's health continued to deteriorate. His leukemia did not respond to treatment and thus Frank did not experience a remission in his disease. Several months following the family's last consultation, Frank was admitted to the hospital to receive palliative treatment and to be monitored for potential infection. During his last weeks of life, however, he was able to find joy in simple pleasures with his wife and family. In addition, with some help from the rest of the family, he was able to complete the dollhouse he wanted to build for his grandchildren. Anne commented, "Frank Jr. helped him build the dollhouse, so it will go to his children first."

Six months following the death of his father, Frank Jr. was still working at his father's business. Frank Jr. reported, "I am coping with my father's death better than my grandfather's passing. I think it is because I felt so helpless with my grandfather. There was nothing that I could do to help him. With my father, I was able to contribute to his last days and improve his quality of life. The conversations we had before he died will stay with me for the rest of my life. And I feel okay about not going back to school. I guess I was just meant to take over my father's shop. I am used to it now. It is the life I know. Besides, my girlfriend lives here in town, and it seems like a waste to go back to college when I have a good job." Anne disagreed with his decision to not return to school: "I would like to see you go back to college, but you have to make your own decisions now." Even though Anne was grieving the death of her husband, she realized the need to allow Frank Jr. to continue with his developmental tasks. Anne commented, "Frank Jr. is moving out of our home next week. I have enough insurance money to last me and the other kids for awhile, and it is time that Frank Jr. builds a life of his own. I am going to miss him so much. I mean, I am grieving the loss of my husband to cancer and the loss of my son as he moves out of the home at the same time. That is a lot for me to handle, but I know that he needs to grow up and be on his own for awhile. I have Alexis and Fred to keep me company at home, and I have started to work at the catering business with my sisters again."

Because of their flexible family system, this family was able to navigate the difficult terminal illness phase. The family's developmental course was permanently altered as a result of cancer, particularly in Frank Jr.'s case. Although he was able to resume his developmental momentum after his father's death, his decisions regarding his life's work were permanently changed due to the circumstances of his father's illness. However, the family system was able to maintain developmental momentum in spite of terminal illness and even to find joy during the final days of Frank's life.

☐ The Family Launching Children during Terminal Illness

CASE EXAMPLE 5 (Continued). Claire's Family

Claire and her husband, Greg, came in for a follow-up consultation. Greg began the session, "Claire hasn't been doing too well lately. Her cancer has metastasized to her bones, and she is in a lot of pain much of the time. We have been carefully monitoring her pain medication and I take care of her around the clock. Katherine and Peter come over on the weekends to see us, but for the most part, it's just me and Claire going through this thing." Claire and Greg had begun to work on their marital relationship soon after Claire was diagnosed with recurrent breast cancer. The recurrent illness brought to light the preciousness of their relationship, especially for Greg: "I don't take Claire for granted anymore. I am so disgusted with myself that it has taken a terminal illness to show me the important things in life. Both of us are learning more about ourselves, our marriage, and our relationship with God."

Claire and Greg discussed the spiritual journey they had begun together over the last several months. Claire stated, "Greg and I have joined a fantastic church that is very near our home. We walk there on Sunday mornings, when I am strong, and we attend Wednesday night Bible study with six other couples. We are learning more about God, family, and marriage than ever before. The awareness of the brevity of our life together enhances our learning, and we have so much to share with the congregation."

Claire and Greg were also able to discuss their biggest fears and the core of any anger they periodically experienced. Claire commented, "I used to be so afraid of death. I didn't have any belief system that helped me to get a handle on what death means, what waits for me when I die. I wasn't sure I even believed in God. The illness has changed all that for me, for us. Now, we believe that there is a God and that God's love and power are watching over us, helping us through the difficulties of dying. While we are not praying for a cure for my cancer, we do pray that our family will be cared for and that my pain will be taken from me. Greg and I meditate together and we practice different forms of relaxation to help reduce my pain. He is also very good at helping me take my medicine before my pain becomes too great." Greg also expressed his anger toward himself that it took a serious turn in Claire's health for the relationship to be enhanced: "I wish that I would have placed my marriage as a priority before we knew about Claire's terminal condition. I feel like we have wasted so much time. I guess that I am going to have to go through the process of forgiving myself and just enjoy the time that we have now."

During Claire's last months of life, she and Greg were able to tackle life's most difficult questions. They were able to connect with their own beliefs in God and to find strength in their religious and spiritual practices. While both of them stated that they don't have all the answers to life's questions, Claire believed that she was able to face her own death without much fear and with faith that God would help both her and her family make the transition from one life to another. Claire stated, "This is the biggest transition that an individual and a family can go through. We are preparing ourselves for this transition by trying to build our relationship with each other and with God. We have been strengthened by our renewed love for each other and by our new faith in God." Claire and Greg both kept journals of the last few months of Claire's life. Claire had even begun to draw abstract art to express some of her more intense experiences: "I never knew that I could draw before, but one evening I decided to try. Everything felt so jumbled inside that I decided to draw a more abstract sketch of my feelings. I was surprised at how great it turned out. Now I draw almost every night. I have even started using colored chalk to add depth to my images."

Claire was able to continue many of her new spiritual activities until the day of her death. Greg brought in a few of her drawings to a follow-up consultation: "Claire drew these on the last day of her life. She was so weak, but she wanted to finish them. Our friends from church came to visit that day, too. Katherine and Peter were both in town that night and stayed with me for a week after she died. Claire and I put together her funeral service while she was still alive. She wanted a small ceremony with only the family and a few friends from church. I read bits and pieces from our journals, and I showed her pictures to Katherine and Peter. We also picked out our favorite poem and I read it to her spirit:

> Farewell to you and the youth I have spent with you.
>
> It was but yesterday we met in a dream.
> You have sung to me in my aloneness,
> and I of your longings have built a tower in the sky.
> But now our sleep has fled and our half waking has turned to a fuller day,
> and we must part.
>
> If in the twilight of memory we should meet once more,
> we shall speak again together and you shall sing to me a deeper song.
> And if our hands should meet in another dream we shall build another tower in the sky.
> Kahil Gibran, *The Prophet*, 1923

Greg concluded, "It was hard for me to go through the funeral service, and I cried openly in front of our children and friends. I have never showed such public emotion before. It's strange, but I didn't care that I was crying in front of everyone. In fact, I felt closer to my family and friends than I ever have in my whole life. Like the poem says, we truly did build a tower together. And that tower is strong enough to get me through anything—because it reaches my Claire, and my God."

During the months following Claire's death, Greg was able to forge new relationships with his daughter and son. Greg reported that he and Katherine and Peter had never been really close before Claire's illness: "But I wasn't going to make the same mistake with them that I had made with Claire. I wasn't going to wait for a terminal illness to start building my relationship with them. Now I see that relationships are like live entities, I need to feed them and care for them. I call Katherine and Peter all the time, and I am a part of their lives now. I need my family. I need to be a good father and grandfather to my future grandchildren. Katherine and I are in the process of putting Claire's journal and pictures into a book to be published. It is the most rewarding project I have ever been a part of. The book is an account of our personal experiences coping with Claire's terminal illness. But it is not so much a book about death, as it is a book about family and spiritual rebirth. It is a tribute to Claire's life and the things she loved most about it. We have decided that all of the proceeds from the book will go toward a breast cancer research fund so that advances can be made in the field and a cure can be found."

For this family, Claire's recurrent breast cancer was used as an impetus for creating a deeper marital commitment and for finding deeper meaning in life. Although the terminal illness was difficult and oftentimes devastating for Claire and her family, they were able to use the intense experience to heal their marriage and their family system. Claire and Greg chose to cope with terminal illness by developing a relationship with each other and with a shared belief in God and an afterlife. This decision left an indelible change in Greg, which rippled outward to his children and will, in time, even affect his relationships with his grandchildren. Greg remained closer to his children and continued to recognize the importance of family and of sharing intimate feelings with others. Thus, Claire and the experience of cancer left a legacy of deepened spiritual understanding and enhanced family relationships.

☐ The Family in Later Life during Terminal Illness

CASE EXAMPLE 10 (Continued). Carl's Family

Ruth came in for an individual consultation soon after a decision to place Carl in the care of a nursing home. She related, "It was difficult for me to come to a counseling session. I am so independent and it feels like I am losing my independence as I get weak and need help. I don't usually discuss private matters with strangers." Ruth also discussed her feelings about putting Carl in a nursing home: "At first I felt so guilty. I felt like such a failure. Carl and I always told each other that we would care for each other until the day we died. My daughter, Mary, talked me into the idea, though. She has been really wonderful about helping me through Carl's illness, but she doesn't realize that I don't want to become dependent on her or on anyone else. She is even trying to get me to move in with her after Carl dies." Although Mary was attempting a role reversal with her mother, Ruth resisted this shift and wanted to maintain her independent status: "I love all of my children, but I am not ready to move in with any of them just yet. I love my home and I can still take care of myself. I could have taken care of Carl, too. But I guess it did get to be too much for me. The staff at the nursing home has been wonderful, though. They have let me keep my promise to Carl by continuing to care for him and comfort him on a daily basis. But now I am beginning to take care of myself, too. When I was taking care of Carl at home, I couldn't do all the things he needed for me to do. I guess it just took some time to see that I couldn't do it all on my own."

Ruth reported how she visited Carl every morning and evening. She was able to talk to him, to help bathe him, and to monitor for any signs of disease progression or increases in pain. She said, "Lately, he doesn't even recognize me. But I believe that somewhere inside his brain, his mind, he knows who I am. I know that he still needs me. I sing to him every day, and I tell him what the kids and grandkids are doing. I don't wear him out, though. Most of the time, I just sit near him and work on my needlepoint. I have to keep myself busy, or I think I'd go crazy." Ruth reported experiencing feelings of extreme loneliness and isolation: "My kids are great, but you can't really talk to them like you can your spouse. I mean, they are my kids—they are not my friends or my husband. They can't understand my generation and everything that we have gone through. I have a few close friends at my church and I really need them right now."

Over the course of the next few weeks, Ruth was able to discuss the losses she had experienced in her life: "Both my mother and father died quite awhile ago. It was difficult for me to accept their deaths. Every year it seems like someone I know dies. It gets sad and scary sometimes. But I guess I am just learning to accept death as a part of life. My faith, my family, and my friends help me get through the bad times." A few weeks after moving Carl to the hospice setting, he died of advanced-stage lung cancer. Ruth was with Carl when he died: "It was so strange to be with him as he died. We had decided well in advance that we would not try and revive him, nor would we have him hooked up to all those machines to keep him alive. Carl and I always wanted to be free from drugs when we met our maker. Carl seemed at peace when he died, and for that I am eternally grateful. Some of the kids were supposed to come in later that evening to see him for a few minutes. But right then it was only Carl and me. I held his hand as he passed away. He died knowing that he was loved and cared for. I believe that he is with God now, and soon I will be with both of them. For now, I have my family and friends to help me continue with my life."

The terminal illness phase brought about its own set of difficulties for this family in later life. Although Ruth had a great deal of familial support to help her adapt emotionally to the death of her husband, she experienced guilt over Carl's not being able to die at home, as promised. In addition, Ruth felt that her daughter wanted to "take over" by attempting a role reversal that was not warranted. Even though Ruth felt lonely at times without her husband, she wanted to maintain her independence following her husband's death, and she was not ready to become dependent on her children. However, Ruth was encouraged to recognize her need for connectedness with her children. She was able to understand that accepting increased support and becoming more deeply connected to her children was not the same as becoming "dependent" upon them. Ruth decided to maintain living in her home, but to regularly invite her children and grandchildren to visit in order to decrease chances of isolation. In addition, Ruth began to understand the importance of her role in the family as a grandmother and provider of family legacies and memories, which serve to strengthen generational family bonds. Ruth was able to find connectedness with her family at the funeral service for Carl. Most of the family was present, including multiple familial generations. Together, the family was able to grieve the passing of Carl as well as celebrate his life. Each family member was given an opportunity to share his or her fond memories of Carl. This allowed for the family to grieve, cry, laugh, and love, which facilitated the process of grieving. Ruth continued to expand her roles as a mother and grandmother after Carl's death and began to recognize her value in the family system. In doing so, she was able to increase her support system and to perceive herself as an important member of the family, rather than as "dependent."

Adults in later life often experience multiple losses: the loss of a job, the loss of health, and the loss of parents, and other family members and friends. Ruth had also experienced several losses, including the recent loss of her husband to cancer. Like many adults in later life, Ruth reported that "faith" and her "family" served as a buffer to her life stresses (Oktay & Walter, 1991).

☐ Summary

The families highlighted in this book and the countless others with whom we have been privileged to work will remain a valued part of our lives. As professionals working with cancer patients and their families we are called on to be of service during a time of incredible vulnerability. As fellow human beings we have been honored to be part of their lives and, sometimes, a part of their deaths. Our work with families suffering from terminal illnesses is a sacred profession. We are called upon to provide hope, guidance, reassurance, and, most of all, compassion. We are sometimes called to lead them across frightening and yet hallowed and intimate ground. We hope our words have served as both a conceptual roadmap along that hallowed ground as well as an inspirational resource for all those whose lives have been touched by cancer—for all of those who continue to live under the sword of Damocles.

☐ References

Babcock, E. N. (1997). *When life becomes precious: A guide for loved ones and friends of cancer patients.* New York: Bantam Books.

Bailey, S. (1998). Comprehensive spiritual care. In A. Berger, R. Portenoy, & D. Weissman (Eds.), *Principles and practice of supportive oncology* (pp. 717–731). New York: Lippincott-Raven.

Barnard, D. (1998). Withholding and withdrawing treatment: The doctor-patient relationship and the changing goals of care. In A. Berger, R. Portenoy, & D. Weissman (Eds.), *Principles and practice of supportive oncology* (pp. 809–817) . New York: Lippincott-Raven.

Bass, D., & Bowman, K. (1990). The transition from caregiving to bereavement: The relationship of care-related strain and adjustment to death. *The Gerontologist, 30*(1), 35–42.

Beckwith, B., Beckwith, S., Gray, T., Micsko, M., Holm, J., Plummer, V., & Flaa, S. (1990). Identification of spouses at high risk during bereavement: A preliminary assessment of Parkes and Weiss' Risk Index. *The Hospice Journal, 6*(3), 35–44.

Bowlby, J. (1977). *Attachment and loss* (vol. 2, Anger). New York: Basic Books.

Bowlby, J. (1980). *Loss.* New York: Basic Books.

Breitbart, W. (1990). Cancer pain and suicide. *Advances in pain research and therapy, 16,* 399–412.

Breitbart, W., Bruera, E., Chochinov, H., & Lynch, M. (1995). Neuropsychiatric syndromes and psychological symptoms in patients with advanced cancer. *Journal of Pain and Symptom Management, 10,* 131–141.

Breitbart, W., & Passik, S., (1993). Psychiatric aspects of palliative care. In D. Doyle, G. Hanks, & N. Macdonald (Eds.), *Oxford textbook of palliative medicine* (pp. 610–626). New York: Oxford University Press.

Breitbart, W., Passik, S., & Rosenfeld, B. (1994). Psychiatric and psychosocial aspects of cancer pain. In P. Wall & R. Melzack (Eds.), *Textbook of pain.* New York: Churchill Livingstone.

Cassel, E. (1982). The nature of suffering and the goals of medicine. *New England Journal of Medicine, 306,* 639–645.

Chochinov, H., Holland, J., & Katz, L. (1998). Bereavement: A special issue in oncology. In J. Holland & J. Rowlands (Eds.), *Handbook of psychooncology* (1st ed., pp. 1016–1027). New York: Oxford University Press.

Christ, G., Siegel, K., Freund, B., Langosch, D., Hendersen, S., Sperber, D., & Weinstein, L. (1993). Impact of parental terminal cancer on latency-age children. *American Journal of Orthopsychiatry, 63*(3), 417–425.

Christ, G., Siegel, K., Palamara Mesagno, F., & Langosch, D. (1991). A preventive intervention program for bereaved children: Problems of implementation. *Journal of American Orthopsychiatry, 61*(2), 168–178,

Coyle, N., Loscalzo, M., & Bailey, L. (1998). Supportive home care for the advanced cancer patient and the family. In J. Holland & J. Rowland (Eds.), *Handbook of psychooncology* (1st ed., pp. 589–606). New York: Oxford University Press.

Creagan, E. (1998). Patient-physician communication in the cancer setting. In A. Berger, R. Portenoy, & D. Weissman (Eds.), *Principles and practice of supportive oncology* (pp. 773–784). New York: Lippincott-Raven.

Cummock, V. (1996). Journey of a young widow: The bombing of Pan Am 103. In K. Doka (Ed.), *Living with grief after sudden loss* (pp. 1–9). Bristol, PA: Taylor & Francis.

Dar, R., Beach, C., Barden, P., & Cleeland, C. (1992). Cancer pain in the marital system: A study of patients and their spouses. *Journal of Pain and Symptom Management, 7*(2), 87–93.

De Conno, F., Saita, L., Ripamonti, C., & Ventafridda, V. (1993). In retrospect—On the last days of life. *Journal of Palliative Care, 9*(3), 47–49.

Du Boulay, S. (1984). *Cicely Saunders.* London: Hodder and Stoughton.

Elliott, W. (1995). *Flow of flesh, reach of spirit* (251). Grand Rapids, MI: Wm B. Eerdmans. Adapted from the beginning of W. Farrell & M. Healy (Eds.). (1952). *My way of life: Pocket edition of St. Thomas.* Brooklyn: Confraternity of the Precious Blood.

Emanuel, L. (1998). Advance directives. In A. Berger, R. Portenoy, & D. Weissman (Eds.), *Principles and practice of supportive oncology* (pp. 791–808). New York: Lippincott-Raven.

Foley, K. (1991). The relationship of pain and symptom management to patient requests for physician-assisted suicide. *Journal of Pain and Symptom Management, 6*, 289–295.

Forman, W. (1998). The evolution of hospice and palliative medicine. In A. Berger, R. Portenoy, & D. Weissman (Eds.), *Principles and practice of supportive oncology* (pp. 735–740). New York: Lippincott-Raven.

Gibran, K. (1923). *The Prophet.* New York: Alfred A. Knopf.

Given, B., & Given, C. W. (1998). Family caregiver burden from cancer care. In J. Holland & J. Rowland (Eds.), *Handbook of psychooncology* (1st ed., pp. 93–109). New York: Oxford University Press.

Herth, K. (1990). Fostering hope in terminally ill people. *Journal of Advanced Nursing, 15*, 1250–1259.

Hill, C., Thompson, L., & Gallagher, D. (1988). The role of anticipatory grief and aged widows and widowers. *The Gerontologist, 28*, 792–796.

Ingham, J. (1998). The epidemiology of cancer at the end of life. In A. Berger, R. Portenoy, & D. Weissman (Eds.), *Principles and practice of supportive oncology* (pp. 749–766). New York: Lippincott-Raven.

Irizarry, C. (1992). Spirituality and the child: A grandparent's death. *Journal of Psychosocial Oncology, 10*(2), 39–58.

Kastenbaum, R. (1986). *Death, society, and human experience* (3rd ed.). Columbus, OH: Merrill.

Kissane, D., & Bloch, S. (1994). Family grief. *British Journal of Psychiatry, 164*, 728–740.

Kissane, D., Bloch, S., Onghena, P., McKenzie, D., Snyder, R., & Dowe, D. (1996). The Melbourne family grief study, II: Psychosocial morbidity and grief in bereaved families. *American Journal of Psychiatry, 153*(5), 659–666.

Lev, E., Robinson, L., & McCorkle, R. (1989). Loss and bereavement. In J. Holland & J. Rowland (Eds.), *Handbook of psychooncology* (1st ed., pp. 110–118). New York: Oxford University Press.

McGoldrick, M., & Walsh, F. (1995). Death and the family life cycle. In E. Carter & M. McGoldrick (Eds.), *The changing family life cycle: A framework for family therapy* (3rd ed., pp. 185–201). New York: Gardner Press.

McKenna, R., Wellisch, D., & Fawzy, I. (1995). Rehabilitation and supportive care of the cancer patient. In G. Murphy, W. Lawrence, Jr., & R. Lenhard, Jr. (Eds.), *American Cancer Society textbook of clinical oncology* (2nd ed, pp. 635–654). Atlanta, GA: American Cancer Society.

Oktay, J., & Walter, C. (1991). *Breast cancer in the life course: Women's experiences.* New York: Springer Publishing Company.

Oratz, R. (1988). Commentary. In C. Cohen (Ed.), *Casebook on the termination of life-sustaining treatment and the care of the dying* (p. 77). Bloomington: Indiana University Press.

Pace, J. (1997). Palliative care. In C. Varricchio (Ed.), *A cancer source book for nurses* (7th ed., pp. 260–268). Atlanta, GA: Jones and Bartlett Publishers.

Parkes, C. (1970). The first year of bereavement: A longitudinal study of the reaction of London widows to the death of their husbands. *Psychiatry, 33*, 449–461.

Parkes, C. (1972). *Bereavement: Studies of grief in adult life.* New York: International Universities Press.

Parkes, C. (1985). Bereavement. *British Journal of Psychiatry, 146*, 11–17.

Parkes, C. (1987). Models of bereavement care. *Death Studies, 11*, 257–261.

Parkes, C., & Weiss, R. (1983). *Recovery from bereavement.* New York: Basic Books.

Pellegrino, E. (1991). Ethics. *Journal of the American Medical Association, 265*, 3188.

Rando, T. (1983). An investigation of grief and adaptation in parents whose children have died from cancer. *Journal of Pediatric Psychology, 8*, 3–20.

Roy, D., Williams, J., & Dickens, B. (1994). *Bioethics in Canada.* Scarborough, Ontario: Prentice Hall Canada.

Schachter, S. R., & Coyle, N. (1998). Palliative home-care: Impact on families. In J. C. Holland (Ed.), *Psycho-oncology* (pp. 1004–1015). New York: Oxford University Press.

Siegel, K., Palamara Mesagno, F., & Christ, G. (1990). A prevention program for bereaved children. *American Journal of Orthopsychiatry, 60*(2), 168–175.

Siegel, K., Palamara Mesagno, F., Karus, D., Christ, G., Banks, K., & Moynihan, R. (1992). Psychosocial adjustment of children with a terminally ill parent. *Journal of the American Academy for Child and Adolescent Psychiatry, 31*(2), 327–333.

Siegel, K., Raveis, V., Bettes, B., Palamara Mesagno, F., Christ, G., & Weinstein, L. (1990). Perceptions of parental competence while facing the death of a spouse. *Amercian Journal of Orthopsychiatry, 60*(4), 567–576.

Siegel, K., & Tuckel, P. (1984). Rational suicide and the terminally ill cancer patient. *Omega, 15,* 263–269.

Stephens Mills, D. (1992). Changes in oncology health care settings. In J. Clark & R. McGee (Eds.), *Core curriculum for oncology nursing* (2nd ed., pp. 205–220). Philadelphia, PA: W.B. Saunders Company.

Storey, P. (1998). Symptom control in dying. In A. Berger, R. Portenoy, & D. Weissman (Eds.), *Principles and practice of supportive oncology* (pp. 741–748). New York: Lippincott-Raven.

Weber, J., & Fournier, D. (1985). Family support and a child's adjustment to death. *Family Relations, 34,* 43–49.

Weir, R. (1989). *Abating treatment with critically ill patients: Ethical and legal limits to the medical prolongation of life.* New York: Oxford University Press.

World Health Organization. (1990). *Cancer pain relief and paliative care.* Geneva: Author.

Zabora, J., & Loscalzo, M. (1998). Psychosocial consequences of advanced cancer. In A. Berger, R. Portenoy, & D. Weissman (Eds.), *Principles and practice of supportive oncology* (pp. 531–545). New York: Lippincott-Raven.

INDEX